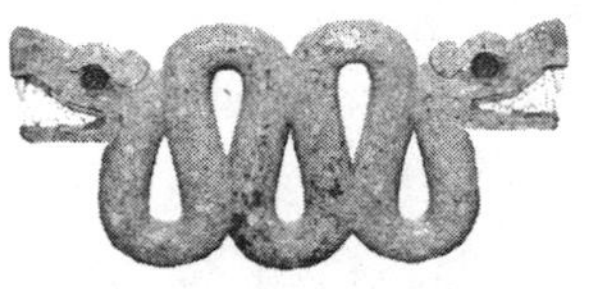

THE AZTEC TREASURE HOUSE

ALSO BY EVAN S. CONNELL

The Anatomy Lesson and Other Stories

Mrs. Bridge

The Patriot

Notes from a Bottle Found on the Beach at Carmel

At the Crossroads

The Diary of a Rapist

Mr. Bridge

Points for a Compass Rose

The Connoisseur

Double Honeymoon

A Long Desire

The White Lantern

Saint Augustine's Pigeon

Son of the Morning Star

The Alchymist's Journal

Mesa Verde

The Collected Stories of Evan S. Connell

Deus lo Volt!

THE AZTEC TREASURE HOUSE

SELECTED ESSAYS

Evan S. Connell

COUNTERPOINT
WASHINGTON, D.C.
NEW YORK, N.Y.

"Messages on a Sandstone Bluff" is reprinted from the July-August 1996 issue of *Preservation*, the official magazine of the National Trust for Historic Preservation. "Mesa Verde" was originally published in a limited edition by The Library Fellows of the Whitney Museum of American Art, 1992.

LIBRARY OF CONGRESS CATALOGING-IN-PUBLICATION DATA
Connell, Evan S., 1924–
The Aztec treasure house : new and selected essays / Evan S. Connell.
p. cm.
Includes bibliographical references.
ISBN 1-58243-162-0 (hc); ISBN 1-58243-253-8 (pbk)
I. Title.
PS3553.O5 A97 2001
814'.54—dc21 2001028899

FIRST PAPERBACK PRINTING 2002

Jacket and text design by Amy Evans McClure

COUNTERPOINT
387 Park Avenue South
New York, NY 10016-8810

Counterpoint is a member of the Perseus Books Group

10 9 8 7 6 5 4 3 2 1

TO

JACK SHOEMAKER

CONTENTS

The soul has many motions, many gods come and go.

D. H. Lawrence

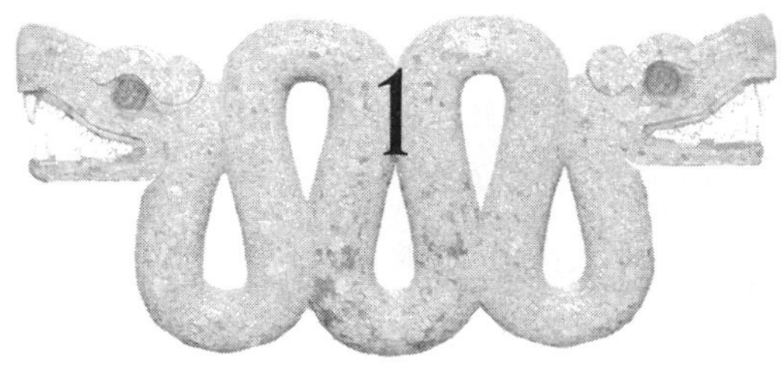

1

Olduvai & All That

JAMES USSHER, BORN IN 1581, attended Trinity College, Dublin, where he was ordained at the age of twenty. Four years later he became chancellor of Saint Patrick's Cathedral. Ten years after that he drafted the articles of doctrine and discipline for the Irish Protestant Church. At forty he was appointed bishop of Meath. Soon he became archbishop of Armagh. He visited England frequently and after his death he was buried, by Cromwell's order, in Westminster Abbey. Widely honored and respected, not merely because of his ecclesiastic eminence but for prodigious scholarship, he was the first to distinguish between the genuine and spurious epistles of Saint Ignatius of Antioch. He wrote as fluently in Latin as in English, and among his most celebrated works is *Annales Veteris et Novi Tentamenti*, a tremendous article of faith which proves that God created the Universe in 4004 B.C.

Considering Archbishop Ussher's erudition and prestige, nobody should have challenged his date for the Creation, but the devil's disciples seldom rest. So we come upon Isaac de La Peyrère who, after examining some oddly chipped stones gathered from the French countryside, wrote a little book in which he asserted that these stones had been chipped by human beings who lived before the time of Adam. The year A.D. 1655 was not a good year to make such observations: M. de La Peyrère's blasphemous monograph was publicly incinerated.

You might think this warning would be sufficient, enabling Christians to sleep comfortably through another millennium; but the Western world had begun to awaken and strict guardians of the status quo could not prevent impertinent questions from blossoming like daffodils in spring.

The Ark, for instance. How big was it? How many animals shuffled up the gangplank?

This problem, although not new, had been complicated by the voyages of Columbus and other explorers who reported seeing strange birds and beasts. In 1559 a monk named Johann Buteo had tried to clear up the matter with a learned disquisition titled *Noah's Ark, its Form and its Capacity*. Alas, Brother Buteo's statement did not assuage certain doubts.

Theologians then explained that these previously unknown creatures came into existence after the Flood just as domestic animals crossbreed and evolve, just as the mating of a cat with a wolf produces a lynx, or a camel with a leopard produces a giraffe.

Sir Walter Raleigh had something to say, as usual. New species might emerge not only through crossbreeding but also because of different surroundings. The European wildcat, when its home is India, grows up to become the panther. The European blackbird changes color and size in Virginia.

Nevertheless, despite every explanation, new and more odious questions bloomed, nourished by such infernal advocates as a French diplomat named Benoît de Maillet who wrote that germs of the first living organisms could have arrived from outer space—an idea considered preposterous until quite recently. These germs inevitably dropped into the ocean because a long time ago there was no land, and here they commenced to evolve. Hence it must follow that Man's ancestors were aquatic: "maritime people who spend part of their life under water and who often have fins instead of feet, scales instead of bare skin." About ninety such creatures had been sighted, we are told, and several females were delivered to the king of Portugal who, wanting to preserve these curious beings, graciously allowed them to spend three hours a day in the sea—secured by a long line. And it is said that they submerged at once and never came up for air. The king kept these maritime women for several years, hoping to communicate with them, "but they never learnt to speak at all."

Maillet also reflected upon the metamorphosis of fish into birds:

> There can be no doubt that fish, in the course of hunting or being hunted, were thrown up on the shore. There they could find food, but were unable to return to the water. Subsequently their fins were enlarged by the action of the water, the radial structures supporting the fins turned to quills, the dried scales became feathers, the skin assumed a coating of down, the belly-fins changed into feet, the entire body was reshaped, the neck and beak became prolonged, and at last the fish was transformed into a bird. Yet the new configuration corresponded in a general way to the old. The latter will always remain readily recognizable.

However bold he may have been imaginatively, Benoît de Maillet in person was altogether discreet. Rather than identify himself as the author of these intellectual flights, he contrived the anagram Telliamed, and further protected himself by attributing his theory to an Indian philosopher who had revealed it to a French missionary. "I confess to you," says the missionary to the philosopher, prudently separating himself from the Indian's outrageous ideas, "that notwithstanding the small Foundation I find in your system, I am charmed to hear you speak. . . ."

Maillet also stipulated that the manuscript should not be published until eleven years after his death, as though there were a statute of limitations on the digging up of heretics in order to burn or otherwise abuse their corpses.

Despite these precautions, copies of *Telliamed ou Entretien d'un Philosophe Indien avec un Missionnaire Français* were circulating through Paris salons during his lifetime; and the great naturalist Georges Louis Leclerc, Comte de Buffon, seems to have been much impressed by the startling essay.

Buffon, we should note, admitted to being one of history's five supreme figures—the others being Newton, Bacon, Leibniz, and Montesquieu. The earth, said he, had been thrown from the sun and congealed until it attained a temperature suitable for life. That being so, the earth's exact age could be deduced without resorting to biblical texts. One needed only to heat some iron spheres, observe how long they required to cool, and correlate this information, taking into account the earth's dimensions. Buffon then announced that he had found our planet to be 74,832 years old. It had sustained life for the past 40,062 years, but because the temperature would continue falling it would become uninhabitable after another 93,291 years, a globe forever sheathed in ice.

Along with these facts, which have not weathered very well, he came close to anticipating Darwin: "It may be assumed that all animals arise from a single form of life which in the course of time produced the rest by processes of perfection and degeneration." And he went on to say that the organic structure of each natural thing illustrates the following truth: life on earth developed gradually.

However, discretion may at times be advisable, and Buffon could appreciate the monumental power of the Church. No, he wrote somewhat hastily at one point, "no, it is certain—certain by revelation—that all animals have shared equally the grace of creation, each has emerged from the hands of the Creator as it appears to us today."

One of Buffon's pupils, Jean-Baptiste Pierre de Monet, Chevalier de Lamarck, encouraged the attack on biblical dogma. He wrote that species cannot be absolutely distinguished from each other; species pass into one another, proceeding from simple infusoria to the magnificent complexity of Man.

Immanuel Kant had similar thoughts: "It is possible for a chimpanzee or an orangutan, by perfecting its organs, to change at some future date into a human being. Radical alterations in natural conditions may force the ape to walk upright, accustom its hands to the use of tools, and learn to talk."

Schopenhauer wrote in 1851: "We must imagine the first human beings as having been born in Asia of orangutans and in Africa of chimpanzees. . . ."

James Hutton, a Scottish geologist and farmer, a gentleman of numerous parts—philosopher, chemist, jurist, Quaker, inventor, physicist—Hutton found the world not in a grain of sand but in a brook gently transporting sediment to the sea. Only one portrait of this extraordinary man survives, revealing a long, sad face. The face of somebody who has looked so far, comments Loren Eiseley, that mortals do not interest him. For the lesson of the industrious brook was this: mountains, plains, rivers, and oceans must be the result of slow topographical changes. The earth's surface must have been lifted and then eroded, which would take a while. Indeed, Hutton wrote, "we find no vestige of a beginning, no prospect of an end." Apparently he did not think this contradicted the Bible because he is said to have been gravely shocked when charged by the Royal Irish Academy with atheism; so shocked that he became physically ill and never quite recovered.

Then along came Sir Charles Lyell who demonstrated in three stout volumes, *Principles of Geology*, how the earth had been modified in the past and how this process continues. If, let us say, you watch some pebbles tumble from a crag, you are watching a mountain disintegrate. Furthermore, he said, any catastrophic flooding in the past had resulted not from a stupendous rain but from glaciers melting.

This latter argument especially troubled the faithful because the Bible was explicit: forty days, forty nights. Rain rain rain rain. Fifteen cubits of water. We had God's Word. Besides, look at the evidence.

In 1726, for example, the city doctor of Zurich, Johann Jakob Scheuchzer, had unearthed a fossilized skeleton near the village of Oeningen. This ancient sinner, according to Scheuchzer's calculations, went down for the last time in 2306 B.C.

"You will like to know, my learned friend," wrote Scheuchzer to the prominent British physician and naturalist Sir Hans Sloane, "that we have obtained some relics of the race of man drowned in the Flood. . . . What we have here is no vision of the mere imagination, but the well-preserved bones, and much in number, of a human skull, quite clearly distinguishable. . . ."

Dr. Scheuchzer then wrote an uncompromising pamphlet titled *A Most Rare Memorial of That Accursed Generation of Men of the First World, the Skeleton of a Man Drowned in the Flood*, which informs us that together with the infallible testimony of the Divine Word we have other proofs of a Deluge: various plants, fishes, insects, snails, quadrupeds, et cetera. Of human beings drowned on that occasion, however, few traces survive because their corpses floated on the surface of the waters and soon decayed. How fortunate that Oeningen Man should be preserved.

Dr. Scheuchzer provided an illustration of his remarkable find: "a carefully executed woodcut now offered for the consideration of the learned and inquiring world. . . . It does not merely present certain features in which a vivid imagination could detect something approximating to the human shape. On the contrary, it corresponds completely with all the parts and proportions of a human skeleton. Even the bones embedded in the stone, and some of the softer components too, are identifiable as genuine. . . ."

And there was the testimony of a German pastor, Johann Friederich Esper, who had uncovered the shoulder blade and jaw of another Flood victim in a cave near Bamberg.

During the nineteenth century additional proof turned up. William Buckland, Dean of Westminster and author of *Reliquiae Diluvianae*, reported a unique burial in South Wales—a female skeleton which became known as the Red Lady because her bones were stained with red ocher. Such mortal deposits, Buckland wrote, "by affording the strongest evidence of a universal deluge, leads us to hope that it will no longer be asserted as it has been by high authorities, that geology supplies no proofs of an event in the reality of which the truth of the Mosaic records is so materially involved."

Just the same, renegade Christians continued boring holes in the Ark:

Scheuchzer's rare memorial, upon close examination, proved to be all that was left of a giant salamander.

Esper's fossils could not be reexamined because they had somehow disappeared, but on the basis of contemporary drawings it would seem that what he picked up were the bones of a cave bear.

Buckland's so-called Red Lady was indeed human—though male instead of female—but nothing about the discolored scraps indicated that this person had drowned. Apart from sex, in fact, all that could be scientifically determined was that his bones, which had been discovered in association with Paleolithic tools, were older than the date of Scheuchzer's flood, perhaps older than the date established by Archbishop Ussher for the creation of the universe. Just how old Dean Buckland's masculine lady might be—ah, that would be hard to say. One can scarcely estimate how long men and women have been going about their affairs. To resolve such questions quite a lot more information would be necessary.

Then, in 1857, while the Neander valley near Düsseldorf was being quarried for limestone, workmen blasted open a cave and the shattering reverberations have not yet died away. Within this cave lay a wondrously complete skeleton. Laborers shoveled it aside because they were after something more valuable; but the owner of the quarry, Herr Beckershoff, either noticed these bones or was told about them and decided to save them. By this time, however, all that could be collected were some bits of arm and leg, part of the pelvis, a few ribs, and the skullcap. Herr Beckershoff thought these might be fragments of a bear, and after keeping them awhile he gave them to the president of the Elberfield Natural Science Society, J. C. Fuhlrott.

Fuhlrott realized that the bones were human. The slanted brow of the skullcap and the thick, bent limbs convinced him that this individual must have lived a long time ago. Possibly he had been washed into the cave while Noah was riding out the storm. In any event somebody important ought to be notified, so Fuhlrott called on Professor Schaaffhausen who taught anatomy at the University of Bonn.

Schaaffhausen carefully appraised and measured Fuhlrott's treasure: "The cranium is of unusual size, and of a long, elliptical form. A most remarkable peculiarity is at once obvious in the extraordinary development of the frontal sinuses. . . . The cavity holds 16,876 grains of water, whence its cubical contents may be estimated at 57.64 inches, or 1033.24 cubic centimeters." Or, in dried millet seed, "the contents equalled 31 ounces, Prussian Apothecaries' weight." This skull and the attendant bones, Professor Schaaffhausen deduced, probably belonged to one of the "barbarous, aboriginal people" who inhabited northern Europe before the Germans arrived.

Not so, replied other experts. The bones of a forest-dwelling hydrocephalic, said one. A cannibal somehow transported to Europe, said another.

Probably a Dutch sailor, said Professor Andreas Wagner of Göttingen.

An old Celt who perished during a tribal migration, said Dr. Pruner-Bey of Paris.

A Mongolian Cossack killed in 1814 while the Russians were chasing Napoleon across the Rhine, said a colleague of Schaaffhausen's, Professor Robert Mayer. Unmistakably a Cossack because, if you will be good enough to observe, the femur is bent inward, which is characteristic of a man accustomed to riding horses. No doubt this soldier had been wounded and crawled into the cave to die.

T. H. Huxley, soon to be Darwin's champion, also thought the skeleton was recent. An odd specimen, granted, but still a member of *Homo sapiens*.

Darwin himself would not comment; he seldom did unless he could be absolutely sure.

The great panjandrum of the era was Rudolf Virchow, director of the Berlin Pathological Institute. In his opinion the bones Fuhlrott displayed were not prehistoric but merely diseased. The bent legs were a consequence of rickets. The bony ridge above the eyes, together with other apparent malformations, were the result of arthritis. What could be more obvious? Also, this individual had suffered a number of blows on the head. Yet in spite of injury and disease he had lived to a ripe old age, which would be conceivable only in a settled community; and as there were no settled communities thousands of years ago it must be self-evident that the Neander valley bones were recent.

Nobody cared to debate Virchow. There is a portrait of him seated tensely in an armchair. A long sharp nose supports thin spectacles; he looks acutely intelligent, crisp, impatient, and merciless.

Years later these bones would be unpacked and scrutinized again, compared with similar finds, and subjected to a variety of microscopic, electronic, and chemical tests, with the result that we now know quite a lot about Fuhlrott's caveman. It has even been determined that he was unable to raise his left hand to his mouth because of an elbow injury.

And we have learned enough from other Neanderthal remnants to make a few tentative generalizations. For instance, it could be deduced from an Iraqi skeleton that the owner was arthritic, blind in one eye, and had a birth defect limiting the use of his right side. Now what this means is that he would have been unable to hunt, which in turn means that somebody had to provide his food. Care of the infirm and elderly is not what comes to mind when the word *Neanderthal* is mentioned.

Something else we don't think of in relation to these people is a concept of life after death; yet the Neanderthals buried their dead, which implies concern. Furthermore, the characteristics of a burial may tell us what the survivors were thinking. At least that is the assumption we make. Fires had been kindled on the graves of two Belgian Neanderthals, presumably to lessen the chill of death. And in France, at La Chapelle-aux-Saints, a hunter was interred with a bison leg—food for his long journey.

Another French site held bits and pieces of a man, a woman, two children about five years old, and two babies. Flint chips and bone splinters were discovered in the man's grave and a flat stone lay on his head, either to protect him or to prevent him from coming back. The woman was buried in a tight fetal position, as though she had been bound with cords. Perhaps, like the stone slab, this was meant to confine her. Or maybe it saved work by reducing the size of the grave.

On a gentle slope near this family plot another child had been buried—its head separated from its body. The head lay almost a yard higher on the slope. Why this child did not lie with the others, and why the head was detached, is not known.

Quite a few Neanderthal graves were found at the Shanidar cave in northern Iraq. Several of these people appeared to have been killed by rocks falling from the roof, possibly during an earthquake. In one trench lay a hunter with a fractured skull, and when the surrounding soil was analyzed it disclosed pollen from a number of brightly colored wildflowers related to the hollyhock, bachelor's button, grape hyacinth, and groundsel. The existence of so much pollen could not be attributed to wind or to the feces of animals and birds. The only other explanation is that flowers were scattered on his grave by somebody who loved him.

A less agreeable picture came into focus at Monte Circeo, fifty miles south of Rome. Laborers at a tourist resort were widening a terrace when they exposed the entrance to a cave that had been sealed long ago by a landslide. The owner of the resort, accompanied by some friends, crept on hands and knees through a tunnel leading deep into the hillside and finally they entered a chamber that had not been visited for perhaps 60,000 years. By lantern light they saw a human skull, face to the earth, within a circle of stones. Anthropologists suspect the skull may have been mounted on a stick and dropped in that position when the wood decayed; but the unforgettable part of this ceremony must have occurred before the skull was mounted, because the aperture at the base had been enlarged, almost certainly in order to extract and eat the brain.

Neanderthal rituals in Switzerland clearly focused on the bear. A number of boxlike stone structures found in Alpine eaves contain bear skulls. One of these crude chests held seven skulls arranged so that the muzzles pointed to the chamber entrance, while farther back in the cave six more skulls had been set in niches along the wall—one with a bone thrust through the arch of the cheek.

What this bear business means, nobody knows. Maybe the earliest human pageantry involved a bear. Even today a few Stone Age tribes conduct ceremonies whose principal figure is a bear, and some ethnologists regard this as the last glint of light from Neanderthal times.

Says Herbert Wendt: "It was in the time of cave bears that the first cultural and religious ideas arose, that the first magicians appeared, that Man achieved dominion over Nature and began to believe in the support of supernatural powers."

What did they look like?—these people we faintly abhor and seldom think about, yet who seem always to be not far away,

Museum dioramas are familiar: shambling, hairy, ape-faced monstrosities wearing animal pelts, the males holding spears or clubs, the females usually crouched beside a fire. This is the image, but it may not be accurate. Our impression is based on a skeleton reconstructed and studied in 1908. The relatively uncorrugated inner surface of the skull suggested that the brain had been simple, with convolutions resembling those of apes. The 1908 examiners also deduced a "simian arrangement" of spinal vertebrae and concluded that Neanderthal man slumped along with knees bent, on feet very much like the feet of a gorilla.

In 1957 this skeleton, which was that of a male, was reexamined. The gentleman was not exactly typical. He might have been fifty years old, which in those days was very old indeed. He suffered from arthritis of the jaws and spine, and perhaps of the lower limbs. The 1957 inspectors issued this statement: "There is no valid reason for the assumption that the posture of Neanderthal man . . . differed significantly from that of present-day man."

And in museum displays their faces are never painted because it was assumed that Neanderthals had not crossed that threshold of humanity where the idea of decorating something—a wall, or themselves—would occur to them. Well, maybe. But powdered black manganese, yellow ocher, and various red pigments are found at their campsites, frequently in stick-shaped pieces that appear to have been rubbed on a soft surface.

As for other artistic efforts, probably there were none. No sculpture has been found, nothing but tantalizing hints. A bone with a hole drilled in it. An ox rib with a collection of unnatural streaks. A bit of ivory polished and artificially stained.

Yet these same people, struggling toward a new plateau, seemed unable or unwilling to distinguish between animal meat and the carcasses of their neighbors. Twenty mutilated skeletons were discovered in a Yugoslav cave, skulls bashed, arm and leg bones split lengthwise to get at the marrow. And in France another grisly accumulation turned up—some of the bones charred, implying a barbecue.

Neanderthal front teeth, when examined under a microscope, often show a number of parallel scratches, the result of an eating habit. Even today certain primitive people stuff big chunks of meat into their months and use a knife to hack off what they are not able to chew, which leaves scratches on their teeth. These scratches almost always run diagonally from upper left to lower right, proving that the gourmets in question are right-handed—as you will see if you act out the scene. Now this information is not as useless as you might think, because man is the only animal that prefers one hand to another, and neurologists suspect there may be some kind of relationship between this preference and the development of speech. If that is correct, those minuscule marks on Neanderthal teeth could help to solve one of the most fascinating questions about our predecessors—whether or not they could speak.

The answer would seem to be: Yes.

Yes, but only a little. So say linguist Philip Lieberman and anatomist Edmund Crelin who reconstructed the vocal tracts of some fossilized men. They concluded that European Neanderthals did not have much of a pharynx, and without a decent pharynx it is impossible to articulate *g* or *k* or several vowel sounds. Consequently a Neanderthal's power of speech would be limited. Furthermore, say Lieberman and Crelin, he could not have pronounced his few sounds in quick succession. He spoke slowly, about one-tenth as fast as we do, perhaps one-twentieth as fast as a Spaniard.

It is alleged that Pharaoh Psamtik in the seventh century B.C. had two infants reared beyond the sound of human voices on the theory that when they began to talk they would necessarily resort to man's earliest language. One child finally said "bekos"—which is the Phrygian word for bread. But that *k* would seem to preclude Phrygian as the Neanderthal language.

James IV of Scotland conducted an almost identical experiment. He gave two babies to a mute woman who lived alone on Inchkeith Island, and we are told that the children grew up speaking perfect Hebrew. However, with a stunted pharynx it would be exceptionally difficult to speak Hebrew. At the moment, therefore, all we can do is speculate.

But the absorbing question about Neanderthals is not what they spoke; it is what became of them.

Did they vanish because of some inability to meet a changing climate?

Could they have been slaughtered, liquidated, terminated with extreme prejudice, by the Cro-Magnon people?

Or could these two supposedly distinct races be, in fact, the same?

Present wisdom holds that the last unadulterated Neanderthal died 40,000 years ago. However, one April evening in 1907 some Russian explorers led by Porshnyev Baradiin were setting up camp in an Asian desert when they noticed a shaggy human figure silhouetted against the late sun on a ridge just ahead. Whatever the thing was, it appeared to be watching them. After a while the creature turned and lumbered away, so they ran after it but were quickly outdistanced. This was the first meeting between Westerners and Yeti, or Sasquatch as the beast is called in the Pacific Northwest of the United States.

Soviets do not treat these encounters with as much levity as do Americans; there are Soviet anthropologists who believe that a few Neanderthals have survived in the deserts and mountains. European and American scientists doubt this. More significant than such reports, they say, are the features of people around us. In other words, although the race is extinct, Neanderthal characteristics have endured.

So they are among us at least in a vestigial sense, and just possibly as an isolated race that exists like the giant condor in remote pockets of the earth. Frequent reports of midnight brushes with humanoid monsters indicate a certain tremulous anticipation—which is to say, an abiding belief—but thus far no hairy pelts have been tacked to the wall.

In any event, while Rudolf Virchow and his nineteenth-century colleagues were disparaging Fuhlrott's caveman, a most outrageous book was published. Its author—a tall, bald, white-bearded gentleman—subsequently became known as the Shy Giant. He read so slowly, wrote so slowly, even thought so slowly, remarks biographer William Irvine, "that he always felt desperately behindhand, like a tortoise concentrating every energy on the next step, as he creeps in frantic haste toward impossible horizons. . . ."

This sounds exactly like a living Neanderthal, but of course it was Charles Darwin. And twenty-eight years earlier he almost did not get to sail on the *Beagle* because Captain Fitzroy, who believed one could pretty well judge a man by his features, mistrusted the shape of Darwin's nose. He thought the young man looked indecisive. We can only guess what might have happened, or failed to happen, had Fitzroy himself been more decisive and stamped his foot and lifted the gangplank so Darwin could not slip aboard.

Then the Scopes trial, that little masterpiece of idiocy, might never have been staged.

Nor should we have had that immortal debate between Thomas Huxley, on behalf of Darwin, and Bishop Wilberforce, known unkindly as Soapy Sam, on behalf of God:

"It would be interesting to know," said the bishop, "whether the ape in question was on your grandfather's or your grandmother's side."

But it is not a sound idea to prick a man as intelligent as Huxley, who whispered, "The Lord hath delivered him into my hands." And getting to his feet he answered aloud: "If you ask me whether I would rather have a miserable ape for a grandfather or a man highly endowed by nature and possessed of great means of influence and yet who employs those faculties and that influence for the mere purpose of introducing ridicule into a grave scientific discussion, then I unhesitatingly affirm my preference for the ape."

Whereupon, we are told, a lady in the audience fainted. And good Captain Fitzroy, trembling with honorable Christian rage, picked up a Bible and was just prevented from throwing it at Huxley. Fitzroy later was promoted to vice-admiral, which seems to be the natural course of events.

One is tempted to caricature Fitzroy. Still, whatever his faults, the man was not a simpleton. He came from a distinguished family, which perhaps proves nothing, but he had traveled around the world on the survey ship *Beagle* once before, and had been appointed a captain at the age of twenty-three. His surveys were accurate and highly valued, and he was a Fellow of the Royal Society. It is said, too, that after getting to know Darwin he changed his opinion. All the same, no matter how hard you try to look without prejudice upon Captain Fitzroy, it seems best to admit that this is an individual you cannot love.

However, the important thing is the debate, not the audience, and those traditional opponents Science and Religion once again entered the arena when Thomas Huxley challenged Soapy Sam.

It is the scientist, of course, armed with some impertinent fact, who attacks first—though the maneuver may be oblique or heavily veiled. Then the ecclesiastic must counterattack, for the very good reason that he perceives a threat to his office and to his life's work. The status quo must be protected, the heretical march of knowledge obstructed, whether it be the development of anesthetics, the experiments of Galileo, or the deductions of infamous bulb-nosed naturalists.

Both attitudes are easy to understand. Science feels obligated to inquire, whereas the Church comes armed with infallible dogma.

Thus we have Dr. John Lightfoot, Vice-Chancellor of Cambridge and Master of Saint Catherine's, nailing down the particulars in Archbishop Ussher's article of faith: "Heaven and earth, center and circumference were created all together and in the same instant, clouds full of water. This took place, and Man was created by the Trinity on the 23rd October, 4004 B.C. at 9 o'clock in the morning."

Gilgamesh the Sumerian may have been eating ham and eggs at that hour, but never mind; what impresses us is Dr. Lightfoot's stately assurance.

By contrast, old Darwin frets about each mistake he makes, telling us he is ready to weep with vexation, referring to himself as "the most miserable, bemuddled, stupid dog in all England." He goes then, we are informed, and walks through the winter morning—this aloof old genius—walking by himself and meditating, so early that he startles foxes trotting to their lairs at dawn.

Accompanying these famous champions we now and again meet an individual who, like some overexcited spectator at a wrestling match, resolves to assert himself by clambering into the ring. Consider a certain Denis or Didier Henrion, a seventeenth-century French engineer, who measured various bones that probably came from a brontosaurus and then announced without qualification that our progenitor Adam stood 123 feet, 9 inches tall. Eve, he said, had been five feet shorter. M. Henrion did not calculate their weight, which is too bad, nor Eve's other measurements, which must have been formidable; but what we would like to know most of all is why he positioned himself so awkwardly in the path of common sense.

Then we have the case of a respected historian named von Eckhart.

Early in the eighteenth century Professor Johannes Bartolomaus Beringer who taught natural history at the University of Würzburg, and who collected fossils, dug up hundreds of stones containing the imprint of fruits, flowers, spiders, turtles, snakes, frogs, and so forth. He studied them carefully because he had never seen anything like them and he therefore assumed that his report would have unusual scientific value. He published his conclusions in a handsome book titled *Lithographiae Wirceburgensis*, illustrated with twenty-two plates of the finest specimens. Unfortunately, von Eckart had persuaded some boys to carve and bury these fakes where Professor Beringer would be sure to find them.

It was a practical joke born of petulant dislike for Beringer, yet something beyond malice seems to have been involved: there is an undertone of hostility toward science.

This brings up the American Goliath, born of animosity toward hard-shell Protestants. An Iowa cigar manufacturer named Hull and a preacher named Turk argued about giants in the earth. Reverend Turk of course defended the Bible. Hull, choking with disgust, resolved to mock him as viciously as Eckhart had mocked Beringer.

In the summer of 1868 Hull bought a five-ton block of gypsum at a quarry near Fort Dodge and sent it by rail to Chicago where a stonemason was hired to sculpt a proper giant. The monster was then aged with acid and shipped to the New York village of Cardiff where Hull had a relative—William Newell—who buried it on his farm.

A year later Newell employed some laborers on the pretext of digging a well. Very soon their picks struck a stony ten-foot corpse, and considering that they knew nothing of the plot their fright does not seem unreasonable.

Thousands of sightseers arrived, so many that the town of Syracuse put a horse-drawn omnibus in service to Newell's farm. Among these visitors was Ralph Waldo Emerson who judged the slumbering colossus to be " undoubtedly ancient." The curator of the New York State Museum called it "the most remarkable object yet brought to light in this country"—a comment that might be variously interpreted. Dr. Oliver Wendell Holmes also paid a visit. Dr. Holmes drilled a hole behind one ear in order to inspect the substance, which suggests that at the very least he was uncertain. Most people thought it was a fossilized antediluvian man.

Whether or not Reverend Turk made a pilgrimage to Newell's farm, we don't know; but it would be safe to assume that when he heard about this giant in the earth he fairly quivered with satisfaction. How vindicated he must have felt. How joyous. How proud. Maybe a little complacent. Even a bit pontifical. If only we knew what he said to the diabolic cigar manufacturer.

And when Hull at last decided to crucify the gullible pastor, how did Reverend Turk respond? Did he pray? Did he forgive? Did he foam at the mouth? Furthermore, one can't help wondering if the experience taught him anything. Probably not. Fundamentalists are apt to be so fundamental.

More sophisticated, more enigmatic, and infinitely more knowledgeable than our cranky American atheist was the British sponsor of Piltdown Man—that veritable missing link with a human cranium and the jaw of an ape.

"Several years ago I was walking along a farm-road close to Piltdown Common, Fletching, when I noticed that the road had been mended with some peculiar brown flints not usual in the district. On enquiry I was astonished to learn that they were dug from a gravel-bed on the farm, and shortly afterwards I visited the place, where two labourers were at work. . . ."

So begins the account of Mr. Charles Dawson, a rotund Uckfield lawyer and amateur antiquarian who discovered the famous skull. He told his story in 1912 at a meeting of the London Geological Society, to which he had been invited by Dr. Arthur Smith-Woodward of the British Museum, and his remarks later were printed in the society's journal. Several renowned scientists were present when Dawson spoke, and for many years a painting titled *Discussing the Piltdown Man* hung on the staircase of the society's headquarters.

Dawson said that after coming upon fragments of a skullcap he got in touch with Smith-Woodward, who examined the bones and considered them so important that he joined the search. Together they turned up quite a lot. According to Dawson: "Besides the human remains, we found two small broken pieces of a molar tooth of a rather early Pliocene type of elephant, also a much-rolled cusp of a molar of *Mastodon*, portions of two teeth of *Hippopotamus*, and two molar teeth of a Pleistocene beaver."

From an adjacent field they recovered bits of deer antler and the tooth of a Pleistocene horse. All the specimens, including those of Piltdown Man, were highly mineralized with iron oxide.

The Piltdown cranium did not quite fit the Piltdown jaw, which made a few scientists uneasy. Yet they had been excavated at the same level, and despite the apelike lower jaw the molars were flat, indicating that the jaw worked with an acceptably human rotary motion. Then too, it would be exceedingly strange if, side by side, a prehistoric man had left only his skullcap while a prehistoric ape left only its jaw. Therefore they must belong to the same beast.

So excited was Dr. Smith-Woodward that he built a little house near the gravel bed, and when visitors arrived he could talk about nothing else.

A few more specimens were picked up: small bones from the nasal bridge and some delicate turbinal bones which support the membrane inside the nasal cavity. These turbinal bones were quite fragile; they fell apart when lifted out, but the shards were collected and glued together. And one hot August day Father Teilhard de Chardin, who had become interested in the project, was seated on a dump heap beside the pit idly running his fingers through the gravel when he noticed a canine tooth.

This tooth caused further debate at the Geological Society. It was very large, perhaps too large, and it appeared to be the tooth of a relatively old man whereas the jaw was that of a young man. Did this tooth come from another skull?

Piltdown Man eventually was accepted by English scientists, not without discomfort, as certain applicants for a social club may be accepted; but among friends and relatives, so to speak, he was admitted to the evolutionary tree. Elsewhere his credentials were not approved. Giuffrida-Ruggeri in Italy, Mollison in Germany, and Boule in France all thought the jaw belonged to an ape. American experts, too, looked skeptically at the reconstruction.

Against their doubts stood the simple argument of the discovery: fossil remains taken from Pleistocene gravel, much of it excavated under the meticulous supervision of Dr. Smith-Woodward of the British Museum.

Year after year the dispute simmered.

Then in 1953 the skull got a new custodian, Dr. Kenneth Oakley, who subjected it to a fluorine test. Buried bones gradually absorb fluorine from water in the earth; the longer the burial, the more fluorine.

Results of Oakley's tests were astonishing and puzzling. On the basis of fluorine content the jaw and skullcap did indeed belong together, yet they held less fluorine than animal bones taken from the same stratum. The contradiction so exasperated Dr. Oakley that he abruptly told a colleague: "This thing is bogus!" But his intuitive thrust was ignored, perhaps because the skull had been in the museum such a long time—almost forty years. One hesitates to denounce an old acquaintance.

A few months later an Oxford anthropologist named J. S. Weiner was driving home at night when he clearly understood that Piltdown Man was a fake. And it is curious how often an insight such as Weiner's is accompanied by actual physical movement. The astronomer Kepler, while drawing a figure on the blackboard for his students, was seized by an idea which led to our modern concept of the universe. The mathematician Poincaré reported that just as he was getting aboard an omnibus, just as his foot touched the step, a brilliant realization unfolded: "that the transformations I had used to define the Fuchsian functions were identical with those of non-Euclidean geometry." Beethoven, writing to his friend Tobias von Haslinger: "On my way to Vienna yesterday, sleep overtook me in my carriage. . . . Now during my sleep-journey, the following canon came into my head. . . ." A. E. Houseman: "Two of the stanzas . . . came into my head, just as they are printed, while I was crossing Hampstead Heath. . . ." And we have the testimony of Bertrand Russell who says that while walking toward Cambridge, capriciously tossing a tin of pipe tobacco and catching it—at the exact instant a ray of sunlight reflected from the metal surface of the tin he understood the basis of a certain philosophical argument. Goethe, too, experienced a swift flowering of knowledge while out for a walk, just as he noticed the whitened skull of a sheep on a hillside.

So it happened with the anthropologist, driving alone at night from London.

Weiner mentioned his startling thought to Sir Wilfred Le Gros Clark at Oxford. Then he took a chimpanzee jaw and spent a while filing down the molars. He was surprised by how quickly the teeth could be redesigned to look like human teeth. He dipped the chimp's jaw in permanganate until it acquired a suitable brownish hue and when it was dry he laid his new fossil on the desk of Le Gros Clark. He is said to have remarked with a look of innocence: "I got this out of the collections. What do you suppose it is?" And Sir Wilfrid, who knew immediately, exclaimed: "You can't mean it!"

They decided to have a conference with Oakley.

Soon after that conference Piltdown Man started falling apart. Those distinctively human molars had been artificially flattened; close inspection revealed that their surfaces were not quite on the same plane, as though the counterfeiter had altered his grip when he moved from one tooth to the next. The delicate turbinal bones were not what previous investigators had presumed them to be; they were merely a few bone splinters of indeterminate origin. The canine tooth found by Teilhard de Chardin was X-rayed and discovered to be a young tooth that had been ground down until the pulp chamber was almost exposed, which would not happen to a living tooth.

New chemical tests showed a nitrogen concentration of 3.9 percent in the jaw, 1.4 percent in the skullcap. There was also, on this occasion, a discrepancy in the fluorine content.

Details were noticed that should have been noticed earlier. Stone "tools" from the pit had been superficially stained with iron salts—except for one that had been colored with bichromate of potash. An elephant-bone pick, when examined under a glass, revealed uncharacteristic marks. This implement, said Oakley, was probably obtained from a Middle Pleistocene brick-earth or sandy formation: "The ends were whittled with a steel knife. . . ."

Various bones taken from the pit were given a newly developed test for uranium salts. If the bones had come naturally to their ultimate resting place the Geiger counter should have clicked along at more or less the same speed, but Oakley noted a wide spectrum, including one "fossil" so radioactive that when left on a photographic plate it took its own picture.

Thus, after forty years, the walls came tumbling down. The pit had been salted from top to bottom. The skullcap was old, perhaps even Neolithic; the jaw was recent and apparently belonged to a female orangutan. Of eighteen specimens collected by Dawson and Smith-Woodward ten unquestionably were fraudulent. As to the other eight, they are not held in high esteem.

Punch ran a cartoon showing Piltdown Man in a dentist's chair with the dentist saying, "This may hurt, but I'm afraid I'll have to remove the whole jaw."

And a motion was put before the House of Commons: "That the House has no confidence in the Trustees of the British Museum. . . ."

Among those trustees were some rather celebrated personages

including Winston Churchill, Anthony Eden, the Archbishop of Canterbury, and a member of the royal family.

Many scientists regarded the great Piltdown farce as not only an embarrassment but a waste of time. Others disagreed. It did stimulate public interest in anthropology; it did remind professionals of the need for accurate data and improved analytical procedures.

One is entitled to ask, of course, how so many eminent scientists could have been fooled for such a long while. There's no satisfactory answer. Dr. Louis Leakey suggested that the Piltdown bones were accepted as genuine because they fitted the pattern of what a very early human skull *ought* to look like. And this preconceived image must have been known to whoever contrived the hoax. Leakey himself had been dissatisfied with the skull, yet the idea of a forgery never occurred to him.

Asking himself how he could have been duped, he recalled a day in 1933 when he went to the British Museum. After explaining to the curator that he was writing a textbook on early man, he was escorted to the basement where the Piltdown fossils were kept in a safe. They were removed from the safe and placed on a table, together with reproductions. "I was not allowed to handle the originals in any way," said Leakey, "but merely to look at them and satisfy myself that the casts were really good replicas." The originals were then locked up, leaving him with only the casts to study. "It is my belief now that it was under these conditions that all visiting scientists were permitted to examine the Piltdown specimens. . . ."

Two other important questions cannot be answered. First, who was responsible? Second, what was the motive?

Charles Dawson, who died in 1916, is thought to have been the villain. Whoever concocted the fake had known quite a lot about anatomy, geology, and paleontology. Dawson qualified. There were no other suspects. "It is certainly not nice to accuse a dead man who cannot defend himself," wrote the Dutch geologist von Koenigswald, "but everything points quite clearly to his responsibility for the forgery."

Besides, Dawson once claimed to have observed a sea serpent in the Channel—although one must admit this is not impossible. Another time he was sure he had found a petrified toad. And he seems to have been fascinated by the concept of missing links. He picked up a tooth that he thought must be intermediate between reptile and mammal. He attempted to cross a carp with a goldfish in order to create a golden carp. He said he had unearthed a strange boat—half coracle, half canoe. Furthermore, he is known to have washed old bones with potassium bichromate.

Very well, suppose we ascribe the forgery to Dawson. Next, why did he do it? Why would Dawson, or anybody, go to all that trouble? For the pleasure of humiliating the authorities? To stir up a drowsy neighborhood? To make money? To obstruct and detour the search for knowledge?

And did he plan to reveal the hoax?

Fictional crimes are more gratifying: the author keeps you writhing in suspense, which is his job, but at last he tells you.

So much for cranks, fakes, jongleurs, and fanatics. Dawson, Hull, von Eckhart, M. Denis Henrion—no matter how diverting these testy eccentrics might be, they contributed nothing. They acted out their compulsions, that was all.

At the same time, offstage, a number of earnest men had been at work.

Eugène Dubois, following Darwin's conjecture that originally we lived in a "warm, forest-clad land," left Holland for the Dutch East Indies where he served with the colonial military forces as health officer, second class. In 1891 on the island of Java he unearthed some extremely heavy, chocolate-brown bones, harder than marble—remnants of a 700,000-year-old creature whose low skull resembled that of an ape, yet whose legs were adapted to walking erect. That the bones were ancient could not be disputed, but Dubois' claim that they represented a transitional form of life was not greeted with much enthusiasm. Most professionals who examined these bones in Europe thought he had brought back the top of an ape and the bottom of a man.

A few years later a fossil-collecting German naturalist who was traveling through China noticed a human tooth in a druggist's shop, where it was regarded as a dragon's tooth and would soon have been ground up for medicine. This tooth, along with other fossilized scraps of humanity, led paleontologists to a hillside near the village of Choukoutien, southwest of Peking, which yielded the remains of some exceptionally old Chinese. But by now the Second World War was gathering and archaeological work became difficult, especially after Japanese forces occupied Choukoutien in 1939. Chinese scientists grew increasingly concerned, and in 1941 they asked that the fossils be taken to America.

It is known that the Choukoutien fossils were packed in two white wooden boxes, labeled A and B, destined for the port of Chingwangtao where they were to be put aboard the SS *President Harrison.* A detachment of U.S. Marines was assigned to guard them.

Almost certainly these boxes left the Peking Union Medical College in a car which was going either to the U.S. Embassy or to the Marine barracks.

Beyond this point the journey of the prehistoric Chinese is obscured by swirling mist. Their bones are said to have been scattered and lost when Japanese soldiers stopped a train carrying the Marines. They are said to have disappeared from a warehouse in Chingwangtao which was twice ransacked by the Japanese. They are said to have been aboard a barge that capsized before reaching the *President Harrison*—although this sounds unbelievable because the *President Harrison* ran aground at the mouth of the Yangtze, quite a long distance from Chingwangtao. Then there is the possibility that an enterprising chemist may have gotten hold of them, in which case we must assume they were pulverized and swallowed.

Even now, decades later, the search for these bones goes on. Considering how much evolutionary evidence has accumulated since 1941, we might ask why anthropologists are so anxious to locate one particular batch of fossils.

There has never been a loss of such magnitude, says Dr. Harry Shapiro of the American Museum of Natural History, "for these ancient bones represented a veritable population of at least forty individuals—men, women and children—from a stage of human evolution previously unknown. . . . Although a few additional representatives of this ancient population have recently been discovered as a result of renewed exploration by the Chinese, it is unlikely that anything approaching the original sample will ever be restored."

Conceivably a few men might still be alive who know exactly what happened. If so, the inscrutable old Chinese could reappear. But more probably, somewhere between Peking and Chingwangtao, they passed from the hands of those who knew their scientific value into the hands of those who either didn't know or didn't care. And it is this last thought that appalls Dr. Shapiro, who reflects upon the dismay and sadness we would feel if we heard that Shakespeare's manuscripts had been found, only to be burned by a maid who looked at them without comprehension.

In Africa it's a different story, less tragic but more incredible because here we are concerned with men who supposedly knew what they were doing. The first important fossil turned up in Africa was contemptuously dismissed.

Momentous news is greeted like this more often than you would suspect. Einstein's germinal bolt of lightning did not attract much notice for eight years. Francis Bacon anticipated Newton's law of gravity by half a century, but the times were out of joint. The linguist Grotefend correctly deciphered an obscure cuneiform script and published his evidence in three reports, all of them ignored. Olaus Roemer, a seventeenth-century astronomer, discovered that light traveled at a fixed rate instead of propagating instantaneously, yet academic scientists rejected this idea for fifty years.

It happened again in 1924 when a Johannesburg anatomy professor named Raymond Dart reported on a miniature skull found in a limestone quarry near a railroad station called Taungs.

Two crates of fossil-bearing rock had been delivered to Professor Dart while he was getting dressed for the wedding of his friend Christo Beyers—"past international footballer and now senior lecturer in applied anatomy and operative surgery at the University of Witwatersrand." Dart immediately opened both crates. The first was a disappointment; he saw nothing but petrified eggshells and turtle shells.

The second crate held a gem: nearly enclosed by rock was the skull.

Dart returned to it as soon as Beyers had been legally committed. With a hammer, a chisel, and one of Mrs. Dart's knitting needles he set to work, delicately, because the little creature he meant to release had been imprisoned for almost a million years.

"No diamond cutter ever worked more lovingly or with such care on a priceless jewel," he later wrote, "nor, I am sure, with such inadequate tools. But on the seventy-third day, December 23, the rock parted. I could view the face from the front, although the right side was still embedded. . . . What emerged was a baby's face, an infant with a full set of milk teeth and its permanent molars just in the process of erupting. I doubt if there was ever any parent prouder of his offspring than I was of my 'Taungs baby' on that Christmas."

The skull seemed to be that of a young ape, yet its cranium was too large—implying a large brain, a brain in which for the first time intellect might outweigh instinct—and its roundness suggested that the creature had walked erect. Dart estimated that when fully grown the baby would have been perhaps four feet tall and would have weighed about ninety pounds.

Cautiously he named it *Australopithecus*, Ape of the South; but in a paper for the British scientific journal *Nature* he pointed out certain human characteristics and indicated that his baby belonged in the family somewhere between Pongidae and Hominidae: "The specimen is of importance because it exhibits an extinct race of apes intermediate between living anthropoids and man."

Not so! Not so in the least! cried European authorities, none of whom had examined the South African infant.

"Professor Dart is not likely to be led astray," commented the British anatomist Sir Arthur Keith. "If he has thoroughly examined the skull we are prepared to accept his decision." But presently Sir Arthur changed his mind: ". . . one is inclined to place *Australopithecus* in the same group or sub-family as the chimpanzee and gorilla. It is an allied genus. It seems to be near akin to both."

"There are serious doubts. . . ." wrote Smith-Woodward of Piltdown fame.

". . . the distorted skull of a chimpanzee just over four years old, probably a female," said Professor Arthur Robinson.

Not a hominid but an anthropoid ape, said Hans Weinert. Not a member of the human gallery, said Wilhelm Gieseler. Related to the gorilla, said Wolfgang Abel. And there were others. The consensus being that Dart's child was a chimpanzee.

Only one ranking professional agreed with Dart. This was Dr. Robert Broom, who looked like everybody's grandfather, who spoke with a Scottish burr, and who had become widely known—however implausible it may sound—for studying reptiles in the Great Karoo. He is described as a small, elderly gentleman who invariably wore a business suit with a high, starched collar, a black necktie, and a black hat. This was his uniform no matter where he happened to be, even in the bush. He was a medical doctor and part-time paleontologist who liked to collect things. In Ardrey's eloquent phrase: "fossils, Rembrandt etchings, postage stamps, susceptible girls."

A couple of weeks after Dr. Broom heard about the Taungs skull he came marching into Dart's laboratory unannounced, ignored everybody, strode to the bench on which the skull rested, and dropped to his knees. He remained for the weekend as Dart's houseguest and spent almost the entire time inspecting *Australopithecus*. He agreed that it was an intermediate form of life.

Because of Dr. Broom's reputation the skull became famous, so famous that witty young men would ask: "Who was that girl I saw you with last night?—is she from Taungs?"

But along with the simpletons, as usually happens, a few intelligent people spoke up. An editorial in the London *Observer* concluded with these lines:

> There must needs be some who will say that the discovery of a damaged skull in subtropical Africa makes no difference. Admittedly it does not affect us materially like the discovery of wireless or electric light. The difference is in outlook. The stimulus to all progress is man's innate belief that he can grasp the scheme of things or his place therein. But this stimulus compels him to track his career backward to its first beginnings as well as to carry it forward to its ultimate end. The more clearly he sees whence he has come the more clearly he will discern whither he is bound. Hence it is not an accident that an age of immense scientific advance produced Darwin with his Theory of Origins, or that a later period of social unrest has stimulated archaeologists to reveal the strength of the social tradition. Viewed in some such intellectual context as this, the Taungs skull is at once a reminder of limitations and an encouragement to further endeavour. Its importance, significant in itself, is enhanced by the fact that its message has been preserved through unimaginable ages for discovery here and now.

The *Observer*'s thoughtful opinion did not convince everybody. Letters from around the world arrived at Dart's office, warning him vociferously, emphatically, with magisterial certainty, that he would roast in Hell. The London *Times* printed a sharp rebuke, addressed to Dart, from a woman who signed herself "Plain but Sane":

"How can you, with such a wonderful gift of God-given genius—not the gift of a monkey, but a trust from the Almighty—become a traitor to your Creator by making yourself the active agent of Satan and his ready tool? What does your Master pay you for trying to undermine God's word? . . . What will it profit you? The wages of the master you serve is death. Why not change over? What will evolution do for you when dissolution overtakes you?"

And, regardless of evolution or dissolution, Profit was much on the mind of a gentleman who owned property in Sterkfontein, northeast of Taungs, for he issued a pamphlet with this invitation:

"Come to Sterkfontein and find the missing link!"

Given any conversation about men, apes, evolution, and all that, somebody inevitably will use the phrase *missing link*, often as a derisive question: "Why can't they find it?"—followed by hostile laughter. The unmistakable inference being that the link can't be found because it never existed, which proves that Archbishop Ussher must have been right. Oh, not 4004 B.C. exactly, but once upon a time the clouds split with a blinding flash, a huge Anglo-Saxon finger pointed down, and immediately the earth was populated with dinosaurs and cavemen. And if, let's say, a bona fide living breathing furry link could in fact be produced—a specimen undeniably half-and-half—you may be sure it would be angrily rejected, identified either as a peculiar chimpanzee or as a hairy little man with rickets.

The skull seems to be the determining factor. If the skull looks reasonably human—well then, the owner must have been human. Otherwise it was some sort of ape.

Consider the brow, the jaw, the dome. Especially the dome. Is it high, capacious, handsomely rounded?—a suitable receptacle for a human brain? If so, we have Man. Hominidae. Glory of the universe.

Does it resemble a football?—flattened, unimposing, diminutive? Then we have Pongidae, brute keeper of the forest.

The problem with such attractive and shapely logic may be illustrated by the fact that Lord Byron's brain measured 2,350 cubic centimeters while that of Anatole France measured just 1,100. It should follow, therefore, that Lord Byron was at least twice as intelligent as Anatole France. You see the brambles on this path.

Besides, the average cranial capacity of Cro-Magnon skulls is 1,650 cubic centimeters while that of modern Europeans is about 1,400—which implies that the human brain is shrinking. It could be. And perhaps for the best.

But this leads in another direction, so let's return to the Transvaal, to Professor Dart patiently sifting the earth for additional scraps of *Australopithecus*.

In the Makapan valley he discovered where a troop of these "chimpanzees" had stopped, and the campsite revealed gruesome proof of human behavior—an assortment of baboon skulls together with that of another *Australopithecus* child. The jaw of each baboon skull, as well as that of the child, had been broken in such a way as to suggest a feast. Chimpanzees customarily eat plants and fruit, not baboons, nor do adult chimps eat their own children. So, Dart reasoned, these creatures a million years ago were evolving rapidly.

He showed his skull collection to an expert in forensic medicine who told him that the *Australo* infant and forty-two baboons had been dispatched by powerful blows with a hard object. Dart suspected that the hard object, or objects, might still be around. Presently he found them: antelope leg bones. In some instances a particular bone could be fitted to the break in a particular skull. The fragile, porcelain-thin skulls of infant baboons had been emptied of their brains, then crushed and tossed aside, says Dart, just as a human child might crush and throw away a breakfast eggshell.

He published an article about these carnivorous Transvaal citizens in 1949, and being a scientist he gave it an appropriate title: "The Predatory Implemental Techniques of Australopithecus." Very few people who read it liked it.

Six years later a scientific congress met at the town of Livingstone near Victoria Falls. Dart was allotted twenty minutes, which meant he scarcely had time to summarize what he had learned. His talk seems to have been ignored. Many of the scientists did not bother to look at the exhibit he had prepared. Those skulls could not have been fractured by our ancestors. Probably a band of hyenas killed the baboons. Or some leopards. Or it could be that porcupines, which occasionally collect bones to chew on—porcupines might be responsible.

Said von Koenigswald, speaking for most of the Establishment: "It is easy to take such bones for implements, and this is in fact often done. But a comparison of the picture produced by Dart shows without any doubt that these bones have been gnawed and split by hyenas."

However, a British paleontologist named Sutcliffe who had spent a great deal of time studying hyenas did not agree. He said it would be uncharacteristic of hyenas to leave all those skulls around. Hyenas pulverize everything. Then, too, some rudimentary "tools" were unearthed in the *Australo* encampment, and the shaping of implements for a specific purpose is a trait that distinguishes *Homo sapiens* from beasts.

Rather cautiously the professionals began revising their opinion of Dart's exhibit.

Meanwhile, Dr. Broom had been attracted to the Sterkfontein limeworks where some fossils were turning up. The plant manager, Mr. Barlow, previously had worked at Taungs and he now understood that there were commodities other than lime; he was gathering fossils and selling them to tourists. Through him Dr. Broom got a few interesting bones, though nothing important. Then one day Mr. Barlow said, "I've something nice for you this morning." And he produced a jaw with recently broken teeth which Broom bought for two pounds. However, because the matrix looked different, Broom suspected it had not been dug out of the quarry. When asked about this, Barlow grew evasive. Dr. Broom therefore returned to the limeworks on the manager's day off and showed the jaw to some workmen. None of them recognized it.

Broom then had a serious talk with the plant manager, who admitted he had gotten the jaw from a boy named Gert Terblanche. Broom drove to the Terblanche home. Gert was at school. Broom drove immediately to the school. He arrived just after noon, during playtime, and spoke to the headmaster. The boy was located and took out of his pocket "four of the most wonderful teeth ever seen in the world's history." These teeth, says Broom, "I promptly purchased from Gert, and transferred to my own pocket."

The boy had noticed the jaw protruding from a ledge. He had worked it loose by beating it with a rock, which accounted for the broken teeth.

In 1939 the price of lime dropped, closing the Sterkfontein quarry, and the Second World War further restricted archaeological work.

After the war Prime Minister Jan Smuts asked Dr. Broom to see what else he could find at Sterkfontein. Barlow was now dead, but from him Dr. Broom had learned to appreciate dynamite, so that very soon the vast African silence was being thunderously violated. And almost at once, remarks William Howells, first-rate fossils began describing small arcs in the air to the tune of his blasts.

The most startling find was an immensely powerful jaw—a jaw so massive that its owner came to be known as the Nutcracker Man. Further bits and pieces of these robust nutcracker people, or near-people, revealed the significant fact that their skulls had been crested like the skulls of orangutans or gorillas.

Dart and Broom now were convinced that East Africa was where it all began, but very few professionals agreed with them. Africa seemed rather distant. One would expect humanity's cradle to be nearer the center of things. Not that our first squiggly tracks ought to show up on Thames mud or the Champs-Élysées, but Africa did seem remote. A more familiar setting—Italy or Greece, let's say—would be perfect. The Dutch East Indies, possibly. Java might be acceptable. Perhaps China.

Louis Leakey then clambered out of the Olduvai Gorge where he had been prospecting for eighteen years, and he brought undeniable news.

Olduvai is a Masai word for the sansevieria plant which grows wild in that area. The gorge is about 25 miles long and 300 feet deep: a parched canyon where anthropologists, rhinos, cobras, and black-maned lions go about their business in dignified solitude, except for an occasional truckload of apprehensive tourists from Nairobi. It is a splendid place to study human evolution because quite a lot was happening here and because erosion has made it possible for scientists to get at the remains.

Archaeologist Hans Reck commented in 1913: "It is rare for strata to be so clearly distinguishable from one another as they are at Olduvai, the oldest at the bottom, the most recent at the top, undisturbed by a single gap, and never indurated or distorted by mountain-building forces."

Leakey, with his wife Mary, camped season after season at the edge, walked down into the gorge looking for bones, and shared a water hole with various large animals. "We could never get rid of the taste of rhino urine," he said, "even after filtering the water through charcoal and boiling it and using it in tea with lemon."

He sounds like the natural descendant of those nineteenth-century British explorers, men and women both, who marched presumptuously in when common sense should have kept them out. Eighty years ago one of his aunts arrived at Mombasa with the idea of touring the continental interior. Local officials, aghast at such madness, told her to go home; instead, she took a firm grip on her umbrella, hired a string of porters, and walked to Uganda. No doubt she approved of a nephew who chose to spend his life associating with dangerous animals and fever-laden mosquitos in the serene conviction that none of them would dare interrupt his work.

Leakey's first diamond in the rough was, as we might expect, a chunk of somebody's skull. It looked human—if compared to Dart's semihuman *Australopithecus*—and was about 750,000 years old. This, as professionals say, hardened the evidence that the African evolutionary line had continued. Leakey's man fitted nicely between ourselves and Dart's bone-wielding cannibalistic baboon killers.

Between 1961 and 1964 the Leakeys uncovered some two-million-year-old bones. The skulls indicated a large brain and the reconstructed hands looked altogether human. But we have trouble granting the existence of humans two million years ago—humans of any sort—not to mention those who may have been sophisticated enough to invent a device still used by various people around the world. By Argentine cowboys, for example, and by Eskimos who use it to capture geese and ptarmigan. That is, the bola. For there is evidence in the form of stone spheres from Bed II at Olduvai that those people used bolas to hunt animals. The spheres, which have been deliberately worked, are the size of baseballs. They might have been nothing more than hammers or clubheads, or balls meant to be thrown individually, though it would be strange to spend so much time shaping an object that could be lost. The reason Leakey suspected they were bolas—the stones encased in hide and connected by thongs—is that they often are found in pairs, or in sets of three.

It's a bit staggering to think that bolas may have been whirling across the earth for two million years.

A number of occupied sites have been located. At one of them the debris forms a curious pattern: a dense concentration within a rectangular area fifteen feet long by thirty feet wide. Outside this rectangle practically nothing can be found for three or four feet in any direction. The ground is bare. Then, beyond this vacant area, the artifacts show up again, though not as many. The explanation is simple. The littered rectangle was their home, surrounded by a protective thorn fence. Trash was tossed over the fence.

At another site there is a ring, about fifteen feet in diameter, consisting of several hundred stones. Occasionally the stones form a mound. The Okombambi tribe constructs shelters like this. For two million years they've been doing it. The mounds of rock support upright poles over which grass mats or hides are stretched to break the wind.

So the chronicle of humanity continues to lengthen. Now and again this record is frankly reassuring. In 1966 on the French Riviera, while a hillside was being excavated to make way for some luxurious apartments, the site of an ancient encampment was revealed. And there, 400,000 years old, lay a human footprint. It tells as much as anything. The footprint proves that we have tenure on earth as certainly as the whale and the crocodile. We, too, have taken part in the grand scheme.

Flipper-bearing lungfish moved ashore in East Africa—in East Africa or some other warm forest-clad land—where they turned into tree shrews which turned into apes. Then, fifteen or twenty million years ago, presumably when forests were dwindling because of a change in climate, some adventurous or desperate apes moved from the trees to the savannas. Here, anxious to see what was happening, because it could mean life or death, they spent most of their time upright.

And on the plain, unprotected, they learned the value of tools and the use of fire.

After that it was downhill all the way, or uphill—depending on your estimate of mankind—from omnivorous thighbone-wielding assassins to those erect Ice Age people with whom we can sympathize, who felt a previously unknown need to worship, to make music, to dance, and paint pictures.

Evidence that our Ice Age ancestors could appreciate music is tentative, unlike the vividly painted animals that register their love of graphic art, yet what seems to be a musical instrument still exists in southern France. In a cave at Pêche Merle a set of stalactites appears to have been worn down unnaturally, and when struck with a chamois-covered stick each column produces a different note. Ascribe this to chance or not, as you like.

At Le Tuc d'Audoubert, half a mile inside the cave, a pair of bison were modeled in high relief on a clay bank—the bull ready to mount the cow. The clay is now dry and deeply cracked, otherwise the animals seem unaffected by the millennia that have passed since they were formed. They surge with vitality. But the arresting thing about this tableau is not the elemental vigor of the bison or the skill with which they have been realized; more startling is the fact that the mud floor of the cave shows a ring of little heelprints, as though children had been dancing. In other words, these two animals were the central images of a ritual, a bison dance. And it is possible that the young dancers wore bison horns and pelts, just as in the eagle dance American Indians wear eagle feathers and represent themselves as eagles, circling, sweeping, fluttering.

Prehistorians agree that this grotto was the scene of a ritual, though some of them are not sure about the dancing; they favor a kind of backward march, a goose step in reverse, which is such an ugly concept that it may well be correct. Neither theory has been certified, however, so let's assume the children were dancing.

In either case, why should this performance have been limited to children? The answer is fairly obvious. At an appropriate age each child was admitted to tribal membership, just as today the Church observes a rite of confirmation. Deep inside Le Tuc d'Audoubert these novitiates danced around a male and female bison, dancing from childhood toward the mysteries of adult life.

Not far away, in the cave known as Les Trois Frères, an entire wall is covered with snowy owls, rabbits, fish, muskoxen, mammoths, and so on—with arrows flying toward them from every direction. This complicated mural may very well illustrate something of profound mystic significance. The numinous spirit of life, for instance. But probably what it represents is more immediate and understandable: Hunger. Meat for the table.

Sex and the stomach, remarks one anthropologist, such are the dominant themes of most philosophy.

Still, in this same cave, cut into the rock twelve feet above the ground with a stone knife, we find a very different philosopher—a prancing round-eyed antlered Wizard who gazes emptily down upon today. Something about the position of his hands is strangely terrible and important, but what does the gesture signify? What is he telling us? If only we knew. All we can be sure of is that he has dominated this wall for thousands of years, dressed in a stag's pelt with the tail of a horse.

Less enigmatic and threatening than the Wizard of Les Frères is the ivory Venus of Lespugue, who now holds court not in her original cave but in a glass cabinet at the Musée de l'Homme in Paris, just a step from the Trocadéro métro. She is flanked by mirrors so that after pressing the minuterie button you have sixty seconds to contemplate her prodigious feminine melons, north and south. Unspeakably poised, tranquil as a water lily, this stained and fractured Aurignacian princess waits, more beguiling than your favorite movie actress. Modern sculpture seldom says as much.

Further evidence of man's complex artistic roots turned up at La Genière, near Serrières-sur-Ain. Excavators came across a limestone plaque tucked into a layer of the Middle Stone Age, and on this limestone scrap had been engraved that popular subject the bison—engraved decisively, powerfully. Most unusual, however, was the fact that this one resembled a polychrome bison on a wall painting at Font-de-Gaume some 300 kilometers distant. So close indeed was the resemblance between these animals that the famous abbé-archaeologist Henri Breuil wrote: ". . . one is forced to consider the possibility that both are by the same hand. Who knows whether that small limestone plaque from Serrières could not have been a sketch for the wall painting. Or was the drawing of La Genière, on the other hand, just a souvenir of a pilgrimage."

Did the artist who painted the wall at Font-de-Gaume carry his preliminary sketch all the way to La Genière? Or did a prehistoric tourist so greatly admire the mural that he, or she, bought or stole the sketch in order to take it home?

Both thoughts are surprising. Who could have imagined such artistic concern during the Stone Age?

Alas, regardless of ancient aesthetics, we are here confronted by a fake. Professor Viret of Lyon observed suspiciously: "On ne saurait pas manquer d'être frappé de la profondeur et de la régularité du sillon de la gravure." In other words, authentic Stone Age engravings almost always are drawn softly, delicately, whereas the beast at La Genière had been delineated with deep regular strokes.

Professor Viret, troubled by this discrepancy, submitted the limestone bison for laboratory analysis, and beneath ultraviolet light one could see that the fluorescence of the line sharply differed from the fluorescence of the surface. This meant the engraving must be recent. Quite recent. And here, too, just as in the case of Charles Dawson, although the faker cannot be positively identified, circumstantial evidence does point to somebody: one of the workmen at La Genière. It's been learned that he was familiar with the Font-de-Gaume wall painting, and he is known to have made an engraving of a deer in the same style. The deer is not as good, probably because he didn't have a model. Forgers are better at copying than at creating.

So, regrettably, the limestone plaque cannot persuade us that our ancestors would travel 300 kilometers to view the latest chef d'oeuvre.

However, when sifting evidence one must be careful. Consider the engravings of mammoths discovered at Les Eyzies. In 1885 these were denounced as fakes. Modern investigators, though, have doubts about the nineteenth-century doubts. For example, certain anatomical peculiarities of a mammoth—which are clearly represented at Les Eyzies—were unknown even to scientists in 1885.

And the Altamira paintings were ridiculed for a long time, mostly because nineteenth-century scholars were able to perceive a "slightly mediocre air of modernity."

All of which should remind us that one can be not only too gullible, but too skeptical.

Besides, as the twentieth-century scholar Luis Pericot-Garcia has remarked: "Without aesthetic ability, the experience gained by apprenticeship in a school, and the background of a tradition, no artist would spontaneously paint a bison such as those at Altamira."

Herbert Kühn, who examined the work at Lascaux, discovered that the figures had been outlined with knives before they were painted, and these outlines first had been delineated with a brush—perhaps made from the plume of a snipe—because such fragile drawing could not be rendered any other way. Parenthetically it may be noted that in German the snipe's plume is *die Malerfeder*, the artist's feather, and when equipped with a bone handle it becomes a perfectly adequate little brush. The Lascaux artwork, however, does not seem to have been brushed on; almost certainly the paint was squirted, very much as we spray-paint automobiles. The surface was prepared with oil and fat, then powdered colors were blown onto the sticky background through bone tubes. Now this is quite a sophisticated technique, which clearly supports Pericot-Garcia's theory. There must indeed have been schools.

Ice Age pigments are genuine oil colors, not much different from those used by artists today, says Kühn. "The ochres would have been pounded fine in mortars, and in many caves ochre-crayons have been found. . . ."

On a rock bench at Altamira lay a supply of crayons, sharpened and neatly arranged, resembling women's lipstick displayed on a cosmetics counter, just as the artist left them 12,000 years ago. Or perhaps long before that. Say 15,000. The mere existence of these crayons seems astonishing, yet still more so is the arrangement—the fact that it was not a disorderly collection but a coherent spectrum from which the artist could select whatever he thought appropriate. It is this evidence of planning which truly surprises us because we assume that those spear-carrying fur-clad hunters did not shrewdly organize their thoughts, did not quite bring their minds into focus. Not unless it concerned survival. Organizing for a mammoth hunt, yes. But one man, a cave muralist, reflectively choosing his palette?

And if you still think Ice Age artists lacked sophistication, it might be observed that a grasshopper incised on a bone at Les Trois Frères was portrayed with such fidelity that the insect's species has been determined.

They seem to have been modern enough in other ways. One engraved bone depicts a man who is either watching or following a voluptuous nude woman—a picture that bluntly points out, with little equivocation, how you and I happen to be here.

Professor Magín Berenguer suggests that man entered the world of art by way of these adipose Venuses, where the entire expressive force is concentrated on fecundity. Then, through his art, man established the immense distance which separates him from all other created things.

So be it.

Lungfish to shrew to ape to man. For better or worse that was the sequence; at least it's a sequence acceptable to many anthropologists. As always, however, there are creepers of dissent pushing in every direction.

According to Richard Leakey, who has continued the work started by his father: "Early man was a hunter, but I think the concept of aggressiveness—the killer-ape syndrome—is wrong. I am quite sure that the willingness of modern aggressive man to kill his own kind is a very recent cultural development. . . ."

Says George Schaller: "Man is a primate by inheritance but a carnivore by profession. . . ."

David Pilbeam: "I have grown increasingly skeptical of the view that hominids differentiated as weapon-wielding savanna bipeds. I am as inclined to think that changes in a predominantly vegetarian diet provided the initial impetus. Also I believe that too little emphasis has been placed on the role of language and communication. . . ."

F. Clark Howell: "We still do not know the source of the hominids, but it is possible that their origin may lie between seven and fifteen million years ago, and perhaps not only in Africa. . . ."

Von Koenigswald: "I definitely believe man's earliest ancestors came from Asia. . . ."

Or you may choose to go along with paleontologist Bjurn Kurten, who thinks man did not evolve from the ape but vice versa. He considers it possible to draw a direct line of ancestry from ourselves to a small-jawed animal called *Propliopithecus* that lived thirty or forty million years ago.

If none of this sounds appealing you can always return to the comfortable certitude of Archbishop Ussher.

The ultimate question, though, toward which all inquiries bend, and which carries a hint of menace, is not where or when or why we came to be as we are, but how the future will unfold.

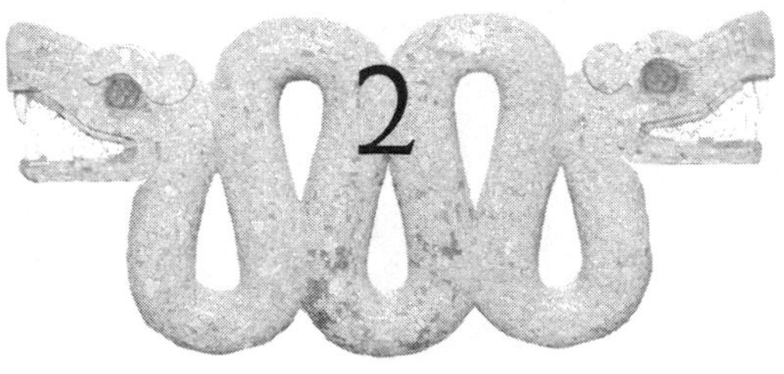

2

Eca Suthi . . .

IN 1828 A PEASANT WHO WAS plowing on the Italian estate of Lucien Bonaparte, Napoleon's brother, crashed through the roof of an Etruscan burial vault. A bailiff was ordered to investigate, and what he saw underground promptly caused Lucien to start raking the countryside for more tombs. Hundreds were found and looted, yielding thousands of painted dishes, statuettes, jewels, rings, bracelets, and so on. The Vulci necropolis, from which Bonaparte recovered most of this treasure, is thought to have given up more valuables than any other ancient site with the exception of Pompeii.

News of the Vulci bonanza whistled through Italy and across Europe while Lucien Bonaparte's neighbors began to contemplate their own fields with deep interest. As a result, more tombs were ripped open and stripped of marketable merchandise, and Prosper Mérimée felt inspired to write *The Etruscan Vase*. The vase that excited him was not Etruscan, it happened to be Greek, either imported or manufactured in a south Italian Greek pottery shop; but Mérimée did not know this, for which we may be mildly grateful. *Le Vase Étrusque* is not classified as a masterpiece but we need all the literature we can get, even if it's written under a misapprehension.

One by one the sites and the important relics were catalogued, scholarly papers rustled, and archaeologists took to quarreling over the debris. They still quarrel, mostly because the language cannot quite be understood and because nobody has proved beyond doubt where the Etruscans came from.

At present we have two legitimate theories concerning their homeland, and a third theory which once was greeted with respect but now is not. Wherever they originated, these people dominated the central Mediterranean for several centuries. We are told by Livy that Etruria's renown "filled the lands and the waters from one end of Italy to the other, from the Alps to the Straits of Messina."

Herodotus thought they emigrated from Asia Minor:

"During the reign of Atys, son of Manes, there was famine throughout Lydia. For a while the Lydians persisted in living as they always had, but when the famine lengthened they looked for a way to alleviate their misery—some suggesting one thing, some another. At this time they invented dice games, knucklebone games, handball games, and other games—except draughts, which they did not invent. They would play all day for two days in order to distract themselves and on the third day they would eat. For eighteen years they lived like this. . . ."

At last, continues Herodotus, the king divided his subjects into two groups and chose by lot which would remain in Lydia and which must go in search of a new home. The king himself remained, while those who were to leave he put in charge of his son Tyrsenos. Then all those who were departing went down to Smyrna where they built ships, and after loading the ships with their possessions they sailed away and "passed by many nations in turn" until they reached the land of the Umbrians.

Summarizing the exodus in this manner makes it sound like a ten-day cruise. The reality—if we are discussing reality—must have been quite different. Assuming a degree of truth in the legend, it seems unlikely that there could have been one vast embarkation; more probably there would be numerous small embarkations over a period of years, just as bands of Crusaders straggled toward the Holy Land for 200 years, in contrast to the popular view of seven Christian armies one after another clanking through Syria. And Herodotus' remark about passing many nations in turn could mean that the emigrants settled here and there, then some of their descendants drifted along, and theirs wandered farther, until at last—centuries after Tyrsenos left home—people with Lydian blood and Lydian traditions reached Italy.

That there was famine in Asia Minor during the thirteenth century B.C. cannot be doubted. Pharaoh Merneptah shipped grain to "Kheta," land of the Hittites, and a communiqué from one Hittite ruler alludes to starvation. There is also the account of a provincial king with an unpronounceable name who led his famished subjects to the court of the Hittite emperor.

Egyptian hieroglyphs speak of an attempted invasion by "Peoples of the Sea" during the reign of Pharaohs Merneptah and Ramses III, between 1230 and 1170 B.C., and it's possible that among these half-identified sea people were some Lydians. Whether or not this is so, the course of the emigrants is reasonably clear: they sailed past Malta and Sicily, at which point a few might have continued west to the famous city of Tartessus in Spain. A majority, however, must have turned north to the Italian mainland where they settled along the coast between the Tiber and the Arno, north of the marsh that eventually would become Rome. Here, in Tuscany, among a Bronze Age people called Villanovans, they built those cities we dimly remember from school—Cerveteri, Tarquinia, Populonium, and the others—and here they became known to the Greeks as Tyrsenoi, to the Latins as Etrusci.

The evidence for such a theory is persuasive. In the first place, Herodotus was not the only historian to describe an ancient Lydian migration. Secondly, it is a fact, with little disagreement among archaeologists, that during the eighth and ninth centuries B.C. a noticeable change occurred in the Tuscan way of life. This commonly is called the "Orientalizing" period. It included the substitution of burial for cremation and the appearance of chambered tombs beneath a *dromo*, or mound, very similar to the earliest tombs in Asia Minor. Religion, too, assumed a different form, apparently related to the eastern Mediterranean. Even the Tuscan devils evolved into first cousins of Assyrian and Chaldean devils. And the livers of sacrificed animals were examined for signs, a Babylonian practice.

Furthermore, the social organization began to display Eastern characteristics, particularly the attitude toward women. The Greeks, in fact, were shocked to learn that Etruscan men treated women as equals. To the Greeks, and later to the Romans, this seemed degenerate.

The style of dress became Eastern. Fashionable ladies wore the round or pointed cap that had been popular with Hittite women. Men wore a belted jerkin with a cloak thrown across one shoulder—which developed into the Roman toga. Men and women both wore pointed shoes with turned-up toes, very much like Hittite shoes.

Then there are linguistic arguments for supposing that these people came from Asia Minor, because Etruscan is not one of the Indo-European languages. Its alphabet is Greek, but the words and sentence construction are not. Nobody has been able to relate Etruscan to any other language, though just about everything has been tried: Sanskrit, Albanian, Hebrew, Basque, Hungarian, and various Anatolian languages. That it should still be indecipherable is not just curious but rather outrageous, because Etruscan was spoken in Tuscany right up to the opening of the Christian era and was used by Etruscan priests as late as the fifth century A.D. This being so, how could it absolutely disappear? We have no explanation, although there are reasons for thinking that the Christian Church obliterated it, just as the Church attempted to silence Aztec, Mayan, and other such ungodly tongues.

However, remnants of a lost civilization tend to be as durable as pottery shards. The archbishop's staff, for instance, developed from the coiled wand of an Etruscan soothsayer. And the mallet used by Charun to smash the skulls of Etruscan dead is employed whenever a pope dies. Not long ago, you may remember, the Vatican secretary of state, Cardinal Villot, tapped John Paul's forehead three times with a silver hammer, calling him by his given name: "Albino, Albino, Albino. Are you dead?" People everywhere, including many who are not Catholic, must have prayed that the elfish little pontiff would smile and sit up. Alas, there was no response; the September pope was gone. Cardinal Villot grasped John Paul's hand, withdrew the gold ring of the fisherman, and smashed it.

And occasionally we speak or write an Etruscan word: *tavern*, *cistern*, *letter*, *person*, *ceremony*, *lantern*. But except for these, only about 100 Etruscan words have been deciphered, mostly funeral announcements which occur again and again so that their meaning is not much in doubt. *Eca suthi*, let us say, followed by a name.

One of the strongest linguistic pillars supporting the Eastern theory is a stela from the seventh century B.C. which was uncovered in 1885 on the island of Lemnos in the Aegean. It depicts a warrior holding a lance and it bears two inscriptions using the Greek alphabet. The language, though, is not Greek; it is Etruscoid. Other fragments of this language have since been found on Lemnos, which does away with the idea that the stela might have been imported. What all of this suggests is that Etruscan-speaking Lydians might have settled there.

Take a narrow look at the statues, pots, tripods, jewelry, sword hilts, murals. So much hints at Oriental ancestry.

If you study the Cerveteri sarcophagus which is now in Rome's Villa Giulia it becomes very difficult to think of these people as primitive Italians: the husband's tilted eyes and stiff Turkish beard, the wife's little cap and pointed slippers, the languorous sensuality surging like a wave between them.

And in the Louvre, not fifty yards from the Winged Victory in her stone nightgown, rests another Etruscan sarcophagus—less erotic than the Italian, a bit more crisp, more architectonic, although they were produced at about the same time in the same city, perhaps in the same workshop. Once again you meet those tilted eyes, the complacent wife's up-curled slippers, the mild husband's carefully shaped beard. And, if you walk around behind the sarcophagus, you see how the hair has been styled in tight Babylonian ringlets.

New York's Metropolitan used to display three impressively sculpted Etruscans with somewhat Asiatic features: a gigantic helmeted head; a six-foot, eight-inch warrior; and the "Big Warrior" who stood eight feet tall. They turned out to be fakes, manufactured sixty years ago by a quartet of young entrepreneurs in Orvieto, but that's not the point; the point is that even a fraudulent Etruscan seems less Italian than Eastern.

I remember the big warrior. I looked at him a number of times when he was considered authentic, and I always felt surprised that such an enormous antique could be in such good condition. When I heard he was a fake I felt incredulous, but only for an instant. Almost at once I heard myself muttering "Of course! Yes, of course! Anybody could see that!"

And what puzzled me then, as it does today, is why the experts were deceived. Because if somebody with no particular knowledge of

Etruscan art could half suspect the truth, as I did—well then, how could professionals be so blind? But for twenty-eight years most of them saw nothing wrong. One or two had doubts. One or two called these giants bogus. As for the rest: they came to marvel, to offer learned praise.

Now in Copenhagen, in the basement of that peculiar Edwardian museum known as the Glyptothek, are several bona fide Etruscan figures: a shattered frieze of black-bearded warriors wearing Trojan helmets and carrying circular shields embellished with a mysterious red, white, and black whirlpool. These thick-legged businesslike fighting men are the real McCoy, and everything about them points east.

So often with Etruscan artifacts one does apprehend these long reverberations from Asia. Nevertheless, a good many prominent archaeologists refuse to buy Herodotus' account; they consider it a fable. They reject the idea of an immense migration—half a nation sailing into the sunset—and insist unromantically that the Etruscans were natural descendants of some Italian farmers. What a gray thought. It's like being told the Kensington runestone is a fake—that the bloody tale of a battle between Indians and Vikings in upper Minnesota never took place. One wants to imagine.

Among the cold-blooded exponents of this autochthonous theory none is chillier than Massimo Pallottino, professor of Etruscology and Italic archaeology at the University of Rome. Indeed, Professor Pallottino sounds exasperated that other professionals could be wrong-headed enough even to contemplate the migration hypothesis, which he goes about dissecting with meticulous disdain and a glittering assortment of scalpels:

> Edoardo Brizio in 1885 was the first to put this theory on a scientific footing: he identified the Etruscan invaders with the bearers of Orientalizing (and later Hellenizing) civilization into Tuscany and Emilia, and he saw the Umbrians of Herodotus—i.e. Indo-European Italic peoples—in the cremating Villanovans. Among the most convinced followers of Brizio's thesis were O. Montelius, B. Modestov, G. Körte, G. Ghirardini, L. Mariani. . . . Herodotus may have been attracted by the similarity of the name Tyrrhenian *(Tyrrhenoi, Tyrsenoi)* with that of the city of Tyrrha or Torrhebus in Lydia. . . .

Nor was there an abrupt change in burial rites from the practice of cremation, typical of the Villanovan period, to Oriental inhumation. Both were characteristic of early Villanovan ceremonies, he tells us, notably in southern Etruria where the idea of cremation predominated. Later, during the eighth century B.C., the practice of inhumation gradually became established—not only in Etruria but in Latium, where no Etruscan "arrival" has been postulated.

"We should now examine the linguistic data. In spite of assertions to the contrary made by Lattes, Pareti and others, a close relationship unites Etruscan with the dialect spoken at Lemnos before the Athenian conquest of the island by Miltiades in the second half of the sixth century B.C. . . . This does not mean, however, that Lemnian and Etruscan were the same language. . . . Further, the onomastic agreements between the Etruscan and eastern languages carry no great weight (as E. Fiesel correctly pointed out) when we consider that they are based upon . . ."

Obviously this is not the stuff of which best-sellers are made, even in light doses, and with Pallottino one is forced to swallow page after page of it. The result is tedium sinking inexorably toward stupefaction, together with a dull realization that whatever the man says probably is correct. To read him is appalling. No dreams, my friend, just facts. Facts and deductions. Deductions followed by occasional impeccable qualifications. One is reminded of those medieval ecclesiastics wondering how many angels could dance on the head of a pin, it is all so academic. The difference, of course, being that these churchmen had not the least idea what they were talking about, while Professor Pallottino knows precisely.

Along the way, before telling us how it actually was, he takes a few pages to demolish that third theory, the illegitimate one. In this version, highly regarded during the nineteenth century, the Etruscans came down from the north. The reason for thinking so was linguistic: traces of an Etruscan dialect had been found among the Rhaetian Alps. But it seems that this material dates from the fourth century B.C., long after Etruscans had staked a claim in Italy.

An additional argument against it, says Pallottino, is the relationship of Etruscan to pre-Hellenic languages throughout the Aegean:

"This could only be explained by accepting Kretschmer's thesis of a parallel overland immigration into Greece and Italy originating from the Danube basin. We would then still have to explain those elements in the 'Tyrrhenian' toponymy. . . ."

In other words, let such nonsense be forgotten.

What remains, then, is the not particularly exciting thought that our sensuous, artistic, enigmatic Etruscans were the natural children of Villanova peasants. The name *Villanova,* if anybody asks, comes from a suburb of Bologna where vestiges of a previously unknown culture turned up: hut-shaped urns filled with human ashes, bronze weapons, amber jewelry, pins and combs. Apparently these ancestors of the Etruscans, if that is what they were, drifted south into Tuscany about the eleventh or tenth century before Christ and overwhelmed whatever inhabitants they encountered.

Perhaps 300 years later the Orientalizing began. This was the time of a Dark Age in Greece, between the decay of Mycenaean civilization and the emergence of those wise marble Pericleans against whom we half-consciously measure ourselves. It was a time when that templed colossus, Egypt, was beginning to crumble. Assyrian armor glinted ominously. Phrygian trumpets bellowed. Phoenician traders drove westward, dipping their sails at Carthage and Tartessus. Fresh currents rippled the length of the Mediterranean.

So, inevitably, the rude Villanova culture was affected. Greek vase painters moved to Cerveteri, bringing the alphabet and other such radical concepts. Pallottino believes that these various intellectual and artistic transfusions have given the impression of Etrurian dependence on the East, an impression to which the ancients—notably Herodotus—succumbed, and which still inhibits the thinking of twentieth-century investigators.

D. H. Lawrence, faced with the cool reason of Pallottino, might have been impatient or just disgusted. His own exploration of the subject, *Etruscan Places*, did not precede the professor's *Etruscologia* by much more than ten years, but Lawrence illuminated a region fully ten light-years away. He was a breast-fed romantic, the Italian a most assiduous scholar. Lawrence plunged into Etruria; Pallottino picks and brushes and trowels away at it.

The experience! cried Lawrence. The *experience*—that was what mattered. Live! Empathize! Feel!

When he visited Tuscany in 1927, three years before he died, he was quite sick; yet the book gives no hint of it, except indirectly. "Ease, naturalness, and an abundance of life," he wrote. "The things they did, in their easy centuries, are as natural and easy as breathing." No need to twist the mind or soul. Death was simply a pleasant continuance of life, with jewels and wine and flutes playing for the dance. Neither an ecstasy of bliss, a heaven, nor a purgatory of torment.

"From the shadow of the prehistoric world emerge dying religions that have not yet invented gods or goddesses, but live by the mystery of the elemental powers in the Universe, the complex vitalities of what we feebly call Nature."

"The goat says: let me breed for ever, till the world is one reeking goat. But then the lion roars from the other blood-stream, which is also in man, and he lifts his paw to strike. . . ."

This sort of thing annoys Pallottino, who has no time for mystics. Painted tombs littered with jewelry and elegant vases have created around his specialty "a peculiar aura of romantic suggestion, which the books of Dennis and Noël des Vergers helped to spread, never to disappear again. Scholarly uncertainties and polemics on the interpretation of Etruscan inscriptions, on the classification of the language, on the problem of Etruscan origins, gave birth to the notion of an 'Etruscan mystery'; and this notion, rather than describing, more or less aptly, a scientific situation . . ."

On and on he goes in his oddly dry, convincing prose—much less gratifying than the rainbows whipped up by Lawrence. And what he is insisting is that these people twenty-five centuries ago were neither more nor less enigmatic than you and I; which is to say that they are interesting by themselves, never mind the blather.

Physically they were small, judged by skeletal remains. The men averaged five feet, four inches, the women just above five feet. On the basis of tomb information their life expectancy was about forty.

Early historians denounced them as decadent and drunken, promiscuous lovers intoxicated by comfort, a reputation they shared with the Sybarites. Theopompus wrote in the fourth century B.C. that they copulated publicly and did not consider it shameful. "They all do the thing, some watching one another. . . . The men approach the women with great delight, but obtain as much pleasure from young men and adolescents. They grow up, in fact, to be very beautiful, for they live luxuriously and shave their bodies. . . ."

Posidonius, a Stoic author of the second century B.C., after observing that the Etruscans once were valorous, attributes their degeneration to the richness of the land—its minerals, timber, and so on. Later critics explained the decline with equal facility. Victorians, for example, thought they collapsed because of a perverse religion. Our twentieth century is less positive: we aren't sure just what happened to their world. From our balcony they appear to be at once naive and sophisticated, artistic and materialistic, radical, conservative, industrious, indolent, foolish, clever, ad infinitum. That is to say, a disorganized bellowing parade of contradictory mortals.

Despite meager evidence we do know a little about their activities and concerns.

Etruscan women liked to bleach their hair—a fancy that has been entertained, it seems, from the female prototype to the latest model. And depilatories were popular. Try this: boil a yellow tree frog until it has shrunk to half its natural size, then rub the shriveled frog on the unsightly area. Now, it's too bad we have no testimonials from satisfied beauties of Vetluna or Caere, but that does not mean the treatment is useless. These people sometimes equaled or surpassed us in the most unexpected ways.

Etruscan hunters understood the compelling power of music far better than we do. Aelian, who wrote in the third century, reveals that after the nets and traps had been set a piper would come forth playing his sweetest tunes. Wild pigs, stags, and other beasts at first would be terrified. But after a while, seduced, they draw closer, bewitched by these dulcet sounds, "until they fall, overpowered, into the snares." And we have the word of Polybius, five centuries earlier, who asserts that Etruscan swineherds walk their charges up and down the beach, not driving them as we would expect, but leading them by blowing a trumpet.

In dentistry, too, one must salute these creative sons of Villanova.

Skulls found at Tarquinia contain teeth neatly bridged and capped with gold.

Insecticides, which we regard as a small miracle of our century, were commonplace. The agronomist Saserna recommends an aromatic vine called serpentaria. Soak the root of this vine in a tub of water, then empty the tub on the infested earth. Or let's say you become conscious of ravenous little guests in your bed at night. Should that be the case, dampen your bed with a potion of ox gall and vinegar.

Take an ordinary business such as the production of cheese. Here again the Etruscan surprises us. Do you know those great wheels made in Holland and Denmark? Listen, my friend, Etruscans in the village of Luni fashioned wheels of goat cheese weighing 1,000 pounds.

Yet right along with such innovations they clung obstinately to the mindless beliefs of their fathers. Even the Romans, who are not celebrated for a liberal imagination, had begun to grasp the nature of things more clearly. Seneca, commenting on the difference between Romans and Etruscans, offers this example: "Whereas we believe lightning to be released when clouds collide, they believe that clouds collide so as to release lightning."

Another difference, more curious, which has not yet been explained, is that the Greeks and Romans and everybody else in that part of the world faced north when attempting to determine celestial influences. Only the Etruscans, those perverse, contradictory individuals, faced south. Why? Tomorrow, if the gods so ordain, we'll dig up the answer.

You can see them as they were, just as they were, on the ragged stone sarcophagus lids. You see the rich and powerful, of course, rather than the poor, because nobody commemorates the poor; but the features of affluent Etruscans have been studiously registered on their coffins. And there can be little doubt that these sculpted effigies are portraits of unique men and women, not blind symbols.

At least so it seems to an impressionable observer. However, one must be cautious. When making little terra-cotta votive heads the Etruscan coroplasts often used molds, then a touch or two with a modeling tool could give an effect of individuality. In other words, a mass-produced standardized face with a few singular characteristics—let's say a bobbed nose, a couple of warts, and a triple chin—is not the same as a portrait. Therefore one should regard the sarcophagus sculpture with mild distrust; maybe these figures, too, were only impersonations of life.

Yet no matter how they were done they do give the sense of being particular people. They are quickly recognizable and somehow appalling, like faces on the society page, and they tell quite a lot.

For instance, toward the end—while Etruscan civilization deteriorates—the sarcophagus men and women grow flabbily plump. They project an air of self-indulgence, of commercial success. And they seem strangely resigned or dissatisfied, as though they could anticipate the falling curtain. Yet if you look back a few centuries, not at these phlegmatic inheritors but at the pioneers who lived seven or six centuries before Christ, you notice a quality of strength or assurance like that found on prehistoric terra cotta statues from India and Thailand and Mexico. It is surprising and alarming to perceive what happens to a nation.

The despair these people felt has been reflected also in the late tomb paintings. Gone are the joyous leaping dolphins, the pipers and dancers. Instead, the hereafter looks grim. Mournful processions of the dead are escorted by gray-green putrescent demons with pointed ears and snakes in their hair. Ghoulish underworld heralds brandish tongs, ropes, and torches; they carry hammers and clubs with which to smash the skulls of the newly deceased. Everything seems to prefigure medieval Christianity.

Perhaps the *Libri Fatales* were responsible, not the minerals and timber, nor a degenerate religion—though it is true that the *Fatales* were religious texts. These books concerned the division of time, with limitations on the lives of men and women, and they placed a limit of ten saecula on the life of the Etruscan nation. A saeculum was a variable period, averaging about 100 years, and it was up to the priests to determine when each had ended. During the eighth and ninth saecula, while their city-states gradually were being absorbed by Rome, the people must have realized that the end was near, that nothing could save Etruria from extinction. Thus the prophecy became self-fulfilling.

In 44 B.C. when Julius Caesar was murdered a comet gleamed overhead, sheeted corpses gibbered in the street, and the Etruscan seer Vulcatius proclaimed an end to the ninth saeculum.

Claudius died ninety-eight years later—the last high Roman to understand the Etruscan language. His wife Plautia Urgulanilla was Etruscan, and Claudius had written a twenty-book history of them, *Tyrrhenica*, which has been lost. At his death, we are told, another brilliant comet appeared and lightning struck his father's tomb, marking the end of the final saeculum. Archaeologists find no evidence of what might properly be called Etruscan civilization after that date.

These ominous books, the *Fatales*, were part of a complex prescription covering rules of worship, life beyond the grave, civil and military ordinances, the founding of cities, interpretation of miracles, et cetera. Much of it has vanished, but some was transcribed by Greek, Roman, and Byzantine chroniclers, so we have—along with the *Fatales*—the *Libri Fulgurales* and *Haruspicini*.

Because it derives from the verb "to lighten," *fulgurale*, the first of these books naturally had to do with divination from objects hit by lightning. According to the sound and color of the bolt, and by the direction from which it came, a soothsayer would deduce which god had ordered the stroke and what it meant. The next step was to consult the *Libri* in order to learn what should be done. This was not easy. Any of nine gods might have thrown it, and Jupiter himself could hurl three different kinds of lightning. Etruscan skill at interpretation seems to have impressed the Romans; they themselves could recognize only one bolt from Jupiter's hand. If the regnant god was enraged he struck, and that was that. Consequently they would call for an Etruscan whenever they wanted a truly subtle reading. It was an Etruscan, Spurinna, who advised Caesar against the Ides of March.

In 1878 near Piacenza in the Po valley a unique object turned up: a bronze model of a sheep liver. The surface was divided into forty compartments enclosing the names of various gods such as Cilens, Ani, Hercle, Thuflthas, Muantras, and Satres. Without a Rosetta stone it has been necessary to proceed inchwise, as Mayan linguists do, but still there has been progress and several of these names have been correlated with familiar Latin gods. Others remain incomprehensible. But the significance of the bronze object is understood. The liver, being the seat of life, was a rich source of information. A priest would examine the liver of a sacrificed animal for blemishes or deformity, and after interpreting what he saw he would consult the *Libri Haruspicini* for an appropriate ritual. The bronze liver unearthed at Piacenza might have been used to instruct apprentices.

How remote it sounds—interpreting divine will through lightning bolts and sheep livers—like something from Stonehenge or the labyrinths of Crete. Yet as late as the fifth century A.D. these services were ordered in Christian Rome: Pope Innocent I, frightened by the approach of Alaric's Visigoths, consulted Etruscan fulgiatores and haruspices.

How remote, psychically, is Etruria? Well, my neighbor knocks on wood, millions consult the horoscope, and I myself don't much care for room 13. Interpret that as you please. Now back to the facts.

This incomplete collection of sacred books is just about all the Etruscan literature we have. Otherwise there are only scraps, threads, allusions, and those brief monotonous remarks on funerary items, on mirrors, weapons, and little boxes:

I BELONG TO LARTHIA.

TARCHUNIES HAD ME MADE.

VEL PARTUNU, SON OF VELTHUR AND RAMTHA SATLNEI, DIED AGED TWENTY-EIGHT.

ASKA MI ELEIVANA, MINI, MULVANIKE MAMARCE VELCHANA, which of course means: "I am an oil bottle donated by Mamarce Velchana."

A contemporary of Cicero mentions some tragedies written by Velna, or Volnius, but that is all we know, not the titles, not even the century. Indeed, there may not have been much Etruscan literature. If there was, it failed to excite the Romans.

In 1964 three rectangular sheets of gold were discovered near the port of Santa Severa. All were inscribed—one in Phoenician, two in Etruscan—perhaps telling a wonderful story, perhaps describing a voyage from Lydia. So, as you might imagine, there was whooping and dancing among Etruscologists. Unfortunately the Phoenician is not a translation of the Etruscan; linguists are convinced of that. Still, the plates have been helpful because the messages are similar: the king of Caere, Thefarie Velianas, is dedicating a shrine to the Lady Astarte in the month of the Sacrifice of the Sun. This ceremony, which must have been widely proclaimed, occurred about 500 B.C.

Latin inscriptions from the period of Roman hegemony often are found on monuments or on the pedestals of statues. One speaks of a military commander who led an army against "C," which would mean Caere. He led another force against Sicily, thus becoming the first Etruscan general to cross the water, and when he returned from this punitive expedition he was rewarded with an eagle and a golden crown. Clearly he was a great general. His name, almost obliterated, appears to be "Vel X, son of Lars."

What seems to resist oblivion, outlasting all other created things, including the greatest plays and the most exquisite poems, outlasting murals, statues, bronze mirrors, and stone sarcophagi, is pottery, the humble craftsman's daily product. It is just about indestructible. Certain plastics may last until the end of the world—maybe longer, if anybody cares—but pottery shards are practically as durable, which is a bit of luck. They are easily glued together, very often they fit to perfection although the object may have been shattered millennia ago, and the most ordinary scraps reveal quite a lot because, almost from the beginning, potters have decorated their pots. Changes of taste, form, and technique accurately measure the passing years. The examination of pots and cups and plates, therefore, becomes a fundamental discipline of the archaeologist.

Kylix, alabastron, rhyton, hydria—Etruscan potters, often adapting Greek forms, steadily manufactured them, century upon century. Thousands have survived intact, or faintly chipped, and we can only guess how many would be around if grave robbers were more considerate.

For instance, the famous blackware called bucchero. Lawrence described these vases and dishes as opening out "like strange flowers, black flowers with all the softness and the rebellion of life." Another Englishman, George Dennis—the same Dennis of whom Professor Pallottino disapproves—tells of being present during an excavation at Vulci in 1843. Under orders from Lucien Bonaparte's widow, the workmen divided whatever they found into two groups: jewelry, richly painted Greek vases and so forth, which fetched a good price, on one side;

everything of slight commercial value, such as bucchero dishes, on the other side. Whereupon, says Dennis, everything of little or no value was deliberately smashed. Widow Bonaparte did not want to dilute the market. "At the mouth of the pit in which they were at work, sat the *capo*, or overseer—his gun by his side. . . ."

One is reminded of Genghis Khan destroying what he was unable to use because he could not imagine what else should be done with it. Or Diego de Landa burning the elegant Mayan codices. Or those Mohammedan soldiers who broke into the library at Alexandria and helped themselves to 700,000 books—fuel enough to heat the public baths for six months.

Today what remains of Etruria?

A stone leopard. Dice. Chariot fragments. Several lead discs. An ivory writing tablet. Those three sheets of gold. Odd, mysterious items such as the bronze handle picked up at Fabbrecce, near Città di Castello, which shows a man wearing a crown of leaves, arms raised, with a dog or a lion on the ring above his head—with a human arm issuing from the animal's mouth! What does it mean? Or the engraved ostrich egg from Quinto Fiorentino. An ostrich egg with Etruscan lettering. What about that?

And the Capitoline wolf—emblem of Rome. We have this wild bronze mother, which probably was cast at Veii during the fifth century before Christ. Romulus and Remus, the sucklings, who crawled beneath her sometime during the sixteenth century, are meant to symbolize how Rome drew nourishment from Etruria.

So we have all this and more. Quite a lot more. But if one item alone testifies to the fugitive existence of these people it must be the ivory writing tablet. On its surface are traces of wax and some very old scratches; therefore we assume that an Etruscan stylus scratched the tablet.

Professor Luisa Banti, terse and formidable, says no. Without qualification: No.

We assume the tablet belonged to a child because of its small size and because an alphabet has been cut into the rim, just as you see our alphabet printed in bold letters on the cover or first page of a child's tablet.

Professor Banti does not waste time on this sentimental hypothesis. Instead, she offers two explanations, not mutually exclusive, for the small size and for the presence of an alphabet. First, the tablet may have been symbolic. Writing was then a new art in Etruria and the personage with whom it was buried wanted everybody to know that he could write. Second, the tablet might have been used for practice. If you have trouble forming letters you need a model.

The argument that Etruscan adults needed a model abecedary is tenuous but convincing: the alphabet was engraved also on quite a few miniature vases and these vases are thought to have been "inkpots"—containers for the red or black liquid that served as ink when writing on papyrus.

Regardless of who owned this tablet or how it was used, it must have been a delightful possession because one could magically erase the letters by waving a baton of hot metal over the wax. A hole drilled through the handle implies that there was a string, meaning it probably was worn like a necklace.

Such things—objects accompanying a funeral—are the most reliable guide to Etruria, as long as they are studied without preconceived theories. They are the one true Etruscan source, says Banti, "the only one unaltered by personal ideas, or by the interpretations and prejudices of the ancient writers whose works we use as historical sources. Archaeological finds are the archive documents of antiquity, documents that have to be studied patiently in museums and in excavation diaries. They are safer and more credible than the scant information handed down by ancient Greek and Latin historians."

We could almost fill a railroad train with Etruscan bric-a-brac. Corroded swords, dented bronze helmets, pots, plates, boxes, flasks, cinerary urns, mirrors, figurines, antefixes, cylinders, and so on. And yet, paradoxically, we don't seem to have nearly enough. We hunt for more and more, perhaps because it's easy to imagine how much has been lost.

What else remains?

Inside those odd funerary beehives that dot the Tuscan hillsides we come upon stained murals whose colors evoke memories of Crete and Egypt—pink, green, black, white, red, yellow—though the sensibility is Etruscan. Some of them cross the centuries between us like a bolt of lightning. A mural at Chiusi shows a charioteer who has just been pitched out of his vehicle: a moment from now he will land on his head. We can understand this. We appreciate and comprehend his problem. One can empathize with him more easily than with a Cretan acrobat somersaulting over the horns of a bull.

All right, we have these disintegrating murals. What else?

Sundry goods. Everyday merchandise. Scraps of apparel. Here and there a tantalizing curiosity.

In the National Museum of Yugoslavia stands a rigid female mummy shaped like a cudgel, or a Giacometti sculpture, or one of those elongated prehistoric Sardinian bronzes; and what is unique about this mummy is that, although it turned up in Egypt, the linen wrappings are covered with Etruscan liturgical formulas. Furthermore, what was written on the bandages has no connection with the burial. The linen contains 1,185 words, evenly spaced, written in red. Allowing for repetitions and illegible areas, there are 530 different Etruscan words, only a few of which can be translated. *Vinum* is obvious, and some others are not difficult for philologists: *fler* meaning an offering or sacrifice, *tur* meaning to give, *ais* or *eis* being the word for god. But most of the text is indecipherable: "ciltħs spurestres enas ethrse tinsi tiurim avils chis . . ."

Now the red-haired young woman stands naked in Zagreb, her leathery brown body stripped of its last garment, the one thing about her that excited professionals. Nobody knows her name or where she came from. *Eca suthi* . . . But then what? She could have been Egyptian, she could have been Etruscan. The linen roll probably was brought to Egypt by Etruscan colonists during their migration from Lydia about the ninth century B.C.—assuming such a migration did take place—or brought by a wealthy Etruscan family fleeing the Roman encroachment.

So much for scholarship.

You can visit Etruria with no trouble. Every morning the tourist buses leave Rome, air-conditioned buses with multilingual guides. They will take you to Cerveteri and Tarquinia and other famous sites. Or you can go by yourself and walk along the dusty paths, which may well be those the Etruscans used—because paths, like pots, last indefinitely. And you get the feeling that not much has changed. In midsummer the bloated purplish flies have no fear; they believe they are entitled to stick to your face. Pale blue blossoms of rosemary decorate the low hills, thick with prickly shrubs, and there is a sense of the Tyrrhenian Sea not far off.

You can visit the places where they lived and search the hills and enter the caves and burrows overgrown with trees. Uneasily you look at the *cippi*—stone symbols outside their tombs, a phallus to show that a man lies within, a house with a triangular roof to indicate a woman. That is to say, you can find the Etruscans—if you pretend. Because of the murals and painted ceramics, because of what you have been told or have read, you dimly perceive them. Almost. But it doesn't quite work. Imagination fails. There is no authentic Etruscan sound, no touch of an Etruscan hand, nor the odor of a plump Etruscan body. They seem to be present, yet they are not.

At last you return comfortably to Rome on the bus, having been told about Etruscans; or you return by yourself, exhausted and sweaty and confused, knowing no more, the past unrecaptured.

A Roman art dealer named Augusto Jandolo got a little closer. When he was a boy in Tuscany he watched as the sarcophagus of a Tarquinian nobleman was opened. The great stone cover was difficult to lift; but finally it rose, stood on end for a moment, and fell heavily aside. Then, says Jandolo, he saw something that he would remember until his dying day:

> Inside the sarcophagus I saw resting the body of a young warrior in full accoutrements, with helmet, spear, shield, and greaves. Let me stress that it was not a skeleton I saw; I saw a body, with all its limbs in place, stiffly outstretched as though the dead man had just been laid in the grave. It was the appearance of but a moment. Then, by the light of the torches, everything seemed to dissolve. The helmet rolled to the right, the round shield fell into the collapsed breastplate of the armor, the greaves flattened out at the bottom of the sarcophagus, one on the right, the other on the left. At the first contact with air the body which had lain inviolate for centuries suddenly dissolved into dust. . . . In the air, however, and around the torches, a golden powder seemed to be hovering.

3

Vinland Vínland

THE MOST COMPLETE ACCOUNTS of early Norse voyages to America are "The Greenlanders' Saga" and "Eirik's Saga." Both were written long after the events they describe and both are copies or variations of earlier accounts that have been lost.

"The Greenlanders' Saga" is part of a large vellum codex known as the *Flateyjarbók*, which was commissioned sometime between 1382 and 1395 by a wealthy Icelandic farmer named Jon Hakonarson who lived—as the title indicates—on a flat island. The book was carefully preserved by his descendants until one of them gave it to an Icelandic bishop, who gave it to the king of Denmark. It is now in the Royal Library.

There are two versions of Eirik's saga. One occurs in *Hauksbók*, which dates from about 1334 and was written by a certain Hauk Erlendsson "the Lawman" with the help of two secretaries. Erlendsson was descended from one of the first Norsemen to visit America; he was quite proud of this fact, and scholars believe he revised history somewhat in order to make his family seem still more illustrious. The other version appears in *Skálholtsbók*, probably written during the second half of the fifteenth century, and because it is later than Erlendsson's version it was at first assumed to be less accurate. But apparently the opposite is true; the *Skálholtsbók* copyist, no doubt descended from a long line of impoverished and lusterless clerks, did not care about history. He only wanted to produce a satisfactory duplicate so that he could get paid. At any rate, if you read medieval Norse and wish to compare them, both are in Copenhagen's Arnamagnaean Library.

"The Greenlanders' Saga" and "Eirik's Saga" recount many of the same events, though not all, and occasionally they contradict each other, which makes historical detective work just that much more difficult. Considering this, as well as the sparse evidence from other sources, and the obscurities, and the centuries that have elapsed since Leif and his half sister Freydis and Thorfinn and the others went adventuring, and the fact that both sagas are either variants or perhaps inaccurate copies of lost manuscripts—considering these handicaps, only an arrogant and simpleminded historian would claim to have deduced the truth absolutely.

Even so, the sagas are not fiction.

It is well known that scholars fight like spiders in a bottle over the interpretation of artifacts and crumbling parchment, and medieval Norse explorations have particularly excited their testiness, making it almost impossible for an ignorant reader to know which gray eminence to believe. All the same, this seems to be more or less what happened:

In A.D. 985 or 986 a young Icelandic trader named Bjarni Herjolfsson returned from Norway to spend the winter with his father, as he customarily did every second year. But when he got to the farm it was deserted, and neighbors told him that his father had accompanied Eirik Raude, Eirik the Red, to Greenland. Bjarni, according to one translation, was "taken heavily aback" by this news, and instead of unloading his cargo he decided to sail on to Greenland. Having never been there, he asked where it was to be found and what it looked like; and after being told that it lay somewhere to the west Bjarni asked his crewmen if they were prepared to go there with him, because Greenland was where he meant to spend this winter.

They said they would go with him.

He told them that the trip might be considered foolhardy, since none of them had been to the Greenland Sea. But they told him they would go, if that was what he had in mind.

After taking aboard supplies they left Iceland, not in one of those classic dragonships with brightly painted shields overlapping the rail but in a broad-beamed wallowing merchant ship called a knarr. They sailed west "until the land sank into the sea." Then, we are told, "the fair wind dropped, and there was a north wind and fog, and they did not know where they were going. Day after day passed like this. Then the sun came out again, and they were able to get their bearings from the sky."

Presently they saw land. They asked each other if this could be Greenland. Bjarni did not think it was, but they sailed closer. The country was low, with many trees and small hills.

They turned away and sailed north.

Two days later they sighted another coast. The crew asked if this might be Greenland. Bjarni did not think it was, for there were said to be huge glaciers in that country while this was flat and heavily forested. The crew wanted to put ashore because they needed water, but he refused.

They continued sailing north.

After several more days they sighted land for a third time. They saw mountains and glaciers, but again Bjarni refused to stop, saying the country had an inhospitable look. So, once more: "they turned their prow from the land and held out to sea with the same following wind."

The wind freshened. They sailed four days and nights until they saw yet another coast.

"From what I have been told," said Bjarni, "this most resembles Greenland. Here we will go ashore."

They put in that evening at a cape and found a boat nearby. Bjarni's father, Herjolf Bardsson, was living on this cape, which has been known ever since as Herjolfsnes.

"The next thing that happened," says the narrator of "The Greenlanders' Saga," "was that Bjarni Herjolfsson came from Greenland to see Earl Eirik"—which refers not to Eirik the Red but to Earl Eirik Hakonarsson who ruled Norway from A.D. 1000 to 1014. During this visit Bjarni described the lands he had seen when he was blown off course fifteen years earlier and people at the court rebuked him for his lack of curiosity, telling him that he should have gone ashore.

The following summer he was back in Greenland. His embarrassment at court must have been the subject of considerable gossip; but more important, the sagas tell us that "there was now great talk of discovering new countries." Eirik the Red's son, Leif, then bought Bjarni's ship and signed up a crew of thirty-five.

Old Eirik was asked to lead this voyage of exploration, just as he had led the colonists from Iceland to Greenland. He consented reluctantly, observing that he was not able to stand bad weather as he used to. But on the day they were to embark, while they were riding horseback to the ship, he was thrown and injured his foot.

"It is not fated that I shall discover more lands than Greenland, on which I live," he said. "We can go no further together."

Eirik Raude then returned to his farm, called Brattahlid, or Steep Slope, while Leif and the crew went aboard. Among the crew was a southerner, probably a German, named Tyrkir, who is identified in some accounts as Leif's godfather.

They followed Bjarni's route backward, coming first to the inhospitable country. "They made for land, lowered the boat and rowed ashore; but they saw no grass there. The uplands were covered with glaciers, and from the glaciers to the shore it was like one great slab of rock." Leif called this barren plateau Helluland. The leading candidates for Helluland seem to be Baffin Island and Newfoundland.

Next they came to the forest land, which they named Markland. It sounds agreeable, "with white sandy beaches shelving gently toward the sea," yet according to the sagas Leif and his men stayed only a short time before hurrying back to their ship as fast as they could. The sagas do not explain why they were anxious to leave. Nor do we know exactly where they were, though it must have been either Labrador or Nova Scotia.

Two days later they reached an island and went ashore. The weather was fine. They saw dew on the grass, which they tasted, "and they thought that never had they tasted anything as sweet." After this they returned to the ship and entered the sound which lay between the island and a cape projecting northward from the mainland.

They sailed westward past this cape. The water was very shallow. At low tide the ship touched bottom, "and it was a long way from the ship to the sea. But they were so impatient to get to land that they did not want to wait for the tide to rise under their ship but ran ashore at a place where a river flowed out of a lake."

As soon as the tide refloated their ship they brought it up into the lake. Here they anchored, unloaded some sacks of hide, and built stone-and-turf huts. Later, after deciding to winter at this place, they built houses. The lake and river were full of huge salmon and they thought cattle would be able to survive without fodder. There was no frost and the grass scarcely withered.

When the house-building had been completed Leif divided his men. Each day one group went out to explore the countryside, with orders that they should not become separated and that they return by dusk. At first things went well, but one evening Tyrkir was missing. Leif was very much disturbed because Tyrkir had been one of his father's companions for a long time.

"Leif spoke harsh words. . . ."

Twelve men set out to find Tyrkir. They had not gone far when he showed up. He was obviously in a good mood, rolling his eyes and laughing and talking in German so that nobody understood what he was saying. "The Greenlanders' Saga" describes him as being small, dark, and seedy in appearance, with a sloping forehead and an unsteady eye, but good at all kinds of odd jobs.

"Why are you so late, foster-father?" asked Leif. "And why did you leave your comrades?"

Tyrkir continued laughing, grimacing, and talking in German. Finally be spoke in Norse. "I have some news for you," he said. "I have found vines with grapes."

"Is that true, foster-father?" Leif asked.

"Of course it's true," said Tyrkir, "because where I was born there are plenty of vines and grapes."

Next morning Leif instructed his men to pick grapes and cut vines and to begin felling trees so that when they returned to Greenland they would have a good cargo. And when they embarked in the spring their ship carried a load of grapes, vines, and timber. Leif named the place Vinland.

All right, where was this lush country?

The sagas give many clues, several quite pointed, others too general to be of much help. That sweet-tasting dew, for instance, has been identified by some investigators as the sweet excreta of certain plant lice and flies—yet this could be found any number of places. Others who have studied the problem say it might have been only the dew which normally collects overnight, and the men had been aboard ship so long that they were eager for a taste of fresh water. Then there's a third possibility: the incident might be a fabrication which should be disregarded.

As for grapes, about thirty varieties grow wild in the northeastern United States and Nova Scotia. Along the coast at the present time they grow no farther north than Massachusetts, which would seem to establish Vinland's northern limit. However, in Leif's day the climate might have been different, which would extend that boundary. In the 1530s, for example, Jacques Cartier saw grapevines on both banks of the Saint Lawrence where none grow today. And botanists who examined pollen found in the ruins of Greenland Viking settlements have concluded that eleventh-century weather was not bad, certainly no worse than it is now, perhaps a little warmer.

The big argument about grapes, though, is not how far north they might have been growing during the Middle Ages but whether Leif's men actually found any. The quarrel hangs like a sword over the syllable *vin* or *vín*. In the original manuscript—long lost—did that syllable, or did it not, have a diacritical mark? Was Leif talking about Vinland or Vínland? Because the minuscule notation makes quite a difference. Without the mark it means meadow, grassy land, pastureland; with the mark it means wine country, grapevine country. In other words, how far north or south the Vikings camped might depend on whether Leif spoke of grass or of grapes. The sagas clearly suggest that Tyrkir was uncommonly exhilarated, and nobody ever has been known to get drunk on crushed grass, which argues that he was loitering amidst the vín, not the vin. But things aren't that simple. Perhaps Tyrkir stumbled upon wild berries, not grapes, and the Vikings sailed home to Greenland with a boatload of berries.

Now about the salmon, a cold-water fish. Today it swims no farther south than New York, which ought to establish a southern boundary for Vinland, thus eliminating Virginia and North Carolina where some students of the problem have placed it. And a warmer ocean 1,000 years ago would have kept the salmon in still higher latitudes, which would eliminate New York.

On the other hand, because of a remark in the sagas concerning the winter solstice, a German scholar located the settlement between 27° and 31°—in Florida. A Norwegian, interpreting this same remark differently, concluded that Vinland must have been on Chesapeake Bay.

A Yankee partisan proved that Leif wintered at Plymouth. He determined not only the exact route from Greenland but the time of year Leif arrived, even the time of day. His argument covers many pages and could hardly be more persuasive. That is, until you listen to somebody else.

A Harvard professor fixed the site in his own neighborhood, less than a mile from campus.

So the squabble persists, point and counterpoint.

In any event, Leif had not been home very long when one of his brothers, Thorvald, volunteered to inspect Vinland more closely.

"Well, brother," said Leif to Thorvald, "use my ship, if you like."

Thorvald picked thirty men and reached the encampment with no trouble. They spent that winter comfortably and the following summer they explored the western coast. They saw no animals or humans, but they did come across a small wooden structure—perhaps the frame of a tepee.

The next summer while exploring the east coast they saw three unusual humps or mounds on the beach, which turned out to be hide-covered boats with three "skraelings" asleep under each boat. "Skraeling" cannot be precisely translated, but it refers to the native inhabitants of Greenland and North America and is contemptuous, meaning barbarian or screamer or wretch. Whether these skraelings were Eskimos or Indians is not known. Some anthropologists believe they were the now extinct Beothuk or Micmac Indians. The hide-covered boats, however, might have been Eskimo umiaks which are larger than kayaks. Whatever they were, Thorvald's men crept up to these boats and killed eight skraelings. One escaped.

Then, we are told, after returning to the headland from which they had looked down on these boats, the Vikings became drowsy. This seems curious, but the saga does not explain. Next "they were aroused by a voice shouting: 'Awake, Thorvald! Awake with all your men! Hurry to the ship and leave quickly if you would save your lives!' Then came a great fleet of skin-boats to attack them."

During this fight Thorvald was hit by a freak shot: an arrow struck him in the armpit. "I think it will be the death of me," he said.

He asked to be carried to a place not far away where he had planned to build a house. There he was buried, with a cross at his head and another at his feet, so the place was named Krossanes.

Thorvald's men remained at Leif's camp that winter, loading their ship with vines and grapes. In the spring they sailed back to Greenland.

Another of Leif's brothers, Thorstein, offered to bring home Thorvald's body. He outfitted the same ship and took along his wife, Gudrid. The voyage was a disaster. They got lost, either because of storms or fog, and ended up not in Vinland but at a small Viking settlement on the upper coast of Greenland. They were obliged to spend the winter there, and Thorstein died of plague.

Shortly after his death, while Gudrid was seated near the bench on which his body was lying, Thorstein sat up and began to speak. Translations vary in detail, but essentially this is what Thorstein said:

"I wish to tell Gudrid her fate, that she may endure my death more easily, for I am comfortable in this place. Gudrid, listen. You are to be married to an Icelander and will live with him a long time. Many descendants will you have—stalwart, fair, sweet, and good. From Greenland you will go to Norway, thence to Iceland where you will make your home. In Iceland you will live many years with your husband, but you shall outlive him. After his death you will travel south but then return to Iceland where a church will be erected. In this church you will take the vows of a nun and this is where you will die."

Thorstein then lay down again on the bench. Later his body was dressed and carried to the ship. Another crew was formed because many of his men also had died of plague, and with Gudrid aboard they returned to the main settlement.

That summer the Icelander arrived. He was a merchant named Thorfinn Karlsefni of noble lineage: we read on his family register such aristocratic names as Thorvald Backbone, Thord Horsehead, and Ragnar Shaggypants. As prophesied, he fell in love with Gudrid and asked permission to marry her. Eirik consented. Or perhaps old Eirik was now dead and his son Leif gave permission. In either case, we know there was great joy at Brattahlid, with gaming, the telling of sagas, and other diversions.

"There was also much talk of Vinland voyages. . . ."

Karlsefni, urged by Gudrid, organized a large expedition consisting of sixty men, five women including Gudrid herself, and various kinds of livestock. It appears that they hoped to establish a permanent colony.

They settled in Leif's houses and the skraelings began to come around, peacefully. But one of the skraelings tried to steal a knife or an ax, he was killed by a Viking, and another battle took place.

At this point "The Greenlanders' Saga" and "Eirik's Saga" do not agree. The first says nothing about Leif's terrible half sister Freydis being a member of the Karlsefni expedition; yet according to "Eirik's Saga" she was present, and during this fight with the skraelings she did something so odd that it could hardly have been invented.

First, though, the ballistic missiles must be mentioned. The skraelings hurled some objects at the Vikings. These could have been Eskimo harpoons tied to bladders which served as floats, or they may have been stones sewn up in leather cases and launched from the poles—which would suggest Indians. Centuries ago the Algonquins are said to have flung leather-bound stones at their enemies, with a hideous face painted on each bundle. Yet there is no reference to Indian arrows. Whatever they were, these blue-black flying objects terrified the Vikings, who turned and ran.

Freydis then appeared. As the skraelings rushed toward her she picked up the sword of a dead Viking, pulled out her breasts, and whetted the blade on them. Some translators say she slapped the sword against her breasts, or made as if to cut them off. Anyway, this spectacle frightened the savages worse than the ballista had frightened the Vikings: "They were aghast and fled to the boats. . . ."

Karlsefni's party spent one more winter in the New World. They liked it and wanted to remain but anticipated further trouble with the natives; so when spring came they returned to Greenland bringing a load of timber, grapes, and furs. With them was a new passenger—Gudrid's baby son, Snorre, born in America almost six centuries before Virginia Dare.

It is said that Karlsefni, his wife Gudrid, and their son, Snorre, eventually went to Iceland where Karlsefni bought a farm at Glaumby. After his death Gudrid and her son managed the farm until Snorre got married. Then Gudrid made a pilgrimage to Rome, became a nun, and lived the rest of her life in accordance with the prophecy.

Next we hear of Helgi and Finnbogi, two Icelandic brothers who may or may not have been planning a trip to Vinland when they were approached by Freydis. She proposed a joint expedition in two ships, sharing equally whatever profit they might make. Each group would consist of thirty men and a few women. The Icelanders agreed to this, so Freydis went to Leif and asked for the houses he had built on Vinland. Leif said he would not give them to her, although she might have the use of them.

The ships sailed together. Helgi and Finnbogi arrived first. Assuming the expedition was to be fully cooperative, they and their men settled in Leif's houses; but when Freydis arrived she ordered them to leave. And now the brothers learned something else about their business partner: she had brought along five extra men.

"We are no match for you in wickedness, we brothers," said Helgi. The Icelanders then moved out and built a shed for themselves some distance away.

During the winter there was more trouble. The two parties began avoiding each other.

Early one morning Freydis got up, put on her husband's cloak, and walked to the shed where the Icelanders lived. The door was half open. She stood by the door and Finnbogi, who was awake, saw her. He asked what she wanted.

"I want you to come outside," she said. "I want to talk to you."

Finnbogi came out of the shed and they sat down together on a log.

"How do you like things here?" she asked.

"I like this country," he said, "but I don't like the quarrel that has come between us. I see no reason for it."

"What you say is true," she answered. "I feel the same. But the reason I came to see you is that I would like to exchange ships. Your ship is larger than mine and I would like to get away from here."

"All right," he said, "if that will make you happy."

Freydis then walked home. She had not worn shoes or stockings and when she climbed into bed her cold feet awakened her husband. He asked where she had been. She had gone to visit the brothers, she told him, and offered to buy their ship, which made them so angry that they had beaten her. "But you," she said, "you wretched coward, you won't avenge our shame! Now I know just how far from Greenland I am!"

Her husband called his men and ordered them to get their weapons. They walked to the shed where the Icelanders lay asleep and tied them up. As each man was brought outside Freydis had him killed. At last there were only five women left alive and nobody wanted to kill them.

"Give me an ax," she said.

One of the men lent her an ax and Freydis slew the Icelandic women.

"After this wicked deed," the saga tells us, the Greenlanders went back to their houses, and it was clear that Freydis felt she had handled the matter very well. This is what she said to her companions: "If we get to Greenland I shall be the death of any man who reveals what took place. Our story will be that they stayed here after we left."

Early in the spring they loaded the brothers' ship with as much as it could carry and sailed to Greenland. There, after bribing everybody to ensure silence, Freydis returned to her farm. But Leif heard rumors. He seized three of her men and tortured them until they confessed. When he learned the truth he said, "I do not have the heart to punish my sister Freydis as she deserves. But I prophesy that no good will come to her descendants."

And after that, we are told, "no one thought anything but ill of her and her family."

How many other Norse adventurers and colonists reached the American continent, either on purpose or by accident, is unknown. There must have been quite a few. Among the first was a certain Bjorn Asbrandsson who vanished after leaving Iceland in the year 1000. The chronicles are not clear as to whether he was on his way to Greenland; but about twenty-five years later, according to the "Eyrbyggja Saga," a merchant named Gudleif who set out from Dublin was blown far to the west by a gale and finally anchored in a cove of some unfamiliar land. There he and his crew were captured by a group of dark-featured natives. They were released after an old white man spoke on their behalf. This man identified himself to Gudleif as Bjorn Asbrandsson. He said he had been living with the natives for a long time and had no wish to go back to Iceland.

In 1059 a Celtic or Saxon priest named Jon is said to have undertaken a missionary voyage to Vinland where he was murdered.

In 1120 or 1121 the bishop of Greenland, Eirik Gnupsson—or Upsi —"sailed in search of Vinland." Or he sailed "to visit" that country, depending on how *leitadi* is translated. Nothing more is heard of him, and presumably he did not return because three years later King Sigurd Jorsalfare—*Jorsalfare* meaning a traveler to Jerusalem—King Sigurd gave the bishopric to a cleric named Arnald.

In 1226 the leaders of Greenland's eastern settlement, Eystribyggd, which Eirik the Red had founded, became greatly disturbed by the arrival of Eskimos. They sent an expedition into Davis Strait, which separates Greenland from Canada, with instructions to find out where the Eskimos were coming from and to learn, if possible, what their intentions might be. Cairns and shelters discovered in that region prove that these men traveled through the extreme north at least to Devon Island—about as far west as Chicago.

Farther south, in the Vinland area, Norsemen were active as late as 1347, probably in the lumber trade. Says the *Flateyjarbók*: "Came a ship from Greenland that had been to Markland, eighteen men on board." With a bit more detail this same ship is reported in the *Skálholt* annals: "Also there came a ship from Greenland, smaller than the small Icelandic boats, which put in at the outer Straumfjord and had no anchor. There were seventeen men on board. They had made a voyage to Markland but were afterwards storm-driven here."

Chests found by archaeologists at Herjolfsnes are made of pine, deal, and larch. Some of this wood might have come from Norway, but the larch did not. It may have been driftwood, though this seems unlikely, not with Canada's tremendous forests just below the horizon.

Indeed, there is a possibility that the entire western settlement, or what was left of it—perhaps several hundred people—emigrated to

America, because in 1350, plus or minus a year or two or three, a cleric named Ivar Bárdarsson was chosen "to goe with Ships to the Westland, to drive away their Enemies the Skerlengers. But hee comming there, found no people neither Christian nor Heathen, but found there many Sheepe running being wilde, of which Sheepe they took with them as many as they could carrie, and with them returned to their Houses."

Bárdarsson saw no indication of a struggle with Eskimos, which means the people must have left voluntarily. Eskimos may or may not have plundered the empty houses; his report suggests that they did. Yet the presence of livestock—not only Sheepe but goats, horses, and cattle—implies that Eskimos had not been near the place because they would have slaughtered the animals for food. If the Vikings did emigrate they must have crossed the strait to Canada.

A dozen theories have been offered to explain the disappearance of these people; each answers certain questions but fails to answer others.

The revolving centuries fought against them, says Gwyn Jones. The climate grew colder, glaciers crept down. And ahead of the ice came the skraelings. Events in Europe also weakened the colony: an increasing preference for English and Dutch cloth rather than Greenland woolens. African elephant ivory instead of walrus ivory. Commerce with Russia. In short, business. It became less profitable for Europeans to trade with those distant colonists. The immediate causes, though, beyond doubt, were skraeling attacks and the encroaching ice.

Gisle Oddsson, Bishop of Iceland at about the time of Ivar Bárdarsson's voyage, thought the colonists had emigrated: "The settlers of Greenland lapsed of their own free will from the true faith and the Christian religion; having abandoned all good conduct and true virtues they turned to the people of America. Some people believe that Greenland lies very near to the westerly countries of the world."

The mystery of this deserted Christian outpost seems to have troubled King Magnus Smek, who directed Poul Knudsson to take a look at that faraway place. Knudsson sailed in 1355: "in honor of God, for the deliverance of our souls, and for those ancestors of ours who brought Christianity to Greenland. . . ."

Nine years later several of Knudsson's men returned to Norway.

What news they brought—if any—concerning Vestribyggd, the western settlement, has not been preserved.

In 1379 the small "middle settlement" near Ivigtut was attacked by Eskimos who killed eighteen colonists and carried off two boys.

The last merchant ship to visit the colonies departed in 1383.

A ship bound from Norway to Iceland in 1406 was driven west by gales and made port in Eystribyggd, where it lay at anchor four years. During this time a crewman named Thorstein Olafson married a local girl, Sigrid Bjornsdatter. Their wedding was celebrated in Hvalsey church on September 16, 1408, "on the Sunday after the Exaltation of the Cross." With the newlyweds aboard, this ship sailed to Iceland in 1410, the last European vessel known to have reached either settlement.

A letter dated 1448—which might possibly be spurious—from Pope Nicholas V to the two bishops of Iceland laments the misfortunes of Greenland colonists: "Thirty years ago, from the adjacent coasts of the heathen, the barbarians came with a fleet, attacked the inhabitants of Greenland most cruelly, and so devastated the mother-country and the holy buildings with fire and sword that there remained on that island no more than nine parish churches. . . ."

A few English ships, mostly from Bristol, might have visited Eystribyggd during this century. And perhaps a joint Portuguese-Danish expedition in 1473, because there is a letter dated March 3, 1551, from the burgomaster of Kiel, one Karsten Grip, addressed to Christian III. Burgomaster Grip reports that "two admirals of Your grandfather, His Royal Majesty Christian I, Pining and Pothurst, on the instructions of His Royal Majesty the King of Portugal, etc., were sent with several ships on a voyage to the new islands and the continents in the north. . . ." But we can only surmise the state of the colonies at that time.

A letter written by Pope Alexander VI in 1492 observes that there has been no priest resident in Greenland for eighty years and the people have nothing to remind them of Christianity except one altar cloth. Alexander fears that they have lost sight of the true faith, and he comments on a Benedictine monk named Mathias who is prepared to live and work as a missionary in Greenland.

About fifty years later a German merchant ship was blown by strong winds into a Greenland fjord. Buildings were visible, so the crew went ashore. They saw a dead European lying on the frozen ground. He was dressed in sealskin and frieze—which is a coarse woolen cloth with a shaggy nap. Beside his body lay a dagger, very thin from constant whetting. Evidently this was the corpse of the last Viking in the New World. There being no one left alive to bury him, he lay on the earth rather than in it.

A resident of Bergen, Absalon Pedersson, writes in 1567 that "many of the nobility hold the deeds of estates in Greenland yet of the country and properties they know nothing. . . ."

Martin Frobisher, who landed on Greenland's west coast in 1578, observed that some of the Eskimos used iron spearheads and bronze buttons and were able to recognize gold, which meant they had dealt with Europeans.

In 1721 a Norwegian missionary, Hans Egede, saw the ruins of a church and the crumbling walls of houses. He asked about them, and described the Christian services, but the Eskimos indicated that they had never heard of such a religion, nor could they tell him anything about the people who built these houses. Despite this rather convincing testimony, as well as the ruins, Egede maintained that Eystribyggd still flourished: "I believe beyond a doubt that it survives and is inhabited by people of pure Norwegian Extraction, which by God's help in due Time and when Occasion offers, may be discovered. . . ."

Hans Egede had a son named Niels who grew up in Greenland and recorded in his diary a curious legend. An Eskimo shaman who camped among the ruins of the lower settlement, "south by the hot baths," told him that in the old days Eskimos and Norwegians had lived together until they were attacked by men who came from the southwest in ships. At first there had been three ships. Then more ships arrived, with much killing and plundering. When these ships came back again the Eskimos fled, taking several Norwegian women and children with them up the fjord. Months later the Eskimos returned, but saw that the houses had been burned and everything taken away. Then they left the settlement forever and the Norwegian women married into the tribe.

The identity of these marauders cannot be established, but German and English pirates often raided Iceland during the fifteenth century. Perhaps they curled westward looking for fresh victims and delivered the coup de grâce to a moribund culture.

In our century, following the Great War that would end all wars, the Danish government dispatched some archaeologists to Greenland. They located the remnants of buildings and of farms—the fields now smothered by weeds and horsehair oats—and many graves.

In the northeast chapel of Gardar cathedral, which was the episcopal seat of Eystribyggd, lay the skeleton of a sturdy middle-aged man who still wore his shoes, though not much else. For some inexplicable reason part of his right foot was gone. He held a crozier made of ash, with an iron ferrule, the upper part carved from a walrus tusk by his wife, Margret, and on the fourth finger of his right hand he wore a bishop's gold ring. This was Jon Smyrill, or Sparrowhawk, who died in 1209.

The grave of a woman named Gudveig was empty, except for a rune rod which served as a proxy. She had died at sea and was buried like a sailor, sewn into sackcloth, a stone at her feet for ballast. A huge stone weighing more than a ton had been placed above the empty grave, either to guard her soul or to keep it from walking abroad.

Ozuur Asbjarnarson died on some island during winter and was buried in unhallowed ground with a wooden stake planted over his chest. Eventually a priest would arrive; then the stake could be withdrawn and consecrated water poured into the hole. That's all we know about Ozuur Asbjarnarson. It seems hardly enough.

The graves of quite a few children were located. Most of them had been buried with their toys.

Herjolfsnes cemetery yielded what was left of fifty-eight adults arranged in neat rows with their heads to the west. When time came for them to sit up on Resurrection Day they would face the rising sun. Each skeleton held a cross with a runic inscription:

GOD THE ALMIGHTY PROTECT GUDLEIF.

THORLEIF MADE THIS CROSS IN PRAISE AND WORSHIP OF GOD ALMIGHTY.

And so forth.

These Herjolfsnes colonists were fashionably dressed in accordance with European styles of the late Middle Ages, although in homespun wool rather than dyed silk or Italian velvet. From this rough material they had cut handsome cloaks and those tall Burgundian caps pictured by Memling, Christus, and other Flemish artists. They had copied the hood with a long tail, called a liripipe—de rigueur for modish gentlemen—which we recognize from descriptions by Dante and Petrarch. And they had imitated the cotte hardie, a man's tight short jacket which fully exposed his legs, except that the Greenland cotte hardie was less revealing. The garment as Europeans wore it must have seemed too bold.

One thing about these cloaked and hooded skeletons is unforgettable: their size. They look like children pretending to be adults. The tallest woman measured just four feet, nine inches. The men were not much bigger.

Half of these people died before the age of thirty, and all of them had been feeble, their bodies deformed. This was not true of the early Greenlanders, Eirik's colonists, nor of their first descendants whose bones indicated that they were healthy enough. But it appears that toward the end, about the time Eystribyggd was raided and plundered, the colonists were suffering from tuberculosis, malnutrition, and rickets.

So it may be argued that the Viking impetus failed. Nothing was born of these people, nothing developed from them.

But that violent westward surge, foaming against the littoral of the New World, has not yet receded from the imagination because even today, a thousand years after Bjarni Herjolfsson was blown off course, we wonder just how far west the Vikings traveled.

This brings up the Kensington runestone, a memorial tablet approximately the size of a tombstone. Medieval Scandinavian characters on its face tell a grim story:

> [WE ARE] 8 GOTHS AND 22 NORWEGIANS ON
> EXPLORATION JOURNEY FROM VINELAND
> THROUGHOUT THE WEST. WE HAD CAMP BESIDE 2
> SKERRIES ONE DAY'S JOURNEY NORTH OF THIS STONE.
> WE WERE OUT FISHING ONE DAY. AFTER WE CAME

HOME, FOUND 10 MEN RED WITH BLOOD AND DEAD. AV[E] M[ARIA] DELIVER [US] FROM EVIL!

HAVE 10 MEN BY THE SEA TO LOOK AFTER OUR SHIP, 14 DAYS' JOURNEY FROM THIS ISLAND. YEAR 1362.

On July 20, 1909, a Minnesota farmer filed this deposition with the local notary public:

> I, Olof Ohman, of the town of Solem, Douglas County, Minnesota, being duly sworn . . . In the month of August, 1898, while accompanied by my son, Edward, I was engaged in grubbing upon a timbered elevation, surrounded by marshes, in the southeast corner of my land, about 500 feet west of my neighbor's, Nils Flaten's, house, and in the full view thereof. Upon removing an asp, measuring about 10 inches in diameter at its base, I discovered a flat stone inscribed with characters, to me unintelligible. The stone lay just beneath the surface of the ground in a slightly slanting position, with one corner almost protruding. The two largest roots of the tree clasped the stone in such a manner that the stone must have been there at least as long as the tree. . . . I immediately called my neighbor's, Nils Flaten's, attention to the discovery, and he came over the same afternoon and inspected the stone and the stump under which it was found.
>
> I kept the stone in my possession for a few days; and then left it in the Bank of Kensington. . . .

Nils Flaten, who accompanied Ohman to the office of the notary, swore to his part in the discovery. This much can be verified, along with a few unimportant details.

Is it a fake, or not?

The runestone's leading advocate was Hjalmar Holand, a Norwegian-born Wisconsin cherry farmer who learned about it in 1907 while he was a student at the University of Wisconsin. He tried to buy it. He offered five dollars, but Ohman wanted ten. Holand could not afford ten. Ohman by this time had put up with a certain amount of ridicule because almost every geologist and philologist who examined the stone had concluded that the carving must be recent, and perhaps because of this he suddenly gave the stone to Holand.

For the next fifty-five years Holand tried to authenticate the grisly tale—which he himself had translated. He even took the stone to Scandinavia for examination. And there have been authorities in one field or another who agreed with him that it could not be a fraud. The American ethnographer Stirling called it one of the most significant finds ever made on American soil. A German geographer, Richard Hennig, said that the stone's authenticity was certain "and consequently the presence of Scandinavians in America a good one hundred and thirty years before Columbus can no longer be doubted." The *Preliminary Report of the Museum Committee of the Historical Society of Minnesota* pronounced it genuine. And so on. Most experts, however, look upon the Kensington stone with distaste, boredom, resignation, and contempt.

The Danish rune specialist Erik Moltke, for instance: "Even the nonspecialist will observe that the text, when it is transcribed into Latin, is easy to read. That is not the language of the fourteenth century, but rather of the nineteenth. In the language of the late Middle Ages 'we had' should be written 'wi hafd hum' not 'wi hade'; 'we were' as 'wi varum' not 'wi var'. . . ." Moltke also pointed out that the carver had invented a runic *j*, and had included a modified *ö* which was not introduced into Swedish until the Reformation.

Among Olof Ohman's possessions when he died was a book with this resounding title: *Carl Rosander, Den kunskapsrike Skolmästare eller hufvudegrunderna uti de för ett borgerligt samfundsliv nödigaste vetenskaper.* It contains a chapter on the development of the Swedish language and gives, as one example, a fourteenth-century prayer ending with "fraelse [os] af illu," which is to say, "Deliver [us] from evil." In Ohman's copy the page on which this prayer occurs had been well thumbed.

Birgitta Wallace of the Carnegie Museum speaks for a majority of professionals when she says that the stone was carved by a nineteenth-century immigrant: ". . . someone with an embryonic knowledge of runes, but who lacked familiarity with medieval Scandinavian languages. The carver could have been almost any one of the early Scandinavian settlers in Minnesota, all of whom knew something about runes but who generally had no philological education." The language employed on the stone, she remarks, is a dialect which developed in the Kensington area and is still spoken by a few old-timers, though it is unknown elsewhere. Furthermore, the tool used in making the inscription was a chisel with a standard one-inch bit, a type sold in American hardware stores.

Quite a few bona fide runestones have been found in Scandinavia. They are big, blunt, ugly things that remind you of menhirs or of the weathered teeth of ancient monsters, and their crude messages are seldom dramatic, although real enough:

RAGNHILD, ULV'S SISTER, PLACED THIS STONE—AND THIS BOAT-SHAPED STONE CIRCLE—TO HER HUSBAND GUNULF, AN OUTSPOKEN MAN, SON OF NÆRVE. FEW ARE NOW BORN BETTER THAN HE.

. . . SER PLACED THIS STONE TO HIS BROTHER AS . . . AND [HE] MET HIS DEATH IN GOTLAND [?]. THOR SANCTIFY [THESE] RUNES.

SØLVE ERECTED . . . SPALKLØSE TO [HIS] FATHER SUSER [AND MADE] THIS BRIDGE [TO] HIS BROTHER TROELS. ETERNALLY SHALL THIS INSCRIPTION BE TRUE, WHICH SØLVE HAS MADE.

THORE ERECTED THIS STONE TO HIS FATHER GUNNER.

After you have contemplated the homeliness and innocence of such epitaphs you are even less apt to be persuaded by that wild Minnesota drama. Still, one wants to believe. THORE ERECTED THIS STONE TO HIS FATHER GUNNER. All right, but who cares? A fight between Vikings and Indians does more for the imagination.

Now, along with that Minnesota runestone, and no less celebrated, we have Rhode Island's Newport tower—alleged to have been built by Knudsson's party either before or after they visited the Midwest, or by some earlier Viking expedition. Or it was built by sixteenth-century Portuguese explorers. Or perhaps by the governor of Rhode Island, Benedict Arnold—not *the* Benedict Arnold—shortly before 1677, the date it first appears in historical records. Those who believe in the authenticity of the Kensington runestone almost without exception believe in the Viking origin of the tower. And, naturally, vice versa.

Here is what we know for certain: it is a cylindrical stone structure approximately twenty-five feet high, with eight arches supported by columns. The walls are about two feet thick with traces of stucco coating. Only the shell of the tower remains, the interior wooden components having disintegrated. It became a proper subject for argument in 1839 after a Danish antiquarian said he thought it was a Norse church or baptistery, and that it had been built by Vinlanders of the eleventh or twelfth century.

True believers point to architectural similarities between the tower and medieval Scandinavian structures: segmental arches, double-splayed casement windows, et cetera. They mention a unit of measurement known as the "Rhineland foot" which they say was used in the design of the tower, whereas all Colonial buildings used the English foot.

Skeptics reply that because of the tower's condition the unit of measurement cannot be determined. Besides, the Rhineland foot was still in use as late as the nineteenth century. Then, too, carefully supervised digging around the foundation has brought up such items as a gunflint and a seventeenth-century clay pipe.

"This is fourteenth-century architecture," said a European archaeologist. "There would be no question as to its age if this were in Europe."

So the dispute continues.

Excluding various knickknacks from L'Anse aux Meadows, there is only one batch of indisputably Norse objects to have surfaced on the American continent. This is the Beardmore find, which consists of a broken sword, an axhead, a horse rattle, and three scraps of iron. In the judgment of almost every authority who has studied these relics, they date from the latter part of the Viking Age: the sword from the tenth century, the axhead and rattle from the eleventh. They were found, according to one report, while dynamiting on a mining claim near Beardmore, Ontario. But another report says they were retrieved from the basement of a home in Port Arthur and that they were brought to Canada about fifty years ago. Both reports are substantiated by witnesses and by circumstantial evidence. Once again, therefore, you have an option.

All in all there are perhaps 100 objects, a couple dozen inscriptions, and at least fifty sites which purport to show that Vikings reached America. By far the most engaging souvenirs are some rusty crescent-shaped little axes from the Great Lakes region, home of the embattled Kensington runestone. Because they are too light to be weapons they have been described as ceremonial halberds. But medieval halberds did not look exactly like that. Furthermore, these specimens apparently were manufactured by the American Tobacco Company in the late nineteenth century for use as plug tobacco cutters—the business end of the hatchet being attached to a cutting board by a hinge. They were given away during an advertising campaign to promote the sale of Battle-Axe Plug and quite a few midwestern housewives probably used them to chop cabbage.

Nevertheless, Hjalmar Holand submitted one tobacco cutter and two of the halberds that he thought were medieval Norse to the department of chemical engineering at the University of Wisconsin. Professor R. A. Ragatz, chairman of the department, examined all three and wrote to Holand: "The metal [of the tobacco cutter] is a rather poor quality of gray cast iron, showing the following micro-constituents: graphite plates, ferrite, pearlite, steadite. The structure is totally different from the frames of the two genuine halberds. . . . I can state positively that the two halberds sent me last fall were not of the same origin as the tobacco cutter recently submitted."

Other disputed evidence of Viking tourists includes "mooring holes," found on Cape Cod and quite plentifully around the Minnesota lakes. These holes, about an inch in diameter and six or seven inches deep, have been drilled into boulders on the shores of past or present waterways. They are said to have been used for mooring a boat temporarily, a line from the boat being tied to an iron pin inserted in the hole. A sequence of such holes should indicate the route traveled; and it so happens that they often appear beside northern rivers and lakes that feed the Mississippi. Now, what this suggests is that Vikings may have traveled up the Saint Lawrence to the Great Lakes, or south from Hudson Bay via the Nelson River into the Wisconsin-Minnesota area. From there they could have gone south with almost no trouble, as far as they cared to float, drifting at last into the Gulf of Mexico below New Orleans. And what a dramatic voyage that would be.

Regrettably we must deal with Birgitta Wallace, archenemy of romantics: ". . . the method is unknown in Norse seamanship, medieval or modern." Ms. Wallace goes on to say that other stones with identical drillings in the vicinity of these so-called mooring holes provide a clue as to what they really are: they are blasting holes drilled by early settlers. It seems that during the latter half of the nineteenth century these settlers obtained foundation stones for their houses by blowing boulders apart. Occasionally the dynamite didn't go off, or the prospective home builder changed his mind, or for some other reason all that endured was the hole, somewhat like the smile of the Cheshire cat.

If Birgitta Wallace & Co. are correct we find ourselves restricted to L'Anse aux Meadows, which is either a grave disappointment or an exciting discovery, depending on your outlook. The name could mean the cove or bay with grass around it, or possibly Meadows is a corruption of Medusa—for the shoals of jellyfish found there during summer. Old sailing charts call it Méduse Bay, Jellyfish Bay. It is on the northernmost tip of Newfoundland, about the latitude of London, within sight of the Canadian mainland, and near this bay are the ruins of a Norse settlement. Carbon 14 tests give a date of approximately A.D. 1000.

Not much is left. There is the ground plan of a big turf-walled house —fifty by seventy feet, with five or six rooms—and the outlines of various smaller structures including a smithy, a bathhouse, five boat sheds, a kiln, and two cooking pits.

Very little handiwork has survived, partly because there is so much acid in the soil. Almost everything made of bone or wood has disintegrated, whatever was not carried off by Eskimos, Indians, and early Newfoundland settlers. There are rusty traces that once were nails, a piece of copper with cross stripings that might have come from a belt, a whetstone, a bone needle, a bit of jasper, a stone lamp of the old Icelandic type, a steatite spindle whorl—meaning there were women in the house—and a bronze ring-headed pin. Pins of this type were used by Vikings to fasten their capes. And in the smithy was a large cracked flat-topped stone—the anvil—together with scraps of bog iron, clumps of slag, and patches of soot.

The great house burned, says Dr. Helge Ingstad, who supervised the excavation, although it is impossible to say whether this happened by accident or design.

L'Anse aux Meadows must have been an agreeable place to live. There were fields of berries and flowers, salmon in the lake, herds of caribou—many more animals and birds than there are now. The sea was alive with cod, seals, and whales, and the weather probably was mild.

Then why was Paradise abandoned? And why is there no sign of other settlements?

The answer seems to be that these people arrived too soon. Europe was not ready to support them, and with only spears, axes, knives, and swords these few colonists could not hold out against the skraelings. Whether they were killed in one overwhelming raid, whether they intermarried with the natives, or perhaps moved farther south, or at last gave up and retreated to Greenland—neither the ruins nor the old vellum manuscripts reveal.

It is certain, though, that they got this far on several occasions, and it would be exceedingly strange if they traveled no farther. Even the most conservative archaeologists admit the possibility of Viking sites on the mainland.

A lump of coal uncovered in a Greenland house strongly implies a voyage to Rhode Island. This house, which stood at the head of Ameralik fjord in the western settlement, may have belonged at one time to Thorfinn Karlsefni and his wife, Gudrid. The coal was found deep in the ruins by Danish archaeologists, and there are two curious things about it. First, there was just one lump, with nothing but wood-ash in the fireplace. Second, it is meta-anthracite, which does not occur in Greenland, nor anyplace along the east coast of North America except in Rhode Island.

And there is an eleventh-century Norse penny, probably struck between the years 1065 and 1080, during the reign of Olaf III, which turned up at an Indian site near Bar Harbor, Maine. It's possible, of course, that the penny was lost by a Colonial American coin collector. Or it might have been brought from Newfoundland by an acquisitive Indian. However, the obvious deduction seems best: eleventh-century Vikings either lived or traded in Maine.

What all of this means is that you are at liberty to follow the mooring holes of imagination as far as you care to. Through the Saint Lawrence waterway, for example, to the Great Lakes and beyond. After all, nobody can prove that a party of Norse adventurers did not reach the Mississippi and follow it to the Gulf, and from there sail west, following the downward coast.

The Mexican Indian legend of Quetzalcoatl says that a bearded white man appeared out of the east on a raft of snakes and later departed in the direction from which he had come, promising to return in 500 years. So you may imagine a Viking ship with a carved serpent head on the prow, with a fair-haired bearded Norwegian in command. And when five centuries had passed a bearded foreigner did arrive, not exactly commanding a raft of snakes, although many people swear he had a complement of snakes aboard. He was, of course, much darker than a Norwegian; and his name, Hernando Cortés, is not unfamiliar.

You will get a chilly reception from anthropologists if you attempt to relate Quetzalcoatl to a Viking, or any other such fabulous theory. But the alternative is to join the conservatives, in which case you will have to be satisfied with a spindle whorl, a bone needle, and some furnace slag.

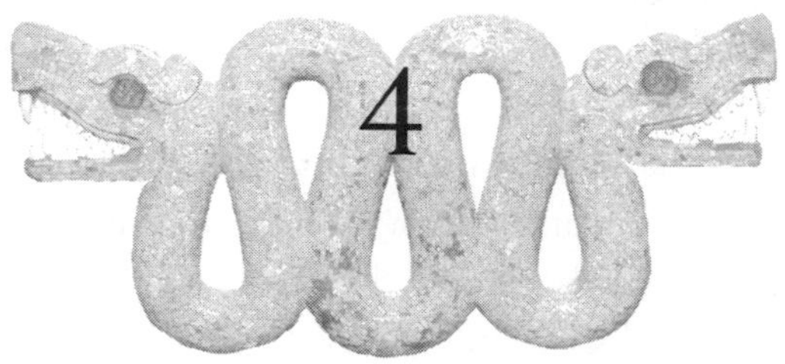

4

Gustav's Dreadnought

KING GUSTAVUS ADOLPHUS was of the opinion that building small ships was a waste of young trees, so when he wanted a new flagship to intimidate his enemies he commissioned a monster. The *Vasa* was 165 feet long, 40 feet wide, 180 feet from the keel to the tip of the mainmast, and weighed 1,400 tons. She carried sixty-four bronze cannons—forty-eight jutting through a double row of gunports on either side, sixteen smaller ones on the top deck—and she was decorated like an opera house. A gigantic golden lion lunged from the prow, a golden lion's head roared from every gunport, and both decks were painted bright red so that the sailors' blood would scarcely be noticed. Above this majestic spectacle floated the orange-yellow and deep indigo colors of seventeenth-century Sweden.

The captain, Söfring Hansson, should have been delighted with such a command, but there were things about the ship that he did not like. He thought the *Vasa* was too long and narrow and the superstructure uncommonly large. He reported as much to the grand admiral of the Swedish Navy, Klas Fleming, but the admiral did not respond; or, if he did, Captain Hansson was not satisfied.

Consequently, a few weeks before the scheduled launching, Hansson invited Admiral Fleming aboard to witness a test. With the ship tied up at her mooring thirty sailors were told to run across the deck. When they did so the *Vasa* heeled "by the breadth of one plank." Hansson immediately ordered them to rush across the deck in the opposite direction. This time the ship heeled by the breadth of two planks. Hansson sent them across the deck a third time and the ship heeled still farther. At this point, according to testimony given during the court-martial, Admiral Fleming ordered the demonstration stopped.

Because the meaning of Captain Hansson's test was perfectly clear you would assume that preparations for the launching were suspended. After all, it would be insane to continue outfitting a ship for disaster.

But of course the work went right ahead.

The explanation for such a paradox is simple and it will not surprise the good student of human affairs. King Gustav had commissioned this vessel. He had selected the builder and personally had approved the plans. Gustav looked forward to the *Vasa* leading his fleet. Nobody wanted to tell him what was going to happen.

So, about three o'clock one Sunday afternoon in August of 1628, while thousands of Stockholm citizens crowded the wharves to wish her Godspeed, Captain Hansson gave orders to cast off. The *Vasa* had been loaded with 2,000 barrels of food, plenty of beer and cannonballs, 133 sailors, assorted bureaucrats and politicians, and a good many wives and children. There may also have been 300 soldiers aboard; the *Vasa* was to carry them, but perhaps they were ashore. They may have been at Älvsnabben, waiting to get on when the visitors got off.

It is said that a mild breeze was blowing across the harbor that afternoon, yet the *Vasa* listed farther than expected when the first sails were broken out. As she righted herself the chief ordnance officer, Erik Jönsson, ran below to make certain the cannons were lashed in place.

A few minutes later a gust of wind blew around the high cliffs of Söder and the *Vasa* heeled sharply. Again she righted herself, but Captain Hansson ordered the topsails cut loose.

The wind dropped. The ship moved heavily toward Beckholmen.

Then a fresh gust struck the sails and for the second time Jönsson ran below. Water was pouring through the open gunports. He gave orders to untie the cannons on the lower side and to haul them up the slanting deck, but this was impossible. Several cannons broke loose, crushing the sailors who unwisely had tried to push them.

The *Vasa* went down almost at once and came to rest nearly upright on the bottom, her mainmast angling above the surface and Sweden's banner fluttering valiantly in the sunshine. She had traveled less than a mile.

About fifty people drowned. Many more would have been lost except that the giant ship was accompanied by a fleet of pleasure boats which picked up survivors.

Captain Hansson, along with every other officer, was arrested that same afternoon. Also arrested were those involved with the construction—excluding the designer, a Dutchman named Henrik Hybertsson who had died the previous year.

On September 5 a formal inquiry opened. The official record seems to have been destroyed, though we do not know whether this was deliberate or accidental. However, copies of certain parts of it have been found so that the procedure, as well as quite a few names and details, can be established. We know there were seventeen members of the court including six councilors of the realm, two naval captains, and the lord mayor of Stockholm. The president was Lord High Admiral Carl Gyllenhielm, King Gustav's half brother.

The court's first purpose was to determine the cause of the disaster, then to fix the blame. Yet it becomes obvious that while they did want to know why the ship went down they were more anxious to learn who was responsible. The suspects may or may not have been aware of this priority; if they were, they must have felt uncomfortable because seventeenth-century punishment was no pat on the wrist.

For instance, according to Swedish naval articles of 1644, a helmsman who ran his ship aground could be keel-hauled, which meant being towed underwater from stem to stern. Or he might be dragged from port to starboard by way of the keel. The penalty for causing a fire aboard ship was more direct: the guilty man was promptly thrown into the flames. Less serious offences, such as whispering during a lecture, brought fourteen days in irons. Nor does there seem to have been much plea bargaining.

If records of the *Vasa* inquiry are accurate, the first crew member of any importance to be narrowly questioned was the ordnance officer, Erik Jönsson. After testifying that the cannons had been secured and could not have rolled across the deck, causing the *Vasa* to capsize, Jönsson added that he thought the ship "was heavier over than under." It would have capsized in any event, he said.

Admiral Gyllenhielm asked why he had not discussed this with the captain.

Jönsson replied that he was an artilleryman and pretended to be nothing else. The captain, he said, should be better able to judge whether the ship was properly ballasted.

Gyllenhielm pointed out that the ship's builder had said that if he had been informed the ship was top-heavy he would have recommended loading her down another foot.

How could that have been done, Jönsson asked, when the gunports already lay but three feet from the surface?

Lieutenant Petter Gierdsson, who had been in charge of rigging, told the court that he, too, considered the ship top-heavy. When asked why he had kept this opinion to himself he replied that ballast was something about which he knew nothing. He did not even know what sort of ballast the *Vasa* carried. He had been concerned only with the rigging.

Jöran Matsson, sailing master, was formally charged with having paid too little attention to the ballast "and other things as his calling and office made incumbent upon him, whereby disaster had befallen His Majesty's ship."

Matsson answered that he had stowed as much ballast as possible. Furthermore, he said, he personally had supervised this work. He had gone down into the bilge with a light to inspect the loading. He felt that he had done whatever was incumbent upon him.

Did he notice that the ship was top-heavy?

Matsson then revealed what everybody in Stockholm except the high officers of the court must have known—that while the *Vasa* was still at her mooring Captain Hansson, in the presence of Admiral Fleming, had ordered a capsizing test. Matsson then repeated a short discussion between himself and the admiral in which the admiral said that the ship rode too low in the water because of so much ballast. To this criticism Matsson had replied: "God grant that she'll stay on an even keel." And to this Admiral Fleming replied: "The builder has built ships before. You need not worry about it."

After questioning several other people the court summoned the builder, Hein Jacobsson. He had not begun the work, but he had completed it after the death of Henrik Hybertsson. He was asked why he had made the Vasa so narrow. He answered that he had not laid the keel, he had only finished what already was begun. Furthermore, King Gustav had approved the plans. There were no blueprints in the seventeenth century, merely a table known as a "sert" which listed the principal dimensions and which was regarded also as a contract to build. Hybertsson had drawn this sert, said Jacobsson, in accordance with the king's wishes.

Arent Hybertsson de Groot, the original builder's brother, was questioned. Why, he was asked, did the *Vasa* have such a large superstructure?

His Majesty had approved it, said de Groot. And all who saw or inspected the ship had agreed that she was irreproachably built.

If that is true, asked the court, why did she capsize?

"God must know," de Groot answered. "His Majesty the King was told by me how long and how broad the ship was, and His Majesty was pleased to approve and wished to have it so."

The court probed this delicate situation. Although the king had approved the sert, should not the builder in good conscience have informed His Majesty as to the correct dimensions?

Neither Jacobsson nor de Groot would argue. Both of them replied: "The King wished it so."

Too many footsteps led toward Gustav's palace. The inquiry ended without establishing a cause and without finding anyone responsible—as far as we know.

If that actually is how the investigation concluded, it's hard to believe. Could everybody be innocent? Fifty people were drowned, either through incompetence or negligence; therefore somebody must be guilty. Yet whom would you convict?

The ordnance officer? Beyond doubt the cannons were tied down. Even if they were not, they couldn't have been the cause.

The sailing master? Unquestionably he checked the ballast. Furthermore, he had spoken to Admiral Fleming about the ship's instability.

The builder? He didn't plan the *Vasa*, he only completed it.

The designer, Henrik Hybertsson?—because it was he who drew the sert and laid the keel. Would you accuse and convict a dead man?

Or perhaps Captain Hansson? He, more than anyone else, had been worried. He had demonstrated very clearly to Admiral Fleming what might happen.

Would you charge Admiral Fleming? He had no part in constructing the ship, nor in the sailing, though he could have prevented the launching. That is, he might have suggested this to his superior, Lord High Admiral Gyllenhielm.

Did Fleming in fact suggest it? We don't know. Yet even if the records were complete they would not likely settle the question. Powerful men seldom expose themselves, as we have learned these past few years. Their fortunes depend too closely on the fortunes of their associates. That could be why Fleming was not charged with negligence.

Let us suppose he did urge his superior to cancel the launching and Gyllenhielm refused. Would you then charge the presiding officer of the investigative court? How many men in Gyllenhielm's position would take such a risk?—because surely it would earn the king's wrath. Gustav himself had approved the ship. He was most anxious for the *Vasa* to be launched.

Well then, the king. Gustav himself must be at fault. But who would be foolish enough to accuse the king?

What a shame the records are incomplete. How many scenes from this eerily familiar drama were lost? Did the court choose a scapegoat? Perhaps a sailor was flogged to death.

Alas, without the full account we can only speculate, and the vaporous conclusion remains not quite believable—until we reflect that, given a change of centuries and circumstances we might be reading yesterday's newspaper. Ask yourself what punishment was administered for the crime at My Lai. Consider what happened. More than 100 civilians were shot by American soldiers: a fact as obvious as Old Glory. Yet the American government, in view of an expectant nation and most of the world, could not find anybody guilty. Years after the massacre one lieutenant was restricted to his barracks for a while, that was all. One lieutenant could not go dancing.

And why was nobody guilty? Because everybody was following orders. The king wished it so.

In other words, nothing changes. As the French aphorism tactfully reminds us: "Plus ça change, plus c'est la même chose."

Well, even before the inquiry opened, almost before the *Vasa* touched bottom, scavengers were descending on Stockholm: a Dutch shipwright, a Scottish baron, a "mechanicus" from Riga, somebody named "Classon," "a man from Lubeck," and various others.

First to obtain permission from the privy council was an Englishman, Ian Bulmer, who started to work less than three days after the catastrophe. He strung ropes from the Vasa's masts to shore, hitched up teams of horses, and managed to pull the ship into a vertical position. What he planned to do next is not known, but the scheme failed and he either quit or was replaced.

For a while Admiral Fleming took charge. In July of 1629 he notified King Gustav: "As far as *Vasa* is concerned, we have been working with all industry, trying to raise her, but until now we have accomplished little . . . I have again fixed seventeen stout hawsers and chains with which, this week, if weather permits, we shall try to see what can be done. It is a heavier weight down there than I could have supposed."

Some time after that the Scottish baron, Alexander Forbes, obtained the rights to all salvage operations in Swedish waters for a period of twelve years, though he knew nothing about marine salvage. When he was unable to raise the *Vasa* he leased the rights to a syndicate that included a Swedish colonel named Hans Albrekt von Treileben. Hans must have been a clever fellow; not only did he jiggle Baron Forbes out of the picture, be managed to get control of the salvage rights and then he went after the prize with a diving bell.

This recent invention, which resembled a church bell, was about four feet high and made of lead. The diver wore gloves, two pairs of leather boots, leather pants, a leather jacket lashed around his body to make it waterproof, and a wool cap. He stood on a platform slung beneath the bell and as he descended the water came up to his chest, leaving a pocket of compressed air at the top. He had a pair of pincers, a hooked pole, and some rope.

It seems impossible that a man with these elementary tools, inside a lead bell in frigid muddy water almost up to his neck, could accomplish much; yet the syndicate divers tore apart the *Vasa*'s superstructure and brought up about fifty cannons, most of which were sold abroad. Von Treileben then lost interest and began making plans for a voyage to the West Indies where he hoped to pick the bones of a Spanish galleon.

A man named Liverton, or Liberton, arrived in 1683 with a "special invention." After being granted a license he recovered one cannon, which he tried unsuccessfully to sell to the Swedish government. That seems to have been the last salvage attempt.

It was now fifty-five years since Gustav's monster went down. The tip of the mast had rotted away, or had been sawed off, so that nothing broke the surface. The *Vasa* was a hulk sinking imperceptibly deeper into the mud. And to the surprise of elderly citizens there were adults who never had heard of the famous ship.

How could it be forgotten? If you consider her size and prestige and splendor, as well as that spectacular maiden voyage—to say nothing of the evasive inconclusive court-martial which must have been talked about for many years—how could people forget the *Vasa*?

But of course it's naïve to think like that. A nation is not anxious to remember its tragic miscalculations. Germany has been unable to forget Hitler, yet you can be sure that today's German children do not think of him as their grandparents do, and by the long measuring rod of history the Nazi war has just ended. America cannot forget Vietnam, but be patient. Several centuries from now—unless our omniscient Pentagon does something cataclysmically stupid—you should be able to read American history without once encountering that painful word.

So, as debris stopped floating to the surface and mud built up against the hulk, and those who knew about the calamity died, the *Vasa* disappeared. Until at last there came a pleasant Sunday afternoon when the wharves were crowded with Stockholm citizens, none of whom could have told you anything at all about King Gustav's benighted flagship.

In 1920 a Swedish historian was searching the archives for information about another seventeenth-century ship—the *Riksnyckeln*, which had sailed into a cliff one dark September night—when he came across the minutes of the *Vasa* court-martial and a reference to Treileben's diving bell. Being an historian he naturally wrote a paper about it, and a boy named Anders Franzén heard about the *Vasa* because his father happened to read what the historian had written.

Now, the Franzéns usually vacationed on the island of Dalarö and there Anders saw a wooden gun carriage salvaged from the warship *Riksäpplet* which foundered in 1676. Although the gun carriage had been submerged more than two centuries the wood was still solid. This fact did not mean anything to him until 1939 when he took a boat trip with his father through the Göta Canal on Sweden's west coast. There he saw the skeleton of another old ship, but its wood was spongy—eaten by the insatiable shipworm, *Teredo navalis*.

Given two long-submerged pieces of wood, one solid and one soft, most of us would say how curious and move on to something livelier. Young Franzén, however, did not let go. He thought there must be a reason for the discrepancy. The reason turned out to be *Teredo navalis*, which likes the taste of salt water. The Baltic around Stockholm has a salinity of 0.7 percent at most. *Teredo navalis* requires a minimum of 0.9 percent.

Again, after noting this tedious fact, most of us would move along. Not so young Franzén.

The Second World War interrupted his plans, but with that out of the way he began to get organized. He listed fifty ships known to have gone down in the vicinity of Stockholm. From this list he chose twelve: *Sastervik*, *Resande Man*, *Vasa*, *Mars*, *Schwan of Lübeck*, *Riksäpplet*, *Kronan* . . .

He started with the *Riksäpplet* because he knew approximately where to look, and because the ship had foundered in shallow water. He found it without much trouble, but he was too late. Very little remained. For 200 years the hulk had been crushed by drifting ice and waves. However, the few planks that he brought up were as solid as the gun carriage.

Franzén decided to hunt for the *Vasa*. Other ships might be easier to locate but this one sounded important.

He talked to Professor Nils Ahnlund, the historian, and after having learned to read seventeenth-century script he spent as much time as possible—by now he was a petroleum engineer—searching the naval archives. At last he knew the names of the men who had built the ship and those who had sailed it, and he knew quite a lot about the salvage attempts. But what he needed most, which he could not find, was a precise reference to the location of the ship. The *Vasa*, if it still existed, lay somewhere in Stockholm Ström "toward Lustholmen, Blochusudden, near Danuiken."

By 1953, having read enough old documents to fill a closet, he was ready. This meant cruising back and forth across an expanse of Stockholm harbor in a motorboat, week after week, sweeping the bottom with wire drags and grapnels. In plain view of anybody who cared to watch he dredged up a great many lost, stolen, or undesirable artifacts: automobile tires, rusty bicycles, stoves, bedsteads, tangled fishing line, Christmas trees, goggles, boots, dead cats, chains, bottles—jetsam of the city.

This is not a job for a man sensitive to ridicule, especially when it becomes known that the man in the motorboat is hunting for a seventeenth-century battleship.

That winter he read another stack of musty documents, and he found an eighteenth-century map on which a cross had been drawn near Stadsgårdskajen. The cross allegedly marked the position of the *Vasa*, so Franzén spent the following summer cleaning that part of the harbor bottom.

Came winter, back to the library.

Summer, sweeping the harbor.

By this time Stockholm's authentic fishermen must have stopped laughing and merely tapped their heads while Franzén reeled in his latest catch.

During the winter of 1956, once again in the archives sifting flaky old records, he came upon a letter from the Swedish parliament addressed to King Gustav, dated August 12, 1628. Gustav had been leading an army through Poland when the *Vasa* was launched. This letter was parliament's report to the sovereign:

"And on that fateful Sunday, which was the tenth of this month, the *Vasa* set sail. But it happened that she got no further than Beckholmsudden, where she entirely fell on her side and sank to the bottom with cannon and all else, and lies in eighteen fathoms. . . ."

Beckholmsudden was doubly significant because while hauling up rubbish in that area Franzén had encountered a long muddy obstruction. Government engineers had told him it was rock blasted out of the island when a dry dock was built, so he had not investigated the strange hump. Now he went back to it, equipped with an instrument he had devised—a steel cylinder with a hollow punch in the front end. He threw this instrument overboard, waited until it struck bottom, and reeled it up. Inside the cylinder he found a plug of old black close-grained oak.

He dropped the cylinder at intervals along the length of the hump. Each time it brought back a plug of oak. So there could be no doubt that a wooden ship of *Vasa*'s dimensions lay on the bottom, very close to the navy diving school.

Franzén did not attempt to claim the ship for himself. He went to the navy, displayed his oak samples, told them what he suspected was there, and asked them to send a man down.

It is easy to guess what would have happened under these circumstances in the United States. After making an appointment and waiting in an air-conditioned lounge the applicant would have been ushered into the office of a lieutenant who would have listened with somnolent courtesy, looked at the plugs, and thanked the visitor for bringing this matter to his attention. The lieutenant might then dictate a brief report which, in due course, would be forwarded to the executive officer of the base, who might conceivably mention it to the commanding officer; and if the commandant happened to be feeling adventurous he might instruct his executive officer to forward a copy to Washington where it would have dried and curled until it resembled the Dead Sea Scrolls.

The Swedes, after listening to Franzén's story, dispatched their most experienced diver.

Chief Diver Per Edvin Fälting went down and reported that he had landed in mud up to his chest. He could not see anything.

Franzén suggested trying another area.

Just then Fälting said that he had felt what might be a wooden wall. It was a big wall, he said, possibly the side of a ship. Fälting then climbed partway up and discovered a square hole—almost certainly a gunport. Higher on the wall he felt another square hole, which meant that he was clinging to the *Vasa* because no other ship with a double row of gunports had been lost in Stockholm harbor.

Everybody got excited. Here was a relic of the days when Sweden had been a formidable power, when every nation in Europe listened apprehensively to King Gustavus Adolphus.

A television camera dipped into the water to prove to the Swedes that what they had been told was there actually was there. And indeed it was. The camera relayed a blurred, sinister image of the giant warship: upright, sealed to the waterline in hard clay. The stubs of her masts thrust violently toward the surface. In the muck that covered her decks lay the tangled chains and irons of seventeenth-century scavengers.

Millions of kronor later the *Vasa* had been pried from the mud, lifted a few feet by two gigantic pontoons, and very cautiously towed like an implausible submarine to nearby Castle Island where, in shallow water, the deposit of centuries was scraped off.

And what came to the surface, dragged from the grasp of The Old One—Den Gamle—was at times unexpected and beautiful and wondrous: gilded carvings of cherubs, musicians, caryatids, mermaids, tritons, knights, dragons, heraldic devices, a bird with an eel in its beak, a man in a rippling cloak, Hercules with the hellhound Cerberus chained at his feet, the god Nereus, King David playing a lyre.

But more often what came up was useful and ordinary and pathetic: mugs, clay pipes, a pocket sundial, a cockaded felt hat, ramrods, axes, smashed beer kegs, tankards, leather boots, pottery, wood bowls, casks of butter, carpenters' tools, muskets, ladles, a slipper, a bronze candlestick, one blue Dutch picture plate showing a bird on a rock, an apothecary's kit, a gold signet ring from which the seal was missing, a seaman's ditty box, another little box holding a lock of hair. Many such personal items Den Gamle released, after being urged by the suction hose.

On the deck beside Captain Hansson's dining table, among shards of crockery that must have fallen when the *Vasa* heeled, lay a tightly stoppered flask containing some dense, dark liquid. When Eisenhower visited Sweden in 1962 he was offered a taste. Ike, not a reckless man, observed and sniffed Captain Hansson's schnapps but declined a drink.

And the great lion figurehead—carved from limewood, weighing two tons, springing toward the enemy—this mighty sculpture was raised from the bottom.

Den Gamle also permitted a number of skeletons to be taken from his ship, most of them still attached to their clothing, and scientists learned that there had been at least two ethnic types aboard. The skulls of one man and one woman were short, with conspicuous cheekbones, suggesting that they were Finnish. The other skulls were typically Nordic. One skull held the residue of a brain.

Among the crew members there had been a man in his late twenties or perhaps thirty, judging by the bones. A scientist who worked on the project had this to say about him: "He was dressed in a knit vest of thick wool and knit wool trousers which showed folds above the hips and were apparently fastened below the knees. Over the vest he wore a long-sleeved jacket with pleated coattails. Under the vest he wore a linen shirt. A pair of sandals and sewn linen stockings completed his dress. A sheath and a knife with a bone handle, as well as a leather money bag, were fastened to his belt. A few coins were in his trousers pockets. Altogether he had about twenty öre in copper money."

In 1628 you could buy a chicken for twenty öre. One chicken and maybe a drink of rum. That was what the sailor had in his pocket when the *Vasa* capsized—enough to buy a chicken. A swallow of rum, perhaps, with a chicken for lunch, or a moment in the arms of a pretty girl.

What else is there to say? Given a description of his clothes, given those coppers in his pocket, we could just about summarize a sailor's life to the hour of his death. And we know when that occurred: August 10, 1628, not long after three in the afternoon, while King Gustavus Adolphus marched fearlessly through Poland.

The White Lantern

In the seventh century, according to Polynesian tradition, a flotilla of canoes under the leadership of Ui-te-Rangiora sailed to a place where the cold was beyond understanding, where the sea was covered with white powder and great white rocks met the sky. Such a legend might have been invented, but probably it was not; it sounds like a report of something actually seen—just as we know, without a twig for evidence, that some Kiowa Indians who claimed to have visited a land where the trees were filled with little men must have traveled to Mexico.

After Ui-te-Rangiora's colossal adventure nobody sailed that far south for the next millennium, which is not surprising when you realize how inhospitable the place is. Sir Douglas Mawson on the coast of Wilkes Land during the early part of this century recorded an average wind velocity for a period of twenty-four hours—average, mind you—of 90 miles an hour. Gusts reached 200 miles an hour. A violent eddy picked up a tractor as though it were an umbrella and tossed it 50 yards. Mawson and his companions lived in a hut submerged in snow, which caused the atmosphere to become so electrically charged that their fingertips glowed blue with St. Elmo's fire. The noise of the storm made conversation impossible, but they got accustomed to this and during an occasional lull when they managed to exchange a few words they felt uneasy because their voices sounded peculiar, almost threatening.

A young Oxford graduate named Apsley Cherry-Garrard, a member of Scott's expedition, went hunting for penguin eggs on Cape Crozier one brisk morning. This was not his idea. He had signed on as an "adaptable helper"—in fact he had contributed 1,000 English pounds for the privilege—and he was told to help the zoologist. In midwinter they started out: zoologist-artist Edward Wilson, Oxford man Cherry-Garrard, and Lieutenant Henry R. "Birdie" Bowers who had once been a gunboat commander on the Irrawaddy River. They were gone five weeks. Cherry-Garrard later wrote a book titled *The Worst Journey in the World*. This is a brash claim but you don't have to read much of his book to conclude that he may have been right.

They took two sledges so heavily loaded that all three of them were required to drag each sledge, which meant dragging one a certain distance, then going back for the other. And it was cold. Their clothes were always frozen and the canvas harness by which they attached themselves to the sledge was so stiff that a man couldn't get properly harnessed by himself; his companions had to bend the frozen canvas around his body.

As for relatively simple matters such as breathing, in the daytime there was no problem; temperatures far below zero merely coated the lower parts of their faces with ice and soldered the balaclavas to their heads. The trouble began at night. They had to enclose themselves in their sleeping bags like caterpillars because the frigid outside air was impossible to breathe: "All night long our breath froze into the skins, and our respiration became quicker and quicker as the air in our bags got fouler and fouler. . . ."

Seventy below zero is not bad, he tells us, not comparatively bad, if you can see where you are going and where you are stepping, where the sledge straps are, and the cooker, the Primus, the food, and so on. But for twenty of each twenty-four hours they lived in darkness. The rest of the time a dull gleam on the horizon helped them along.

They set a course by the planet Jupiter and retraced their steps to the second sledge by candlelight. Once when the sky grew overcast a brief ray of moonlight was all that saved them from plunging into a crevasse just three steps ahead.

They suffered from optical illusions, hunger, frostbite, and—although this sounds odd—snow blindness. On an average day they progressed a couple of miles, traveling ten miles to do it. For one entire week the thermometer registered sixty below, or worse.

During a blizzard, contrary to what you would expect, the temperature began rising. It climbed fifty degrees to a delightful nine below zero.

Cherry-Garrard insists that one morning when he peeped out of the tent his clothing froze instantly, trapping his head in that position. He claims that for the next several hours he had to pull the sledge with his head screwed around at an angle. Now this is ridiculous. This is the sort of thing you see in a Hollywood cartoon, but our Oxford egg-collector is no humorist. Presumably it happened.

At last they got to the penguin rookery and after zoologist Wilson had completed his research they stole five eggs and started home. En route Cherry-Garrard broke two of these precious eggs. He was carrying them inside his mittens and he explains simply that they "burst." Maybe. Maybe it happened. But eggs seldom break unless they have been rudely handled. Nevertheless, he tells us without further clarification, his eggs "burst." All right, let it go. He emptied one mitten but kept the broken egg in the other because he thought that when they stopped to eat he would pour it into the cooker. For some reason he neglected to do this, "but on the return journey I had my mitts far more easily thawed out . . . and I believe the grease in the egg did them good."

Not long afterward, while they were camped, a hurricane sucked away their tent and they could do nothing except huddle in their sleeping bags.

The loss of the tent was critical; if they had to sleep outside they might not survive.

"Face to face with real death," he writes, "one does not think of the things that torment the bad people in the tracts, and fill the good people with bliss. I might have speculated on my chances of going to Heaven; but candidly I did not care. I could not have wept if I had tried. I had no wish to review the evils of my past. But the past did seem to have been a bit wasted. The road to Hell may be paved with good intentions: but the road to Heaven is paved with lost opportunities. . . . Well has the Persian said that when we come to die we, remembering that God is merciful, will gnaw our elbows with remorse for thinking of the things we have not done for fear of the Day of Judgment."

Two days after the tent vanished the weather improved enough for them to prepare a meal—tea and pemmican flavored with burnt seal blubber, penguin feathers, and hair from the sleeping bags.

Then, miraculously, they found the tent at the base of a slope half a mile distant; and their lives, which had been taken by the wind, were given back.

When they returned to the base the first thing they heard was an astonished voice crying: "Good God! Here's the Crozier party!"

Somebody decided to weigh their sleeping bags. At the start of the trip the bags weighed forty-seven pounds. Now, with the accumulation of snow inside and out, they weighed almost three times that much.

Scott was troubled by the appearance of his men: "They looked more weather-worn than anyone I have yet seen. Their faces were scarred and wrinkled, their eyes dull, their hands whitened and creased with constant exposure." A photograph taken after they got back is even more expressive. At first you think you have seen it before, then suddenly it reminds you of pictures taken at Dachau and Buchenwald.

Three of the five eggs at last reached the Natural History Museum in London where they were accepted and studied with no particular excitement. The value of this trip, therefore, depends on your interpretation. One biographer commented that it had drawn Cherry-Garrard and his companions together in permanent spiritual bondage, which makes it sound almost worthwhile. Another said that few men ever have absorbed so much punishment for the sake of adding such an insignificant brick to the edifice of knowledge. In other words the rookery had as much meaning, or as little, as the Pole itself.

And though this has nothing to do with our story it might be remarked that the bird—the Emperor penguin as distinguished from the smaller Adélie—seems to be not very bright but is uncommonly powerful, an association of traits often found at home. Five crewmen of the whaler *Baleana*, intent upon capturing an Emperor, tried to wrestle one to the ice but were disdainfully flung aside. They leaped on the bird again and after a furious struggle managed to get two leather belts strapped around it. The Emperor then took a breath, snapped both belts, and shuffled away.

Now, in regard to harrowing journeys, if Cherry-Garrard's does not sound sufficiently arduous you might go back to Sir Douglas Mawson. He, too, was a scientist—a physicist, geologist, and the first man to use long-distance radio in the Antarctic. He wanted to map some territory east of Wilkes Land, so when the paralyzing storm blew over he emerged from St. Elmo's hut with two companions: a young officer of the Royal Fusiliers, Lieutenant Belgrave Ninnis, known as "Cherub" because of his complexion, and a big Swiss-German ski champion named Xavier Mertz, called "X."

They loaded three sledges, harnessed eighteen dogs, and set out on November 10, 1912.

They crossed two valleys through which glaciers were flowing toward the coast like immense ice tongues and Mawson named them after Ninnis and Mertz. The weather was good. They traveled about 300 miles with no difficulty except that Ninnis suffered from an infected finger, and one sledge which got rather banged up had to be abandoned.

On December 14, a bright clear day, Mertz was skiing ahead, serenading the inconceivable emptiness with Teutonic drinking songs, while Mawson rode on a sledge not far behind him. Ninnis was riding the other sledge.

Mertz abruptly lifted a ski pole: the danger signal.

Mawson stopped to inspect the snow. He could find no indication of a crevasse. Then he looked around. Ninnis was gone. However there was a low ridge that might possibly have obscured him.

The two men hurried back.

On the other side of the ridge they saw an enormous hole. Mawson, a precise man, states that it was eleven feet across. Two sets of sledge tracks led up to the hole, but only Mawson's led away from it.

When they looked down through binoculars they could see a shelf of ice projecting from the shadowy turquoise depths. On this shelf lay a pair of dogs, together with a section of the big tent and a canvas bag holding a ten-day supply of food. One of the dogs appeared to be dead.

The other, named Franklin, was moaning; its back seemed to be broken, and very soon it died.

Ninnis' sledge had been pulled by the strongest dogs and was loaded with equipment. In addition to the food and the tent, it carried some waterproof clothes that Mertz had not worn because of the mild weather, most of their plates, cups, eating utensils, a number of implements—including a pickax, which might be crucial—and all of the dog food. The most important thing was their own food. On the shelf lay enough to sustain three men for ten days.

To find out how far down it was they tied a theodolite to a 150-foot fishing line and lowered the instrument into the crevasse. The legs of the theodolite just touched Franklin's body.

Mertz wanted to lower himself to the shelf on a rope, but Mawson convinced him that this would be suicidal.

For several hours they remained at the lip of the hole, gazing into it, listening, and occasionally calling Ninnis. Not a sound came from the depths, only a draft of frigid air.

At last Mawson read a burial service and they decided on a course to the base; they could not waste any more time pretending Ninnis might be alive or that his body could be recovered. They were so near the Magnetic Pole that the compass swung back and forth like a pendulum, and the sky had grown overcast, which meant they would not have the sun for a guide, but they knew they must start at once. Whether or not they survived would depend on how fast they traveled. They were 300 miles out with no supply depots.

Mawson recorded the location of the crevasse: "It is 35 miles east-southeast of the headland. . . ."

The dogs no longer could be treated decently. In this situation their existence had just one purpose—to contribute toward the survival of their masters. Without food, because there was nothing to feed them, they were mercilessly lashed forward: Haldane, Ginger, Pavlova, Mary, George, and Johnson.

At the site of the abandoned sledge the men inspected the supplies they had discarded a few days earlier. What had seemed useless might now be valuable. The huskies were starving so Mawson sliced up a pair of wolfskin gloves, some worn-out finnesko boots, and a leather strap, divided this into six portions and offered it to them. The dogs gulped down everything and licked the snow. Mawson and Mertz, attempting to conserve their own rations, did not eat anything that night.

Next morning the dog named George could not stand up. Mawson shot the husky and butchered it. The lid of the Nansen cooker became a skillet in which they fried George's hind legs, but there was so little fat on the animal that the meat only scorched. Mertz disliked the taste. Mawson pretended to enjoy it, although he admitted it was somewhat musty and strange and exceedingly tough.

Two days later he was stricken with snow blindness but they could not afford to stop. On they went, Mertz probing the ice for danger, while Mawson—with cocaine and zinc sulfate tablets beneath his eyelids and one eye bandaged—took George's place among the huskies.

Johnson provided the next meal. Mertz shot him through the ear, skinned him, and threw the least appetizing parts to his former friends who instantly crunched his bones, tore his pelt to shreds, and even swallowed his teeth. We are told that Johnson had a strong odor when alive, and after death, although the choicest cuts were sliced into tiny pieces and stewed, he continued to smell.

Mertz and Mawson looked forward to eating the livers of the dogs, not because they were good—in fact they were slimy and stank of fish—but because it seemed to them that the liver must be nourishing. This part of the animal was saturated with a substance which would be isolated eight years later by laboratory technicians and named vitamin A. Twenty years after that discovery the effects of an overdose would be catalogued: nausea, vertigo, loss of hair, cramps, skin fissures, extreme fatigue, dysentery, delirium, and convulsions, often ending in death. Still later it would be learned that eating a Greenland husky's liver was especially dangerous. As Lennard Bickel points out, under the evolutionary pressure of centuries during which these dogs had been fed so much polar bear meat and seal meat the husky's liver had built an abnormal capacity for storing vitamin A. Four ounces of a husky's liver is enough to be considered poisonous. Mawson and Mertz, who ate six livers, swallowed about thirty toxic doses apiece on the assumption that it was good for them.

Haldane and Mary soon disappeared into the pot, then it was Pavlova's turn.

Mawson shot her, smashed her bones with a spade so they could be more easily boiled, and cut off her paws which he added to the soup. This must have been difficult because Pavlova was his favorite. She was named after the great dancer who had come aboard ship in England and talked to him awhile. There on the Thames he had asked if she would be godmother to his ship; so Anna Pavlova poured a little wine on the forestem and reminded God to watch over this voyage. Before going ashore she stopped to pet one of the huskies.

On Christmas Day at the bottom of the world they brightened the stew with a dollop of butter, after which Mawson set up his theodolite to fix their position: "We are some eighteen miles farther south on the glacier than when we were here a month ago. . . ."

Christmas did not end happily. They examined themselves and realized that their bodies were beginning to rot. Patches of skin could be lifted off. Hair was falling out. Teeth were loosening.

The last dog on the menu was Ginger, and because they had thrown away the rifle in order to lighten the sledge it was necessary to kill her with the spade. Mertz could not do it, so Mawson took the spade and broke her neck. Then he cut off her head, which they boiled for an hour and a half. Now, unless you have had some experience it's hard to know when a dog's head is properly cooked. Mawson is not specific, but we must assume that from time to time they uncovered the pot and looked in to see how Ginger was progressing. The idea may seem repugnant, but of course our values fluctuate depending on circumstances.

When they decided she had been cooked enough Mawson drew a line with his knife over the top of the skull, symbolically dividing it, and they took turns eating—gnawing away the lips, jaw muscles, and eyeballs. Their metal spoons had gone down the crevasse with Ninnis, but Mawson had whittled two wooden spoons out of a sledge strut which enabled them to scoop up the brains. In his diary he noted that Ginger's head made a good breakfast.

The death of this animal left them with a sense of loneliness they had not anticipated. They seem to have felt Ginger's absence emotionally as well as physically.

Mertz was beginning to fall apart. He developed stomach cramps and often rested on the sledge while Mawson struggled to pull it. Some days they made no more than a couple of miles.

On January 6 Mawson wrote: "Both our chances are going now." The implication being that if he abandoned Mertz and went on alone he might reach the base. But it is doubtful that he even considered such a thing, though he knew the man was dying.

About ten o'clock the next morning Mertz screamed. Then he thrust one of his fingers into his mouth—the little finger of the left hand, if such details interest you. He thrust this yellow frostbitten little finger into his mouth, chewed it off, and spat it out.

Mawson bandaged the stump and persuaded him to drink some cocoa, which quieted him. After a while he went to sleep, but woke up several hours later and thrashed around so violently that Mawson was obliged to sit on his chest. He complained that his ears ached, he lost control of his bowels, and during the night he died.

Mawson was now alone, at least 100 miles from the base, with very little food: pemmican, raisins, almonds, cocoa, chocolate, dog meat, and a kind of jelly he had made from boiled dog bones.

He began to modify the sledge and camping equipment "to meet fresh requirements," as he puts it. He threw away whatever was not essential and cut the sledge in half, discarding the rear section. He constructed a mast and a spar, and fashioned a sail out of a clothes bag and Mertz's jacket in order to take advantage of any wind. He then dragged the body a short distance from camp, piled blocks of snow around it and raised a cross made from the discarded sledge runners.

"As there is now little chance of my reaching human aid alive," he wrote in his diary, "I greatly regret inability to set down the coastline as surveyed for the 300 miles we traveled. . . ."

When the weather cleared he set out, pulling the front half of the renovated sledge.

En route, aware that his feet seemed numb and rather squelchy, he stopped to inspect them. He had not taken off his socks for quite some time. He remarks that after taking off the third and final pair the sight of his feet gave him a bit of a jolt. The thickened skin of the soles had become entirely detached, forming a separate layer, and the socks were saturated with "an abundant watery fluid." Several of his toes had turned black and the nails were loose. "I began to wonder," says Mawson, "if ever there was to be a day without some special disappointment."

However, one must make the best of a bad situation. He smeared his raw feet with lanolin, tied the soles in place with bandages, put on six pairs of thick wool socks, fur boots, and finally his crampon overshoes. These overshoes, having large stiff soles, spread the weight nicely, he tells us with unmistakable satisfaction, and helped protect his feet from the jagged ice he encountered soon afterward. But it was sticky going. He walked for a while on the outside of his feet, then on the inside, and when he could not endure the pain either way he went down on all fours and crawled—towing his sledge, pausing occasionally to wet his throat with melted snow or nibble at a stick of chocolate.

Presently he got caught in a blizzard.

Then the sledge nearly dropped into a chasm—"a great blue chasm like a quarry" is how he describes it.

And he felt so put upon by these tribulations, one right after another, that he resolved to treat himself to an extra bowl of dog soup.

The next special disappointment occurred the following day when he slipped into a crevasse. Now the predicament in which he found himself is absurd; if it appeared on a movie screen the audience would cackle and hoot. The old Saturday serials used to conclude like this: our hero inextricably, fundamentally, unconditionally, and grievously trapped.

Here is what we have. We have Sir Douglas, harnessed to his sledge for easier pulling, dangling at the end of the rope. Below him the camera reveals a bottomless gorge. Above him the sledge has caught in deep snow but at any instant it may break loose. If that happens Sir Douglas will plunge into frozen eternity.

He is exhausted by his ordeal, having already outlasted two other men. He is dizzy, freezing, poisoned, and half-starved. His feet are not just killing him, they are literally falling apart. He is alone in the Antarctic, the grimmest place on earth, no help within miles. Even if somebody should come looking for him, which nobody will, he could not be rescued because he could not be found. He is out of sight—invisible—not figuratively but actually out of sight, dangling below the surface of the glacier.

So there you have it, a real disappointment. Pauline's perils were nothing. And Sir Douglas certainly thinks he has enjoyed his last bowl of dog-paw soup.

You may wonder how he got out.

Don't miss next week's episode.

"I began to look around," he says in the great tradition of hopelessly mired heroes. Then he goes on to tell us that the crevasse was "somewhat over six feet wide and sheer walled, descending into blue depths below. My clothes, which, with a view to ventilation, had been but loosely secured, were now stuffed with snow broken from the roof, and very chilly it was. Above at the other end of the fourteen-foot rope, was the daylight seen through the hole in the lid."

All right, we have the scene in focus. What next?

"In my weak condition, the prospect of climbing out seemed very poor indeed. . . ."

One would think so. Nevertheless he started up and finally clawed his way to the surface, but all at once was dropped into the abyss a second time when a little more of the crust broke away.

"There, exhausted, weak and chilled, hanging freely in space and slowly turning round as the rope twisted one way and the other, I felt that I had done my utmost and failed, that I had no more strength to try again and that all was over except the passing."

It would be an ignoble, humiliating departure, but what troubled him most was the thought of the food on the sledge that he might have eaten. He had starved himself because there was practically nothing left; now even that little bit was going to be wasted. So, dangling in his harness, looking down and looking up, his palms bleeding, he tried to decide whether he should just wait for the end, or untie the rope and get it over with, or try once more to haul himself out. Then, if you can believe this, he remembered a couple of lines from Robert Service:

Just have one more try—it's dead easy to die,
It's the keeping-on-living that's hard.

You might expect him to think of something by a major poet. Donne, for instance. Or Coleridge or Milton or Blake. No, not at all. He was inspired by Robert Service.

Apparently this wretched poetry saved his life. The incredible man again scrambled to the top. He emerged from the hole feet first, wriggled on his belly to safe ground, collapsed, woke up an hour or two later covered with new snow, and then pitched his tent, figuring he had done enough for the day.

But came morning, on went Mawson, indefatigable, sustained by poetry—this time by Omar Khayyám whom he calls "the Persian philosopher." And if, through some anomaly of nature, he had found his way blocked by a polar bear it seems likely he would have torn the beast apart with his hands, swallowed it, and marched on. Nothing would stop him. If he had dropped into another abyss and plummeted half a mile to the bottom you would expect, after six hours or so, to see him pop out of the ice, resentful of these unwarranted calamities.

One is tempted to exclaim: Oh, come off it, Mawson! And yet, reading the account, one gets the feeling that not only did everything happen just that way, his trial may in fact have been worse than it sounds. He is so anxious not to overstate the case. Very chilly it was, he remarks, describing himself spinning over eternity like a spider on a thread. Very chilly. Yes, no doubt it was.

Somewhat absently he mentions that his toenails continued to fester, numerous boils on his face and body required daily attention, and prolonged starvation abetted by the unwholesomeness of dog meat was affecting him in various ways. Minor inconveniences. And he has thrown away the soles of his feet.

Here is his report of setting up the tent:

"It proved a protracted operation. When the outside was finished off satisfactorily the inside was discovered to be filled with drift snow and had to be dug out. Everything was stuffed with soft damp snow including the sleeping bag, and it took a rare time to put things right."

A couple of nights later the snow-laden tent weighs so heavily upon the sleeping bag that he has trouble moving, and he concludes that if he waits until daylight it may be impossible to dig himself out. Industrious as ever, he sets to work although "the skin was coming off my hands, which were the last parts of my body to peel. A moulting of the hair followed the peeling of the skin. Irregular tufts of beard came out and there was a general shedding of hair from my head, so much so that at each camp thereabouts the snowy floor of the tent was noticeably darkened."

After crossing Mertz Glacier in late January he had thrown away his iron crampons, along with some other equipment. Even the precious diary had been stripped of its cardboard binding. Every ounce mattered. But now he is again crossing wind-polished ice, slipping and falling so often that he worries about breaking a leg, which of course would bring down the final curtain. Obviously a set of cleats would help. He therefore dismantles the mahogany theodolite case and carves a pair of sandals, studding the underside with nails and with the long screws that held the box together.

Having strapped these contraptions to his feet with lampwick Mawson harnessed himself to the sledge and set out again, rather pleased because the ersatz crampons seemed to be working. Imperfectly, to be sure, but he did not slip quite as often.

After a few miles, though, his feet hurt worse than ever. He stopped to find out what had gone wrong. The ice was so hard that it had forced the screws and nails up through the wood—through the socks and bandages—until they were biting into his flesh.

Mawson hammered them down, bound the swollen bloody suppurating lumps that used to be his feet, and went on. He had traveled a fair distance by this time and saw no reason to quit.

Farther up the road his mahogany sandals cracked. He carved a new pair—double-deckers—which carried him a few more miles.

On and on the man goes, day after day, lurching forward, dragging that truncated sledge, now and then with the wind at his back sailing crazily over the ice, leaving an occasional tuft of beard to mark his passage.

Presently he is reduced to twenty chips of boiled dog meat, half a pound of raisins, and several ounces of chocolate. He is still many miles from safety. But Mawson's problems hardly sound alarming anymore, you know he will get through. If the food runs out he will start eating rope. Then he will eat the sledge.

Needless to say, as we say, he got back alive, curiously bald, and somewhat under the weather as he might express it, but he did return. He got back because, first of all, he was Mawson. That's the principal reason. Secondly, he was no amateur. He knew the Antarctic. In 1908 he and the gentlemanly fifty-year-old Professor Edgeworth David had been members of an expedition led by Ernest Shackleton. Shackleton meant to reach the South Pole. Nobody had done this, therefore Shackleton wanted to do it.

He failed. He got within 100 miles before the likelihood of starvation obliged him to turn around. The men had gone as far as they could go, almost too far. They started out with four ponies, three of which they butchered. The other fell into a crevasse. On the way back they were so hungry that they stopped at the place where one of the ponies had been slaughtered and dug into the snow for its congealed blood. However, that's a different story.

While preparations were being made for Shackleton's dash toward the Geographic Pole, Professor David and two associates went off to find the Magnetic Pole. These do not necessarily lie close together. The Magnetic Pole, in fact, drifts across a considerable area because the earth's magnetic field fluctuates, which explains why the first Antarctic explorers could not agree on its location. At present it is not where Professor David and his assistants, Mawson and Dr. A. F. Mackay, found it. But that, too, is a different story.

While they were heading toward it they camped one day on some rather touchy ice. Mawson was in the tent examining photographic plates and Professor David was outside loading the sledge when Mawson heard the professor ask in a strangely resonant voice if he was busy. Yes, Mawson replied through the canvas, he was busy.

A few minutes later Professor David asked the same question. Mawson again answered that he was busy. Then, "with infinite politeness and apology," as Mawson describes it, Professor David said: "I am so sorry to disturb you, Mawson, but I am down a crevasse and I really don't think I can hold on much longer."

Farther up the glacier Mawson himself abruptly dropped from sight, and you get the feeling that these men who trudged around the Antarctic spent half their time rescuing each other.

On top of a high plateau they fixed the position of the Magnetic Pole at 72° 25' S., 155° 16' E. on the sixteenth of January, 1909. Considering that it drifts, you cannot help asking why anybody needed a precise location. Maybe the facts were important in 1909, though today they have about as much value as Cherry-Garrard's penguin eggs.

The good ship *Nimrod* was to meet them at the coast near Professor

David's glacier, but they were late for the rendezvous. No ship was in sight, so they camped and waited. Surely somebody would pick them up because, after all, they were the only people on earth who knew where the Magnetic Pole was.

Two days later they heard a cannon shot.

Mawson, Mackay, and Professor David bounded from the tent and there just offshore lay the *Nimrod*. They began running across the ice, Mawson in the lead, when once again he vanished.

Mackay skidded to a stop beside the hole and looked down. Mawson was clinging to a ledge. Mackay asked if he was all right.

"Yes," said Mawson.

He had fallen twenty feet and if he slipped from the ledge he would never be seen again.

I say, Mawson, are you all right?

Yes.

Well, the question was logical and the response was clear, so perhaps one shouldn't wonder at it.

Mackay and the professor lowered a sledge harness into the hole, assuming they could pull him out. Instead, they were almost pulled in. More help would be needed. Mackay, cupping his hands, shouted to the *Nimrod:* "Mawson has fallen down a crevasse and we got to the Magnetic Pole!"

The grand prize, though, was the mystic southern core, the symbolic end of the earth, the Geographic Pole. Shackleton almost made it but stopped ninety-seven miles short. Ninety-seven miles from immortality.

"We have shot our bolt," he writes in his journal. "We hoisted Her Majesty's flag, and the other Union Jack afterward, and took possession of the plateau. . . . While the Union Jack blew out stiffly in the icy gale that cut us to the bone, we looked south with our powerful glasses, but could see nothing but the dead-white snow plain. There was no break in the plateau as it extended toward the Pole. . . ."

Amundsen and Scott are the illustrious names. They got to the Pole within five weeks of each other, which suggests nothing more than good luck and bad luck; but there was such a difference in what happened subsequently that luck cannot explain it. The explanation must be found in the characters of the two men, just as Mawson's trip can be explained only by his outrageous determination.

Roald Amundsen's opinion of luck is terse and revealing:

"Victory awaits those who have everything in order. People call this luck. Defeat awaits those who fail to take the necessary precautions. This is known as bad luck."

There we have it. To be lucky you must know what you are doing.

At the age of fifteen, after reading about Sir John Franklin's disastrous attempt to find a northwest passage, Amundsen began to get ready. He trained his body to endure hardship. He detested football, but forced himself to play it. He went skiing in the mountains whenever possible. He slept with his bedroom windows open all winter. He looked forward to the obligatory term of military service "both because I wanted to be a good citizen and because I felt that military training would be of great benefit to me as further preparation for my life."

When he was twenty-two he persuaded a friend to go with him on a miniature polar passage. West of Oslo is a mile-high plateau extending nearly to the coast. In summer it is used by Lapp herdsmen pasturing reindeer, but when winter arrives the Lapps descend to the valley and the plateau is deserted. There is no record of anyone ever having crossed it during winter. Amundsen resolved to cross it.

In the middle of their third night on the plateau he woke up because of a temperature change. Instead of sleeping on top of the snow he had burrowed into it, hoping to escape the wind, and while he lay snugly in the hole he had been pleased with himself for such a clever idea. He woke up lying on his back, feeling cramped. Without opening his eyes he tried to roll over but was unable to move. The damp snow of early evening had filled the entrance to his burrow, sifted over his sleeping bag, and then had frozen into a solid block of ice. He began struggling and shouting, but he was helpless—absolutely unable to move—and his voice probably was inaudible at the surface. He very soon quit shouting, he says, because it was hard to breathe, and he realized that if he did not keep quiet he would suffocate. Presumably his friend also had burrowed into the snow, which meant he must be trapped in the same way. Unless there should be a quick thaw they both would die in these ice coffins.

Amundsen does not know whether he fell asleep or fainted, but the next time he became conscious he heard the sound of digging. His friend had slept on the surface, too exhausted to do anything else, and was astonished when he woke up to find himself alone. The only trace of Amundsen was a tuft of hair at one corner of his sleeping bag. Another snow flurry would have hidden him until the Lapps returned.

They got back in such poor shape that people who had seen them eight days earlier did not recognize them.

Commenting on this experience years later, Amundsen remarks that an "adventure" is merely an interruption of an explorer's serious work and indicates bad planning.

This trip across the Norwegian plateau seems to have been rigorously educational. What he learned from it, beyond the danger of burrowing, cannot even be estimated; but it is obvious that, like most extraordinary people, he knew how to distinguish the shape of the world from a grain of sand. Again and again he talks about preparation. Planning. Attention to detail.

He chose the site of his South Polar base only after studying every existing description of the Ross Ice Shelf from the day it was discovered in 1841. Each member of his expedition was judiciously selected. Every bit of equipment, right down to the tent pegs and buttons, was inspected for weakness or inadequacy. He ordered the boots ripped apart and rebuilt according to his own ideas of comfort and safety. He insisted that a new dog whip be designed.

Aboard the *Fram*, in addition to nineteen men, were almost 100 huskies. Amundsen was convinced that dogs were essential to success and he had a false deck constructed on the ship to protect them from the tropic sun. He watched their health as closely as he watched the health of his men. He had calculated the day-by-day weight of the sledges that must be hauled to the Pole, and he knew how much weight each animal could pull. As the journey progressed the sledges would become lighter, which meant that fewer dogs would be required. Logistics demanded, therefore, that at a certain point a certain number of dogs be slaughtered. Yet even in death they must contribute. He had calculated that the average dog carried fifty pounds of edible meat. He worked out the precise day on which he intended to kill each dog, and he adhered to this schedule almost exactly.

Amundsen says nothing about the liver, but Arctic Eskimos had known for a long time that you should not eat a husky's liver and he probably was aware of this. He would not have known just why the liver was dangerous, but it would be characteristic of him to credit the Eskimos with some valid reason for their belief.

On the central plateau twenty-four huskies were killed.

"We had agreed to shrink from nothing," he wrote. "The pemmican was cooked remarkably quickly that evening and I was unusually industrious in stirring it. I am not a nervous man, but at the sound of the first shot I found myself trembling. Shot now followed shot in quick succession, echoing uncannily over the great white plain. Each time a trusty servant lost his life."

The Norwegians afterward referred to this campground as the Butcher's Shop.

At first they were reluctant to devour their trusty servants, but the cook Wisting knew his trade. He selected a young animal named Rex.

"I could not take my eyes off his work," says Amundsen.

> The delicate little cutlets had an absolutely hypnotizing effect as they were spread out one by one over the snow. They recalled memories of old days, when no doubt a dog cutlet would have been less tempting than now—memories of dishes on which the cutlets were elegantly arranged side by side, with paper frills on the bones, and a neat pile of petits pois in the middle. Ah, my thoughts wandered still farther afield—but that does not concern us now, nor has it anything to do with the South Pole. . . . The meat was excellent, quite excellent, and one cutlet after another disappeared with lightninglike rapidity. I must admit that they would have lost nothing by being a little more tender, but one must not expect too much of a dog. At this first meal I finished five cutlets myself, and looked in vain in the pot for more. Wisting appeared not to have reckoned on such a brisk demand.

About three o'clock on the afternoon of December 14, 1911, Amundsen's men calculated that they had reached the end of the trail.

There were no cheers, no orations. All together the five men grasped a Norwegian flag and thrust it into the snow: Amundsen, Sverre Hassel, Oskar Wisting, Helmer Hansen, Olav Bjaaland.

"Thus we plant thee, beloved flag, at the South Pole, and give to the plain on which it lies the name of King Haakon VII's plateau."

That brief speech was the only concession to ritual. One gets out of the way of protracted ceremonies in these regions, says Amundsen. The shorter they are, the better.

The Norwegians were in no hurry to leave. The trip had not been difficult, the weather was mild, and they had more than enough food. They stayed several days, taking measurements, circling the area on skis to be sure they truly had encompassed the Pole, and otherwise enjoyed themselves.

They were camped in the middle of a continent almost as large as Australia and Europe combined. The Ross Ice Shelf, over which they had traveled at the beginning, appears to be only a deep indentation on the map of Antarctica, although it is about the size of France. Ice has buried the entire continent—all of its mountains, plains, and valleys, with very few exceptions—in some places to a depth of two miles. Astronauts say that it is the earth's most noticeable feature and that it radiates light from the bottom of the world like a great white lantern.

Once upon a time Antarctica was different. There were pine forests, swamps, and fern jungles. Shackleton's party found a seam of coal eight feet thick near the top of Beardmore Glacier. Scott, following the same route, came across fossilized twigs and leaves:

"The best leaf impressions and the most obvious were in the rotten clumps of weathered coal which split up easily to sheath-knife and hammer. Every layer of these gave abundant vegetable remains. Most of the bigger leaves were like beech leaves in shape and venation, in size a little smaller than British beech."

On the Palmer Peninsula are traces of fig leaves, sequoia, and an evergreen called araucaria that reached a height of 150 feet and still grows in South America. At Mount Weaver, close to the Pole, is a petrified log eighteen inches in diameter; it dates from the Jurassic period, the age of dinosaurs. What reptiles, animals, and birds lived in prehistoric Antarctica is not known—except for some ancestral families of the penguin, one of which grew as tall as a man.

Nor does anybody know what changed the climate. There are theories, but not much agreement.

At present more than a million people live within a radius of 2,000 miles of the North Pole, yet within that radius of the South Pole—excluding the men at weather stations—there is no human life. There are no land animals or birds, only the indestructible aquatic penguin. There is not a single living tree. There are lichens clinging to exposed rocks, a little moss, some coarse grass, a few spiders and flies. The spiders do not spin webs because of the wind and the flies have no wings. These tiny creatures, as obstinate as Sir Douglas Mawson, spend most of their lives frozen stiff, but thaw out several days a year and hurriedly go about their business in order to maintain the species. Such is life today in Antarctica, which may explain why King Haakon's real estate has never been developed.

Before starting the return journey Amundsen lashed a small Norwegian flag to a tent pole. Inside the tent he left a bag containing a letter to the king, just in case they should not make it back to their ship. He discarded some items: reindeerskin foot bags, mitts, a sextant, a hypsometer case—which is an instrument for measuring heights above sea level. And he addressed a letter to Scott.

"He will be here sooner or later," Amundsen told a member of the party. "I hope for his sake it will be sooner."

What Amundsen meant was that the weather could only get worse.

Their trip home sounds idyllic. They had marked the route, and the wind and sun were at their backs. They planned to travel eighteen miles a day, which they did without effort in less than five hours. There was so much food that sometimes they threw away biscuits and pemmican, and fed chocolate to the dogs. The dogs had such an easy time pulling the sledges that they began to get fat.

"We were in high spirits and bowled along at a cracking pace. . . ."

They reached their base on January 25, the date Amundsen had selected two years earlier in Norway. A week later the *Fram* sailed with all aboard in perfect health.

Scott at this time was hundreds of miles away, writing in his diary: "February 2. Three out of five of us injured. We shall be lucky if we get through. . . ."

On March 18 he wrote: "Ill fortune presses. . . ."

March 19: "The weather doesn't give us a chance. . . ."

Earlier he had told a Melbourne journalist: "We may get through, we may not. We may lose our lives. We may be wiped out. It is all a matter of providence and luck."

Shortly after that while en route to the Antarctic: ". . . fortune has determined to put every difficulty in our path."

Again, the following week: "I begin to wonder if fortune will ever turn her wheel."

At the start of the final journey: "The future is in the lap of the gods. . . ."

While struggling up Beardmore Glacier, unaware that Amundsen had just reached the Pole: "Our luck is very bad."

Eight days later: "I trust this may prove the turning point in our fortunes. . . ."

Near the end of March as he lay dying he wrote to the mother of one of his dead companions: "The ways of Providence are inscrutable. . . ."

And in his *Message to the Public*, found beside his body, he begins: "The causes of the disaster are not due to faulty organisation, but to misfortune. . . ."

Perhaps. Perhaps he was right. Maybe all things rest in the lap of the gods. Maybe "faulty organisation" was not the cause, though it is hard to forget something he had said ten years before:

"To my mind no journey ever made with dogs can approach the height of the fine conception which is realized when a party of men go forth to face hardships, dangers, and difficulties with their own unaided efforts, and by days and weeks of hard physical labour succeed in solving some problem of the great unknown. Surely in this case the conquest is more nobly and splendidly won."

It's arguable, of course, whether one should extract particular phrases from a man's life to offer as proof of anything. On the subject of luck, for example, Amundsen himself occasionally referred to it without disdain, in a rather idle fashion, as something to be hoped for.

Still, there's a difference. And the difference becomes more significant when you learn what others thought about Scott. As a child he was so lethargic and preoccupied that he was called "Old Moony." He seems to have been the storybook sissy: emotional, horrified at the sight of blood, physically weak, pampered by his mother and an older sister. A doctor who examined him before he joined the navy advised him to choose a different career.

Scott himself recognized his languid disposition and tried to do something about it; and considering how rapidly be was promoted in the navy he must have changed. Yet in every photograph he looks bemused, tentative, almost doubtful. His stance, his expression—he lives far away from the frigid brutal world of Roald Amundsen. Biographer Peter Brent speaks of a brooding, melancholy air. "His mouth, with its full rounded lips, suggests a leaning toward sensuality and pleasure. . . ."

Scott's resemblance to his romantic kinsman, Sir Walter Scott, is startling; they look like brothers. And his written "impressions" of the Antarctic are what you might expect from a mystic poet, not an explorer:

> The small green tent and the great white road.
>
> The drift snow like finest flour penetrating every hole and corner—flickering up beneath one's head covering, pricking sharply as a sand blast.
>
> The sun with blurred image peeping shyly through the wreathing drift giving pale shadowless light.
>
> The eternal silence of the great white desert. Cloudy columns of snow drift advancing from the south, pale yellow wraiths, heralding the coming storm, blotting out one by one the sharp-cut lines of the land.

Given such a temperament, why was he chosen to lead an expedition? The answer seems to be that as a midshipman he won a whaleboat race. This sounds like a petty triumph, but among the excited spectators was Sir Clements Markham, president of the Royal Geographical Society. He invited Scott to supper and later commented: "I was much struck with his intelligence, information, and the charm of his manner."

Because of Markham's patronage, when a British exploratory party sailed for the Antarctic in 1901 its commander was Scott. Even then he admits he is out of place: "I may as well confess that I have no predilection for polar exploration. . . ."

Subsequently he married an actress, Kathleen Bruce, and began to associate with actors, authors, painters, and musicians—a doubtful lot. How much these people unsettled him can only be imagined. Once he wrote to Kathleen: "I seem to hold in reserve something that makes for success and yet to see no worthy field for it and so there is this consciousness of a truly deep unrest."

Now listen to Roald Amundsen on the same subject: "Success is a woman who has to be won, not courted. You've got to seize her and carry her off, not stand under her window with a mandolin."

In 1910 when the South Polar expedition departed, Scott once more was put in charge. And it is a little strange—or perhaps not—that the London *Evening Standard* should remark: "We may never see them again."

Scott's wife also had premonitions, confiding to her diary:

"I had rather a horrid day today. I woke up having a bad dream about you, and then Peter came very close to me and said emphatically, 'Daddy won't come back,' as though in answer to my silly thoughts."

"I was very taken up with you all evening. I wonder if anything special is happening to you. Something odd happened to the clocks and watches between nine and ten p.m."

"I was still rather taken up by you and a wee bit depressed. As you ought about now to be returning to ship I see no reason for depression. I wonder."

Ernest Shackleton wrote to a New Zealand friend: "I suppose that we shall soon hear of Scott. I am inclined to think that we will hear from Amundsen first."

Today, from this distance, as one reads about the expedition, a feeling of doom soars overhead like an albatross. Aboard ship—even before they reach Antarctica—things do not go well. Icebergs appear farther north than expected. Then a storm threatens the *Terra Nova* and ten precious bags of coal which had not been lashed down must be jettisoned. At four in the morning the pumps become choked, water rises in the engine room, the men start bailing with buckets. A dog drowns. Two ponies die.

Upon reaching Antarctica they were unable to establish winter quarters on Cape Crozier as they had planned. Three motor sledges were brought along for heavy work but one sledge broke through the ice and sank, so that in order to get the ponies' fodder ashore the men harnessed themselves to bales of hay. And the expedition's photographer, standing quite literally on thin ice, was almost knocked into the water by a scheming killer whale.

About this time they got news of Amundsen, who had set up camp on an indentation sixty miles nearer the Pole. Scott wrote in his diary: "I never thought he could have got so many dogs safely to the ice. His plan for running them seems excellent. . . ."

Three more ponies died while the first depot was being stocked. Two more drowned when the ice disintegrated beneath them. And Scott writes: "I could not rid myself of the fear that misfortune was in the air. . . ."

Despite every problem he scrupulously kept his journal.

January 15: "We left our depot today with nine days' provisions, so that it ought to be a certain thing now, and the only appalling possibility the sight of the Norwegian flag forestalling ours."

January 16: "The worst has happened. . . . Bowers's sharp eyes detected what he thought was a cairn; he was uneasy about it, but argued that it might be sastrugus. Half an hour later he detected a black speck ahead. Soon we knew that this could not be a natural snow feature. We marched on, found that it was a black flag tied to a sledge bearer; nearby the remains of a camp; sledge tracks and ski tracks coming and going and the clear trace of dogs' paws—many dogs."

Next day Scott reached the Pole: "Great God! this is an awful place. . . ."

Inside the tent was Amundsen's message.

Poleheim
15 December 1911

Dear Captain Scott:

As you are probably the first to reach this area after us, I will ask you kindly to forward this letter to King Haakon VII. If you can use any of the articles left in this tent, please do not hesitate to do so. The sledge left outside may be of use to you. With best regards, I wish you a safe return.

Roald Amundsen

The British party stayed just long enough to verify the location. By their measurements, Amundsen's tent was only a few hundred yards from the geographical center.

It is hard to understand why they loitered on the way back. They did not have much food, the weather was savage, and they had 900 miles to go. But here is Scott's journal entry on February 8: "I decided to camp and spend the rest of the day geologising. It has been extremely interesting. We found ourselves under perpendicular cliffs of Beacon sandstone, weathering rapidly and carrying veritable coal seams. From the last Wilson, with his sharp eyes, has picked several plant impressions, the last a piece of coal with beautifully traced leaves in layers, also some excellently preserved impressions of thick stems, showing cellular structure. In one place we saw the cast of small waves in the sand."

Why did they do this? Two explanations have been proposed. If they could bring back some scientific information that the Norwegians had overlooked their defeat would not be total. Certainly they knew that. The other explanation, which seeps through Scott's journal like a stain, is that they sensed they could never make it. By now they were crippled and suffering from the cold. Wilson had pulled a tendon in his leg. Evans' hands were so badly frozen that his fingernails had begun to drop off. Oates' feet were turning black. Scott had injured his shoulder. Bowers seems to be the only one in good shape.

Yet the next day they again stopped to collect geological specimens. Scott remarks on "the delight of setting foot on rock after 14 weeks of snow and ice."

A few days later Evans died.

Temperatures dropped so low that in the mornings it took them an hour to put on their footgear. The cooking oil was almost gone. Food rations were cut. Scott meditates: "I wonder what is in store for us. . . ."

On the fifteenth of March while they waited in the tent for a blizzard to let up Oates said, "I am just going outside and may be some time." His feet had become so painful that he could hardly walk, and he did not want to delay the other men.

The bodies of Scott, Bowers, and Wilson were discovered eleven miles from a food depot. Their tent was almost buried by snow. The men lay in their sleeping bags, Wilson with his hands folded on his chest. Bowers also appeared to have died without anguish. Between them lay Scott, the flaps of his sleeping bag open. His diaries were in a green wallet underneath the bag, the last letters on a groundsheet beside him. His left arm was extended, his hand resting on Wilson's shoulder. The interior of the tent had been kept neat. There was an improvised lamp, a bag of tea, a bag of tobacco, and their scientific notes.

Outside stood the sledge. Along with the necessities, it carried thirty-five pounds of rock.

Scott's wife was aboard ship en route to New Zealand to meet him when she learned of his death—five days after the captain got the news by radio. The captain had been so distressed that he could not approach her. She reports in her diary that his hands trembled when he finally showed her the message. After reading it she said to him: "Oh, well, never mind! I expected that. Thanks very much. I will go and think about it."

Then, as she usually did each morning on the ship, she took a Spanish lesson. Then she ate lunch and discussed American politics and in the afternoon spent a while reading about the *Titanic*, determined to avoid thinking of her husband's death until she was sure she could control herself.

She mentions that because it was too hot to go to her cabin she stayed on deck the whole day. Immediately after this commonplace statement, and without a pause, as though it were the most natural sequence in the world, she writes the following passage: "My god is godly. I need not touch him to know that. Let me maintain a high, adoring exaltation, and not let the sorrow of contamination touch me. Within I shall be exultant. My god is glorious and could never become less so. Loneliness is a fear that I have never known. Had he died before I had known his gloriousness, or before he had been the father of my son, I might have felt a loss. Now I have felt none for myself. Won't any body understand that?—probably nobody. So I must go on and on with the tedious business of discretion. Must even the greatest visions of the heart be blurred by discretions?"

That last line, once you have memorized it, cannot ever be forgotten, although when analyzed it doesn't make much sense. It suggests some deep communication with her husband, nothing more. But that's all right, many of Shakespeare's indelible lines don't make sense.

What is curious and moving about this passage is the radiance emanating from Scott through the adoration of his wife. To arouse such transcendent feelings in a woman, he must have been extraordinary. And that such a man should have been misplaced seems all the more pathetic.

Just as curious—perhaps more so—is the fact that Amundsen, the victor, is not as renowned as the loser. Quite a few people think Scott was the first man to reach the South Pole. There is no logical explanation for this belief, though his dramatic death may account for it, together with the fact that he and his companions are still there—frozen like insects or splinters on the side of the great white lantern. However, they won't stay there indefinitely. Calculations by scientists at McMurdo Sound indicate that the bodies now lie fifty feet beneath the surface and fifteen miles closer to the edge of the ice shelf. What this means is that sometime in the future Scott and his companions will be carried out to sea on an iceberg.

As for Roald Amundsen, who knows what became of him? Almost no one. He died on a gallant but useless errand, searching for General Umberto Nobile whose dirigible crash-landed in the Arctic. Amundsen's plane may have developed engine trouble; pieces of it were found off the Norwegian coast. The plane had been lent by the French government, which had at that time two modern seaplanes: one with a water-cooled engine, the other with an air-cooled engine. The French, exhibiting that singular wisdom we have come to associate with all federal government, provided Amundsen with the water-cooled engine for his long flight through subzero temperatures.

A Swedish pilot later rescued the Italian general.

Scott is now remembered and honored throughout the English-speaking world while Amundsen is not. One might say this is folly, because Amundsen has more to teach us. But in the end, of course, they are equally instructive.

6

Syllables Here and There

THOSE OF US WHO ARE not overly familiar with the nuances of Ugaritic, Luvian, Hittite, Mesopotamian cuneiform, Palaic, or Creto-Mycenaean Linear B do know a little something, nevertheless, about the Rosetta stone. Ah yes!—the Rosetta stone! Of course, of course. Haven't thought about that in years. Let's see now, they dug it up someplace. The thing was covered with hieroglyphics. Yes indeed, the old Rosetta stone.

More specifically—just where and when it was found, who deciphered it, what the message was—on these points we grow a bit hesitant. And soon the subject becomes tiresome. After all, the translation of dead pronouncements scarcely relates to our daily round. Still, some people consecrate their lives to such matters. For example, George Smith.

That name sounds almost as fictitious as John Doe, but our George Smith was a particular individual—a nineteenth-century London bank-note engraver employed by Messrs. Bradbury and Evans of Bouverie Street. Forsaking this career with its many benefits, Smith advanced to the British Museum where he was taken on first as a restorer, then as assistant keeper of Oriental antiquities. Day after day he spent gluing together and reading shattered clay tablets excavated at Nineveh. We are told that the job fascinated him; his only complaint was the London fog which obliged him to study the tablets by lamplight.

Soon he had become not only an expert on Akkadian cuneiform but had partly deciphered the Cypriot syllabary, which sounds just as exciting. However this was nothing compared to the day in 1872 when, bending over some newly delivered tablets, George Smith understood that he was reading a story. Those little wedges, like so many chicken tracks, spelled out not just one more Assyrian memorial inscription but the adventures of the hero Gilgamesh, one-third human and two-thirds divine, who built the walls and temples of the ancient city of Uruk. Then came the hairy antagonist Enkidu, an account of his fight with Gilgamesh, and their subsequent exploits together.

On the chance that you might care to know what a hairy antagonist looks like, there is in the Louvre a miniature gold pendant from Mesopotamia, almost 5,000 years old and about the size of your thumb, which shows Enkidu flanked by two bison standing on their hind legs. The bison appear to be embracing him, and for some reason—perhaps their tiny gold ringlets and smooth gleaming haunches—they bring to mind a couple of preposterously costumed chorus girls. Enkidu himself gives rather that same impression. He has a bison rump complete with tail, and bison legs right down to the hooves, although his torso belongs to a natural man and he is not wearing horns. What he and his precocious friends might be up to, I have no idea. Anyway, there stands Enkidu as a Mesopotamian goldsmith imagined him, but if you plan to inspect him you should take along a magnifying glass.

Now back to George Smith and those baked clay tablets.

The tablets revealed how Gilgamesh and Enkidu overpowered Khumbaba, Lord of the Cedar Forest, and cut off his head, and how they overcame a fierce bull sent by the goddess Ishtar. At last, searching for eternal life, Gilgamesh sought the advice of his ancestor Ut-Napishtim, the one survivor of the Deluge.

It is said that Smith continued reading "feverishly" because Gilgamesh certainly would ask his ancestor about the Deluge, although to hear Smith tell it you might think he had only deciphered a Mesopotamian recipe for bouillabaisse. Listen to this phlegmatic recital:

"On looking down the third column, my eye caught the statement that the ship rested on the mountains of Nizir, followed by the account of the sending forth of the dove, and its finding no resting-place and returning. I saw at once that I had here discovered a portion at least of the Chaldean account. . . ."

He was unable to find the piece be wanted—a dialogue between Gilgamesh and Ut-Napishtim about the Flood—possibly because his collection of shards was incomplete; but what he already had learned was important enough, and on December 3, 1872, he informed the members of the Society of Biblical Archaeology.

The London *Daily Telegraph* then offered 1,000 guineas to finance an expedition to search for the missing text, on condition that the search be directed by Smith. His employers, in a surprising display of logic, gave their ace philologist a six-month leave of absence and off went George Smith to Nineveh.

Now it must be understood that he was looking for some dirty bits of clay almost indistinguishable from thousands and thousands of other bits scattered across the ruins, which measured eight miles in circumference. Smith might just as well have shuffled through the woods in autumn looking for half-a-dozen specific leaves, yet he picked up the pieces in a week. Considering the amount of rubble, how did he do it? Nobody knows. You couldn't get away with this in a novel or a movie because the odds against such a thing happening are outrageous.

Was Mr. Smith himself amazed? Not much.

"On the 14th of May . . . I sat down to examine the store of fragments of cuneiform inscriptions from the day's digging, taking out and brushing off the earth from the fragments to read their contents. On cleaning one of them I found to my surprise and gratification that it contained the greater portion of seventeen lines . . . fitting into the only place where there was a serious blank in the story."

He brought back 384 scraps from Nineveh, which almost completed the epic:

What I had loaded thereon, the whole harvest of life
I caused to embark within the vessel; all my family
and my relations,
The beasts of the field, the cattle of the field,
the craftsmen, I made them all embark.
I entered the vessel and closed the door. . . .

For six days and nights
Wind and flood marched on, the hurricane
subdued the land.
When the seventh day dawned, the hurricane
was abated, the flood
Which had waged war like an army;
The sea was stilled, the ill wind was calmed,
the flood ceased.
I beheld the sea, its voice was silent. . . .

When the seventh day came,
I sent forth a dove, I released it;
It went, the dove, it came back,
As there was no place, it came back.
I sent forth a swallow, I released it;
It went, the swallow, it came back,
As there was no place, it came back.
I sent forth a crow, I released it;
It went, the crow, and beheld the substance
of the waters;
It eats, it splashes about, it caws,
it comes not back.

The tablets were from the library of King Ashurbanipal, circa 650 B.C. But the story is older, much older, older than Abraham.

In 1929 Sir Leonard Woolley uncovered its origin. Mucking about in Mesopotamia beneath remnants of the 5,000-year-old Erech dynasty, he probed an eleven-foot layer of silt brought down from the upper Euphrates valley—the residue of a gigantic flood—and saw traces of reed huts. According to Genesis the water was fifteen cubits deep, about twenty-six feet. Woolley calculated that the depth of the Mesopotamian flood must have been at least twenty-five feet, which would have inundated everything for 300 miles.

So there we are. A few reed hut dwellers guessed what was coming; they leapt into their boats and escaped and never stopped talking about it.

Woolley seems to have been a man of rare equanimity. You would assume that anybody who had just put his finger on the source of a great Christian legend would display some excitement. Not Sir Leonard.

"I was convinced of what it meant," says he, "but I wanted to see whether others would arrive at the same conclusion. I brought up two of my staff and, after pointing out the facts, asked for their conclusions."

If his staff members were disconcerted, Mrs. Woolley was not. As cool as Sir Leonard, she remarked, "Well, of course, it's the Flood."

Whereupon everybody went back to work.

George Smith was more unpredictable: one moment jubilant, then altogether self-possessed when a little exuberance might be expected, or at least tolerated. For instance, during the Gilgamesh affair he sounds calm enough, methodical and scholarly; but on another occasion he looked up from a cuneiform cylinder and startled his associates by exclaiming in a loud voice that he was the first person to have read it in 2,000 years.

Now, among professionals such ebullience is thought rather gross. But the disorderly scene was not over. George Smith then stood up and went striding back and forth "in a high state of excitement."

And then he began taking off his clothes.

This occurred, mind you, on an upper floor of the British Museum, in the room directly above the office of the Royal Asiatic Society's secretary.

What happened next, we don't know. In other words, after having removed his laboratory smock, his necktie, his shirt, and possibly his trousers, did he—as we say—come to his senses?

Meanwhile, what were his fellow archaeologists doing? One would suppose they frowned. At the very least they must have frowned. But did any of them protest? Did they ask each other what was going on? Or, having lifted their eyebrows in order to register disapproval, did they consider it prudent to mind their own business?

Several years ago in Los Angeles during the evening rush I was driving along Wilshire when a naked woman appeared on the sidewalk.

She was about forty years old, plump, an average sort, neither beautiful nor homely. She wore ballet slippers, that was all, and she was scowling when she marched past me with immense resolution toward—toward what? I can't guess. Toward an inconceivable destiny. But the way that sea of Los Angeles citizens rolled apart, she could have been Madame Moses. Nobody stared. Very few looked at her twice. Obviously, unquestionably, undeniably the woman was mad, and we cannot endure much contact with those who are mad. We cannot even estimate what such a person might say or do, which means that we avoid the encounter. Instinctively we give way, submitting to the incomprehensible strength of madness.

Not only did every man avoid this mad naked creature, so did every woman. She dominated the street, no question about it. She may have realized this, but if so she was indifferent. Or perhaps not. Perhaps that was her purpose. All I can be sure of is that nobody—not one person in that vast polluted city of savages—would have been reckless enough to touch her.

Now about our man in the museum. Was he, also, cautiously ignored? Did his colleagues pretend to find nothing odd about his behavior? Did they go right on reading their baked clay tablets? Or did some fearless staff member speak up?

"I say, George old chap, aren't you carrying things a bit far?"

We don't know because whoever kept the records in those days didn't think it was important. It was, though. Such details, like savory fruit, ought to be carefully plucked.

So much for George Smith. The young genius who unraveled Egyptian hieroglyphics, Jean-François Champollion, is altogether as engaging and neurotic as our British exhibitionist. One appealing thing about him, which has been nearly overlooked because of his success with hieroglyphics, is the title of his first scholarly paper, written when he was twelve: "A History of Famous Dogs." Information of this sort should be preserved.

Anyway, glyph by glyph, year after year, Jean-François had been working on the puzzle but with no significant results until September 14, 1822. That morning he either received or began to study a consignment of drawings from the architect Huyot, who was traveling through Egypt and Nubia.

On the first page of Huyot's drawings from Abu Simbel he saw a cartouche beginning with the circular sun-symbol: *Ra*. Beside it was a sign he could not translate. Then came the sign representing folded cloth: *os*. And the *os* was repeated. In hieroglyphic writing, as everybody knows, the Egyptians dropped their vowels, so that what Champollion had within the boundaries of this cartouche was the ancient equivalent of *R-ss*.

Could it be the pharaoh Ramses?

On the second page of Huyot's drawings he saw a cartouche beginning with the ibis, a bird sacred to the god Thoth. Beside the ibis stood the unknown symbol from the first cartouche. Next to this was the folded cloth: *os*.

There could no longer be any doubt. If the unknown symbol represented *m*, which it must, here were two great names: Ramses and Thotmes.

The lock would not open easily, but Champollion had the key. In time it would be possible to read hieroglyphics, and Egypt's enormous history—lost for 1,500 years—would never be lost again. Provided, of course, that the symbol did represent *m*.

He was certain it did because the identification of two famous names could hardly be coincidence. Still, one does not like to make a fool of oneself. He therefore spent the entire morning bent over Huyot's sketches looking for additional proof. At last he was convinced. Gathering up the papers he rushed to the Institut de Paris where his elder brother Jacques-Joseph worked. It is said that he burst into the library of the Institut and threw the papers on Jacques-Joseph's desk:

"Je tiens l'affaire!" he cried in a hoarse voice.

Then he fell over in a dead faint and spent the next five days in bed.

Champollion's excitement seems appropriate, in contrast to George Smith's vulgar display, although of course the important thing is not a linguist's personality but his accomplishment. And because of Champollion's detective work the Rosetta stone, which had baffled everybody for twenty-three years, would not be an enigma much longer.

The fact that the stone was not translated for twenty-three years surprises people. Since its message was trilingual—given twice in unknown languages and once in Greek—why couldn't the unknown scripts be quickly correlated with the Greek? Because not until Champollion identified Ramses and Thotmes had anybody realized that the hieroglyphic system was partly phonetic, partly symbolic.

As to where the stone was found, and how this came about, we are indebted to Napoleon. At least, if there had not been a Napoleon it is unlikely that the stone would have turned up. Whether one justifies the other is not a bad question, but outside the limit of this discussion.

Napoleon invaded Egypt in 1798, which displeased the Turks whose domain it was, as well as the British who had become uneasy about their expansive neighbor. So a bombardment was undertaken, and in the course of this a French captain named Bouchard ordered his men to dig in at Rashid, or Rosetta, close to the mouth of the Nile.

Now, while they were digging trenches an Arab soldier's pick clanged against something inexpressibly hard: a slab of black basalt covered with unintelligible writing. Bouchard, smarter than most captains, thought this object might be important.

The stone was carted off to the Institut d'Égypte in Cairo, which Napoleon had founded, where copies were made of the text and sent at once to France—almost as if everyone had a presentiment that something unfortunate was about to happen. In Paris, Professor Du Thiel translated the Greek. The stone was a memorial, dated fourth Xandikos, equivalent to the eighteenth Meshir of the year 9, equivalent to March 27, 196 B.C. What it said, in brief, was that the priests of Memphis wished to express their gratitude to Ptolemy V Epiphanes. Ptolemy had evidently crossed various palms with silver, a most ancient custom, and the priests declared that because of his virtue this endorsement should be posted in all Egyptian temples of the first, second, and third class.

Meanwhile the stone had been shipped to the house occupied by General de Menou in Alexandria, where presumably it would be safe.

Then the British landed.

"I shall defend myself to the last extremity within the walls of Alexandria," wrote Menou to Napoleon. "I know how to die, but not how to capitulate."

This is a noble sentiment, the utterance of a proud and valiant soldier. Just the same, under certain conditions it may be advantageous to restate one's views, and after a good many poilus had been rudely deprived of their existence General Menou exercised his prerogative to suggest the possibility of negotiation. As a diplomat he succeeded triumphantly, obtaining terms identical to those obtained by other French generals who surrendered. Now it happens that Menou himself had been offered these terms somewhat earlier and had scornfully rejected them, insisting upon peace with honor—which may remind you of events elsewhere. But of course one does not expect high logic on the battlefield or at the conference table.

So it came about that the Rosetta stone journeyed to the British Museum, though not before some stiff words between Generals Menou and Hutchinson:

The stone, Menou declared, was his private property.

Article XVI of the treaty of capitulation, replied the British general, specifies that such objects, as well as everything else collected by French scientists in Egypt, must be surrendered.

"I have just been informed," Menou wrote to Hutchinson a few days later, "that several among our collection-makers wish to follow their seeds, minerals, birds, butterflies, or reptiles wherever you choose to ship their crates. I do not know if they wish to have themselves stuffed for this purpose, but I can assure you that if the idea should appeal to them, I shall not prevent them. I have authorized them to address themselves to you."

Hutchinson either did not want a cargo of butterflies and crocodiles detracting from the glory of his return to England, or he was moved by the loyalty of the French scientists to their pickled specimens. Whatever the reason, he told them to keep their crates. But he insisted upon having the stone.

Menou responded: "You want it, Monsieur le général? You can have it, since you are the stronger of us two. . . . You may pick it up whenever you please."

Even so, the mills of God grind exceeding small; it was not to be an Englishman but the neurasthenic Jean-François Champollion whose name would be associated forever with that big black slab of basalt.

Grotefend and Rawlinson are names as redoubtable in their field—Old Persian—as are the names of Smith and Champollion. Grotefend was a Göttingen schoolteacher, Rawlinson an employee of the East

India Company. Although their lives overlapped by some thirty years it is doubtful if they met.

Grotefend first. The son of a cobbler, born in a small town, never a professional Orientalist, he is your basic Outsider. According to some scholars, he undertook the job of deciphering Persian cuneiform as the result of a bet made while he was drunk. Others say a librarian persuaded him to try it. What we know for certain is that he liked puzzles. An evening packed with acrostics, rebuses, palindromes, wordplay of any sort—that was young Grotefend's idea of a jolly time.

Quite a few schoolteachers, along with a great many less bookish people, share this odd passion, so the question comes up as to why, or how, one undistinguished crossword puzzle fan did something important enough to get his name in the encyclopedia. The answer is that we don't know. The computer cannot be built that will tell us why one brain may seize and interpret in a fresh way the data accessible to all. Therefore we use the term *genius*, a word sucked dry through misapplication. Now it may be extravagant to call Grotefend a genius. However, Karl Marek has this to say: "Among many other things, genius implies the ability to reduce the complicated to the simple, and to recognize inclusive structural principles. Grotefend's inspiration was astoundingly simple."

Whatever guided or motivated him, he broke the spine of the Persian riddle. Not altogether by himself—which never happens, or very seldom. Linguists as well as inquisitive tourists had studied the crisp little marks chiseled here and there across Iran and had tried without success to make sense of them. Only once in a while a clue would be noted.

Near the end of the tenth century a traveler named ibn-Haukul visited the colossal bas-relief at Behistun. This huge and almost unapproachable sculpture high on a rust-colored cliff illustrates the victory of Darius the Great over some rebellious princes; but ibn-Haukul, after contemplating the figures, stated that in his opinion they represented a schoolmaster chastising a group of disobedient pupils.

Two centuries later the Arab geographer Yaqut thought it represented the Sassanian hero Khusru Parviz astride his stallion Shabdiz, accompanied by Queen Shirin. Yaqut must have been smoking something because it is hard to visualize a lady in the tableau, and certainly there is no horse.

A nineteenth-century French traveler to Behistun thought he saw twelve apostles beneath a crucifix.

An Englishman, Sir Robert Ker Porter, saw the conquest of Israel by Shalmaneser: the ten little victims facing Darius being members of the ten tribes. This must be so, Ker Porter said, because the pointed bonnet worn by the last rebellious prince was undoubtedly the miter of a Levite priest.

All of which should remind us that what we see, wherever we go, is usually what we expect to see.

The Spanish ambassador to Persia, Don García de Silva Figueroa, after examining "a remarkable inscription carved on black jaspar," provided one of the first authentic clues. These letters, he said, "are neither Chaldean, nor Hebrew, nor Greeke, nor Aribike, nor of any other Nation which was ever found of old, or at this day to be extant."

A wealthy young Roman named Pietro della Valle, touring the East to regain his equilibrium after a disastrous love affair, met and married a bewitching maiden in Baghdad—which sounds implausible because a foreigner, even a wealthy young Roman, is not apt to meet a Baghdad maiden. Nevertheless he did; and with his bride, Sitti Maani, Pietro resumed traveling. At the ruins of Persepolis he copied some announcements which he brought back to Italy, the first examples of Persian cuneiform to reach European scholars.

Then came Sir Thomas Herbert who saw and studied "lynes of strange characters . . . so mysticall, so odly framed . . . consisting of Figures, obelisk, triangular and pyramidall, yet in such Simmetry and order as cannot well be called barbarous." They might, he thought, "conceale some excellent matter, though to this day wrapt up in the dim leaves of envious obscuritie."

A wandering jewel-trader, Jean Chardin, correctly guessed that the odly framed lynes should be read from left to right and noted that they often occurred in groups of three, though he did not suspect that three languages were involved.

Next came Engelbert Kämpfer and Samuel Flower and Cornelius van Bruyn and Carsten Niebuhr, experienced and dedicated philologists even if they do sound like suspects in a British murder mystery.

Kämpfer spent three days at Persepolis: "To copy the sculpture and inscriptions of all these buildings with the measurements, decorations, and all that is worthy of being noticed would take more than two months. I shall communicate faithfully all I have been able to acquire. . . ."

Neibuhr assiduously copied several tablets and was the first to delineate an Old Persian alphabet. He insisted that he could recognize forty-two letters among the chicken tracks, and in fact he did identify thirty-two.

Then there was Abraham Hyacinthe Anquetil du Perron, a theological student in Paris who became obsessed by the idea that he must read the sacred literature of the Parsees, the *Zend Avesta*. He obtained a grant from the French government and sailed to Pondicherry, at that time a French outpost, where he set about learning modern Persian. Having accomplished this, he ventured north in search of Parsee fire-worshipers. He found some, which was not difficult, though it was dangerous. He made friends with the dasturs, the priests, and seven years later returned to Europe with a copy of the *Zend Avesta* written in the ancient script. Nobody could read it—not even the dasturs—but until then no European had so much as seen the book.

Thus, from here and there, came bits and pieces that occasionally fitted together, but most often did not, until one day Grotefend perceived an underlying pattern.

You would suppose that the academic world—at least the philologists—would rush to congratulate the young schoolteacher. Especially after they had read an excerpt from his stimulating article "Praevia de cuneatis quas vocant inscriptionibus Persepolitanis legendis et explicandis relatio" which appeared in the *Göttinger Gelehrten Anzeigen*.

Not so. Well, you may ask, why not?

Alas, the reply is familiar. Its author lacked credentials. He was not a recognized Orientalist. For this reason the journal's editors refused to print the complete essay. The full text did not appear until 1893, forty years after his death.

And while Grotefend's manuscript began to acquire the fine patina of age, Henry Creswicke Rawlinson was born. Grotefend, the puzzle-master, lived indoors; Rawlinson, a vigorous athletic man, wanted some action. At sixteen he joined the East India Company which shipped him to Bombay. There he worked as paymaster of the first grenadiers, but languages came easily to him—Arabic, Persian, Hindustani—and before long he was regimental interpreter.

When the Afghan Wars seemed about to erupt he was dispatched to Kermānshāh because of his linguistic skill. Here he learned of Behistun, twenty miles away. He rode over to take a look.

His first view was from the Khurasan road, a caravan route that had been in use for at least 5,000 years, and he returned many times. Should you wish to locate Behistun, where so many early tourists had seen whatever they wished to see, it is about 200 miles northeast of Baghdad. And when discussing this with a professional you must say Bisitun, not Behistun, the latter being a popular corruption. Professionals care about these things.

An experienced armchair traveler can seldom be startled, but the cliff at Behistun appears quite astonishing from any angle. The bas-relief commemorating Darius' great victory is perhaps 150 feet long and 100 feet high, and the bottom of the carving is at least 300 feet above the ground. Invincible Darius, twice the size of his defeated adversaries, stands nonchalantly with one foot on the stomach of a supine captive and seems to be addressing nine unhappy princes who are roped together by the neck, each with his hands tied behind his back. Darius gestures in a rather benevolent way, which no doubt is misleading; he must be signifying displeasure, or else he is acknowledging the salute of a winged deity who hovers nearby. One gets the impression that Darius and the deity are on familiar terms.

Rawlinson, having admired the giant memorial through a telescope, decided to copy the part he considered most important. This meant, first, a dangerous climb up the rock face.

Here is what he has to say about the situation:

"On reaching the recess which contains the Persian text of the record, ladders are indispensable in order to examine the upper portion of the tablet; and even with ladders there is considerable risk . . . the upper inscriptions can only be copied by standing on the topmost step of the ladder, with no other support than steadying the body against the rock with the left arm, while the left hand holds the notebook, and the right hand is employed with the pencil."

In brief, Rawlinson was high above the Khurasan road without a net, with absolutely nothing for protection except nerve and his sense of balance. You can, if you are imaginative enough, get a touch of vertigo just thinking about it.

Visualizing him at the top of a rickety ladder propped on a rock ledge 300 feet above the ground, with a notebook in one hand, meticulously copying some little wedge-shaped marks—seeing him in that position one is reminded of other nineteenth-century English men and women: Mawson and Shackleton at the South Pole, Franklin in the Arctic, Fanny Bullock Workman in the Himalayas, "Chinese Gordon" in Egypt, Mary Kingsley having tea with cannibals, Lady Hester Stanhope costumed as a Bedouin riding in triumph through the ruined streets of Palmyra. Faced with such people, one can't help thinking that the nineteenth-century English must have been utterly bonkers.

Now back to Rawlinson on his ladder:

"To reach the recess which contains the Scythic translation of the record of Darius is a matter of far greater difficulty."

Why? Well, there was a split in the cliff and the only way to get across was to bridge this gap with a ladder. Rawlinson calls his first attempt "unfortunate." Because of the narrowness of the ledge he was obliged to turn his ladder on its side. That is, with the rungs in a vertical position. He planned to walk across the underside while holding on to the upper side.

All right, here we go:

"If the ladder had been a compact article, this mode of crossing, although far from comfortable, would have been at any rate practicable; but the Persians merely fit in the bars of their ladders without pretending to clench them outside, and I had hardly accordingly begun to cross over when the vertical pressure forced the bars out of their sockets, and the lower and unsupported side of the ladder thus parted company with the upper, and went crashing down over the precipice."

Rawlinson now is dangling by his hands from a broken ladder that may snap at any moment. Below him, empty space. Nor can anybody help him. Good luck, Henry.

Hand over hand be went. You may remember this tingling sensation from childhood—nothingness underneath as you worked your way out a tree limb with the ground at least ten feet below. Rawlinson was a bit higher. From the Khurasan road he must have been about the size of a bug.

Somehow he scrambled back up the Persian side of the cliff. The Scythic translation would have to wait awhile.

A third account of Darius' victory, written in Babylonian, was more difficult to approach than either the Persian, where one need only stand on the topmost rung of a ladder, or the Scythic, where one must cross a chasm.

After studying this new challenge Rawlinson decided it was too dangerous. Peasants who lived nearby and who were accustomed to tracking mountain goats across the face of the mountain told him that the Babylonian legend could not be reached.

While he was wondering how to obtain this text "a wild Kurdish boy" volunteered to try. Rawlinson promised him a fat reward so the boy started up. Using ropes, driving wood pegs into the cliff, hanging by fingers and toes, he crossed a twenty-foot sheet of perpendicular rock "in a manner which to a looker-on appeared quite miraculous." From this point it was easy.

"He had brought a rope with him attached to the first peg, and now, driving in a second, he was enabled to swing himself right over the projecting mass of rock. Here with a short ladder he formed a swinging seat, like a painter's cradle, and, fixed upon this seat, he took under my direction the paper cast of the Babylonian translation of the records of Darius."

The question that remains, though, is this: If an agile Kurdish boy, risking his life, could just manage to reach the text, how was it carved? Unless you believe in levitation the answer seems to be that a fantastic scaffold was attached to the cliff in 516 B.C.

Rawlinson says no more about the Kurdish daredevil. Presumably the boy got down, collected his reward, lived more or less happily ever after, and bored his grandchildren with the details of his famous climb. Concerning the mad Englishman, we do know that he lived happily ever after, more or less, wrote learned papers which were read to the Royal Asiatic Society in London, and sometimes was pointed out on the street—although today you would have a hard time finding anybody who recognized his name. But of course if you should mention

Darius the Great these days everybody would think you were talking about a wrestler.

And if—at a cocktail party, let's say—you should mention Michael Ventris or Sir Arthur Evans you probably would get an uncomprehending stare. Evans might possibly draw a response. He excavated the palace at Knossos and there are people who remember that, just as they remember the Rosetta stone.

Knossos! Ah yes, let me think. It was on Crete or Mykonos, one of those islands, and there were murals showing acrobats somersaulting over bulls. Also, some kind of labyrinth. Yes indeed, the old palace of Knossos! King Minos lived there, I believe. Or was that Theseus? Or Croesus? Or did Knossos have something to do with the sword of Damocles? Those Greek names all sound alike.

Mykonos, no. Crete, yes. Damocles and Croesus, no. Minos, yes. Theseus, not quite; he found the apartments exciting but it cost an arm and a leg to live there.

Now back to Michael and Sir Arthur.

In 1889 the Ashmolean Museum at Oxford received a collection of artifacts, the bequest of a wealthy traveler. The museum's steward was Arthur Evans, an extremely nearsighted little man who always felt his way around with a cane, and while examining this bequest he was puzzled by a carnelian seal with oval sides bearing unfamiliar hieroglyphs. It was said to have come from Sparta.

Four years later Evans himself visited Sparta where he noticed several of these curious objects. He was told they came from Crete.

The following year he visited Crete and saw quite a few village girls wearing them as amulets, calling them *galópetrais*, milkstones. It was important to wear a milkstone while pregnant.

He bought as many as he could, traded modern cameo brooches for others, and managed to copy the hieroglyphs on most of those whose owners would not give them up. Occasionally he saw one with linear characters suggesting an alphabet. This, in turn, suggested the possibility of not one but two unknown systems of writing.

The next step, logically, would be to excavate. The site of Knossos seemed a good place, but Turkey controlled the island and there was difficulty with Turkish bureaucrats. Schliemann had run afoul of them years earlier. Evans was balked until 1899 when the Turks left Crete. Then he got a permit. He dug into King Minos' palace, cemented it together, and painted it as he imagined it must have looked in 1500 B.C. His re-creation was not very convincing; a number of archaeologists are upset, and today even the tourists look suspiciously at those ponderous brown Victorian colonnades. However, the job seems to have satisfied Evans. Anyway he was less concerned with architectural niceties than with the people who used to live there.

In the ruins he found almost 3,000 baked clay tablets and after studying them he concluded that the linear inscriptions were of two sorts.

"Much study and comparison will be necessary for the elucidation of these materials," he wrote in March 1901, for *The Monthly Review*.

> If, as may well be the case, the language in which they were written was some primitive form of Greek we need not despair of the final decipherment of these Knossian archives, and the bounds of history may eventually be so enlarged as to take in the "heroic age" of Greece. In any case the weighty question, which years before I had set myself to solve on Cretan soil, has found, so far at least, an answer. That great early civilisation was not dumb, and the written records of the Hellenic world are carried back some seven centuries beyond the date of the first known historic writings. But what, perhaps, is even more remarkable than this is that, when we examine in detail the linear script of these Mycenaean documents, it is impossible not to recognize that we have here a system of writing, syllabic and perhaps partly alphabetic, which stands on a distinctly higher level of development than the hieroglyphs of Egypt or the cuneiform script of contemporary Syria and Babylonia. It is not till some five centuries later that we find the first dated examples of Phoenician writing.

In 1909 he published a handsome volume entitled *Scripta Minoa I* which had to do mostly with the hieroglyphs. Subsequent volumes, he announced, would focus on scripts A and B.

Up to this point, excepting the doubtful reconstruction of Minos' palace, Arthur Evans was highly esteemed by his colleagues and celebrated by the public. But now he insisted on keeping the tablets to himself. He would not permit other specialists to examine them, and because he himself could not translate them the ancient Cretan language, or languages, remained a mystery. Situations like this are always surprising: one never expects an intelligent, brilliantly educated humanist to play dog-in-the-manger. But because of Evans' recalcitrance the second volume of *Scripta* was not published until 1952, eleven years after his death.

Michael Ventris and his associate Chadwick, who share credit for the decipherment of Linear B, would later say, "Two generations of scholars were thus deprived of the possibility of doing any constructive work on the problem."

Yet it was Evans, despite himself, and without realizing it, who encouraged Ventris.

In 1936 Evans gave a lecture at Burlington House in London where one member of the audience was young Michael, fourteen years old. He did not attend by chance, nor because his parents wanted to hear the elderly scholar discuss Minoan riddles; he was there because he enjoyed linguistic challenges. At the age of six, for example, while other children were struggling with English, he taught himself Polish. "He had not only a remarkable visual memory," says Chadwick, "but, what is rarely combined with it, the ability to learn a language by ear."

Ventris would go on to become an architect specializing in prefabricated schoolhouses; at the same time, though, he followed the progress of linguistics as closely as a flower tracks the sun. How much Evans influenced him can only be guessed, but when he was just eighteen he published an *Introduction to Minoan Writing*, based on the tablets Sir Arthur did not have locked up in his closet and whatever else was available. Ventris thought the language might be Etruscan, an opinion he maintained for several years.

During the Second World War he served as a navigator in the RAF and later with the British Army of Occupation in Germany, but no matter where he went he managed to take along some copies of Minoan documents. After the war, between prefabricated schoolhouses, he continued chipping away at the problem.

This kind of thing: "certain words of the same type afforded in their endings variants which could be considered as flexional endings of declensions, whereas other words of the same type showed notable modifications . . ." and so on. The point is that Ventris, an amateur, was making more progress than the professionals, and some of his notes were handed along to a young Cambridge philologist, John Chadwick.

Chadwick was busy but he took a look at what Ventris had done. Then he looked again. Later he would write: "Those four days were the most exciting of my life. . . ." He had recently been married, so it would be instructive to know what his wife thought of that statement.

Ventris and Chadwick began corresponding and a time would come when they chose to address each other in Mycenaean Linear B—which surely establishes a record for snobbery. Although it should be mentioned that Champollion occasionally talked to himself in Coptic.

With Chadwick's help, Ventris proved that the language was an early form of Greek. This surprised philologists, who thought the Greeks of that era had not known how to read and write. Even those hoplites who later besieged Troy were assumed to be illiterate. However, there could be no doubt about the age of the Minos tablets because a style of pottery found with them also turned up in the Nile valley among ushabtis and mummies from the Eighteenth Dynasty: 1580 to 1350 B.C.

So we have learned when Linear B was in use, and it must have developed from Linear A, thus pushing back the literary frontier several more centuries. And because Linear A probably evolved from the hieroglyphs it seems quite possible that Aegean children started going to school 5,000 years ago. But the first day of class is less interesting than the fact that some tablets discovered on the mainland refer to Achilles and Theseus as well as to unlucky Hector and his comrades.

Achilles, Hector, Priam, Ajax—such names would lead anybody to expect a bloody confirmation of Homer's bestseller. Unfortunately, what the tablets have preserved almost without exception are common lists—invoices—of people or things. References to carpenters, masons, bath attendants, weavers, gods, goddesses. List upon list of commodities. Figs. Olives. Tunics. Spices. Lamps. Helmets. Cauldrons. War chariots. Goats.

"Most of the phrases are quite short," said Ventris. "The longest sentence I can find has eleven words and occurs on a tablet from Pylos which seems to be an assessment of tithes, somewhat as follows: 'The priestess holds the following acres of productive land on a lease from the property-owners, and undertakes to maintain them in the future.'"

How tedious. Nothing about Europa aboard her white bull, not even Icarus plunging into the Aegean from 30,000 feet. Nothing but inventories and leases.

Not only is it disappointing that the Cretans bequeathed us such mundane information, it is also rather odd. You would expect them to hand along the big news, as Darius the Great did on his tremendous Behistun panel, or Hammurabi on his black diorite legal stela, or the various pharaohs who celebrated on sandstone their immortal triumphs. The explanation is thought to be this: important Cretan records were written on some sort of expensive paper, whereas the inventories were scratched on clay which could be discarded or broken up to be used again. But the terrible fire that swept Knossos and destroyed Cretan civilization burned all the paper and baked these inconsequential clay tablets for posterity.

That there was such a fire, and that it devastated King Minos' palace, seems undeniable. If you visit the ruins you will see, despite Sir Arthur's handiwork, many dark and sinister tongues of soot; you can even tell which direction the wind blew on that calamitous day 3,500 years ago—from the south, which means that the palace burned in late April or early May, because that is the season when a south wind blows across Crete. Whether the palace was burned by invaders or by some natural catastrophe, perhaps the eruption of Thera, will usually get you an argument in academic circles.

Evans himself suspected a militant invasion: "Under the closely compacted pavement . . . there were built in, between solid piles of masonry, double tiers of stone cists lined with lead. Only a few were opened and they proved to be empty, but there can be little doubt that they were constructed for the deposit of treasure. Whoever destroyed and plundered the Palace had failed to discover these receptacles. . . ."

Whatever happened, the wrath of the gods broke over Knossos. Nobody argues that.

One further catastrophe, very small by comparison, must be inscribed on the Cretan record. We cannot yet read Linear A or the primitive hieroglyphs. Ventris would have gone to work on them, of course, but time ran out. In 1956 at the age of thirty-four he was killed in the ugliest way: a car accident.

Chadwick, himself an ex-serviceman, carefully avoided taking credit for deciphering Linear B: "I have always endeavoured to make it clear that all the merits of the discovery are due to Ventris; my role was that of the first infantry division sent in to widen the breach. . . ."

It's a sad conclusion. Working together, they might have solved Linear A and then the hieroglyphs. Maybe. Maybe not. We'll never know. As it stands, the first Aegean stories wait. Eventually, we assume —because we dislike the assumption of defeat—eventually a new cryptographic prodigy will appear, entranced by linguistic puzzles. Then we may look forward to some laundry lists, to the names of forgotten kings, perhaps to a new epic which begins:

It was a dark and stormy night . . .

If we do not know much about the earliest language of Crete, we know practically nothing about that of India, except what it looked like. Hundreds of amulets and incised seals made of copper or soapstone have been collected from the ruins of Harappa and Mohenjo-Daro in the Indus valley. They date from the second or third millennium B.C. and, like Cretan milkstones, they bear a variety of symbolic signs together with representations of monkeys, tigers, parrots, doves, humped cattle, squirrels, crocodiles, et cetera.

As yet these curious objects have not met their Champollion, nor does he seem to be waiting just offstage; almost no progress has been made toward understanding the symbols or the exquisite little pictures. Ordinarily the script should be read from left to right, but sometimes the opposite is true. Sometimes it should be read as the ox plows, one way and then the other—a method called boustrophedonic. We do not even know how many separate signs there are. One scholar claims to have distinguished 900, although 250 is a more commonly accepted number, the rest being variants.

The script is a stiff, precise mélange of stylized images and "alphabetic" symbols unrelated to any other language except, perhaps, that of Easter Island—and we will come back to Easter Island in a moment. It cannot be linked to the oldest comprehensible language of India, a precursor of Sanskrit, because Sanskrit-speaking people did not enter the Indus valley until about 1500 B.C. The *Rig-Veda*, in fact, refers to these first citizens as *dasyus* or *dāsas:* a swarthy, pug-nosed race of infidels who spoke gibberish.

Harappa and Mohenjo-Daro—which means Mound of the Dead—

seem to have been their great cities, but the ruins of many others have been located, and it is thought that the Indus culture extended from the Simla hills to the Arabian Sea, a distance of 1,000 miles. The area covered by all of their dead cities is twice the size of the old Egyptian empire.

Harappa and Mohenjo are twins, so much alike that archaeologists believe they could have been built by the same ruler, despite the fact that they are 400 miles apart. They may have been twin capitals. They did not grow by chance, as most cities do; they were planned as deliberately as Brasília or Salt Lake City and are just as predictable. Everything was arranged. The mechanical, conservative, windowless, unchanging architecture—block after block after block—implies a totalitarian attitude. These are barracks, not apartments. There is a terrible efficiency about this culture, observes Stuart Piggott, which recalls the worst of Rome, and with it "a stagnation hard to parallel in any known civilization of the Old World." And he goes on brusquely: "There is something in the Harappa civilization that I find repellent."

Where did such people come from? Because the earliest inhabitants of the valley lived in ragged, disorderly villages. But then, 2,500 years before Christ, out of the dust and mist came these unimaginative, dark, flat-nosed builders who knew exactly what a city should look like. And they lived in their geometrical barracks for ten centuries without changing a thing. The style of building never changed. The language did not change. The first carved amulets are the same as the last.

The longest inscription contains seventeen characters. Most contain five or six. They may be invocations to a god, or laundry lists. No Harappan poems have been found—unless they are as brief as haiku. Obviously there are no historical records. This means that even if the script could be deciphered we wouldn't learn much. What it does tell us, though, is something about the monotony of their life. Egypt was conservative, yet over the centuries its language changed. So did Mesopotamian. So do all languages, or almost all. At Harappa and Mohenjo-Daro nothing changed.

They were, it must be said, a clean race of people. Mother India today is less than that, but the ancient mounds have disclosed bathhouses and sanitation systems. In fact these people used the seat toilet: a channel through the wall connecting with a pottery receptacle or a brick drain outside. The drains were engineered as skillfully as those at Knossos; they empty into a central drainage system beneath the street.

Very little else can be deduced about the Indus people. They traded with Mesopotamia, that much has been established. Sumerian cylinder seals were discovered at Harappa, and Harappan seals have turned up in the Tigris-Euphrates ruins. And cuneiform tablets from the Near East speak of a marvelous land where the sun rises, called Dilmun or Telmun, whose ships bring pearls and cosmetics and stone beads and much copper and silver and ivory combs. Dilmun might refer to Bahrein in the Persian Gulf, a port of call, or it might mean the source of this wealth, the great Indus civilization.

Just how far the commercial interchange extended, and when it declined and ultimately stopped, is uncertain. One Harappan bead—dated about 1600 B.C.—was found on the island of Crete. Trade with Persia might have lasted another century.

Then came the Sanskrit invaders.

Harappa and Mohenjo-Daro fell quickly. Their civilization may already have been disintegrating, which usually is the case when a nation succumbs to an invader. There is evidence of this in the cheap construction of later buildings, in subdivisions, and so forth—things we ourselves are familiar with.

But the end was abrupt. Thirteen skeletons were uncovered in a room at Mohenjo: all showed signs of violent death. One skull had been split by an ax or a sword. In a different arrondissement nine skeletons huddled together, five of them children. Nearby lay two elephant tusks. The adults may have been ivory workers who had planned to escape with the valuable tusks.

If these people chose not to write about themselves, and apparently they did not, we might expect them to describe their lives some other way. After all, we find nothing so consistently absorbing as our own unprecedented existence. But again, they left practically nothing. No Pompeiian mural, no crushed golden harp, not even a basketball court. As for sculpture—tiny fragments. Fragments of tiny people, goggle-eyed ceramic caricatures, as though they considered themselves too insignificant to be remembered. There are not more than half a dozen genuinely revealing figures. One is an insolent dancing girl loosely modeled in bronze, with lanky arms and legs, extremely sure of herself, nude except for a necklace and bracelets, with her long hair twisted into a rope, one hand cocked on her hip, and a look of hard experience. Another is a carved stone figure—an important, bearded ruler with slit eyes and thick lips, coldly arrogant. They do go well together, this antipathetic couple, the dancing girl—who might have been a slave—and the merciless middle-aged man: they seem to represent two persistent types. Or you could say they symbolize life and death.

One more thing. In the rubble of a little city called Chanhu-Daro an archaeologist noticed a brick with the print of a cat's paw slightly overlapped by the paw of a dog. These were not symbolic designs but actual prints left by the animals as they raced across a wet brick. And it was clear from the impress of the pads that both had been going full speed, the dog chasing the cat.

There you have the Indus testament. Beads. Copper and stone seals. Pots with brief legends. A few rings. Bracelets. Clay caricatures. Crumbling skeletons. Elephant tusks. Millions of bricks. Two sculpted individuals altogether different, equally expressive.

At present this is one of the most desolate regions on earth—hot, windy, colorless, salty, and dry. The trees are twisted and small. Bushes are gray, cloaked with dust. No civilization could have developed here unless the land at one time had been fertile. As indeed it was. Excavators found dikes, which means that the valley often was flooded. Nor are the bricks sun-dried, they are kiln-baked. If the Indus never had much rain there would be no reason to bake bricks; only in wet weather do you need durable building blocks. So there must have been plenty of drizzly days once upon a time in that blistering valley.

As to why the climate changed, we must guess. It may have been a natural sequence; or the people, not realizing what they were doing, may have altered the climate. An immense supply of wood was needed to fire the kilns to bake those millions of bricks, but as they chopped down the trees they reduced the amount of water vapor provided by the forest, and water vapor returns to the earth as rain. Thus the kilns were fueled, bricks plopped off the assembly line while the forest shrank, and one day the rain stopped.

The Indus valley civilization vanished like the trees and the rain. The people are gone, their language a mystery. In a sense, of course, they have become an eternal part of India; but as a race or a nation with an intricate history of kings, or a politburo, and holy days and public events and famous ball players and dignitaries—they are gone.

Now about Easter Island, that isolated South Pacific rock halfway around the world from the Indus valley. Nothing connects these two. They could hardly be farther apart, chronologically there is a 3,000-year gap, and no language pertaining either to the Indus script or to the Easter Island "talking boards" has been found anywhere else. Yet the languages appear to be related. It is not a matter of occasional similarity but of a great many similarities. This must be coincidence because all knowledge of the Indus language was lost soon after the Aryan invasion about 1500 B.C., whereas the Easter Island script is recent; it was understood well into the nineteenth century A.D. and seems to have developed only a few centuries before that.

Kohau-rongo-rongo, the talking boards, may be less spectacular than the monstrous stone heads but to a philologist they are more exciting. The island must have been studded with them in 1722 when Admiral Jaakob Roggeveen landed on Easter Sunday, but after the arrival of Belgian and French missionaries, who did not like the look of such devilish lettering, the boards started to disappear. Only twenty-one have survived. Or nineteen, because two of them might be fakes.

A certain Father Zumbohm, more inquisitive and less bigoted than his brothers, asked some natives for an explanation. The sight of a tablet pleased them, he reports, and one immediately began to read the text by singing. "But others shouted 'No it is not like that!' The disagreement among my teachers was so great that, in spite of my effort, I was not much more informed after their lesson than beforehand."

About 1870 a few of the boards reached Bishop Jaussen in Tahiti. Rather than start a fire, as clerics are apt to do when confronted by mysterious objects, Jaussen tried to find somebody who could interpret them. A former citizen of Easter Island, Metoro Tauara, was at that time working on a nearby plantation and the bishop asked him to read a board. Metoro was happy to oblige. He chanted a line, then he turned the board upside down in order to chant the following line. This, most scholars agree, is correct. Every other line of Easter Island script is inverted. Nobody knows why.

The first scientist to study these boards was a British anthropologist, Mrs. Katherine Routledge. In 1914 she interviewed the last surviving native who had been trained to read them; but the old man, dying of leprosy, did not say very much.

Then, in 1954, a German ethnologist named Barthel came upon a bilingual document in the Roman archives of the order to which Bishop Janssen had belonged: Metoro's Polynesian along with the bishop's French translation.

This should have been a great help. It wasn't. Metoro, anxious to please, had given the impression that he understood what the boards were talking about, when in fact he understood very little. Even so, Barthel managed to obtain a few fixes, enough to determine that there were approximately 500 signs and that the language was based upon what specialists call the phonetic rebus. For example, the Polynesian word *pure* means shell but it can also mean prayer. Now, if you know most of the words or syllables in a sentence and come to *pure* you could probably interpret it correctly; but if most of the words were unknown—and so far very little of the Easter Island script has been deciphered—you would be forced to guess. And, of course, one mistake encourages another.

Nevertheless, Barthel kept at it and came up with a sensational line: "Then they addressed their prayers to the god of Rangitea."

Rangitea means "bright field." It is the name of one of the Tonga or Friendly Islands close to Fiji, about 1,500 miles west of Easter Island. If Barthel's translation is correct he has provided a clue to the origin of the Easter Islanders—something which has caused squabbles among ethnologists, historians, and archaeologists.

Metoro's reading, however inadequate, was the best that could be obtained. Other natives gave totally different translations of the same text.

If or when the language is resolved we might learn about a connection with the Indus valley. It's at least very curious that present-day Islanders speak a form of Munda, a language once spoken in India.

Professor Piggott, an authority on the Indus civilization, does not think they are related and he is displeased by such conjecture: "One can only say that, apart from attempts to connect it with the nineteenth-century 'script' of the natives of Easter Island in the Pacific, the Harappa script has perhaps suffered less from lunatics than the Minoan. But perhaps it is only the shortness of the available Harappa inscriptions that has deprived us of such entertaining fantasies as the transliteration of the Phaistos Disc into Basque hexameters."

Professor Hans Jensen, with appalling erudition, has summarized the argument in his thick study of practically everything ever written anywhere, *Die Schrift in Vergangenheit und Gegenwart:*

> Hevesy believes the Easter Island script to be very old; in addition, he is convinced of the reliability of the native tradition that Polynesian immigrants brought sixty-seven inscribed wooden tablets with them some 900 years ago. Now he puts forward the hypothesis that the Easter Island script and the Indus script go back to a common primordial form. . . . The close correspondence between the strange stone monuments on the island of Guam and ones just like them on Easter Island seems to him to indicate the route the script followed in its migration from southeast India. Even the oldest Chinese picture-script, he believes, in agreement with the views of Heine-Geldern, Rottauscher and Shirogorov, must be regarded as closely related. . . .

In short, you'll have to wait awhile.

When it comes to Old Mayan we have another kettle of glyphs and a new scenario. The locale is neither an island in the South Pacific, Homer's wine-dark sea, nor a sun-blasted Asiatic valley, but the breathless green jungle of Yucatán, and this time the principal actor is villainous. It was churlish of Sir Arthur Evans to lock up his Minoan tablets, but for authentic wickedness in the department of linguistics you must look to Diego de Landa; although it should be pointed out that he did only what he thought was proper—an impenetrable defense—and there are those who do not consider him malevolent. Dr. Michael Coe, for instance, whose Mayan credentials should not be doubted, refers to "the great Bishop Landa."

However he is to be judged, this is what happened.

A shipment of Franciscan monks arrived at Mérida in 1549, among them Diego de Landa, twenty-five years old and abristle with Christian energy. He wasted no time. Scarcely had he unpacked his bags when native shrines began dropping like tenpins, their idols smashed, and young Diego definitely became a monk for the Indians to remember.

Then, on July 12, 1562, he staged an auto-da-fé that still—after four centuries—brings down curses upon his tonsured head. Into the fire on this occasion went several thousand examples of Mayan sculpture, as many painted books as Diego and his associates were able to find, and a number of distressed Yucatecans who lifted incomprehensible prayers to the Great Spirit.

Serious charges require scrupulous attention, so it must be pointed out that Diego de Landa was not the first vandal cleric; the deliberate destruction of Mayan culture was underway when he arrived. It must also be mentioned that his pious orgy shocked many Spaniards. The bishop of Yucatán, Francisco Toral, had been in Mexico City when de Landa supervised the auto-da-fé, and upon his return to Mérida he was so outraged that he ordered an investigation. He wrote angrily to King Philip II that the monks responsible for this act were men of little knowledge and even less charity, and he submitted the case to the Council of the Indies. Because of Bishop Toral's protest, de Landa was recalled to Spain.

In Spain, preparing to defend himself against charges that he had usurped the bishop's authority and that his attempt to crush idolatry had been unnecessarily harsh, de Landa wrote his famous account of life among the New World barbarians: *Relación de las cosas de Yukatán.*

It is in this account that we meet the terrible yet familiar justification for book-burning:

"These people use definite signs or letters to record in their books their early history and their lore. By means of those letters, as well as by drawings and figures, they can understand their own story and make others understand and learn from it. We found a great number of books, and since there was nothing in them but superstitions and lies of the devil, we burned them all, to the great woe and lamentation of the people."

In 1573, after having been censured for excessive zeal, Diego de Landa was promoted and returned to the New World as Bishop of Yucatán, a fact which may or may not surprise you.

And because of his *Relación*—the most important document concerning sixteenth-century Mayans—we are left to muse upon this paradox: a man who did everything possible to annihilate their civilization is the man who preserved what little we know about it.

The painted books that he incinerated were, to those with an eye for such things, almost unbearably beautiful. They were made from hammered plant fibers sized with lime, they unfolded like a Chinese screen and were exquisitely illustrated in various colors: orange, blue, red, black, yellow, white, blue-green. Many of them were bound in wood or leather inlaid with semiprecious stones, so that they resembled those sumptuous European books from the Middle Ages. Our friend and future bishop Diego burned all but three, which somehow escaped his dragnet.

One is in Dresden. It is known to be a copy of an earlier manuscript dating from the peak of Mayan artistic activity, the so-called Classic Period, which ended around A.D. 900. Of the three, this codex—eight inches high and twelve feet long, consisting of seventy-eight pages—is the most exotic; and though Mayan writing has been only partly deciphered, enough has been learned to know that this book contains mathematical and astronomical tables.

The priests of Copán, incidentally, understood our planetary system better than did the ancient astronomers of the Near East; they were calculating on a scale of hundreds of millions of years at a time when sophisticated Europeans thought the earth was 5,000 years old; and they measured the length of a solar year more accurately than does our modern calendar. Yet, says Leo Deuel, for these people the concern with time did not imply a tyranny of time. The past and the future might merge. "This world would come to an end, but it would have a new beginning."

The Codex Tro-Cortesianos in Madrid is the longest, and its cumbersome label needs to be explained. Part of this codex turned up in 1865, the property of a Madrid paleographer named Tro y Ortolano, after whom it was called the Troano. Fifteen years later another manuscript was found in Estremadura, called the Cortés because this famous conquistador might have owned it. Then a French scholar realized that these were not independent codices; they belonged together. But somehow, somewhere, for some reason, the book had been cut almost in half.

Like the Dresden codex, the Tro-Cortesianos is a replica of a Classic Period manuscript. It seems to consist of ceremonial directions that relate to hunting, rainmaking, and planting, together with the dates of religious festivals. Most authorities believe it was copied just for the information, without regard to aesthetics, by somebody who was not an artist—maybe a priest. If that assumption is true the Mayans must have been supernaturally talented because the artistic level of the Madrid codex is beyond the reach of an untrained person today.

You can see this book at the Museo de América, and despite the faded colors and half-obliterated drawing it is not an exhibit you overlook. The halves are displayed separately. The "Fragmento Cortesiano" is perhaps ten feet long, the "Fragmento Troano" a bit longer. Each of the 56 sheets—112 pages because they are painted on both sides—each is about the size of a modern book page, but there all similarity ends. The information that unfolds is singularly unfamiliar.

For instance, among the birds, beasts, and glyphs you will come upon a sequence of sixteen little panels in which an animal, possibly a dog or a deer, has been tied to a tree—either a tree or a hat rack—by its right foreleg. In several panels the rope has been looped around the creature's neck and it is grimacing as though it were being strangled. Now, the pragmatic observer will say this clearly depicts game caught in a snare. Myself, I have doubts. After studying the remorseless scene for a few minutes it is easy to persuade yourself that what you are looking at is a parable of man's existence.

These two fragments of a single codex just might not have been painted by the same hand. The Troano is in slightly better shape—the black, blue, and reddish brown colors less faded; but what is significant is that the drawing appears sharper, more precise, more accomplished. It is unmistakably more satisfying than the Cortesiano. If indeed these halves were painted by different men that fact might almost explain the mysterious separation.

The Codex Peresianus, in the Paris Bibliothèque Nationale, contains various prophecies and is thought to have been painted during the tenth or eleventh century. It was found beneath some waste paper in the basement of the library, the name *Pérez* scrawled on its wrapping. So tell me, if you can, how it got there. How could anybody handle such a thing—an extremely old, richly illustrated book in a totally unintelligible language—how could anybody pick it up and toss it aside?

Only these three codices escaped the fanatic Franciscan, although there is in Mexico City a fourth whose authenticity has been questioned. Thus we can study three books for clues to the Mayan civilization. As Coe remarks, it is as if future historians of the English-speaking world were obliged to evaluate us on the basis of two prayer books and *Pilgrim's Progress*.

But there are rumors of a fifth book, owned by an individual—somebody in Mexico—who would be willing to sell it if the price is right; if he, or she, could do so without being prosecuted. The Mexican government would seize this book, of course, if it could be located. If it exists.

And de Landa tells us that priests sometimes were buried with their books. Scraps of paper flecked with color occasionally have been found in Mayan graves, which seems to verify his statement, so another Dead Sea treasure might turn up, though that would be miraculous.

Then there are glyphs on the gloriously decorated bowls you see in galleries, museums, private collections, and textbook reproductions, in addition to glyphs carved or painted on temple walls at archaeological sites. So there does remain quite a lot to work with, but not enough, not nearly enough. Except for Diego de Landa we probably would understand Mayan as well as Egyptian.

Still, we are indebted to this violent priest. If it weren't for his curiosity about Mayan picture writing we would have no Mu. The line of descent may appear circuitous, but in fact it is easily traced.

Young Diego, while smashing idols and baptizing converts, decided to find out what these un-Christian symbols meant. He therefore attempted to reduce them to an alphabet, more or less as Bishop Jaussen did—or tried to do—with the Easter Island symbols. He went through the letters of the European alphabet as they are pronounced in Spanish and he asked a Mayan prince, Nachi Cocon, to draw for each letter the appropriate glyph. If Prince Nachi had been subjected to this exercise by an English-speaking inquisitor the result, obviously, would have been different. There was no Englishman present to amplify the confusion, but what de Landa got by himself deserves some kind of a prize:

Como se escribe a?

The Spanish *a*, as everybody knows, does not sound like the English *a*. To Nachi it sounded like the Mayan word for turtle. He drew a stylized picture of a turtle's head.

Como se escribe b?

Nachi drew an oval which he divided into three sections by means of two horizontal lines, and in the center section he drew an irregular oval accompanied by three dots. *B*, or *bay*, sounded like the Mayan word signifying a path or a journey; he therefore had drawn parallel lines to indicate the borders of a path and he had placed a foot between them. The irregular oval represented the sole, the dots indicated toes. It was logical, perfectly clear, and it had the charming incoherence of language spoken in a dream.

Como se escribe c?

And so on until *zed.*

De Landa presumably was satisfied with this Alice-in-Wonderland equation, and if one considers the witless auto-da-fé for which he was responsible there is something fine and just about his accomplishment.

Nachi, one might suppose, was handsomely rewarded for his part in the translation. Well, we are told that some time after his death his body was exhumed and his bones were scattered by order of the bishop of Yucatán, Diego de Landa. Why? It seems that de Landa grew suspicious. He feared that Nachi Cocon's apparent conversion to Christianity might not have been genuine; the Mayan prince might secretly have clung to the idolatrous faith of his fathers.

In any event, the alphabet which these two had created was lost and forgotten until 1863 when *Relación de las cosas de Yukatán* turned up in the Madrid archives. And the man who found it, the remarkable French abbé Charles Étienne Brasseur de Bourbourg, soon crowned the bishop's peculiar achievement with fantasy. Out of de Landa's alphabet he concocted Mu.

Mu has not become as famous as Atlantis, but of course Plato's story has been on the market quite a bit longer. Mu is doing all right, and if you don't think so you have not looked in the pseudo-science department of any large paperback bookstore. There you will see *The Lost Continent of Mu, The Sacred Symbols of Mu, Cosmic Forces as They Were*

Taught in Mu, ad infinitum. The French abbé did not write any of these; he was far too intelligent, and the fact that he was intelligent makes him all the more preposterous.

He is described as a tall, courtly man, a savant who could speak twelve languages and read twenty. He traveled a lot and seems to have spent relatively little time at his trade. "I am an abbé in the Church," he told an American acquaintance in Rome, "but my ecclesiastical duties have always rested very lightly on me."

He was fascinated by the pre-Hispanic cultures of America, a predilection growing out of the books he read as a child, especially an account of the ruins of Palenque in Yucatán, and he resolved to become an archaeologist. However, without a wealthy father or an indulgent government, he was obliged to earn a living.

This he did in Paris by laboring as a journalist for *Le Monde* and *Le Temps*, meanwhile writing novels with such splendid titles as *l'Exil de Tadmor* and *Sélim ou le Pacha de Salonique*.

Five years of the literary life seems to have left him exhausted or depressed: he enrolled in a seminary at Ghent. And from there, after wandering about Switzerland, he settled in Rome to complete his theological education.

Upon being ordained he got himself shipped to the Sacred College of the Propaganda in Quebec—farther north than he wished, but at least it was the right continent.

Soon he popped up in Mexico City where he studied Nahuatl, the Aztec language, and wrote a little book on antiquities. He then went back to Rome where he spent a while searching the archives for material on early explorations in America. His position with the Church must have been somewhat ambiguous because he took time off to fabricate several more dreamy novels which he described as works of "lesser importance," meaning that he hoped they would make money. Apparently they did not because on his next trip to America he sold his portable missionary chapel. This may sound shocking, but of course when you are in the grip of an obsession you have no choice.

So, back and forth he went from continent to continent, studying, producing potboilers as well as erudite papers, making a name for himself. Then, among stacks of musty documents at the Academy of

History in Madrid, he saw de Landa's *Relación*, which had been ignored for almost 300 years.

Greatly excited, thinking he would now be able to translate Mayan, Brasseur went to work on a section of the Codex Tro-Cortesianos.

Nobody has been able to explain what went wrong. That is, we know what happened but we cannot account for it. Here was Abbé Brasseur, a man of high intelligence, a bona fide scholar—a man who had spent years in Mexico and Central America studying the Indians—who actually spoke several native languages. In other words, he was thoroughly qualified. Yet he failed to perceive that the story unfolding from the Madrid codex was a very odd story indeed. Intuition ought to have told him that something somewhere was dreadfully wrong. Nevertheless he went right on translating.

Professor Robert Brunhouse, who has richly summarized this baroque era, observes with neat academic restraint: "Why his fertile imagination got the better of him is not clear."

Others have suggested that perhaps he was overwhelmed by the mass of information he had accumulated, or that the complex Indian mythology affected his judgment. Whatever happened, the abbé's translation of the Tro-Cortesianos, inscribed with a turkey-quill pen and a bottle of homemade reddish brown ink, commences thus:

"The master of the upheaved earth, the master of the calabash, the earth upheaved of the tawny beast . . ."

Halfway through this epic he encountered two symbols more or less resembling the *m* and *u* of de Landa's wondrous alphabet, and he concluded—by what logic, unfortunately, we do not know—that the name of the upheaved real estate was Mu.

This brings us to Dr. Augustus Le Plongeon—"Dr." because at some point in his serpentine career he decided that he was a physician and should be addressed as such. Quite a few peculiar individuals have gone poking through the Mexican jungle, but it is likely that Augustus Le Plongeon with his patriarchal white beard, gleaming blue eyes, great round bald head, and "beautiful brick-dust complexion" was the most unconventional.

He was born in 1826 on the island of Jersey, his father a commodore in the French navy, his mother the daughter of the governor of Mont-

Saint-Michel. He went to military school, later attended the Polytechnic Institute of Paris, and one fine day embarked for California on a yacht that foundered off the coast of Chile. Only two men survived. What became of Augustus' companion has not been recorded, but he himself washed ashore at Valparaiso where he learned Spanish and taught school while his clothes dried out. Then he made another attempt to reach California. Again he met foul weather—"the ship was reduced to a pitiable condition"—and for the second time Augustus Le Plongeon nearly ended his career some fathoms down.

Arriving in San Francisco too late for the gold rush, he got a job as county surveyor but this was a bore so he moved along. Hawaii. Tahiti. Australia. Back to San Francisco. Then to Peru where he wrote a book about the Incas, which nobody would publish, though he did break into print with a treatise on earthquakes. And he may have invented a seismograph.

He showed up in New York with three valuable paintings—two by Murillo, one by Juan del Castillo—which he claimed to have discovered in a Peruvian church. He wanted to sell them. He could not find a buyer but he did find Miss Alice Dixon of Brooklyn. Augustus at this time was forty-seven, Alice was twenty-two. They got married and went to Mexico.

For several years they explored deserted cities on the Yucatan peninsula. An 1875 photograph shows them at work in their field headquarters. Augustus, his imperial dome handsomely sun-browned, is seated on a box and appears to be reading aloud. Alice, dressed in white, as immaculate as a Hollywood heroine, listens pensively. Propped against the wall are two perfect symbols of a nineteenth-century marriage: his shotgun and her guitar.

In the spring of 1877 they are on the island of Cozumel. Le Plongeon writes a thirty-page letter to the Honorable John W. Foster, United States Minister to Mexico, announcing a definite similarity between Mayan and Greek: ". . . Who brought the dialect of Homer to America? Or who took to Greece that of the Mayas? Greek is the offspring of Sanscrit. Is Maya? or are they coeval? A clue for ethnologists to follow the migrations of the human family on this old continent. Did the bearded man whose portraits are carved on the massive pillars of the fortress of Chichen-Itza belong to the Mayan Nations? The Maya language is not devoid of words from the Assyrian . . ."

One day at Chichén something occurred that recalls Schliemann's intuitive feeling for Troy. A party of tourists from Mérida came across him meditating among the ruins. They saw him jump up, rush to the top of a little mound, stamp on it, and order his workmen to dig. Very soon they unearthed a carved tiger with a human face. Le Plongeon ordered them to dig deeper. Twenty-three feet down they uncovered the famous statue of Chacmool that you see in Mexican travel brochures.

Decoding glyphs was as easy as divining the location of buried statues. After all, he explained, the inhabitants of Yucatán were Mayans who still spoke the language of their ancestors even if they could not read the hieroglyphs. And there was de Landa's instructive alphabet.

So, to prove that he knew what he was talking about, he wrote a history of the Mayan people, basing it on Brasseur's fantastic translation of the Madrid codex. His version makes the abbé's account of an upheaved land sound like a neighborhood mud slide. He gave the story dimension and structure. A doomed country with a brilliant civilization, a beautiful queen, a fearless king, intrigue, love, hate, war. Two princes named Cob and Aac in love with their sister, Queen Kinich Kakmo, sometimes called Móo. Cob murdered by Aac, who fled to Uxmal, and so forth. At last the gods speak up:

"In the year 6 Kan, on the 11th Muluc in the month of Zac, occurred terrible earthquakes . . . ten countries were torn asunder and scattered. Unable to stand the force of the convulsion, they sank with their sixty-four million inhabitants . . ."

Queen Móo escaped to Egypt where, under the name Isis, she founded Egyptian civilization. A few other refugees populated Central America.

In 1885 Dr. and Mrs. Le Plongeon returned to New York where he published an unusual study of the Mayan alphabet. The language spoken by Jesus, he said, was not Aramaic but Mayan. "Eli, Eli, lama sabachthani!" did not mean what everybody thought it meant. Instead, the outcry was pure Mayan—"Helo, helo, lamah, xabac ta hi!"—and should be translated: "Now, now, I am fainting; darkness covers my face!"

Eleven years later he published his masterpiece, *Queen Móo and the Egyptian Sphinx*.

After that Augustus himself began receding into the darkness. Not Alice, his second self. She went on writing. *Queen Móo's Talisman* appeared in 1902. Five hundred rhymed couplets embellished with songs and pictures. Here is a sample:

Loved by the Will Supreme to be reborn,
In high estate a soul sought earthly mourn;
Life stirred within a beauteous Maya queen
Of noble deeds, of gracious words and mien.

It did better than you might suspect. The songs were scored for harp, piano, and violin, and the assemblage was produced as "a tragic drama of ancient America, in five acts and ten scenes."

Augustus died not long afterward. There does not seem to be a connection between his death and his wife's drama. Probably he died of heart failure and disappointment. His reputation had evaporated; he was ridiculed and his work ignored. Several times he threatened to destroy his Mayan papers. Instead, he lent them to an ex-Bengal Lancer named James Churchward who was living in Mount Vernon, New York, and who liked to be addressed as "Colonel."

Augustus Le Plongeon and Charles Étienne Brasseur and Bishop Diego de Landa are names that very few people recognize, but you can drop Colonel Churchward's name with some expectation of a response. He is a famous author. His earliest work, quite possibly his most important, was *A Big Game and Fishing Guide to North-Eastern Maine*, but his reputation depends on Mu.

He claimed to have learned about it while serving in India. A friendly temple priest allowed him to see, and later helped him to interpret, the Naacal tablets—seen by nobody else before or since—which revealed to him that Mu had occupied an area of the central Pacific. It was a flat, lush territory, supported by belts of gas, however improbable that may sound. Some 12,000 years ago the gas escaped, hence the deluge.

Your basic commercial hack might squeeze a book out of this which would earn enough to pay the rent for six months, but Churchward knew a really good item when he saw it. Utilizing the ectoplasmic

Naacal tablets and several kilos of information supplied by Augustus Le Plongeon—who depended on Abbé Brasseur's upheaved land—derived from Diego de Landa's surrealistic alphabet—Churchward was able to crank out one best-seller after another detailing the life, times, sacred symbols, and cosmic forces of the fabulous continent. Those are the paperbacks you still see in print after fifty years.

Mu does sound like an ideal vacation spot:

> Over the cool river, gaudy-winged butterflies hovered in the shade of trees, rising and falling in fairy-like movement, as if better to view their painted beauty in nature's mirror. Darting hither and thither from flower to flower, hummingbirds made their short flights, glistening like living jewels in the rays of the sun. Feathered songsters in bush and tree vied with each other in their sweet lays. . . . On cool evenings might be seen pleasure ships, filled with gorgeously dressed, jewel-bedecked men and women. The long sweeps with which these ships were supplied gave a musical rhythm to the song and laughter of the happy passengers. . . .

For all of which, let the record show, we are indebted to a sixteenth-century Spanish priest. Had Diego de Landa not incinerated the classic Mayan books, nearly obliterating the written language, we could not enjoy this Muvian idyll.

Of course there are other ways of looking at it, such as the fact that even now, after four centuries, despite the work of many scholars, only about half of the Mayan glyphs can be understood: names, dates, relationships—shards of a painted bowl that once was lovely and complete.

You can get some idea of the Mayan world as it used to be if you visit Palenque. Every morning there is a bus from Villahermosa to the village of Santo Domingo de Palenque, and on down the road a few miles you come across a silent, mildewed, ivory city in the jungle. No matter when you go it will be hot. The sun dangles above your head all day like a burning spider.

What this place was called by the Mayans who lived there, we don't know. Palenque, meaning Palisade, is Spanish, but the site had been deserted for almost 1,000 years when Spaniards learned about it. Pottery crushed beneath some of the structures prove that the area was inhabited several centuries before the time of Christ.

From the seventh to the ninth centuries A.D. the Mayan culture bloomed at Palenque, but archaeologists noticed Totonac votive axes—meaning that enemies from the Gulf Coast may have invaded the city, killed its leaders, and destroyed in a matter of days what had taken many generations to create. This sounds plausible because it sounds familiar.

Other explanations have been offered for Palenque's collapse: earthquakes, hurricanes, disease, depletion of the soil. Or maybe the people just got fed up and revolted against a complacent aristocracy. Whatever happened a millennium ago, the center failed to hold. Peasants subsequently used the vacant buildings for shelter—crude grinding stones have been found in the rubble—and during this period the jungle, which had been slashed and held at a distance by the sophisticated Maya, again crept forward. The city's last inhabitants were parrots, lizards, jaguars, and butterflies.

Cortés rode past Palenque, but it was then so thickly overgrown that he saw nothing. Even the natives who lived nearby, descendants of the founders, were unaware that each tree-covered mound concealed a temple.

John Lloyd Stephens, who visited the place in 1840, wanted to buy it. The ground was reasonably flat, the coast lay not far distant, and he thought he would not have much difficulty shipping the best monuments to New York. Today, of course, Stephens' excellent logic sounds outrageous, but at that time the state of Chiapas was anxious to sell the land: 6,000 acres, ruins included, for $1,500. There was one catch. Mexican law stipulated that no foreigner could buy land unless married to an *hija del país*, a daughter of the country.

Stephens, reflecting upon this, considers it a brilliant stroke, designed to seduce men from their natural allegiance, "for, when wandering in strange countries, alone and friendless, buffeted and battered, with no one to care for him, there are moments when a lovely woman might root the stranger to any spot on earth. On principle I have always resisted such tendencies, but I never before found it to my interest to give way. The ruined city of Palenque was a most desirable piece of property."

However, the situation became embarrassing and complicated. The girl he fancied was already married. Otherwise, there were two middle-aged *hijas del país*, "equally interesting and equally interested," and a fourteen-year-old. For some reason he let these three opportunities pass, so the abandoned city lay unmolested a few years longer.

It was a religious sanctuary, a necropolis, a political seat, an artistic and scientific rendezvous, an unconquered fortress on a lush viridian slope, impregnable until the Totonacs arrived. How large it is—even today nobody knows because much of Palenque remains hidden: symmetrical hills lavishly camouflaged by foliage. In the moist oppressive heat an endless net grows sensuously, almost perceptibly, above Palenque's buried temples.

Those that have been excavated seem to be arranged in groups.

The so-called palace is the largest, constructed on an artificial platform 300 feet long and 240 feet wide: an imperial complex of chambers, galleries, stairways, and gloomy little passages that may have been used by priests who wanted to move from one room to another without being seen. Traces of murals and fantastic stucco masks cling almost everywhere to the lime-streaked walls. Even the damp shadowy passageways have been incised with glyphs—now veiled by moss and calcium deposits, occasionally hidden behind clusters of stalactites that resemble opaque greenish icicles. Bright yellow flowers splatter the rocky slope outside, but within the palace you meet only death, moisture, and indifferent emptiness.

Three murky white buildings blackened by tropical growth and freckled with orange lichen—abstract art at its best—stand on terraces behind the palace: Temples of the Sun, of the Cross, and of the Foliated Cross.

The first was a four-story pyramid. Inside on the back wall is a handsome carved panel. Two priests, one obviously more important because of his size, have offered something to the sun, which is symbolically represented by a round shield and a pair of crossed lances. Enough glyphs have been deciphered to provide a Christian date: A.D. 642.

The Temple of the Cross, matted with vines, rises from a high pyramidal structure that has not yet been excavated. A crumbling black honeycomb on the roof gives it the look of a Dresden apartment firebombed during the Second World War. Much of it has collapsed, but another religious scene can be distinguished on carved slabs flanking the door to the sanctuary. Again we have two priests, one accompanied by a panel of glyphs. The other, who wears an elaborate tigerskin headdress, is smoking a cigar. They are worshiping a cross. Here also we find the date A.D. 642. Why that year was significant is not known.

The Temple of the Foliated Cross was built against a hillside which helps to sustain it. Parts of the building have slipped down the hill, but the panel for which it is named still can be seen—the cross ornamented with maize leaves and human heads. The heads are not those of sacrificial victims; they represent ears of corn. Masks of the sun god and rain god surmount the cross, and among several dates registered in the glyphs the most important seems to be A.D. 692.

There is a curious, very human thing about this temple. Carved slabs embellish the stairway leading up to it and on one of these slabs a Mayan sculptor cut the wrong date. It sounds presumptuous for present-day investigators—especially when they can read only a few glyphs—to announce that somebody 1,300 years ago did not know what he was doing. Nevertheless, Alberto Ruz states flatly that in the Secondary Series the number of the *Uinal*, or twenty-day months, should be ten instead of eleven. The obvious question is: How many citizens of Palenque noticed the botched *Uinal*? Did any of them complain? If so, what happened to the sculptor?

The Temple of Inscriptions, close by the palace, stands on top of a large pyramid so that it rises above everything else. From the doors of this temple you can look twenty or thirty miles, though there's not much to see except a flat green bowl of jungle, and now the railroad station.

Inside are a great many carved panels with some sort of chronology embedded in the text. Several dates have been identified and here again we find A.D. 692. What happened that year?

The stone floor consists of broad slabs carefully joined. Ruz, who directed the exploration from 1949 to 1958, noticed that one slab had a double row of holes plugged with stoppers. Nor did the walls end at floor level, which indicated that there might be a room underneath. The perforated slab was lifted, revealing a staircase deliberately choked with rubbish. Almost a year was required to clean it out.

These steps led deep into the pyramid and apparently ended at a plastered wall—an obvious fake. Excavators broke through and saw the bones of five or six young men. Beyond this macabre display the passage did come to an end. But on the left side of the sacrificial compartment a triangular stone had been set in the wall, and when the triangle was removed they were able to look into a royal crypt.

This funerary chamber at the bottom of the staircase is eighty feet beneath the temple floor and below the level of the plaza outside. It is thirty feet long, thirteen feet wide. The vaulted ceiling, reinforced by girders of yellow-veined stone, is twenty-three feet high. The walls have been decorated with stucco reliefs of nine priests who probably represent the Bolón-ti-kú, Lords of the Night and of the Nether Worlds. Although they might be ancestors of the man who was buried here. If we could read the text, we would know.

Most of the crypt is occupied by a monolithic sarcophagus, the largest ever encountered in North or South America. The elegantly sculpted lid shows a man with a plumed headdress who is either falling or reclining at the base of a cruciform tree of life. According to some scholars he has been portrayed at the instant of death, falling into the jaws of a subterranean monster. A ceremonial belt—three miniature masks and several flat stones in the shape of axes—had been left on top of the sarcophagus. On the floor stood a number of clay bowls that probably held food and something to drink.

After the lid—weighing almost five tons—was jacked up, archaeologists could see that the monolith had been hollowed out in a peculiar, sinuous form. A beautifully polished stone cover exactly fitted this strange, undulant pattern.

Within the cavity, which had been reddened with cinnabar—color of the east where the sun is born and reborn—lay the skeleton of a man who, by Mayan standards, was huge. He had been loaded with jade: necklaces, bracelets, earspools of jade and mother-of-pearl, a breastplate made from concentric rings of tubular jade beads, a jade ring for each finger. Two impressive jades rested among the bones of his hands. Another had been placed in his mouth. A mosaic jade mask, with inlaid shells for eyes and obsidian discs to symbolize the iris, concealed his face. He was buried in a red winding-sheet which long ago disintegrated, but traces of red pigment clung to the jewels and to his skeleton.

The glyphs tell us that his name was pa-ca-la, or Pacal, meaning Shield. He married his sister, Lady Ahpo Hel, and he reigned over Palenque for sixty-eight years, from A.D. 615 to 683. Sixty-eight years! He lived into his fifth *katun*, which is to say that when he died he was at least eighty and possibly one hundred. How long the average citizen lived in those days, we have no idea; but it should be a fair guess that only a few watched the sunrise half as many times as Pacal.

If we take into account how much longer people live today and how much larger they are—considering these factors, if we cast Pacal in the present we might be talking about a king seven feet tall who reigned for a century. It's inconceivable. The Western world has never seen such a man. The nearest thing to him might be Charlemagne, who is alleged to have been of great stature and who reigned forty-six years, two-thirds the length of Pacal's reign.

Could the glyphs be exaggerating? Not likely. Beneath that pyramid rests the skeleton of a king so much taller than his subjects that they should not even be compared.

This astonishing man must have radiated an aura of supernatural wisdom and strength; no doubt the glyphs proclaim his greatness and his achievements. Had he lived in England or France every schoolchild would recognize his name.

One thing more. When Alberto Ruz first peered through that triangular hole into the crypt he saw an immense snake fashioned of mortar crawling from the sarcophagus. It crawled across the stones to the entrance, at which point it became a hollow molding that flowed up the steps all the way to the perforated slab in the temple floor, in this way establishing a magic connection between the dead regent and the priests above. Through them Lord Pacal might hear and speak, and thus look after his subjects forever, interceding with the deities on their behalf to protect them from hunger, invasion, and disease.

So he did, for a few centuries. At least we assume everything went well for Palenque until the Totonac armies approached. One need not read Old Mayan to know what happened then. The story seldom changes.

Peasants moved in when things calmed down, never mind if the floors and walls were smeared with blood. Soon the jungle returned.

Lichen mottled the neat white surfaces and discolored the murals. Vines obscured the entrances.

Now you may drive to the ruins in your air-conditioned Cadillac, or take the leisurely Villahermosa bus, and climb the majestic outside staircase to the Temple of Inscriptions. Here, by shading your eyes, you can squint across the forest and think hieroglyphic thoughts until sundown. Below you on the uneven plaza there will be puddles of water so greenly poisonous you can almost count the bacteria; unquestionably there will be a dog because there is always a dog, asleep or scratching, several turkeys, an occasional gringo tourist, perhaps some laborers in a rusty truck.

Nobody will pay the slightest attention to you. One visitor more or less means nothing, no more than the new day. Palenque is too old to care. People lived and worked and died here long before the classic Mayan age, at a time when pharaohs ruled Egypt. And because of this it might occur to you, standing in the shade of the temple with a lime-stained frieze of priests at your back, high above Pacal's red bones, that Ikhnaton's "Hymn to the Sun" could be invoked as appropriately here as at Tell al-Amarna on the Nile:

Thy light rises in the mountains to the East,
And thou fillest the country with thy beauty.
Thou art beautiful and great, lucent and sublime over every land.
Thy rays burn them to the end of what thou hast created.

Thou hast subjected them to thy beloved son.
Thou art remote, but thy rays shine upon the earth.
Thou dost illuminate mankind but none sees thy path.

Lord, how great and numerous are thy works,
Hidden from the face of men.

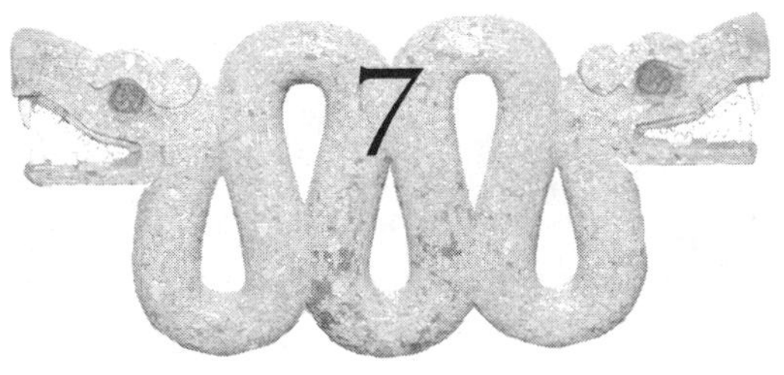

7

Abracadastra

Isaac Newton said that if he saw farther than most men it was because he stood on the shoulders of giants. Such words from a bona fide giant sound agreeably modest, even self-effacing; but the remark happens to be true because scientists—more so than butchers, bakers, and candlestick makers—benefit from the cumulative wisdom of their predecessors.

We are indebted to various Babylonians and Egyptians for the beginning of our celestial inheritance, though we have no idea who they were; not until pre-Christian Greece do we meet any individuals. Thales of Miletus, 2,600 years ago, seems to have been the first astronomer. His conclusions are now meaningless and therefore boring, but he is remembered because in 585 B.C. he predicted an eclipse. He is known to have been a traveler and was thought to have learned the mysterious art in Egypt, but modern scholars say the Egyptians themselves could not predict eclipses. It's possible, of course, that he divined the event. After all, Jonathan Swift located the moons of Mars 150 years before they were discovered.

What Thales did do, beyond doubt, was to earn a pile of drachmas by some astute weather forecasting based on his knowledge of meteorology and local tradition. One winter, after having deduced that next summer would be favorable for olives, he bought options on all the presses. Came summer the countryside grew thick with olives waiting to be pressed, whereupon Thales applied the screws to his neighbors. We remember him also as the first absent-minded professor. One starry night, enraptured by the twinkling spectacle overhead, he neglected to watch where he put his feet and stepped into a well.

With the Pythagorean school and a certain Parmenides of Elea we approach astronomical reality: the moon illuminates the earth through borrowed light, and the earth revolves around a central fire. Strangely, though, this central fire was not the sun. How obvious the truth seems to us, yet some contour of the Greek mind determined that the sun merely reflected heat and light. The actual source was invisible, forever hidden behind a "counter-earth"—a counter-earth being required for the sake of harmony.

Old Pythagoras himself never could accept the idea developed by his students of an earth spinning around a fire; he maintained that the earth was motionless. And it was he who generally is credited with being the first to distinguish between odd and even numbers, an article of wisdom you would think must be within the grasp of an average child.

So we progress, possibly by mutation.

Anaxagoras in the fifth century B.C. stated that the moon consisted of soil and the sun was a red-hot rock, and he understood eclipses. A lunar eclipse would occur "when the earth, and sometimes the bodies below the moon, are in line between the moon and the sun. The sun will be eclipsed when the moon, at the dark phase, is between the sun and the earth."

About this time Democritus of Abdera speculated that innumerable stars too small for us to see might account for that hazy white ribbon overhead, a fact not confirmed until 2,000 years later when Galileo looked through a telescope. Democritus also proposed the existence of other worlds.

Next we come to a pair of cautious geometers, Aristarchus and Eratosthenes, who flourished three centuries before Christ.

Little is known about the first, not even where he worked, but he understood that all of the planets, Earth included, revolve around the sun. He argued that the stars were fixed; their apparent movement must result from the earth turning on its axis.

Nothing developed from these brilliant insights, perhaps because he could offer no observational proof or because the age could not absorb such original ideas. Plato, Eudoxtus, Aristotle, and other accredited philosophers had contrived a model of the universe made up of fifty-six crystalline spheres which—however awkward and false—did explain the apparent motions of the sun, the moon, and the planets. One could, therefore, accept this carefully reasoned theory or one could bet on a wild hypothesis. Given a parallel choice today, the response would be no different. Aristarchus' explanation was regarded as charming and curious, but not something an intelligent man would take seriously.

Eratosthenes, a director of the great Alexandrian library, sits in the hall of fame because he measured the circumference of the earth. He was not the first to do this, but his figures are surprisingly accurate, and his procedure was so simple that quite a few Alexandrians probably went around muttering that anybody could have done it.

Below Alexandria lay the town of Syene, the modern Aswan. At noon on the longest day of the year the sun's rays illuminated a deep well at Syene, meaning that the sun must be vertically overhead; yet at the same time the sun cast a shadow at Alexandria. The angle of the rays at Alexandria was a little over 7°, which made it one-fiftieth of a circle. Ergo: if you multiply the distance from Syene to Alexandria by fifty you have the approximate circumference.

Aswan is not precisely south of Alexandria, nor directly on the Tropic of Cancer, nor was the measured distance strictly accurate; but just by luck these mistakes canceled one another so that Eratosthenes' figure of 24,647 miles is less than 250 miles off, which is rather good for a backyard operation.

At this point we come to the Antikýthēra device, recovered in 1900 from the wreck of a Greek ship that sank near the island of Antikýthēra in the first century B.C. It is a deeply corroded chunk of bronze with toothed gears and graduated circles. Nothing comparable has ever been found, and no ancient writing describes or refers to such an object, which allows the gods-from-other-worlds hucksters to hint that it must be from outer space. There is, however, some writing on its surface, mostly illegible, which indicates that the machine correlated celestial movements; and researchers have traced this inscription back to an astronomical calendar used on Rhodes.

Careful cleaning has shown the device to be fairly complex. Some of it is missing, and what remains is not altogether understood, but the gears were driven by an axle, enabling an astronomer to take a reading from three dials. The large dial contains zodiacal signs and almost certainly marked the annual course of the sun. The small dials announced the rising and setting of the moon and gave the motions of five planets.

On one dial was a ring that established a date in accordance with the Egyptian calendar. The Egyptians counted exactly 365 days a year, ignoring those troublesome hours that create leap year, but the remarkable Greek machine could make allowances for this. The ring had last been adjusted to a date corresponding to 80 B.C., quite possibly the year the ship sank.

Where the ship came from and where it was bound, we have no idea. It was loaded with bronze and marble sculpture—some of which is now in the Athens museum—causing scholars to suspect that it may have been one of the tyrant Sulla's treasure ships.

And although this is irrelevant, we are indebted to the Antikýthēra device for proof that those celebrated Greeks did not spend all their time debating, philosophizing, hurling the discus, and carving alabaster nymphs; once in a while they designed rococo little instruments to astound and mystify the future, which speaks well of them.

The earliest post-Christian astronomer was an Alexandrian Greek named Claudius Ptolemy, or Ptolemaeus, whose contribution to scientific knowledge was that he popularized the epicycle, and so great was his reputation that the epicycle became sanctified. Now an epicycle is not something to be ridden; it is merely a small circle moving around the circumference of a larger circle, and Ptolemy employed a clutch of them to illustrate the mechanics of the universe. Epicycles were necessary because he insisted upon a false premise—that the earth hung suspended and motionless in the middle of things.

Ptolemy's system of interlocking wheels, his Ferris wheel universe, lasted longer than you might think—about fourteen centuries—because it confirmed what we wish to believe: that the system has been arranged for our benefit.

Thus, with Claudius Ptolemy, who was not Cleopatra's uncle, Greek astronomical science ends, not with a revelation but an absurdity. You see the same thing happening in late Greek art, in those graceful Tanagra statuettes where the nude elegance of the Periclean age degenerates into costumery.

Next came the interregnum, the Dark Ages. During these centuries very little was learned, at least not much that now seems valuable, while much that already had been learned was forgotten. Spores of Greek knowledge floated through the Middle East, reentering Europe by way of Arabic Sicily and Spain, but whatever failed to coincide with medieval dogma got a miserable reception. When the erudite Byzantine statesman Georgios Akropolites explained an eclipse to the empress she laughed at him.

Here and there, nevertheless, intelligent men persisted.

Some forgotten genius at the Norwegian court wrote in the *Konnungsskuggsja* for the edification of his lord: "You should understand that the earth is spherical and not equally close to the sun at all points. Its curved orbit . . ."

Pope Pius II declared that in the judgment of educated people the earth was round.

Bishop Nicole Oresme asked if the apparent rotation of the heavens might not be an illusion caused by the rotation of the earth.

Cardinal Nicholas of Cusa insisted that not only was the earth a globe, but the stars were other worlds. "We know already," he said, "that our earth moves, even though this motion is not visible. . . . Only God, who constitutes the center of the universe, may be motionless."

At the beginning of the seventeenth century, during a less tolerant period, Giordano Bruno would be roasted alive on the Square of Flowers in Rome for endorsing such ideas:

> Justice done on an impenitent heretic. . . . Hence, at the sixth hour of the night, the Comforters and the chaplain assembled at S. Ursula and went to the prison in the Tower of Nona, entered the chapel, and offered up the prayers. To them was consigned the man Giordano Bruno, son of

> Gni. Bruno, an apostate friar of Nola in the Kingdom, an impenitent. He was exhorted by our brothers in all love, and two Fathers of the Order of St. Dominic, two of the Order of Jesus, two of the new Church and one of St. Jerome were called in. These with all loving zeal and much learning, showed him his error, yet he stood firm throughout and to the end in his accursed obstinacy, setting his brain and mind to a thousand errors and vaingloryings; and he continued steadfastly stubborn while conducted by the Servants of the Justices to the Campo di Fiori, and there being stripped and bound to a stake, was burned alive. Throughout, our Brotherhood sang litanies and the Consolers exhorted him to the very last to overcome his obstinacy. But thus ended his agony and his wretched life.

After all this time it would be impossible to catalog Bruno's thousand errors, yet that unctuous justification of torture and murder still revolts us—despite the Nazis, Hiroshima, and as many more twentieth-century aberrations as you choose to name. We know that he did speak his mind. He spoke defiantly, imaginatively: "In space there are countless constellations, suns, and planets. We see only the suns because they give light; the planets remain invisible, for they are small and dark. There are also numberless earths circling around their suns, no worse and no less inhabited than this globe of ours. . . ."

So it's a bit surprising that Copernicus, Niklas Koppernigk, who plucked the earth from the heart of the Christian scheme, was not excommunicated and flogged by an ever watchful Church. Had he been born a few years later, or if he had lived in southern Europe, he might have been torn apart by wild horses. Liszinski was decapitated, his body burnt, and the ashes blown out of a cannon for teaching that Man created God instead of vice versa.

Church authorities were disturbed and puzzled by Copernicus, but indecisive. People in the street ridiculed him. It is said that during a carnival procession two fools danced side by side: one gave away indulgences for whoredom while the other whirled a pig's bladder on a string and screeched, "I am the sun! See how the earth flies around me!"

Evidently he was protected—perhaps without his knowledge—by a Lutheran clergyman named Andreas Osiander, which is curious because the astronomer himself was Catholic.

Young Niklas grew up steeped in Catholicism. His father died when he was ten so an uncle, Bishop Lucas Watzelrode, became his guardian. Off went Niklas to study theology at the University of Cracow. Four years later Uncle Lucas sent him to Bologna where he studied ecclesiastic law, but he also studied medicine, astronomy, and mathematics.

He seems to have been best known as a physician, which sounds odd, considering that most of his adult life was spent as canon of Frauenburg Cathedral. However, life was less stratified in those days; a poet might also be a king. Indeed, King Sigismund thought of Copernicus as an economist and asked his help in reforming the monetary system. Accordingly, he went to work on the problem, because it is seldom advisable to refuse a king, and being altogether logical he started with a definition: "Muncze wyrdt genennet geczeichennt Goldtt, adir Sylber." Obviously, coin is the name given to stamped gold or silver. And during his examination of the troubled currency he recognized a process that now is called Gresham's Law—bad money forcing good money out of circulation. Bishop Oresme had commented on this phenomenon two centuries earlier, but no matter.

He was also an artist. A self-portrait in the Dürer style shows a bony-featured young man with a book. His right hand, which rests on his left forearm, looks unconvincing, probably because he faked it, being obliged to hold the burin in that hand while glancing at himself in a mirror. Otherwise the picture is forceful and competent, not the work of an amateur. An engraving from the collection of the British Royal Society, clearly by a different artist, again reveals this bony face, the sensual underlip, and a slight—very slight—trace of amusement. In 1509 he published a Latin translation of some "ribald letters" by a minor Greek poet, one Theophylactus Simocatta, and dedicated the volume to Uncle Lucas—which just might account for that suspicion of humor. In neither portrait, though, do we see the face of an affable, jocular man; Niklas Koppernigk is not anybody you would find at the neighborhood tavern.

However adept he may have been at portraiture, fiscal policies, hemorrhoids, or the neat distinctions of canon law, his mind focused insistently on the night sky. And after a while he realized that he mistrusted epicycles.

Of course he was not the first to arrange our local system in its proper order. Various Greeks had understood the situation pretty well—a fact he noted in his iconoclastic book, *De Revolutionibus orbium coelestium.* That he should frankly credit the Greeks would seem to reflect a nature as modest as Isaac Newton's, but this is misleading; his purpose, almost certainly, was to reassure the Church. Resurrected theories are seldom threatening. As canon of Frauenburg Cathedral and nephew of a bishop his credentials were good, but here and there the Church was stretching, mashing, twisting, strangling, and incinerating people who thought they had original ideas. Under such circumstances one should not be adventurous.

To insure himself further he pointed out that, since churchmen had been asked to help reform the calendar, this heliocentric theory might be of some assistance.

Then he took out another policy by addressing the work to Pope Paul III:

> I can certainly well believe, most holy Father, that, while mayhap a few will accept this my book which I have written concerning the revolutions of the spheres of the world, ascribing certain motions to the sphere of the earth, people will clamor that I ought to be cast out at once for such an opinion. . . . Thus when I considered with myself what an absurd fairy-tale people brought up in the opinion, sanctioned by many ages, that the earth is motionless in the midst of the heaven, as if it were the center of it, would think it if I were to assert on the contrary that the earth is moved; I hesitated long whether I should give the light to my commentaries. . . .

Still he dawdled, and finally said the book should not be published until after his death. But a young mathematician named von Lauchen, who chose to call himself Rhaeticus, at last persuaded the anxious astronomer to go ahead with publication.

Some Copernican scholars, though, don't see it that way. The English astronomer and astrophysicist Herbert Dingle, for one, finds no evidence that Copernicus worried about publishing "unless a shrinking from the ridicule of the unlearned may be so classed. The popular idea that he kept his thoughts secret from fear of persecution is entirely baseless. What he did shrink from was the laughter. . . ."

In any case, we will now ride an epicycle.

Von Lauchen changed his name because he had been born in the Austrian Tyrol, which used to be called Rhaetia. The logic is this: Gutenberg's printing press disclosed the classical Greek and Roman authors to a great many European readers for the first time and northern intellectuals responded by attempting to Latinize themselves. Johann Müller, born in Königsberg, called himself Regiomontanus after that regal summit. Philipp Schwarzert exchanged his black Germanic name for a black Greek pseudonym, Melanchthon. Christopher Schlüssel, whose surname means key, would become Father Christopher Clavius. The physician-alchemist whose family name was Hohenheim would call himself Paracelsus after the first-century Roman encyclopedist and doctor, Celsus. Koppernigk became Copernicus. Et al.

Our epicycle is now complete.

De Revolutionibus was delivered to a Nuremberg printer; and here, at Nuremberg, we meet the Lutheran priest Andreas Osiander.

Copernicus wrote to him, asking what sort of reception the book might expect.

Osiander replied that, first of all, the motions of planets as they appear to us may be explained by any of several theories, and ecclesiastic authorities perceived no harm in such speculation—provided the originator of a system in conflict with Church doctrine did not insist that his proposal was more than speculative. Therefore it might be wise to introduce the heliocentric theory in some such light.

Osiander wrote also to Rhaeticus: "The peripatetics and theologians will be readily placated if they hear that there can be different hypotheses. . . ."

But the astronomer, having resolved to publish, now became obdurate. He would neither disguise nor modify his position: the earth wheeled around the sun, there could be no question about it.

His book appeared with an anonymous preface implying that what followed should be treated as mere supposition.

This preface had been carefully drafted by Osiander, who refrained from signing it in order to give the impression that its author was Copernicus—thereby protecting Copernicus from a charge of heresy.

It is said that the first copy of *De Revolutionibus* was handed to the astronomer on his deathbed; he was then only half-conscious, unable to read his work, and died without knowing about the Judas preface. It is also said that he did read this preface and the shock hastened his death. Either account might be true, but there is a third possibility, supported by a letter from the Nuremberg printer which says in part: "Rhaeticus used to assert . . . that this Preface of Osiander's was clearly displeasing to Copernicus, and that he was more than a little irritated by it. . . ."

Hermann Kesten states that in May of 1542, a year before Copernicus died, he saw galley proofs of the first two pages and was not altogether pleased: "When he saw Osiander's arrogant forgery he fell into the most violent rage; his grief and fury may have aggravated his illness, for he had a hemorrhage followed by a paralysis of the right side and remained unconscious for several days."

In other words, although Copernicus knew exactly what Osiander had written he agreed to it. This would have been the wise thing to do, if wisdom and prudence are at times synonymous. Most of us in that situation would do as the astronomer did. Still, one would like to think he died without knowing.

Osiander had reason for concern; rumors were reproducing like fungus. In 1533, ten years before the book was printed, Pope Clement VII had asked his secretary to explain the ideas of Copernicus. And in 1539 the arch-Protestant Martin Luther said during one of his Table Talks: "Mention has been made of some new astrologer who wants to teach that the Earth moves around, not the firmament or heavens. . . . This fool seeks to overturn the whole art of astronomy."

The blistering remark sounds more emphatic in German: "*Der Narr will die gantze Kunst Astronomiae umkehren.*"

Luther's friend and collaborator, Melanchthon, also addressed a few words to the upstart Pole: "Our eyes bear witness against Copernicus, sensual perception speaks against him, the authority of the Bible speaks against him, and the one-thousand-year consensus of learned men. Therefore he is absurd."

John Calvin resorted to the ninety-third Psalm, which assures us that the Lord reigneth and is clothed with majesty. The Lord is clothed with strength wherewith He hath girded Himself. And the world also is established, that it cannot be moved. Calvin then asked—expecting no answer—who would venture to place the authority of Copernicus above that of the Holy Spirit.

Osiander seems to have feared the Catholic response more than that of his own Protestants, whom he understood somewhat better. Indeed there is a jovial undertone to Luther's remarks which suggests that he did not really care what Copernicus had in mind.

And perhaps because of Osiander's disarming preface the Catholics paid little attention. Cardinal Baronius remarked, with an undeniable trace of levity: "The Holy Spirit intended to teach us how to go to Heaven, not how the Heavens go."

But the insubordinate, disagreeable book survived mockery as well as neglect; it refused to wither, it refused to evaporate. And seventy-three years after publication *De Revolutionibus* was placed on the *Index librorum prohibitorum*. There it stood, if you like to keep track of such matters, until 1835.

What is odd, though, is that the preface, which was meant only to shield Copernicus, turned out to be a valid criticism of his theory. He did situate the sun instead of the earth at the center of things, but in other respects his mechanism was false. The planets, as we now know, do not orbit the sun in perfect circles. Copernicus assumed they did, which obliged him to manufacture forty-eight epicycles, eight more than Ptolemy needed. Not until Johannes Kepler went to work on the Copernican system did it become the truth. Only then, as Thomas Digges wrote, would this be recognized: "The sun like a king in the middest of all raigneth and geeveth lawes of motion to ye rest."

Digges, who was English, deserves a moment because in 1576 he published a translation of Copernicus, together with a diagram of the heliocentric system which he himself had drawn. Now, around this circular diagram occurs an astonishing inscription, and if you loosen the knots of Digges' sixteenth-century prose you will see why, because he soars beyond Copernicus, beyond the idea of a closed universe: "THIS ORBE OF STARRES FIXED INFINITELY UP EXTENDETH HIT SELF IN ALTITUDE SPHERICALLYE, AND THEREFORE IMMOVABLE THE PALLACE OF FOELITICTYE GARNISHED WITH PERPETUALL SHININGE GLORIOUS LIGHTES INNUMERABLE. FARR EX-

CELLINGE OUR SONNE BOTH IN QUANTITYE AND QUALITYE THE VERY COURT OF COELESTIALL ANGELLES. DEVOID OF GREEFE AND REPLENISHED WITH PERFITE ENDLESSE IOYE THE HABITACLE FOR THE ELECT." And on his diagram Thomas Digges drew stars outside the outermost circle so that his meaning could not be mistaken.

Incidentally, *De Revolutionibus* was not a best-seller. Being so controversial, how could it fail? Yet, commercially speaking, it flopped. The first edition of 1,000 copies never sold out, though you would have to mortgage a hotel to buy one of those copies today. The most popular astronomy book was by a certain Johannes de Sacrobosco, or John Holywood, which sounds more appropriate; Holywood's smash hit raced through fifty-nine editions.

But if that is true—if very few people read Copernicus—how did his obscure and faulty book transform the world? Nobody knows. Arthur Koestler suggests that ideas powerful enough to influence human thought do not act only on the conscious mind, but seep through to underlying strata which are indifferent to logical contradictions. Or, let us say, truly promising thoughts may not develop in the usual ground, but need different nourishment, like those tiny Japanese paper flowers that require a bowl of water in which to unfold and bloom.

If neither of those images suits you, my friend, go ahead and explain the paradox yourself.

Now, why some people should be celebrated beyond their worth and profit accordingly, such as John Holywood, while others obtain less credit than they deserve is another riddle. Ask passersby in the street what they know about Johannes Kepler. Nothing. Substitute Galileo or Newton or Copernicus and the name, at least, will be recognized. Which is not to suggest that these men are undeservedly famous; it is only that there have been a few, like Kepler, whose contributions have been of equivalent magnitude yet who remain unknown. And how displeasing, if you stop to think about it, that before we see one of history's supreme astronomers on a United States postage stamp we undoubtedly will see the face of a mendacious California politician, which could be interpreted as another instance of Gresham's Law.

Kepler's great stroke may not have been dramatic but it was necessary in order to comprehend the solar system. He demolished a belief held since the time of Pythagoras; he understood what his predecessor Copernicus had not, that the planets in spite of their serene and steady light behave erratically. This may seem no more consequential than a swallow in a barn, but it is deceptive.

Kepler probably was not the first to notice the erratic course of planets. An Arab who studied the sky above Toledo during the eleventh century suspected it, but he was ignored. Arzachel was the man's name. Or if you want to be pedantic: ibn-al-Zarqâla. And if you think Kepler is unknown in the street try ibn-al-Zarqâla. As to why his brilliant hypothesis was overlooked, we can't be sure. The times may have been out of joint. The Queen had a headache. A Christian horde was yowling at the gate. There's always a reason. Still, one feels dissatisfied and puzzled. Arzachel should get some credit.

Anyway, here is the first of three laws conceived for the Western world by Johannes Kepler:

"Planets move in elliptical orbits with the sun at one focal point."

His next two laws are equally soporific:

"The radius vector sweeps over equal areas in equal times."

"The square of a planet's period is proportional to the cube of the semimajor axis."

These laws just might be the reason nobody recognizes Kepler's name; they reek of the textbook, of airless classrooms in April, of theorems, conjugations, participles, and forgotten treaties, of blackboards, chalk, and musty teachers. Yet without them we still would be illustrating the solar system with a Rube Goldberg agglutination of epicycles.

Furthermore, that dreary second law about the sweep of the radius vector indicates that he had found his way to the edge of one of the greatest discoveries of all. Had he pushed ahead one more step he would be at least as famous as Isaac Newton. What Kepler's second law means is that a planet traveling an elliptical path around the sun travels faster as it approaches the sun. Yet why should it? Nobody, including Kepler, could explain this. He guessed that the sun must be responsible; somehow the sun controlled planetary motion: "What else is it but a magnetic emanation of the sun? But what is it that makes the planets excentric with regard to the sun, that compels them to come close to it and move away from it? Nothing else but a magnetic emanation from the planets themselves. . . ."

How very close that is, almost a century before Newton, to the concept of gravity.

And the implications, if reduced from the cosmic to the personal, are enough to make anybody restless. In other words, how often have I myself stopped an instant too soon?

Well, by Kepler's time—about ninety years after Copernicus—the Church was feeling less tolerant. His electric imagination, therefore, did not win many friends among the clergy. He was a devout Lutheran, yet certain aspects of Calvinism and Catholicism attracted him: "It hurts my heart that the three factions have miserably torn the truth to pieces between them, that I must collect the bits wherever I can find them, and put them together again. . . . My attitude, so help me God, is a Christian one; theirs, I know not what."

Naturally he was excommunicated. And in 1630, when he lay dying, the Protestants and Catholics both refused him Communion.

He was buried in the cemetery of Saint Peter outside Regensburg. His grave must have been marked, but three years later—after Swedish, German, and Bavarian troops employed the churchyard as a battlefield—it could not be located. At that hour, no doubt, the battle seemed important. Perhaps it was. Only now it seems less so than the grave of an individual who deduced how the planets turn and who dreamt of celestial music.

This last observation might be clarified. Like other scientists, Kepler at times grew wondrously unscientific. He convinced himself that the planets evoke melodies unheard by human ears, this indescribable concert being played for the benefit of a sublime entity whose soul inhabits the sun.

Then there were the multiplying moons. When he learned that Galileo had seen four moons orbiting Jupiter he decided that Mars would have two. Why two? Because it would be mathematically harmonious. Departing from the sun we find that Venus has no moon, but Earth has one. Therefore Mars, next in line, should have two, because Jupiter, which is next, has four. Obviously then, Saturn would have eight, Uranus sixteen, Neptune thirty-two, Pluto sixty-four, and so on for whatever bodies might be sweeping the latitudes beyond. Regrettably, it doesn't work out. At last count Jupiter had twelve, Uranus five, Neptune two, and we are uncertain about Pluto. Besides, Kepler ignored Mercury whose orbit swings closest to the sun.

He happened to be right about Mars, but that was coincidence.

With Jonathan Swift, though, we might be nearer clairvoyance than coincidence. Gulliver in the course of his fabulous travels visits an aerial island called Laputa whose astronomers have observed two Martian moons. Laputian scientists compute the orbit of the inner moon at ten hours, that of the outer moon at twenty-one hours and thirty minutes. They also calculate the distances of these moons from the planet: 12,600 miles and 21,000 miles.

Swift must have gotten his idea from Kepler, or possibly from a later book by a Capuchin monk, but neither the monk nor Kepler provided much detail. And nobody on Earth was able to see those moons until an ex-carpenter named Asaph Hall found them in 1877 with a big refracting telescope at the Naval Observatory outside Washington, D.C. Hall measured the periods of rotation: seven hours and thirty-nine minutes for the inner moon, thirty hours and eighteen minutes for the outer. He calculated that they were 5,820 miles and 14,615 miles from the planet.

How, then, with all the time and space in the universe to choose from, did Swift predict the rotational periods and distances so accurately? The average error in distance—over 6,000 miles—at first seems rather large, but not if you are talking about two tiny satellites of a planet fifty million miles from the earth. And these "moons" are mere particles—pinpricks of light in Hall's telescope—flying chunks of rock with estimated diameters of five and ten miles.

In Gulliver's day these satellites had not been discovered, yet Swift established their periods of rotation within a few hours and their distances within a few thousand miles. How? Various theories have been offered, but these are the most common:

He got hold of a telescope more powerful than any known to exist during the eighteenth century.

He was informed by ESP or some such process.

He was a Martian.

If you like none of these answers you are reduced to saying it was luck. Very well, call it a lucky guess. In any event, Jonathan Swift and the Martian moons is another epicycle; suppose we return to the central gears and wheels.

Kepler's baroque ideas—multiplying satellites, heavenly music and so forth—may have sprung from his personal afflictions. The man was a seventeenth-century Job. In childhood he endured boils, mange, smallpox, hemorrhoids, constant stomach trouble, and such bad eyesight that he occasionally saw his world doubled or quadrupled. Things did not improve as he grew up: "I suffered continually from skin ailments, often severe sores, often from the scabs of chronic putrid wounds in my feet which healed badly and kept breaking out again. On the middle finger of my right hand I had a worm, on the left a huge sore. . . . At Cupinga's I was offered union with a virgin; on New Year's Eve I achieved this with the greatest possible difficulty, experiencing the most acute pains of the bladder. . . ."

But instead of succumbing to these tribulations Kepler somehow utilized them to charge himself with furious energy; he grew fanatical in his pursuit of the winking mysteries overhead. And despite his natural ugliness the hopeless frog almost turned into a prince, darkly Mephistophelian with wiry linear features and a geometrically sculpted little beard.

Even so, life was difficult: "In me Saturn and the Sun work together in their sextile aspect; therefore my body is small, dry, knobby, my soul suspicious and timid; I reject honors, crouch over books, know no pleasures of life aside from science. All this corresponds to my preference for bitter and sharp tastes, for gnawing bones and hard bread. . . ."

He seems to have been impatient, sarcastic, cowardly, and stingy, and he almost never bathed. His disorderliness was alleged to be very great; his good qualities, if any, remarkably few. He married a miller's daughter named Barbara, already twice-widowed, a Chaucerian pilgrim "simple of mind and fat of body." The wedding took place April 27, 1597, "under a calamitous sky," and nine months later Frau Kepler's first child arrived, a boy with seriously deformed genitals. The astronomer, regarding his son, speaks of "a boiled turtle in its shell."

And there never was money enough. "My hungry stomach looks up like a little dog to its master who used to feed it."

Kepler's purgatory does not end. His wife despised him because he did not earn as much as her father. His brother was epileptic. And he himself, in addition to the authentic complaints, was a hypochondriac: "You ask me about my illness. It was a lingering fever which came from the gall and returned four times because I often committed dietary indiscretions. On May 29, my wife ruthlessly compelled me at last to wash my body; she thinks baths are dangerous. She plunged me in a basin full of very warm water; the warmth did not agree with me and gave me cramps in my bowels. . . . I think I am one of those whose gall bladder has an opening into the stomach; such people are usually short-lived."

Then, too, an age of witchcraft was bearing down and his mother Katharina stood accused. She is described as a hunchbacked little crone, swarthy, quarrelsome, and malicious, the archetypal hag. Ominous things happened while she was present. The twelve-year-old daughter of Jeorg Haller, a workman, was carrying bricks to the kiln when she felt a needlelike pain in one arm just as old Frau Kepler hobbled by. The schoolmaster Beutelspacher grew lame after chatting with her. The tailor Schmid's twin babies died after she rocked their cradle. Everyone knew she could glide through locked doors. And she had begged the sexton of Eltingen churchyard for her father's skull, saying she wished to have it silver-plated so that her son might use his grandfather's skull as a drinking goblet.

On August 7, 1620, the seventy-four-year-old woman—who had been living with her daughter—was seized, thrust into a linen chest, and carried from the house late at night. The weird abduction sounds familiar, reminding us of the Gestapo and of the fact that such men are always among us.

Kepler at this time was living in Austria, but when he heard from his sister that their mother had been imprisoned as a witch he hurried back to defend her. He found her locked in a stone cell, dressed in chains. She was about to be tortured. Kepler hired an attorney, Christoph Besold, and also worked on the case himself—searching out natural explanations for the apparently supernatural occurrences. He submitted a 128-page argument on her behalf, much of it written in his own hand, which just saved her from the stake.

So it becomes a little less absurd, considering his private calamities and the fetid atmosphere in which he worked, that he imagined celestial music.

The astronomer with whom Kepler is associated—Tycho or Tyge Brahe—was equally cracked, though of course there was a reason. There always is. He lost his nose. Not all of it, but quite a piece of it, enough to influence everything he said or did from then on; and we will return to Tycho Brahe's missing nose in a moment.

Brahe is linked to Kepler because they worked together for about a year at Benatky Castle near Prague. Kepler then packed his bag and left, very much displeased that Brahe treated him like an apprentice instead of a colleague.

"I found everything insecure," he wrote to a friend. "Tycho is a man with whom no one can live without exposing himself to the greatest indignities."

Brahe seems to have been puzzled by Kepler's dissatisfaction. He was twenty-five years older and he was famous as the Emperor Rudolph's personal astrologer-astronomer-mathematician. Apart from this, he had invited Kepler to stay at the castle. He therefore considered it natural that Kepler should be subordinate.

The quarrel may not have been Brahe's fault because Kepler subsequently apologized, but throughout his life Tycho Brahe was difficult company. When he was a student at Rostock University he got into an argument with one Manderup Parsbjerg about which of them was the better mathematician. The argument resumed several days or weeks later and was not decisively settled until a third confrontation when they whipped out their swords.

Just where this third encounter took place is disputed. Historians tend to be vague when they aren't sure. It occurred "out of doors," "in total darkness," or, romantically, "at midnight in a vacant house." But there's no doubt about the result: Manderup proved himself the superior mathematician by slicing away the bridge of Tycho's nose.

There is some question about the nature of the replacement, which was thought to be silver, or an alloy of gold and silver. It may have been painted. If indeed it was painted we would assume that Tycho selected an inconspicuous flesh tone. And one might, if one wishes, imagine him embellishing it with little blue and gold stars. Admittedly this sounds odd, though certainly no more so than a lady with a tattooed rump or a gentleman wearing a diamond in his teeth. But let it pass.

An etching dated 1586, when he was forty, shows Tycho dressed up like an Elizabethan sea dog in a lace ruff and lace cuffs and a huge cloak and a velvet hat, with a sommelier's chain around his neck and an ostentatious ring on his index finger. He is portly, almost puffy, with a Vandyke beard, and his nose looks unreal, as well it should. He must have kept the bridge in place with glue because he carried around a tiny box filled with some sort of gelatinous ointment, and in no portrait of him is there any sign of a strap.

You might think very few people would care about Tycho's nose after three centuries, but in 1901 the citizens of Prague were so nagged by curiosity that they dug him up. Lo and behold!—the metallic bridge had vanished.

Now, if we assume that somebody—let's say the mortician—pocketed this curious item, we are entitled to ask what became of it. Presumably it was melted. After all, that's not the kind of souvenir you want around the house. Although I once knew a man in Chicago who had an impressive collection of walrus and whale penises, which proves that just about anything will appeal to somebody. But let us assume that Tycho's baroque appendage was cast into negotiable form. Then who can say what coins were minted from it?—perhaps that old gold florin your grandmother was given on her wedding day.

There is another possibility. In 1901 a greenish stain typical of oxidized copper was observed on his nasal bone, which suggests, alas, that the replacement was neither gold nor silver, that Mother Nature gradually devoured it, and the mortician should not be slandered.

Enough speculation. Tycho's life both before and after the duel indicates that he, not Parsbjerg, was the troublemaker. Arrogant, conceited, avaricious, impatient, the typical son of an aristocrat, he seems to have understood quite early that most people were created inferior. He himself was studying Latin at the age of seven. Six years later, accompanied by a tutor named Vedel, he enrolled at Copenhagen University to study rhetoric and philosophy.

On August 21, 1560, he watched a solar eclipse. This eclipse had been predicted and the realization that such events could be foretold excited him. He bought a book of astronomical tables and for two thalers—talers, dalers, dollars—a copy of Ptolemy's *Almagest.*

After three years in Copenhagen he was sent to the University of Leipzig to study jurisprudence. Again he bought astronomical charts and books, as well as some instruments. He also bought a celestial globe about the size of an orange which he hid from his tutor, examining it late at night when Vedel was asleep.

He appears next at the University of Wittenberg, but only for a while. Plague broke out, so he moved to Rostock where the swift right hand of Manderup Parsbjerg shortened his face.

In 1570 he returned to Denmark because his father was dying. He might have stayed there, seduced by the easy life at Helsingborg Castle, but on November 11, 1572, heaven intervened. He witnessed a supernova:

"One evening when I was contemplating, as usual, the celestial vault, whose aspect was so familiar to me, I saw, with inexpressible amazement, near the zenith, in Cassiopeia, a radiant star of extraordinary magnitude. . . ." He concludes his description by saying with a deplorable lack of originality: "I could hardly believe my eyes."

He thought it miraculous, the greatest miracle since the beginning of the world. Or at least equal to those miracles attested by Scripture: Joshua commanding the sun to halt, and the face of the sun darkening when Christ was crucified. "For all philosophers agree, and facts clearly prove it to be the case, that in the ethereal region of the celestial world no change, in the way either of generation or corruption, takes place; but that the heavens and the celestial bodies in the heavens are without increase or diminution, and that they undergo no alteration. . . ."

His amazement seems justified because supernova are uncommon. Only four—possibly six—have turned up in our galaxy. The brightest was seen by Oriental astronomers on July 4, 1054, although the light reaching the earth that day had been en route for 6,000 years. Yang Wei-te, chief astrologer at the Sung court, prostrated himself before this luminous spectacle and wrote: "I have observed the appearance of a guest star." It could be seen not only at night but during the day for three weeks, and he forecast good times because it was yellow. Yellow was the Sung imperial color.

Astronomers today believe that the supernova so respectfully acknowledged by Yang Wei-te gleamed with a brilliance equal to half a billion suns. Had it been as near to us as the nearest star, Alpha Centauri, it would have been brighter than a full moon. It is now referred to as the Crab nebula in Taurus and still is visible through a telescope because the explosion has not ended. The nebula, which is a cloud of turbulent gas, continues to expand at a speed of sixty million miles a day.

This supernova was also registered by Indians of the southwestern United States who drew symbolic pictures of it. On a cliff near Zuñi, New Mexico, is a pictograph showing a cross with a crescent moon just beneath it to the right. A similar design was found on the wall of Navajo Canyon in Arizona. The argument that they represent the supernova is simple, but convincing: potsherds collected at these sites date from the eleventh century, and astronomers know that the star appeared just above and to the left of a crescent moon.

Medieval European intellectuals failed to report the guest star; they may have been too busy squabbling over neat theological distinctions.

By 1572, however, when Tycho's supernova materialized, Europe was ready. Stargazers across the continent and in England tried to determine just what it was. A German painter named Busch wrote two pamphlets about the cosmic display in which he maintained that it was created "by the ascension from Earth of human sins and wickedness, making a sort of gas which was then set on fire by the anger of God." This noxious gas, he continued, drifted down on people's heads, causing "all kinds of unpleasant phenomena such as diseases, sudden death, bad weather, and Frenchmen."

Tycho studiously observed the star. He fixed its position in the sky, just northwest of Cassiopeia's huge *W*, measured its brilliance against that of other stars, and charted the final diminution. He followed its progress for seventeen months. He also tried to establish the star's parallax—parallax being a change in the apparent direction of something when viewed from different points. Look at your wife with your right eye shut, then with your left eye shut, and she will appear to have moved slightly, which is her parallax.

The exploding star showed no parallax. This was a surprise because most people thought it must be extremely near the earth, closer than the moon. Brahe concluded that since the star showed no displacement it must be located on that remote celestial sphere which, according to Aristotle, was perpetually changeless. In other words, the infallible Greek—that supreme authority on just about everything—had to be wrong.

After much hesitation, because it seemed to him that writing for the public was undignified, he published *De Nova Stella*, a rather tasteless potpourri of letters, meteorological data, and astrological predictions. But *De Nova* did include twenty-seven pages of facts about the new star.

That same year be began living with Christine, who was a servant girl and/or a farmer's daughter. In any case she was not—socially speaking—a lady, and it has been suggested that he chose a lower-caste woman because of his unique nose. After "three winters," according to Danish law, they became man and wife, and they must have liked each other because they produced eight children.

Tycho's reputation at home increased speedily when the Danes learned that he was recognized abroad, which is the way it goes; and in 1576 King Frederik gave him the island of Hveen near Elsinore Castle on which to build an observatory. He was also granted money enough to build it however he pleased, and as landlord he would collect from every tenant and "servant of the Crown" on the island.

What he built was a Gothic complex protected by an eighteen-foot wall—an assemblage of turrets, spires, galleries, onion-shaped domes, gables, and balconies that might be described as an alliance between the Kremlin and the Copenhagen Glyptothek. It covered an acre of ground, and apart from the observatory there was a house for himself and his family, with sumptuously appointed rooms for distinguished guests, a library, an alchemical workshop, a paper mill, a printing press, servants' quarters, and a jail for Hveen citizens who got behind in the rent.

He named this singular growth Uraniborg. Its interior mechanism sounds like the work of da Vinci. Several rooms had running water pumped from a well in the basement. The printing press and paper mill were driven by water from a series of fish ponds. Hidden wires connected the banquet hall with the kitchen, enabling Tycho to evoke his servants by magic, and there were statues with concealed speaking tubes whose only purpose seems to be that they gave him a chance to terrify unsuspecting guests.

On the walls of Uraniborg hung portraits of history's eight supreme astronomers: Ptolemy, Hipparchus, Timocharis, al-Battani, King Alphonso of Castile, Copernicus, Tycho himself, and Tychonides—this last being Tycho's son and successor, who at that time had not been born.

Then there was a dwarf named Jeppe who crouched under the table during meals. Jeppe had the gift of second sight. If a citizen of Hveen fell sick the dwarf invariably foretold whether he would die or recover. Once he exclaimed: "Behold how your men wash themselves in the sea"—whereupon Tycho dispatched a servant to the roof. The servant returned quickly, saying he had seen a capsized boat and two men dripping wet on the shore.

The only thing Uraniborg lacked was Tycho's pet elk, so he ordered the animal brought from his family estate at Knudstrup, but along the road the groom who was leading it decided to stay overnight at Landskroner Castle. Now what happened at Landskroner Castle sounds absurd. We are told that Tycho's elk climbed a flight of steps, entered a vacant apartment, got drunk on beer, then fell downstairs and broke a leg. However implausible this sounds, it must be true; nobody could make up such a story.

Uraniborg with all those gadgets may have impressed visitors, but the sixteenth-century peasants of Hveen failed to look upon their lord with respect and affection. The jail especially did not charm them. So, as years went by, while Tycho enjoyed himself at the observatory, at the laboratory, at the printing press, and at his magic dining table, a rustic muttering could be heard.

King Frederik died of booze in 1588. The new king, Christian IV, did not much care for stargazers; he thought the money Tycho was collecting and spending at Hveen could be better spent by the navy.

The wizard of Uraniborg, whose nature does not seem to have improved since the day he crossed swords with Manderup, finally packed up his globes and quadrants and notebooks and objets d'art and led his family and his private retainers out of Denmark into Germany. Apparently he thought the new king would ask him to come back. When this did not happen he wrote several obsequious letters to Christian, which made the situation worse. At last, dismayed and bewildered, he tried to express himself in rhetorical poems:

Denmark, have I deserved this ingratitude of yours?
Have I, my native land, ever knowingly harmed you?
Is not the fault you find with me after all one and the same
With the magnificent glory which through me alone you have gained?

This kind of verse did not win King Christian's approval either, so he moved to the court of Emperor Rudolph in Prague.

Rudolph, who could not surround himself with enough artists and scientists, installed Tycho and his entourage at Benatky Castle. But the humiliation of being squeezed out of Denmark must have weakened him; he died two years later, October 24, 1601, from some kind of gastrointestinal malfunction. Although long before his death Kepler had remarked: "The feebleness of old age was upon him." It sounds as though he was ninety, instead of fifty-four.

On the last night, delirious, he asked the same question several times: "Ne frustra vixisse videar?" Have I lived in vain?

Uraniborg disappeared. The peasants stole whatever was worth stealing as soon as their lord was on the road, and Christian saw no reason to preserve the extravagant buildings. Now, on the site of the fabulous workshop, there is only a grassy depression and some trees.

Tycho Brahe is not considered a genius. He made just one fruitful discovery and it doesn't sound like much: he realized that precise, continuous data was needed. Today this is such a scientific commonplace that we can't imagine a time when it was thought unnecessary. But because of this concept, and because he kept detailed records of his observations, his disgruntled associate Johannes Kepler was able to formulate those three great and tedious laws.

In Italy during this period lived another of the giants Newton was talking about—a chunky, rheumatic, red-headed individual with somewhat brutish features: Galileo. And how curious that three eminent astronomers should arrive almost simultaneously: Brahe in 1546, Galileo in 1564, Kepler in 1571. Marlowe and Shakespeare were born the same year as Galileo, proving beyond doubt a favorable planetary conjunction; though it's true, unfortunately, that 1564 also marked the deaths of Vesalius, Calvin, and Michelangelo.

At this same time lived two imaginative Dutchmen, Zacharias Janssen and Hans Lippershey. One or the other, or perhaps a Neapolitan named della Porta, invented the telescope. Janssen, a spectacles maker, is alleged to have seen a little telescope belonging to a traveler and copied it, but the story is vague. Lippershey's claim a few years later is documented. At any rate Galileo soon heard about the looking-device, constructed one for himself, and began inspecting the stars instead of women in the next block. He would have been better off with his telescope fixed in a horizontal position because what he found overhead disturbed the Church enormously and brought him to his knees before the Inquisition.

The sequence of events usually is regarded as inevitable. Given one nettlesome intellect, given a despotic religion, given a powerful new instrument and the mysterious sky at night, what would you expect?

Koestler, for one, disagrees: "The conflict between Church and Galileo . . . was not in the nature of a fatal collision between opposite philosophies of existence, which was bound to occur sooner or later, but rather a clash of individual temperaments aggravated by unlucky coincidences."

However the facts should be interpreted, Galileo did certainly strike at the sacred idea of an earth-centered universe when he observed Jupiter's four moons. Now, four moons on a Las Vegas slot machine wins the entire casino but in seventeenth-century Italy all it meant was trouble. Giovanni Magini, professor of mathematics at the University of Padua, declared that he would have Jupiter's satellites extirpated from the sky. Rome's leading mathematician, Father Clavius, peered through Galileo's diabolic instrument and insisted he could not see any moons. The professor of philosophy at Padua refused even to look.

And in December of that year, 1610, Galileo perceived that Venus underwent phases—from sickle to full disc—which was proof that it revolved around the sun. He made no public announcement of this; instead he contrived a baffling anagram:

"Haec immatura a me iam frustra leguntur o.y."

His purpose was to establish himself as the discoverer, but at the same time conceal what he had learned so that nobody else might profit by it. He filed this anagram with Giuliano de Medici, whom he trusted and who would be a powerful witness on his behalf.

Properly arranged the letters read:

"Cynthiae figuras aemulatur Mater Amorum."

Cynthia being the moon—a generally understood poetic metaphor—whose figures or shapes were emulated by Venus, Mother of Love.

This kind of business was not uncommon. The Dutch astronomer Huygens, for instance, protected an important discovery by writing in his book *Systema Saturnium:* "aaaaaaa ccccc d eeeee g h iiiiiii llll mm nnnnnnnnn oooo pp q rr s ttttt uuuuu."

A cryptographer might deduce that the letters should be organized as follows: "Annulo cingitur, tenui plano, nusquam cohaerente, ad eclipticam inclinato." In other words, obviously, Saturn is encircled by a flat ring inclined to the ecliptic and nowhere touching the planet.

Galileo himself decoded the Venus message somewhat later, and this revelation—that Venus sailed around the sun—brought him one step closer to the stake. Such telescopic observations might be real, said the professor of philosophy at Pisa, but it was heresy to suggest that the sun could be the center of the universe.

Galileo next antagonized the Jesuits. Father Scheiner, together with a young assistant named Cysat, had been studying the sky above Ingolstadt in Bavaria. In 1612 they reported sunspots. Cysat reputedly noticed them first and exclaimed, "Either the sun sheddeth tears or she is blemished!"

Father Scheiner's superior was not pleased by this news: "I have read all the works of Aristotle several times from beginning to end, and I assure you that I have not found anything in them which could be what you are telling me. Go, my son, and calm yourself. I assure you that what you took to be spots on the Sun are only flaws in your glasses or in your eyes."

But the spots did exist and Scheiner felt entitled to some credit.

It is now thought that four observers were aware of sunspots at that time: Fabricius in Holland, Harriot in England, Scheiner-Cysat in Bavaria, and Galileo. Who saw them first is an academic point, but the abrasive Italian loudly claimed them for himself and then proceeded to disparage Father Scheiner. It is almost as though he wanted to challenge the full strength and majesty of the Church.

Cardinal Dini cautioned him: "One may write freely as long as one keeps out of the sacristy."

Cardinal Bellarmine wrote to a priest who supported Galileo: "To affirm that the Sun is really fixed in the center of the Heavens, and merely turns upon itself without traveling from east to west, and that the Earth is situated in the third sphere and revolves very swiftly about the Sun, is a very dangerous thing, not only because it irritates all the theologians and scholastic philosophers, but also because it injures our holy faith and makes the sacred Scriptures false."

Pope Paul then spoke up: Galileo was admonished for the publication of heretical ideas.

This ominous charge worried him, as well it might; still he persisted, commenting in a letter: "I believe there is no greater hatred in the world than the hatred of ignorance for knowledge."

And before long he managed to irritate the next pope, Urban VIII.

On June 22, 1633, after ten weeks of trial, Galileo was "vehemently suspected of heresy" for having advocated Copernicus' theory of a moving earth "which is false and contrary to the sacred and divine Scriptures."

He knelt, a tired old man wearing the white shirt of a penitent, in the Dominican monastery of Santa Maria Sopra Minerva, and confessed under threat of torture that he abjured, cursed, and detested his previous belief: "I, Galileo, son of the late Vincenzo Galilei, Florentine, aged seventy years, arraigned personally before this tribunal and kneeling before you, Most Eminent and Reverend Lord Cardinals Inquisitors-General against heretical pravity throughout the entire Christian commonwealth, having before my eyes and touching with my hands the Holy Gospels, swear that I have always believed, do believe, and by God's help will in the future believe all that is held, preached, and taught. . . ."

He was confined to his villa Il Giojello in Arcetri, near Florence, not far from the convent where his two daughters lived. Until 1639, by which time he was blind, no visitors were allowed without permission of the Holy Office. After that he had all the company he wanted, such guests as Milton, Descartes, and Hobbes.

Milton reflected with little pleasure upon this visit to Italy: "I have sat among their learned men, and been counted happy to be born in such a place of philosophic freedom as they supposed England was, while they themselves did nothing but bemoan the servile condition into which learning amongst them was brought. . . . There it was that I found and visited the famous Galileo, grown old, a prisoner of the Inquisition for thinking in Astronomy otherwise than the Franciscan and Dominican licencers of thought."

Kepler, to some slight degree, may have been responsible for this. Galileo wrote to him on August 4, 1597, thanking him for a book and remarking on the fate of Copernicus who was jeered and mocked by an ignorant public. "I have written many direct and indirect arguments for the Copernican view, but until now I have not dared to publish them. . . . I would dare to come forward publicly with my views if there were more people of your way of thinking. As this is not the case, I shall refrain."

Kepler replied on October 13, saying that he himself would rather be criticized by one intelligent man than be praised by the masses. After the great work Copernicus had initiated, he went on, would it not be appropriate for those who understood the truth to join forces? "Be of good cheer," he suggested, "and come out publicly."

How much Galileo was influenced by this advice is impossible to estimate, but he could not have forgotten it. At last he did venture from his closet, and for revealing unacceptable facts the Inquisition drove him to his knees.

In 1642, when the crusty old heretic died, Grand Duke Ferdinand proposed a monument in his honor. Urban VIII objected, claiming that such a monument would insult papal dignity.

According to legend Galileo muttered "E pur si muove!" as he stood up after confessing to the Inquisitors, meaning that in spite of his formal abjuration he knew the earth did move. Scholars insist this is a fable. Just the same, he might have said it, even if nobody was close enough to hear. The story appeared first in *The Italian Library* by Giuseppe Baretti, published in 1757. However, there is a painting of the trial by Murillo, circa 1650, which includes those words, so the story goes back at least that far.

The other Galileo legend—dropping cannonballs from the tower of Pisa—makes scholars grind their teeth. It started when he began to question Aristotle: "Aristotle says: 'An iron ball of 100 pounds, falling from a height of 100 cubits, reaches the ground before a one-pound ball has fallen a single cubit.'"

Aristotle said no such thing, but that's irrelevant; Galileo thought he had, and suspected the statement was untrue, and set out to demonstrate its untruth. What Aristotle did say about moving bodies was less specific and depends on how you translate Greek. For instance, *rhopé* can mean speed or momentum or trend or tendency or impulse.

But the quarrel revolves around the experiment. Did Galileo, or did he not, drop anything from the tower?

Thiel: "His doubts led him to the famous climb up the leaning tower, from which he dropped balls of all sorts."

Ronan: "Unfortunately the story seems untrue, dramatic and to the point though it is: Galileo *may* have dropped weights in this fashion but he probably gave no public demonstration. . . ."

Dickson: "What Galileo did was to let the balls roll down an incline, which in principle is the same as letting them drop vertically. . . ."

Hawkins: "On several occasions he dropped weights from the leaning tower. . . ."

Moore: "He did not, incidentally, drop any stones off the Leaning Tower of Pisa; this is a story of the Canute-and-the-Waves type."

Ley: "Wohlwill was perfectly correct in denying that 'the event' described by popularizers ever took place. But that does not mean that Galileo did not drop things from the Campanile . . ."

One of Galileo's pupils, Vincenzio Viviani, wrote that the master had disproved Aristotle's statement: ". . . demonstrating this with repeated experiments from the height of the Campanile at Pisa in the presence of the other teachers and philosophers, and the whole assembly of students. . . ."

Columbia Encyclopedia: ". . . the story has been disputed."

So he did or he didn't. Choose your scholar. Myself, I'll take Viviani because he brings to mind our recent campus spectaculars. You can practically see a bearded young teacher haranguing the crowd from the top of that old grain silo, whipping his students into a frenzy with scurrilous remarks about Aristotle and rolling cannonballs off the parapet while an FBI agent in a cassock sniffs the wind for heresy.

Well, not only was an autocratic Church shocked by the outrageous Florentine; he seems to have distressed the most sophisticated minds of the day. Johannes Kepler himself exclaimed again and again, with stark anguish, that the idea of infinity was unthinkable.

Galileo died the year Newton was born, which is either a meaningless coincidence or indisputable proof of reincarnation, according to your outlook. He, Newton, arrived on Christmas Day, a farmer's son, so unimpressive that he was not expected to survive. He lasted eighty-four years—lonely, arrogant, irascible—beyond doubt one of the most perceptive men who ever lived. He coordinated the work of that eccentric triumvirate Brahe-Kepler-Galileo and gave us a view of the universe that worked elegantly for three centuries—until the discovery of quasars, black holes, and so forth, when Newtonian laws had to be supplemented by Einsteinian laws.

He also invented the reflecting telescope—the Dutch device had been a refractor—and he created fluxions, which sounds like an indisposition suffered by eighteenth-century ladies, maybe a prelude to the vapors, but is in fact the science of calculus. The German mathematician-philosopher Leibniz invented calculus at exactly the same time, a development as strange as Wallace and Darwin independently and simultaneously comprehending evolution. In brief it's said that, with the possible exception of Darwin, or Wallace-Darwin, or maybe Copernicus, Newton has influenced our view of life more than any other man.

The Swiss physicist Bernoulli once sent the most redoubtable mathematicians of Europe a problem which he challenged any of them to solve within six months. Why he failed to notify the English genius is rather odd, but apparently Newton only learned of it six months later when Bernoulli renewed the challenge. Newton was at this time in poor health, physically and mentally, yet he solved the problem before going to bed. The next day, without identifying himself, he submitted his answer to the Royal Academy. And we are told that Bernoulli, upon receiving the answer, exclaimed "Ex unque leonem!" One knows the lion by its claws.

Leibniz must have felt a bit scratched by this performance because a number of years later he, too, concocted a puzzle—directing it especially at Newton who was then in his seventies:

Find the orthogonal trajectories of any one-parameter family of curves.

Sir Isaac was handed this exercise at five o'clock one evening. Naturally he picked it apart before blowing out the lamp.

Yet this same man, whose intellect may never have been equaled, argued that the Egyptian pyramids were built in 808, 824, and 838 B.C., and that in 989 B.C. the art of carpentry was invented by Daedalus. He also thought Bohemian alchemists were transmuting iron into copper—though any high school chemistry student can explain what happens when iron is combined with copper vitriol. It does make you wonder.

Life's little amenities failed to seduce him, even after he had been appointed Master of the Mint and his income jumped from 60 to 500 pounds. By ordinary standards his house was plain—even austere—except for crimson curtains and crimson upholstery. Most of us could tolerate one or the other, but that combination sounds excessive, practically Byzantine. Crimson, crimson everywhere. Just thinking about it is enough to turn your stomach.

He lived without women. When he was a boy he pursued the village apothecary's stepdaughter so passionately that several years later they became engaged. Luckily for science, perhaps, something went wrong and she married a Mr. Vincent. Never again did young Isaac approach a female.

Nor was he fatally attracted to such bourgeois temptations as playing cards and drinking rum. During undergraduate days at Cambridge he closely watched expenses. His account book does register an occasional session at the pub, but only two gambling losses. Two. Just two. That was enough gambling. And you begin to wonder if he never—ever—lost his head.

He squandered no time on music, art, or dancing. He didn't keep a pet. As for rich food, vintage wine, stylish garments—well, our twentieth-century genius Albert Einstein was less than celebrated as a fashion plate and somebody once asked what governed his taste in clothes. Said Einstein: "Indifference." Sir Isaac evidently felt the same. The abbé Alari, having been invited to supper at Newton's home, later confided that the meal was "detestable." The great man seems to have been satisfied with a leg of mutton, a glass of cider, a game of chess, and time enough to harvest that prodigious brain.

Years after his death a retired officer of the Royal Engineers who was writing a biography of him turned up an old document: *True and Perfect Inventory of all and Singular the Goods Chattels of Sir Isaac Newton*. It listed 362 books in folio, 477 in quarto, 1,057 smaller books, and " above one hundred weight of pamphlets." There were a few histories, a few books on commerce and travel. Everything else was science.

A longtime friend and associate, Dr. Edmond Halley—the astronomer for whom the comet is named—once essayed a little joke about some theological or scientific matter and Newton rebuked him. The subject of the joke is unimportant; what matters is Newton's austerity. And those Edgar Allan Poe curtains! But such irregular patterns must be expected, of course, if you know anything about human behavior.

Still, you can't help liking the man, no matter how sick you might be of the falling apple story. They say that when he was a boy on the farm he was very good at making kites, lanterns, and water clocks; and during a storm, instead of leading the cows to the barn, he was observed jumping against the wind in order to measure its force. And when he was president of the Royal Society he caused a newly designed cannon to be rejected because, he said, "This diabolic instrument will only multiply mass killing." How times change.

Ever since he deduced the existence of gravity we have been accumulating splinters of confirmation, which now and again become unexpectedly relevant. Newton's celebrated law states that all things in the universe, from the heavenly bodies to the least particles, hold some attraction for one another. Now, the strength of this attraction is in direct proportion to the product of the masses of the bodies concerned and varies inversely as the square of the distance between them. Very well, you say, but what has that to do with me? In personal terms it means this much: two people standing at arm's length from one another experience an attraction that has been calculated at one-millionth of an ounce. The implications, as you see, are stupendous.

Newton's friend Halley, a natural man, had no trouble understanding this; he fell in love, which Newton never did—unless you count that interlude of madness with the apothecary's daughter. Halley fell in love with Miss Mary Tooke, whom he married, with whom he spent fifty-five years "happily and in great contentment."

Halley seems not only to have recognized but to have taken pleasure in the genius of Newton, though that must have been difficult for a man as outstanding as himself. Indeed, it was while trying to relieve Newton of some tedious work concerning the paths of comets that Dr. Halley made the discovery for which he himself is famous.

"I am more and more confirmed that we have seen that comet now three times since ye year of 1531," he wrote to Newton.

Somewhat later he was able to present the Royal Society with a table showing the orbits of twenty-four comets.

This sounds like the magnum opus of a dilettante, but Halley's table meant that comets were predictable. Consequently they shouldn't be frightening; and we know how erratically people behave when an unfamiliar light streams overhead. For instance, we are told by the great surgeon Ambroise Paré that in 1528 a hideous apparition bloomed in the sky above France: ". . . so horrible and dreadful . . . some died of fear, others fell sick. . . ." It was the color of blood, Paré insists. It was shaped like a human arm holding a sword, while on either side could be seen axes, knives, and monstrous faces with beards and tangled hair.

Now, we take it for granted that Ambroise Paré was a man with reasonably good eyesight. We assume furthermore that no such phenomenon as he describes could possibly have materialized in the sky. So it's a little troubling. If Ambroise Paré could misrepresent a cloud to this extent—well then, consider what panic must have addled the wits of ordinary men. Some died of fear. Others fell sick. Sinister tidings, my friend.

And in 1664 when a comet was pointed out to Alphonsus VI of Portugal—not to be confused with Alphonso of Castile who hung in Tycho's hall of fame—when Alphonsus of Portugal beheld this luminous visitor he rushed across the palace grounds threatening it with a pistol.

Theologians, one might suppose, would display better sense than common folk or kings. Do you think so? Listen. Bishop Gislebert of Lisieux, having reflected upon a radiant shower of meteorites in 1095, interpreted it as a signal calling for a militant invasion of the East; God must be urging young men to join the First Crusade.

The bishop's interpretation sounds positively Etruscan, but let it go.

Now consider the following:

On the night of November 12, 1883, a Carolina cotton planter was awakened by appeals for mercy and shrieks of horror from the plantation Negroes. While lying in bed wondering about the cause, he tells us, "I heard a faint voice near the door calling my name. I arose, and taking my sword, stood at the door. At this moment I heard the same voice beseeching me to rise, saying, 'Oh, my God! the world is on fire!' I then opened the door. . . . The scene was truly awful; for never did rain fall much thicker than the meteors fell toward the earth,—east, west, north, and south, it was the same!"

In other words, the annual Leonid shower had arrived, brighter than usual.

Planets, too, are capable of raising blisters on the brain. Once in a while they coalesce—which is to say, occasionally they form clusters because they travel at different speeds in different orbits, thereby overtaking each other. And when this happens, so that from Earth the planets appear to have congregated, God Himself has trouble predicting how His inconstant children will react. For example, in the year 1186 an awesome sevenfold conjunction was observed. What else could this foretell but some incomprehensible calamity? As a result thousands of underground shelters were built, which should remind you of more recent alarums. And the Byzantine emperor Isaac II ordered his palace windows boarded up. And the Archbishop of Canterbury declared a three-day fast.

You might feel entitled to ask what occurred. If anything.

Let me put it like this. At that time the chronicles of York were kept by a rather droll clerk who wrote: "We have experienced nothing but the tempest emitted from the pulpit by His Eminence."

In 1524 another portentous conjunction developed. Being in the sign of the Fish it advised humanity to prepare for a disastrous flood.

President Auriol of Toulouse University therefore recommended the immediate construction of an ark. The Margrave of Brandenburg shepherded weeping members of his court to the top of a little hill in Berlin. Et cetera.

Again we might ask what happened. Well, that particular year was noted throughout Europe for unusually cool temperatures and frequent rains. Whether this fulfilled the prophecy and justified the hysterics—who can say? It depends on your evaluation of singular events.

Here's one more. Dr. Halley's table of orbits accurately forecast the brilliant comet of 1773, and because of this scientific accomplishment nobody got upset when the thing materialized. True or false?

Listen. So many people thought the world must be coming to an end in 1773 that clergymen sold seats in Paradise for the twentieth of May, that being the date it was expected to strike and demolish the earth. Skeptics who asked how these tickets had been acquired, and to whom they should be presented, were denounced as atheists.

What next?

Suppose we let a couple of generations go by.

Biela's comet approaches. It, too, is on schedule, which means the universe has not slipped a cog. So far so good. But here we meet Dr. Heinrich Wilhelm Olbers who—after some narrow calculating—predicts that the glowing tail of this comet will brush the earth. And with that announcement Dr. Olbers absolutely electrified his fellow men. Artists sketched the forthcoming holocaust, journalists described it. Millions would die. Cities would burn. Very possibly everybody on Earth would suffocate or be poisoned by noxious gases.

And if you think we have grown more sophisticated, my friend, read your paper the next time a planetary conjunction, a shower of meteorites, or a handsome comet favors us. You will learn that in some farmhouse or on some green Mississippi hilltop a tight knot of zealots, disposing of all earthly possessions, has gathered to await the Day of Judgment.

Many remarkable things may be explained, but why we are so faintly instructed by the past does not seem to be among them.

Well, one thinks of Dr. Halley—assuming one does think of him—as somebody who, like Biela, contrived to get his name in front of a comet. Other than that he may be remembered as Sir Isaac Newton's devoted amanuensis: a polite, timid, modest fellow. But this fails to coincide with seventeenth-century memoirs. We are told that Edmond Halley sopped up brandy like an old sea captain. And in 1691 when he applied for the job of professor of astronomy at Oxford the authorities refused even to consider him, partly because John Flamsteed, the first Astronomer Royal of Britain, feared that he might "corrupt the youth of the University with his lewd discourse." As anyone with any sense knows, such a thing is impossible, but Flamsteed's remark does bring the man into focus. Actually it brings both men into focus.

Then one fine day Czar Peter came to town. Ultimately he would be known as Peter the Great, but in those days he was a young prince touring western Europe more or less incognito to study industrial methods. He had worked awhile as a ship's carpenter in Holland and now he was in England to study boat building. He leased Sayes Court, a property owned by the diarist John Evelyn—who subsequently put in a heavy claim for breakage. Among other outrages, we are informed, the youthful czar mutilated Evelyn's bowling green, destroyed fruit trees, and had himself carried in a wheelbarrow back and forth through the holly hedge. All of which is irrelevant. Somehow, perhaps at a pub, young Peter got acquainted with Edmond Halley. They became friends. They ate together, talked science until late at night, merrily addressed themselves to the keg, and threw a number of undignified parties.

Halley's portrait gives no indication that he was such a bon vivant. He appears to be a discreet eighteenth-century gentleman. His periwig has not slid askew, his mouth is controlled, his eyes are large, dark, and lustrous. The impression is of intelligence and sobriety. He resembles his critic Flamsteed, although Flamsteed does not look refined.

Halley did at last make it to Oxford and we have no evidence that his students were corrupted. However, he was teaching geometry instead of astronomy, which perhaps moderated his lewd discourse. In any event, during the Oxford years he established himself as a distinguished astronomer, quite apart from Newton's blinding radiance. He suggested that those indistinct fields of light visible through a telescope might be clouds of gas, which some of them are. He thought the lovely shimmering polar aurora might be associated with earth's magnetic field, which it is. He argued that the universe could be infinite—a matter still troubling us. And he proposed a way to measure the distance from the earth to the sun.

This could be accomplished, he said, when Venus passed across the sun's disc. Observations would have to be made simultaneously from different points on earth.

Now it so happens that Venus does not very often travel between us and the sun. She makes the trip twice within a period of eight years, then there is a lapse of more than a century. It may not sound reasonable, but that's how things are.

The next transit of Venus would not occur until June 6, 1761, at which time Halley would be 105 years old and therefore unlikely to appreciate it; but he lobbied insistently for his idea, knowing that if you want the government to finance something you must plan well ahead. And it came about after much discussion by various European bigwigs, all of whom wanted to know how far away the sun was, because of course this might have military significance—it came about finally, years after Dr. Halley died, that several expeditions were dispatched to observe the transit of Venus.

The French detachment consisted of one astronomer. Guillaume Joseph Hyacinthe Jean Baptiste Le Gentil de La Galaisière was not a lucky man. Pondicherry, at that time a French enclave, was his destination, so in March of 1760 he sailed from Brest. Good students of the human circus will recall that a war was in progress—the Seven Years' War—and one fine day our hero was quite naturally troubled to perceive a British fleet on the horizon. His ship escaped, though, and reached Mauritius where Le Gentil learned that Pondicherry was besieged. However, a French fleet was about to embark with the intention of liberating Pondicherry and he obtained permission to sail on one of the gunboats.

Scarcely had he settled himself in his new quarters when a hurricane struck. He almost drowned. And because the expedition would need to be reorganized—in other words, postponed—it occurred to him that perhaps he would be able to observe the transit of Venus from Batavia. He therefore wrote to the French Academy in Paris and explained his plan.

While waiting for an answer he was afflicted with a disgusting malady known to many tourists.

Up again, still without word from Paris, he decided that after all he should go to Pondicherry. And because the troopship *La Sylphide* was just about to depart he hurried aboard.

As they were approaching Pondicherry the captain of *La Sylphide* received word that it had surrendered to the British. Who but a fool proceeds on a useless mission? *La Sylphide*'s captain wisely reversed course.

June 6, 1761, proved to be an excellent day for viewing and Le Gentil could see a little black dot on the face of the sun, but with *La Sylphide* rocking over the Indian Ocean he could not take measurements.

Once again in Mauritius he attempted to book passage home.

Unfortunately, no ships were going to France.

Le Gentil was not a man to waste time: he resolved to study the geography, geology, and folklore of the island.

In those days, of course, very few ships bound for Europe put in at Mauritius, and at last M. Le Gentil decided that since he had come this far he might as well wait for the 1769 transit. He therefore began to make preparations. And it occurred to him that possibly he could get a better view from Manila—4,000 miles east—so he wrote to Paris explaining his desire to change the program. He requested the academy to obtain permission from Spain, which governed Manila.

Then a Spanish warship bound for Manila put in at Mauritius. Le Gentil, having heard nothing from the academy, persuaded the Spanish captain to take him along.

In August of 1766 he reached Manila where at last, three years after the war ended, a letter from Paris caught up with him. Pondicherry no longer was besieged. The academy would prefer that he stick to the original plan.

M. Le Gentil, that obedient servant of science, packed up his instruments and sailed once more, although he left a telescope with a missionary in Manila and showed him how to operate it when the great day arrived.

The British, who now ruled Pondicherry, welcomed the French astronomer. They provided everything he asked for. They even constructed a little observatory in the ruins of the old fort. And here, with everything arranged, he settled down to wait.

On the eve of the big event he was too excited to sleep; he remained beside his telescope all night. It had been calculated that Venus would touch the sun's rim at 7:00 A.M.

At 6:50 A.M. in a clear sky one small cloud materialized. As though upon command it drifted over Le Gentil's observatory.

There it stopped.

In his diary he wrote: "Such is the fate which often awaits astronomers. I have wandered almost 10,000 leagues over great stretches of sea, exiling myself from my home country, only to watch a fatal cloud which came to disport itself in front of the sun at the exact moment of my observations, robbing me of the fruit of my troubles and labors."

And because Venus would not again visit the sun for more than a century Le Gentil started back to Paris. He arrived after a difficult journey, having been gone almost twelve years.

You might think that after so many tribulations Providence would look favorably upon M. Le Gentil de La Galaisière. Wrong. Such a long time had elapsed since anybody had heard from him that the courts adjudged him dead. His estate was in the process of liquidation, and it is said that he did not have an easy job recovering his property.

Later he heard from the missionary. The sky above Manila that day was perfect.

Le Gentil cannot be blamed for the fact that in all those years he accomplished nothing. If this malignant cloud had not blown over Pondicherry he would have lived to see his name wedged into the astronomy books as a contributor to the determination of the position of the planet Venus during the solar transit of June 3, 1769. Well, these things happen.

It's good to learn that eventually M. Le Gentil fell in love, got married, and became the father of a charming daughter.

Meanwhile, investigation of the solar system continued. Mercury, Venus, Mars, Jupiter, and Saturn, all being obvious and obviously traveling through the constellations, had long since been identified as planets. There seemed to be nothing else revolving around the sun.

Then one brisk evening in 1781 the organist of the Octagon Chapel at Bath, the German-born Mr. William Herschel, who resembled one of Hogarth's massive squires and whose hobby was stargazing, noticed something in the constellation of Taurus:

"On Tuesday the 13th of March, between ten and eleven in the evening, while I was examining the small stars in the Neighbourhood of H Geminorum . . ."

Organist Herschel—whose status can be judged by the fact that when he first stepped into the limelight his name was spelled Herthel, Mersthel, and Herrschel—Mr. Herschel thought he had spotted a comet in H Geminorum. Later observations by professional astronomers proved the traveling speck of light to be a planet. King George III, much impressed, created a new job—King's Astronomer—for the organist of Bath, quite a plum for one who started his career as an oboist in the band of the Hanoverian Foot Guards. And because the discoverer of a celestial object is entitled to name it, Herschel proposed "Georgium Sidus" in honor of his benefactor. The Royal Society disapproved of this because it violated classical tradition, and scientists on the Continent objected for political reasons, so the new member of the system was named after the sky god Uranus.

Herschel had not been the first to see this planet, nor the first to catalogue it. Flamsteed observed it in 1690 but thought he was looking at a dim star; in fact he noticed Uranus on five occasions and charted the position each time. Lemonnier in France observed it thirteen times without realizing what it was.

Beyond Uranus lies Neptune, which was located before anybody saw it. This sounds implausible, if not impossible, but the explanation shows how thoughtfully men had begun to plot the firmament.

Between 1800 and 1820 Uranus did not perform quite as expected. It seemed to be lagging. Several mathematicians attacked this puzzle, using Newton's gravitational theory, and concluded that some unknown object must be acting as a brake. They then plotted this object's hypothetical orbit. A young mathematician named John Couch Adams was the first to complete the work, which surprised nobody familiar with the situation because Adams was rather good at mathematics. During final examinations at Cambridge he accumulated twice as many marks as the runner-up—a certain Bashford who was himself no slouch, subsequently being appointed to a chair of mathematics. There was, indeed, a wider gap between the scores of Adams and Bashford than between Bashford and the lowest man on the scale, which tells you a bit about John Couch Adams.

This nascent genius called on Sir George Airy of the Greenwich Observatory, but Sir George had been summoned to France because of the "Cherbourg breakwater investigation"—whatever that was.

Adams went home, continued work on the problem, revised his calculations, and tried once more.

Sir George chanced to be out. He was attending a meeting of the Railway Gauge Commission.

Adams tried again. Sir George was at supper; he could not be disturbed. Adams seems to have become a trifle weary. He had brought along a paper concerning the hypothetical object and he gave this to a servant.

In due course Sir George got around to reading Adams' paper but the calculations failed to arouse him. Then he got a letter from a French mathematician, Urbain J. J. Leverrier, whose arithmetic was almost identical. Sir George now requested a Cambridge astronomer named Challis to look into the business.

Challis could not get started for several weeks, and then he did not concentrate on the area pointed out by Adams and Leverrier. If he had, he undoubtedly would have charted the planet.

In Paris, meanwhile, Leverrier grew impatient. He already was disgusted with the somnolence of French astronomers; now it appeared that the British were no more alert. So he wrote to Professor Johann Galle at the Berlin Observatory: "Train your telescope on the point of the ecliptic in the constellation of Aquarius (longitude 326°) and within a degree of that point you will find a new planet, looking like a 9th magnitude star and showing a small disk."

This letter was delivered to Professor Galle at home on his birthday. That evening he went to the observatory where he asked to use the telescope.

"Tun wir doch den Herren in Paris den Gefallen," said the director. Let us accommodate the French gentlemen.

Galle located Neptune within an hour.

Challis may possibly have seen it before news of Galle's discovery reached England because he mentioned to a friend named Kingsley, with whom he was having supper, that he thought he had noticed a disc among the stars. Kingsley was so excited that he suggested they visit the observatory at once. Challis agreed, but Mrs. Challis prevailed upon them to have a cup of tea before starting out, the night being rather chilly. And by the time they finished tea the sky had grown overcast. And before it cleared up there came tidings from Johann Galle.

M. Leverrier was pleased when told that his theoretical object actually existed, but he never bothered to look at it. The mathematics of the problem interested him, the reality did not. One suspects that Leverrier and Newton would have enjoyed a glass of cider together, and perhaps a rousing game of chess.

Those phlegmatic villains Airy and Challis live forever in a kind of scientific purgatory; Adams now shares a marble niche with Leverrier and Galle. So the mills do grind, neither rapidly nor invariably to the right degree, but one shouldn't ask too much.

Soon after Neptune had been bracketed Leverrier theorized that there could be yet another planet. Various astronomers were thinking the same, and presently they determined that Neptune, like Uranus, was dragging his feet. Thus the lord of darkness, Pluto, stood revealed—smaller even than the earth, so small that it, or he, may be only an escaped satellite of Neptune, cruising in a slow elliptical orbit four billion miles from the sun.

Yet here, again, discrepancies in the predicted course hinted at something beyond.

Just where, one may ask, does our solar system end?

The most celebrated planet always has been Mars because of its sanguine color. Greeks called it Ares, which derives from a word that means vengeance or disaster or killing. Persians called it Pahlavani Siphir, the celestial warrior. Chaldeans named it for the god of battle, Nergal. And the earliest symbolic representation consists of a spear and a shield. So the military implications grow like red roots into our half-remembered past.

Even when people were able to look at Mars through a telescope they continued to see it through the filter of imagination. In 1664 the Jesuit

Father Kircher reported: "The surface is extremely hard, rough, sooty, and sulphurous, but incombustible, sweating tar and naphtha, surrounded by poisonous vapors. From mountain gorges brownish flames burst forth with a frightful stench; the seas are viscous sulphurous mud." Clearly a parable of summer in New York.

The idea that it might be inhabited is not new, nor is the desire to communicate with Martians. In the nineteenth century many schemes were debated, not only by imaginative hod carriers but by such eminent personages as the director of the Vienna Observatory, Joseph von Littrow, and the mathematician Karl Friedrich Gauss.

Dig a geometric pattern of canals in the Sahara, fill these canals with water, pour kerosene on top, and set the network afire.

Plant a stupendous triangle of wheat in Siberia—wheat because of its uniform color.

Build a complex of mirrors to reflect Earth's sunlight.

An ingenious Frenchman, Charles Cros, proposed that a gigantic mirror be used as a magnifying glass to focus the sun's heat, thereby making it possible to etch blazing words on the Martian surface. M. Cros did not specify what words should be written, though undoubtedly they would be French; nor did he suggest what to do if, in response, enormous Martian words suddenly began to scorch the Luxembourg Gardens.

One evening in 1877 when the seeing was good, as astronomers say, and Mars spun close to the earth—less than thirty-five million miles away—Giovanni Schiaparelli peered through his 8.5-inch refractor at the Milan Observatory and noticed on the Martian disc a pattern of lines which he referred to as *canali*, meaning channels.

What happened next can be ascribed either to sloppy translation or a deliberate attempt by journalists to sell newspapers. The *canali* became canals, implying artificial construction. Canals also imply irrigation. Ergo: not only were there intelligent beings on Mars, they must be progressive farmers. Probably Socialists, but never mind; the important thing was to find out what they were up to. An engineer calculated how much energy would be needed to pump water from the Martian polar cap to its equator and people began asking where the capital city might be located.

Schiaparelli seems to have been dismayed by the excitement:

"It is not necessary to suppose them the work of intelligent beings, and notwithstanding the almost geometrical appearance of all of their system, we are now inclined to believe them to be produced by the evolution of the planet, just as on earth we have the English Channel and the Channel of Mozambique."

Nobody listened to these cautionary words. A dialogue with Mars was expected to begin at any moment.

Madame Clara Goguet, a rich widow, promised 100,000 gold francs "à celui qui aura trouvé le moyen de communiquer avec un astre autre que la planète Mars." Conversation with Mars being practically a fait accompli, in Madame's opinion, the prize should be awarded for something truly difficult: a method of communicating with more distant beings.

At this point we meet Percival Lowell of the Lowells, who dressed like a banker, whose brother Abbott was president of Harvard, and whose sister was cigar-smoking verse-writing Amy. The existence of life on Mars seemed to him quite possible and when he heard that Schiaparelli's eyesight was failing he built an observatory near Flagstaff, Arizona, in order to continue the investigation.

One does not associate the Lowells of Massachusetts with Flagstaff, a place where a cowboy is not apt to remove his Stetson while having lunch, but the air was clean and dry in 1894 just as it is today. Lowell's observatory stands on a hill west of town. The neat buildings—if you except one monstrous silver bubble—suggest a Baptist summer retreat, the paths between them irregularly decorated with old pinecones as hard as hand grenades. The astronomer, who died in 1916, has been entombed near his telescope under a Persian blue dome, and almost every day the desert wind rushes around his vault with soft insistence.

Guided by Schiaparelli's map, Lowell and his associate William Pickering had no trouble identifying the canals, which radiated from dark regions into lighter areas like the spokes of a wheel. Calculations indicated that they were at least twenty miles wide, so it was thought they might be strips of irrigated land with an aqueduct in the center. Some of these spokes appeared to be double, which might mean that one of them functioned as a return conduit. Thus the water could circulate to and from the Pole. Yet how could water flow across a relatively flat surface for 2,500 miles? The Martians must have contrived some sort of pumping apparatus.

"Irrigation, unscientifically conducted, would not give us such truly wonderful mathematical fitness. . . . A mind of no mean order would seem to have presided over the system we see—a mind certainly of considerably more comprehensiveness than that which presides over the various departments of our own public works."

It's hard to tell, reading that last sentence, whether Lowell was attempting a touch of academic humor.

Because of the pumping stations and the double-barreled canals he is easily ridiculed, but he was not just an odd millionaire. Mars obsessed him, causing him to believe what he wished to believe, yet he did carefully observe the planet for a long time—eleven years—accumulating a formidable amount of data. If only he had not insisted on the public works. Eleven years of reputable work almost forgotten because of one spectacular mistake. But sometimes that happens. Who cares about Casey's batting average?

In any event, Lowell was neither the first nor the last scientist to visit Wonderland. Consider old William Herschel, King George's private eye. Look at Herschel's credits. The man was internationally recognized for his study of nebulae and for his great star catalogue. He charted not only Uranus but the sixth and seventh satellites of Saturn. His research into the nature of double stars, which are called binaries, demonstrated that these very distant systems are held together by gravitation and that they revolve about a common center. All of which should emphasize Herschel's scientific respectability as well as his analytic mind. Yet this lucid, sober gentleman managed to persuade himself that civilized beings were living on the surface of the sun.

Then we have the German selenographer, J. H. Schröter, who inspected the moon night after night for thirty years—until 1813 when French soldiers, who had nothing particular in mind, burned his drawings and his books and smashed his equipment. Schröter thought he had detected industrial activity on the moon. He believed he had seen factories with smokestacks. And so impressed by his observations were French astronomers that they petitioned Louis XVI for a telescope 10,000 feet long which would enable them to take a closer look.

How can it be? How is it possible? Schröter, Herschel, Lowell, the astronomers of King Louis, and any number of others—these must all have been intelligent, judicious men.

There's no answer. No answer except that we live in a world of drifting shadows.

Today, squinting backward, we feel remotely amused by such preposterous misapprehensions. We feel smug. Given those circumstances, we believe, we would have done better. But this is a slippery conceit. Given our present universe of quasars, pulsars, black holes, white dwarfs, neutrinos, photons, and so forth, only a grinning thumping fool would interpret the news with much assurance.

Try neutrinos. This is not a breakfast food. A neutrino is a ghost, a moment of spin, a particle of nothingness formed at the core of a star. It has no electrical charge and no substance, yet it flies through everything with the greatest of ease. It flies through space, it flies through earth. Our bodies are riddled by neutrinos: perhaps 50,000 a second flit through us. Perhaps many times that number. Now, we assume that in the sinister basement laboratories of places like MIT and the University of California there are solid lead walls designed to stop mysterious particles from escaping and killing everybody, and we imagine these walls to be a couple of inches thick, maybe a foot thick. Such walls naturally would stop neutrinos. You think so? Listen.

Neutrinos dance through lead walls the way mosquitos dance through a chicken-wire fence. Of course the analogy isn't strictly accurate, but never mind. Theoretically a lead wall could stop a neutrino, and physicists very much would like to stop one at least long enough to skin it. The problem is the wall. For example, the yellow star Arcturus is about forty light-years away, which, as most people know, means that light traveling from Arcturus at 186,000 miles a second takes forty years to get here. Now listen. A lead wall forty light years thick would almost stop a neutrino. Not quite, but almost. Obviously this makes no sense. Theoretically, you may argue, it does. Yes. All right. But still, something like that is inconceivable.

Pulsars. A pulsar is a source of radio waves emanating from whatever is left of a massive stellar explosion. You might think all stellar explosions are massive, as indeed they are, but everything is relative. Some are more so than others. Our sun, less than a million miles in diameter, is too little to explode. One fine day six billion years hence the sun will expand until it becomes a red giant, enlarging until its surface touches the planet Mercury. By this time the oceans on earth will have boiled away, most of the rocks will have melted, and the atmosphere will have dissipated—which should eliminate the shysters, quacks, generals, and politicians. Next the sun will shrivel and change color, becoming a white dwarf. At last it will lose heat and color and become an invisible cinder coasting around the nucleus of the galaxy until the entire galaxy explodes.

Is that comprehensible? Can you understand it? If not, we might return to the relatively simple business of pulsars.

The core of these pulsing apples is magically small. Some are thought to be no more than a mile in diameter and they blink on and off as frequently as thirty times a second. As for weight, a chunk the size of a matchbox, if you put it down gently, would break through the crust of the earth and keep right on falling toward the center. Anybody can visualize a falling matchbox; the problem begins when we try to imagine material of such density. Expressed another way, a rock the size of a sugar cube would weigh more than a fleet of battleships. And this, we are told, is not science fiction.

That should take care of pulsars but the show is not over. The next act—provided we have a large pulsar—is, quite literally, a sensation. It manages to leave the universe. Nothing remains, only a black hole.

En route to this condition of negativeness—of turning into a hole—the material contracts further. Time slows down. A second becomes eternity. Space has no meaning. And so extreme is the pull of gravity that light itself is trapped. A ray of light could no more escape from one of these collapsing stars than a man could pitch a baseball into the stratosphere. Nor could any sort of electromagnetic radiation escape. And the only evidence that there used to be something where finally there is nothing would be the presence of gravity.

A spaceship cruising near a black hole would be swallowed. The earth itself, if it sailed past a good-sized hole, would be stretched out of shape like silly putty and inexorably devoured.

A miniature black hole may have been responsible for the 1908 Siberian cataclysm which annihilated two villages, barbecued a herd of reindeer, and flattened a forest. Witnesses agreed that something brighter than the sun arched over the southern horizon and hurtled northward. Then, said one who was near the site of the explosion, the ground rose and fell like a wave in the sea and a column of fire spiraled upward. Passengers on the Trans-Siberian express saw it; but the engineer, no doubt conscientiously watching the tracks ahead, only felt a tremendous shock and thought his train had exploded, so he braked to a stop. Whatever the thing was—black hole or meteorite—it had buried itself in the earth 300 miles away. The shock wave registered on microbarographs in England.

Many years later Professor Leonid Kulik of the Russian Academy of Science located the site: "The whole region of the river basins Kimchu and Khushmo is covered with windfallen trees lying fanwise in a circle, their tops pointing outward. . . . The peat marshes of this region are deformed and the whole place bears evidence of an immense catastrophe. . . ."

Another huge explosion in Siberia, in 1947, undoubtedly was caused by a meteorite because twenty-three tons of meteoric material have been collected. Russian scientists think it originally weighed seventy tons. In this case, too, an object as bright as the sun streaked across the sky, thousands of trees were crushed, and a fiery column boiled from the earth. In 1947, you may recall, the Russians and the Americans stood tiptoe to tiptoe, each waiting for the other to make one violent move before retaliating with a storm of nuclear bombs. Even now, after all these years, one doesn't like to think about what would have happened if that meteorite had curled over the horizon and exploded not in Siberia but in the suburbs of Moscow or Washington.

At any rate, because of similarities between these two Siberian spectaculars, both may have been caused by meteorites. However, not a single meteor fragment has been found in the Kimchu-Khushmo basin, which is strange. Consequently, the unthinkable is being thought not only by your basic science-fiction huckster but by serious academic types. That 1908 explosion, they argue, might have been created by a black hole no larger than a virus.

Opponents argue that a black hole would then have passed completely through the earth and emerged in the North Atlantic where it would have caused a tidal wave. No such wave was recorded.

Well then, suppose we try something else. How about a nuclear-powered vehicle from Messier 33? Say it burned a bearing and crashed. Yet this should have left a measurable degree of radiation.

Perhaps a small comet hit Siberia—your average little comet of no significance with a diameter of several hundred feet, weighing a million tons. Or let's imagine a fragment from a larger mass such as Encke's comet. The argument for this theory is persuasive. In 1965 a fearful concussion shook southwestern Canada. Witnesses described a fiery object approaching, illuminating the sky for hundreds of miles before the impact. Scientists who flew over that area in a helicopter could find no trace of a meteorite, but they did observe and collect some black dust; and this dust had the same composition as a particular sort of meteorite which, many astronomers believe, occurs in the heads of comets. All of which may sound irrelevant until we learn that people who saw the 1907 Siberian blast also reported black dust.

Sooner or later the lab technicians—our white-frocked alchemists—will deliver a verdict. Spaceship, comet, black hole, or something still more alarming. But that's not the point. The point is that, regardless of what blew up in a Russian river basin seventy years ago, we've come a long way from Isaac Newton physics.

If you studied physics in high school you were taught that matter and/or energy could not be destroyed.

Well, maybe. Now they are suggesting that such laws apply only to the observable universe. The next question, as you might guess, is what other universe could there be?

Listen. Here is what they are telling us about these incredible black holes—these "puckers in the fabric of space." They may be conduits through time. Say we dove into one: we might emerge not merely in a different universe but during another epoch.

Believe such absurdities if you want to. Myself, I'm dubious.

Inevitably there is talk of trying to build a black hole. Why? Because the energy potential is stupefying. The Pentagon, of course, would dearly love to have a few, or a warehouseful, and just about here we should note that Einstein's curious equation led to Hiroshima. Say a manufactured black hole on the order of 1,600 tons were to escape from the U.S. Army's Dugway Proving Ground—that place in Utah where several thousand sheep abruptly died of natural causes. All right, what would happen? This probably won't surprise you, but the thing would drop out of sight, so to speak: it would begin eating the earth. And nothing could stop it.

The trouble with knowledge is that, contrary to what we expect, as understanding increases so does ignorance.

If you'd like something more formidable than black holes, try quasars.

Nobody is certain what they are, as you might deduce from the word itself which is a contraction of "quasi-stellar"—meaning an apparently starlike object. Astrophysicists seem perplexed by the information they have been gathering from quasars because some of these objects emit 100 times more energy than the largest galaxies in the universe. In other words, to generate that amount of energy a quasar must annihilate a mass equivalent to one billion suns every second.

Suppose we try it again: a good quasar shines as brightly as 100 galaxies of 100 billion suns each. Furthermore, during a period of weeks or months the light flashes like a traffic signal. One of these things, 3C–345 —the 345th item in Cambridge Observatory's third catalogue—registered a fluctuation of 50 percent within twenty days. At present such data is unintelligible. But we do know that the objects radiating this light must be located at the edge of the observable universe several billion light-years distant, and they are not very big.

Unless, of course, the so-called "red shift" could be duplicated by other means, in which case they may not be as bright as they appear to be, nor as distant. The red shift is simple. If light shifts toward the rear of the spectrum the object emitting that light is receding, just as you determine whether the cops are coming or going by the pitch of the siren.

Now, statistics can be interpreted in various ways to provide various answers; all that seems undeniable is that quasi-stellar objects exist, or else we are being confounded by a superlative magician. And if they do exist, unless there has been a gross misinterpretation of the facts, quasars must be drawing energy from some source or by some method about which our physicists know absolutely nothing.

Certain theorists have suggested that they could be ports of entry to our universe, just as black holes could be ports of exit.

They could be galaxies in the paroxysm of birth.

Of course there's always a chance that whatever they are, they no longer are; they may long since have winked out. But if indeed they are billions of light-years distant then we are looking billions of years backward in time.

One further aspect of the great quasar controversy should be mentioned. Radio astronomers at the big dish in California's Mojave Desert have found indications that quasar components may be flying apart at speeds exceeding the speed of light, which contradicts the law that nothing travels faster than light.

So tell me, if you can, confronted by a sky filled with quasars and multiple universes, where time has lost significance, what constitutes reason?

In words that we all understand, how do you grasp the wind?

Not long after Neil Armstrong went lumbering across the face of the moon I happened to be in New Orleans, and I happened to visit the city art museum while an exhibit of wood and tin sculpture by an old self-taught black man named David Butler was on display. A brochure published by the museum showed him standing in his backyard, unmistakably at peace with the universe, dressed in a comfortable sweater and a soiled felt hat which he probably had worn all day every day for at least ten years.

According to the brochure he was born in 1898 in Saint Mary Parish in the town of Good Hope, Louisiana. He was the eldest of eight children. His father was a carpenter, and his mother—when she could salvage a little time for herself—participated in neighborhood religious activities.

He built roads, mowed grass, and worked at the sawmill until a few years ago when he was injured and partly disabled. Since then he has depended on a government check. His check arrives the first of each month at a nearby post office, and after cashing it he fills a paper bag with candy and trinkets which he distributes to children he meets along the way. The neighbors used to think he was peculiar, but now that his art has been recognized they are proud of him.

His favorite subjects are dogs, snakes, rabbits, ducks, skunks, roosters, peacocks, alligators, sheep, fish, and so on; but occasionally he will construct a flying elephant, a dinosaur, a sea serpent, or possibly a mermaid. Sometimes he does arrows, stars, hearts, or mysterious abstract symbols. Or he may reproduce a familiar biblical scene: the wise men bearing gifts.

Ideas come to him while he lies in bed and he sketches them with chalk on old sheets of tin roofing. Then, with a nail punch, a hammer, and a knife, he cuts out various shapes which he wires together. Next he attaches light bulbs, bottle caps, reflector buttons, brass bells, plastic toys, umbrella handles, or whatever else seems appropriate. Usually he paints his creations black and silver, but once in a while he will paint them red, white, and blue out of respect for the American flag.

Accompanying the exhibit of David Butler's work was a documentary that had been filmed at his home. And as the camera slowly spiraled around this world of painted tin, whose features he had perceived while lying dreamily on his bed, he was asked what he thought about the astronauts' trip.

The interview went like this, more or less, partly in his soft black Louisiana dialect:

Aw, they ain't nobody on the moon.

You say those men weren't on the moon?

Wasn't on the moon, naw.

But you saw them, didn't you? Didn't you see them on television?

I seed them, yeah. Aw yeah. My grandson, he got a TV. Come git me, say he want me to see the mens on the moon. Aw yeah. I seed the picture. But wasn't nobody on the moon, naw.

Well, how do you explain that?

Do it in the stu-dio. Tha's how they do it. Make ev'body think they's lookin' at the moon. Fix it up in the stu-dio. Ev'body say "Whooee! Jes' look there! Walkin' round on the moon! What you think bout that?" Naw. Naw. It's a il-lusion. What they call a il-lusion.

You're telling me they weren't actually there? It was a trick? We never went to the moon?

Wasn't nothin' but a trick. Make folks think they's seed the mens up there, yeah. Tha's all. A trick, yeah.

But why? Why would anybody go to all that trouble to trick us?

Aw, sometime they do that. Jes' do it. Yeah. Yeah. Dunno why. I 'spect you have to aks them. Have to aks them folks in the stu-dio. But wasn't never no mens on the moon. Naw.

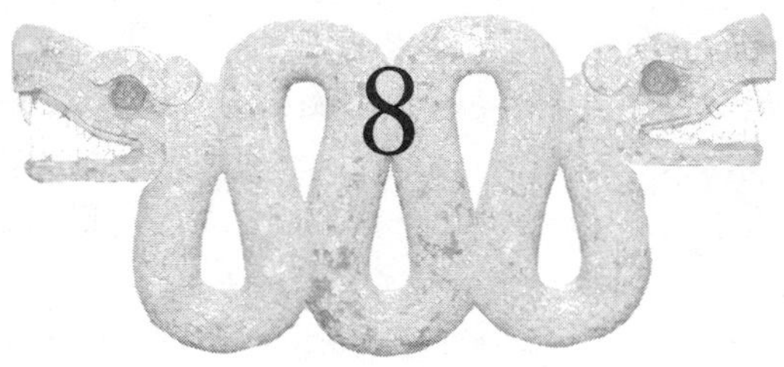

8

Various Tourists

In 1939, when Richard Halliburton tried to cross the Pacific in a Chinese junk, I was a fourteen-year-old stamp collector. Never doubting that he would make it, I paid something like $1.50 to have him deliver a commemorative envelope. It seems to me that he was supposed to initial the envelope, or hand-cancel the stamp, or otherwise authenticate each letter he was carrying. I may be wrong, it's been a while; but I clearly remember how I felt when I heard that the junk was overdue. I felt annoyed and resentful. I wanted my commemorative envelope. And when, finally, there could be no doubt that the junk was lost at sea I felt I had been swindled. I was nominally sorry for the people on the junk and I spent a little time wondering what happened, but I could not get over feeling peevish that my envelope was not going to arrive. In fact I thought there might be a chance the junk would be found and the cargo rescued. I remember being uncomfortable with this attitude, nevertheless it was so; Halliburton's life, I could not deny, meant less to me than a letter he was carrying.

Now, having had some years to reflect upon it, I find that still I am not proud of my reaction; but I have concluded also that I am no more inhuman than most. A trifle, perhaps, if you insist. But this isn't the point. The point is that when Halliburton vanished I realized for the first time that certain people do not travel the way most of us travel; not only do they sometimes choose odd vehicles, they take dangerous and unusual trips for incomprehensible reasons.

I don't think I wondered why he wanted to cross the Pacific in a tiny boat. He did such things. He climbed the Matterhorn and swam the Hellespont and slept beside the Taj Mahal and so on. That was Richard Halliburton. It was why everybody, boys especially, knew his name. *The Royal Road to Romance* was one of our classics, along with *Kidnapped*, *White Fang*, *The Call of the Wild*, and some unforgettable epics by Zane Grey which I have forgotten. So his trip made sense; it was altogether logical that he would set out on an utterly insane voyage across the world's largest ocean in a boat designed for sailing up and down the coast.

He himself had no doubts. In a letter to his parents dated September 10, 1938, he wrote: "Dad, if I could talk to you about the junk trip, I'm sure you would lose all your hesitation over it. Never was an expedition so carefully worked out for safety measures. I've a wonderful captain and engine and engineer. . . ."

Two weeks later he wrote: "The name? I chose that long ago—the *Sea Dragon*. On the day of launching, the prettiest Chinese girl whom I can find will break a bottle of rice wine on the *Sea Dragon*'s nose. And as the junk slides down the ways we'll beat gongs and shoot off firecrackers, in proper Chinese fashion, to drive away the demons of storm and shipwreck. . . . We'll leave China early in January and reach Treasure Island—God willing—the middle of March."

December 12, 1938: "I have complete faith in the captain and the engineer, and feel certain that we'll arrive without the slightest mishap—except a lot of seasickness."

January 1, 1939: "I've lost none of my enthusiasm, and none of my confidence."

In a newspaper article he described how the ship was painted:

> The hull is a brilliant Chinese red, edged at the rail with bands of white and gold. The "glance" of the eyes is black. On either side of the poop a Chinese artist has painted a ferocious red and yellow dragon twenty feet

long, not counting the curves! Our foresail has been dyed yellow; the mizzensail, vermilion. . . . On the *Sea Dragon*'s stern, the central section is brilliant with a huge painting of a phoenix—the Chinese good-luck bird.

We'll be twelve aboard, all American: the captain, engineer, radio-man, seven seamen including myself, a cook and a cabinboy. And because one solitary mascot would make the total thirteen, which superstitious seamen regard with horror, we're taking along *two* mascots—a pair of white Chinese kittens. This means that the *Sea Dragon* will be responsible for twelve souls and (counting the cats) thirty lives.

In late January came the shakedown cruise. He notified his parents that there were a few defects to be corrected, and that the junk sailed slowly, very deep in the water. He did not sound concerned.

Early in February the *Sea Dragon* left Hong Kong.

Two days out during a storm one of the crewmen fell down a hatch and broke an ankle. Another ruptured himself. Halliburton ordered the captain, John Welch, to return to port.

This is his account of the false start: "We turned up the coast of China, as the peak above Hongkong faded behind us, as a warm twilight came, as a huge moon rose out of the sea. The northeast monsoon, which, on nine days out of ten at this season would have been blowing a gale against us, had faded to a pleasant starboard breeze. . . . The *Sea Dragon*, as we wanted it to be, as we had labored hard to make it, had turned into a fantasy of a ship, a picture of a dream-junk from some ancient Chinese painting, a poetry-ship devoid of weight and substance, gliding with bright-hued sails across a silver ocean to a magic land."

On the second day, however, things looked less poetic. Black clouds swirled overhead. Waves began to mount. The radio aerial was ripped loose. Everything not fastened down was tossed about. The messboy lay in his bunk half dead from seasickness. The auxiliary engine was turned on but because of heavy seas it was necessary to close the hatch, with the result that fumes from the newly painted tanks and bulkheads almost suffocated everybody.

"At six o'clock on the second afternoon we caught sight of a lighthouse on the China coast. At six o'clock in the morning the same lighthouse was still in the same place. We had not gained an inch."

Bearded, exhausted, and dejected, they sailed into Hong Kong harbor on the sixth day. The injured crew members were taken to a hospital, then another collapsed with appendicitis, and the messboy resigned, calling the trip six days of terror.

Halliburton decided to add a fin keel because the *Sea Dragon* rolled heavily. He expected to have this done and new crew members signed up by the end of the week.

Two weeks later he was still in Hong Kong, exasperated but optimistic.

"Mother and Dad: One more—one last—goodbye letter. We sail, again, in a few hours—far more seaworthy than before. The delay has been heart breaking, but worth it in added safety. . . . All our leaks have been plugged, and the hull tarred. Our fin-keel will keep us from rolling—so we'll be dry, comfortable and even-keeled. . . . So goodbye again. I'll radio you every few days, so you can enjoy and follow the voyage with me. Think of it as wonderful sport, and not as something hazardous and foolish."

On March 5, 1939, he left Hong Kong.

Eight days out he radioed: 1200 MILES AT SEA ALLS WELL

On March 19 he sent word that they expected to reach Midway Island by April 5 and would not be stopping at Honolulu.

This message was heard on March 24: CAPTAIN JOHN WELCH OF THE SEADRAGON TO LINER PRESIDENT COOLIDGE SOUTHERLY GALES RAIN SQUALLS LEE RAIL UNDER WATER WET BUNKS HARDTACK BULLY BEEF HAVING WONDERFUL TIME WISH YOU WERE HERE INSTEAD OF ME

The next day Halliburton's parents were told that there had been no further radio contact. "Well," his mother said, "that's it. It's all over. It's the end."

Captain Charles Jokstad, master of the liner *President Pierce*, had inspected the *Sea Dragon* in Hong Kong at Halliburton's request. Jokstad said later, "I had the awful feeling that I would never see that young man again, and I urged him not to attempt the voyage. It is my guess that the rudder snapped off in a heavy following sea, the ship broached-to in the trough, the masts went out and she broke up—probably in minutes."

Halliburton seems to have been the last great traveler. Eventually somebody may circumnavigate the world in a canoe, but it won't be the same. Now and then an eccentric in a totally inappropriate vehicle does get across the Pacific, or the Atlantic, or survives some other formidable passage, but it reminds us more of Niagara Falls in a barrel than of that sensual urge which Anatole France called "un long désir."

A number of Victorian ladies were gripped by that urge. Isabella Bird Bishop. Marianne North. Fanny Bullock Workman. May French Sheldon. Kate Marsden. Mary Kingsley. Annie Taylor. To read of their adventures leaves one feeling incredulous and puny. To look at those nineteenth-century photographs—Isabella about to inspect a Chinese village, buttoned up to the neck and wearing a pith helmet, indomitable, serene, and dumpy, posing beside a tripod camera taller than herself—well, nobody who sees that picture is going to forget Isabella Bird Bishop. Or Fanny Bullock Workman high in the Himalayas, standing truculently beside an ice ax thrust into the snow, stoutly displaying a placard headlined VOTES FOR WOMEN. Kate Marsden en route to Siberia, dressed in a coat big enough for the Cardiff Giant. Mary Kingsley, looking remarkably like Dr. Livingstone, being poled across the Ogowé River in a dugout.

And those prodigious adventurers whose names we know, who couldn't rest because of that long desire. Magellan. Columbus. Marco Polo. Ibn Batuta. Hsüan-tsang. Captain Cook. There's no end to the list, of course, because gradually it descends from such legendary individuals to ourselves when, as children, obsessed by that same urge, we got permission to sleep in the backyard.

The first of these compulsive tourists about whom we know anything is a Greek from Marseilles, Massilia it was then called, by name Pytheas—a geographer and astronomer of no small reputation. If we reach back further, beyond Pytheas, we find just what we should expect: footsteps growing less and less distinct, often obliterated, so that we must settle for allusion, reference, and conjecture. We have no idea what half-mad transients passed through Europe or Africa or Asia 5,000 years ago, though there must have been a good many, and each presumably had a name and various in-laws, and worried about snakes and alligators and avalanches just as explorers worry about such matters today. Still, some awful anxiety kept those anonymous travelers traveling: there was always a mountain or a river in the distance.

We do know of a few generals who predate Pytheas, because their expeditions are documented; but they went where they went for obvious reasons. Besides, they had thousands of companions. It is the singular person, inexplicably drawn from familiar comforts toward a nebulous goal, lured often enough to death—it is he, or she, whose peregrinations can never be thoroughly understood, who is worth noticing.

In regard to Pytheas, scholars quibble about his route. And because his own account of the trip has been lost we can only reconstruct it from various sources: long-dead writers, some of whom were very nearly his contemporaries, while others depended in turn on previous authorities. That is to say, what you believe about his tremendous voyage depends on whom you've read.

This much does seem clear. He was born in Massilia not quite 400 years before Christ and was about fifty when he set out to visit the Tin Islands—the Cornish peninsula of Britain, which was thought to be a cluster of islands. Probably he was commissioned by a group of Massiliot businessmen, because in those days Carthage controlled the Straits of Gibraltar and thus controlled sea trade outside the Mediterranean. The businessmen of Massilia, being businessmen, naturally wanted a piece of whatever might be outside—all of it, if possible. They knew about those misty isles to the north and the adjacent mainland, and knew that besides tin there was amber to be found along the coasts, and somewhere in that faraway land there must be gold. So it is thought that these merchants commissioned Pytheas to explore the situation, to find out what the British savages wanted and what they might give in exchange.

It would seem, therefore, that be undertook the trip for commercial reasons. But he was essentially a student of the natural world rather than an employee of the commercial world, and when you read his report—filtered though it is through other sensibilities—you can only conclude that Pytheas, like Halliburton, left home mostly to see what he could see.

For example, he was curious about the tides, and the deep estuaries of Britain would be a wonderful place to study this phenomenon. He suspected that the moon, of all things, had something to do with this long ebb and flow, an idea that his countrymen found hilarious. And it is too bad we don't know how he felt about being mocked, whether it pained him or exasperated him, or whether he knew how to ignore fools. What he wanted to study in addition to the tides can only be surmised; he may have wanted to map the northern constellations, examine the flowers and fish and birds and beasts, listen to primitive music, dance the jig, and get a taste of British cooking. He was that sort.

His ship—if it was typical—would have been quite seaworthy, about 400 or 500 tons and maybe 160 feet long, larger and safer than the *Santa María.*

As to the trip, if we accept the route proposed by some historians, he sailed more than 7,000 miles, which is farther than Columbus sailed. Just why Columbus should remain a bright legend while Pytheas has been forgotten by everybody except connoisseurs of the arcane is puzzling. Time, of course; Columbus is scarcely gone. But more important, nobody followed Pytheas to verify his account. The folks at home enjoying a balmy Mediterranean climate seem to have looked upon him as the fourteenth-century Venetians looked upon Marco Polo—charming fellow, marvelous dinner companion, but an outrageous liar. After all, who could imagine a land where there's no night, where the sun spins overhead like a weathercock? Or a frozen sea? Come now!

The lesson here, of course, is that you should not strain the credulity of your audience, even if what you say is true.

In any case, the book or narrative that Pytheas wrote was titled *On the Ocean* or *About the Ocean*, and it is thought that the manuscript survived for a number of centuries, crumbling to dust in a Massiliot library. Whatever happened, it's now gone, and we must depend on such estimable authors as Pliny, Diodorus, Strabo, Polybius, Timaeus, Solinus, et al. Like more recent scribes, these gentlemen had their passions and prejudices, and sometimes rearranged things closer to the heart's desire. Consequently, you are at liberty to believe or disbelieve.

So, let's begin:

Once upon a time, one fine day, Captain Pytheas sailed westward from Massilia toward the Pillars of Hercules, which we now call the Straits of Gibraltar. . . .

Or, if you like, we might begin again:

One dark and stormy night Captain Pytheas started north up the Rhône along the ancient river route. . . .

His destination, though, is not disputed; and whether he slipped the Carthaginian blockade at Gibraltar, or whether he sailed up the Rhône and subsequently down the Loire to the Atlantic is unimportant. By whatever route, he reached the southwestern tip of England where be introduced himself to the Cornish tin miners and found them quite hospitable.

From Cornwall he must have sailed north through the Irish Sea to Scotland—going ashore at a number of points, but just where and to what extent we don't know. In the missing manuscript he evidently wrote that he walked all over Britain, because Polybius refers sarcastically to such a claim. Whether he walked, picking up information in the pubs, or merely paused here and there along the coast, he did learn that the island's shape was loosely triangular. He gave measurements, much too large, for its three sides—825, 1,650, and 2,200 miles—and announced that its corners were Belerium, Cantium, and Orca.

He considered the natives altogether primitive: "simple in their habits, far removed from the cunning and knavishness of modern men." The country was thickly populated, he said, with many kings and other potentates and had a disagreeable climate, so we know beyond doubt that he was in England.

He may have visited Ireland. At least he saw it, because he noted its position, which enabled the Greek geographer Eratosthenes to pin Ireland to the map.

From Scotland he sailed on up to the Shetland Islands and perhaps to Thule—Ultima Thule—the end of the world. It was his account of this fearful place that provoked the bitterest arguments. Here, "at the time of the solstice, when the sun passes through the sign of the Crab, there is no night. . . ."

Greek and Roman scholars quarreled about whether or not Pytheas was lying; modern scholars in their wisdom quarrel not about his observations but about the location of Thule.

According to Strabo, who lifted the material from Polybius, who got it almost straight from the horse's mouth, Thule is the northernmost of the British Islands, six days' sail beyond the mainland, one day's sail from the frozen sea. And around Thule is neither sea nor air, but a mixture called "sea-lung" in which both are suspended. There is a little more information about Thule, but not much. The natives "thresh their grain indoors in large barns because the climate is dull and wet. They make bread, and those who have both grain and honey brew a drink from them. Northward by the frozen zone are few animals, which all are sickly; nor do cereals flourish, except millet, though there are wild fruits, vegetables, and roots."

The principal contenders for "Thule" are Norway and Iceland, with some attention paid to Greenland.

Norway would seem to be eliminated because, of course, it is not an island, nor does it lie to the north of England. But still, geography in those days included much guesswork. Pliny, for example, refers to Scandinavia as an island. And directions were vague because the compass had not been invented, so "north" might have meant " northeast." And Norway does extend to the land of the midnight sun. And off the upper coast a clammy sea fog develops. And in the south are bees to furnish honey for mead drinkers. Some authorities believe Pytheas reached the vicinity of Trondheim.

As for Iceland and Greenland, it is tempting to think of a Mediterranean ship approaching North America thirteen centuries before the Vikings. Here again, "north" could have meant "northwest." Also, there are wild bees in Iceland, and at that high latitude the sea fog forms.

Anyway, after visiting Thule—or sailing close to it—Pytheas headed south, probably down the east coast of Britain, crossed the channel, and followed the European coastline "beyond the Rhine to Scythia . . . as far as the river Tanais." This, too, is puzzling because Tanais is the old name for the Don—which flows nowhere near the Rhine. What he took to be the Tanais must have been the Elbe or the Vistula. If it was the Vistula he was the first Mediterranean sailor to enter the Baltic. And here he either saw or heard about, among other wonders, an island called Balcia or Basilia where amber is cast up by the spring tides—"an ejectum of the curdled sea."

Then, by land or water, he started home; and all things considered, it is both marvelous and astonishing that he saw Massilia again.

As to what became of Pytheas after his tremendous trip, nobody knows, except that he was ridiculed—which does happen to storytellers. Nor can we say just why he went on such a long and perilous voyage, nor why he felt a time had come to turn around.

The same is true of Hsüan-tsang, a scholarly Buddhist monk who set out from Liang-chou near the western end of the Great Wall during the Christian year 630. That is, Hsüan-tsang had a conscious purpose, just as the American did, and the Greek. But with him, as with them, we can sketch only what is visible. In his case, we know that he decided to visit India, the fountainhead of Buddhism, because he was troubled by imperfections and discrepancies among the sacred texts.

He is said to have been highly precocious; by the age of thirteen he could remember everything in a book after it had been read to him once. But it is more engaging to learn that he was "rosy as the evening mists and round as the rising moon, sweet as the odor of cinnamon. . . ." He grew up tall and handsome, instead of fat and disgusting as we might expect, "with beautiful eyes and a good complexion" and a rather stately manner. He was twenty-eight when he started for India.

An imperial edict forbade leaving the country but he went ahead, fortified by a dream. At the beginning of the Gobi Desert his companions turned back so he continued alone, without a map or a guide, following the caravan route by bones and camel droppings.

Presently he saw a vast mirage—thousands of fur-clad soldiers with glittering lances and shining banners. They were mounted on richly caparisoned horses, sometimes at an immense distance, then close at hand, changing, dissolving. At first he thought they were robbers, but because they vanished whenever they approached he knew they must be hallucinations, so he rode on.

At the first watchtower he was showered with arrows, palpable arrows, from suspicious soldiers guarding the frontier. Such a brusque greeting, though, did not distress Hsüan-tsang; it merely convinced him that he should make friends with the garrison, which he did.

Supplied with fresh water, food, and introductions to officers at other forts, he continued his journey.

However, things did not go well. Having been warned about the soldiers at one particular fort, he left the caravan route in order to avoid them and attempted to proceed by observing his shadow. He got lost, dropped the water bag, and rode around in circles for five days. Both he and his horse were almost dead when the horse scented a pool of water. Greatly refreshed after a pause at this oasis, Hsüan-tsang climbed into the saddle once more and made it to Turfan where he encountered a new problem. The king of Turfan asked him to remain as head of the Buddhist Church. Hsüan-tsang declined, explaining that he must visit the West "to seek interpretations of the Scriptures not yet known outside India so that the sweet dew of the expanded Law might also water the regions of the East."

Then the king said: "The Ts'ung Ling Mountains may fall down, but not my purpose."

Hsüan-tsang again declined. The king insisted. Hsüan-tsang replied that if he were not allowed to leave Turfan he would starve himself to death, and to prove he meant it he stopped eating.

So, after a while, equipped with a new water bag, food, money for expenses, various gifts, an escort of soldiers, and a letter introducing him to Yeh-hu, khan of the western Turks, Hsüan-tsang rode on.

Yeh-hu, wearing a green silk robe, greeted him respectfully. The khan's loose hair was bound with a silk ribbon ten feet long that trailed behind him, and he was surrounded by 200 officers in brocaded robes. On either side were his troops armed with lances and bows, mounted on camels and horses, so many that nobody could tell where they ended. He advised Hsüan-tsang not to go to India, saying it was very hot and the people had no manners, but the monk could not be dissuaded.

On to Samarkand, then south to Balkh where he saw a washbasin used by Buddha, one of Buddha's teeth—yellowish white, pure, and shining—and the Enlightened One's sweeping brush, its handle set with gems.

Over the snowy Hindu Kush to Bamiyan with its ten monasteries. By way of the Khyber Pass to Gandhara. Across the Indus gorges. The roads were dangerous, he said, the valleys gloomy. "Sometimes one had to cross on rope bridges, sometimes by clinging to chains." But there were memorable places to visit, such as a stupa marking the spot where Buddha pierced his body with a bamboo splinter in order to nourish an exhausted tiger with his blood. The plants around this stupa are blood red, said Hsüan-tsang, and the earth is full of prickly spikes. "Without asking whether we believe the tale or not, it is a piteous one."

On to Kashmir, whose citizens he found "light and frivolous, weak and pusillanimous."

While sailing down the Ganges he was captured by river pirates who decided to sacrifice him to Durga. Hsüan-tsang requested a period of meditation before being sacrificed in order that he might enter Nirvana with a calm and joyous mind. The pirates did not find this unreasonable, but while they sat around waiting for him to conclude his meditations a storm blew up, smashing trees and sinking boats. The terrified pirates fell at his feet begging forgiveness.

Hsüan-tsang forgave them and moved on to Benares where he met a saintly instructor. He spent a year in this city, visiting holy sites and studying the philosophy of Idealism.

Next he traveled to Bengal—"a low and humid land with plentiful grain." Then it occurred to him that perhaps he should visit Ceylon; but upon reaching southern India he heard reports of famine and civil war, so he turned around. Having come down the east coast, he went up the west coast through the Gujerat peninsula where he admired the imported Persian carpets and heard of a country to the west called Fo-lin—probably Babylon.

He now began to think of going home, although there was no great hurry.

He accepted an invitation to visit King Kumara of Assam, and while he was there his presence was requested by the omnipotent lord of northern India, King Harsha. Kumara responded that he would sooner send his own head to Harsha's court than his revered guest; but then, horrified by what he had said, Kumara tried to apologize by escorting the monk to Harsha's court in extravagant style. Twenty thousand elephants were mobilized and thirty thousand boats sailed up the Ganges.

King Harsha flung himself to the ground in front of Hsüan-tsang, scattered flowers at his feet, and recited poems in his honor.

What happened next is a bit confused, but Harsha seems to have arranged a public debate lasting eighteen days, featuring the wisdom of Hsüan-tsang against all comers. Hsüan-tsang won, perhaps because Harsha did not permit any serious rebuttals. This did not go over so well with some of the contestants and it is said they plotted to kill the wandering scholar.

It was now the year 643. Rejecting all gifts, except a coat of pressed buffalo down which would protect him from the rain, Hsüan-tsang set off for the Punjab.

In 644 he again crossed the Hindu Kush and spent a month visiting the governor of Badakshan. The governor provided an escort to the high Pamir plains. "The cold is glacial," said Hsüan-tsang, "the wind is furious. Snow falls throughout spring and summer. Fruit will not grow here. Trees are few. There is a lake filled with frogs in this desolate valley; it is situated at the center of the world on a plateau of stupendous height."

Descending from the Pamir, he was attacked by thieves in the Tangitar Gorge but managed to escape with most of the manuscripts, statuary, and Buddhist relics he had collected. After that he seems to have made good time.

At Khotan he dispatched a letter to the emperor, describing his travels and much of what he had learned and asking permission to enter China. Seven months later the emperor replied: "When I heard that you who had gone to distant lands to study Buddhism and to seek for religious texts was now returning, I was delighted. I pray you come quickly. . . ."

Hsüan-tsang was given a magnificent official reception and then settled down at the Monastery of Extensive Happiness, to which he bequeathed twenty pony-loads of treasure including 150 tiny particles of Buddha's flesh, a variety of icons, and 657 volumes of Scripture. It is believed that he lived peacefully ever after, on close terms with the emperor, who sometimes consulted him about the strange countries he had visited and the rulers he had met. Only one thing grieved him:

while fording the Indus he had lost some manuscripts and his collection of flower seeds.

Abu Abdullah Mohammed, better known as Ibn Batuta, that relentless explorer of the Arab world, left home on the fourteenth of June, 1325. Unlike Hsüan-tsang, Ibn Batuta knew precisely where he was going: "I left Tangier, my birthplace, one Thursday, the second day of the month of God, Rajab the Unparalleled . . . with the intention of making a pilgrimage to the Holy House and to the Tomb of the Prophet, on Whom be God's richest blessing and peace. I departed alone, with no companion to delight me, nor with any caravan, my inspiration arising from a limitless desire . . ."

Across North Africa from Tangier to Mecca is approximately 3,000 miles, but Ibn Batuta was young—twenty-one or so. Time hardly mattered.

In Cairo he took a boat up the Nile, expecting to be ferried over the Red Sea at Aidhab, but a war was in progress so he returned to Cairo, spent a while touring Syria, and then approached the holy cities from the north.

After seeing Medina, where be touched a fragment of the palm tree under which Mohammed stood while preaching, he joined a caravan to Mecca. There he walked seven times around the cubical temple as prescribed and kissed the sacred meteorite—a ruby fallen from Heaven that had turned black because of human sin. These obligations performed, Ibn Batuta decided to take a trip. He crossed Arabia to the mouth of the Euphrates, paralleled the Tigris upstream past Baghdad into Turkey, and returned to Mecca where he spent the next three years studying the Koran.

In 1330, anxious to have a look at East Africa, he went sailing down the Red Sea. Somehow—possibly by trading—he had acquired money enough to travel à la mode, with a clutch of wives, servants, and slaves, as well as several children of his own. The party stopped at Aden, crossed the equator and continued south to Mombasa and Kilwa, turned around and sailed through the Indian Ocean to Oman and up the Persian Gulf. Then, hungry for spiritual nourishment, Ibn Batuta made a third pilgrimage to Mecca.

Having steeped himself further in Holy Writ he was off again: slaves, wives, children and baggage. He thought it might be worthwhile to visit Sultan Mohammed ibn Tughlaq who lived in India and who was renowned for his hospitality to learned travelers.

Apparently he tried to get a ship for India but could not find anything suitable, so he set off by land in the opposite direction—first to Egypt, then up the eastern littoral of the Mediterranean, pausing at Ephesus where he bought an attractive Greek slave girl for twenty dinars.

Across the Black Sea to the Ukraine, southwest to Constantinople—a rather lengthy side excursion—and then, having remembered that India was the other way, he continued east as far as the Volga. Here, instead of angling south, he went several hundred miles up the icebound river, evidently planning some sort of business with the fur traders, but whatever he had in mind did not work out.

Around the top of the Caspian and Aral Seas, down to Samarkand, and so to the Indus, bordering the promised land. That was in September 1333.

Having received an invitation from Sultan Tughlaq, whom he describes as "very fond of bestowing gifts and shedding blood," Batuta led his merry band to Delhi. At this time Delhi was the largest Moslem city in the East, though sparsely populated when he arrived because the sultan had taken a dislike to the citizens and ordered most of them to move out. Those who objected, or tried to hide, were killed. Among these was a cripple who was hurled from a mangonel—a military device ordinarily used for catapulting stones—and a blind man whom the sultan ordered to be dragged from Delhi to Dawlatabad. The blind man fell apart on the road and only one leg reached his new home.

Tughlaq liked Ibn Batuta, appointing him guardian of the mausoleum of Sultan Qutb-ad-Din at a salary of 12,000 dinars per annum, with another 12,000 for immediate expenses, an estate with an income of about the same amount, and a splendid horse.

Batuta took the job seriously. He spent eight years at Tughlaq's court, although his career and his life very nearly were cut short when he was suspected of participating in a conspiracy. Four slaves were sent to watch him, which customarily meant that the watchee was doomed. "The first day I was watched like this was a Friday," Batuta writes. "It pleased God on High to allow me to speak these words: 'God is our help and Sovereign Lord!' On that Friday I pronounced these words 33,000 times."

Miraculously restored to grace, Batuta was told by his capricious employer to lead an embassy to the emperor of China. In the summer of 1342 they started out: fifteen diplomats accompanied by women and servants, Ibn Batuta with his personal entourage—all protected by 1,000 cavalrymen and a stout company of foot soldiers. But they met some rebels, there was a fight, Batuta was captured, and once again he came very near to closing the Koran permanently.

This fight disrupted the expedition so much that historians do not agree on what happened. Some say it continued on its way, others think the cavalcade retreated to Delhi where Tughlaq overhauled it and started his ambassadors off a second time with Batuta still in command. How Batuta escaped from the rebels is not clear. At any rate, Tughlaq's diplomats planned to reach China by sea, because we next hear of them in the Gulf of Cambay, then at Goa and Calicut.

What happened at Calicut also is disputed. If we believe one account, which sounds too neat, a storm blew up, sinking the boats and drowning everybody except our hero who chanced to be ashore praying in a mosque. Another account also mentions drowning, so probably there was a disastrous storm, but in addition there seems to have been a massive desertion which left Batuta by himself on the Calicut beach.

He next turns up in the Maldive Islands, again doing very nicely. Now he is a kazi, a judge, and has married four new wives including a daughter of the vizier. You can't keep a good man down. Batuta, though, disclaims credit. Says he: "It is not difficult to get married in these islands." And here, as at Delhi, he is conscientious about his work, attempting to drive the agnostic islanders to the mosque with a whip, trying to get the Maldive ladies to wear some clothes. At last the vizier began looking at him suspiciously so he decided the time had come to resume traveling.

He booked passage for himself and one wife to the Indian mainland, but the ship was blown off course and they landed in Ceylon. There he saw on the forehead of a white elephant "seven rubies larger than hen's eggs. And at the palace of Sultan Airi Sakarvati I saw a spoon made of precious stone as large as the palm of a hand and filled with oil of aloes. At this I marveled. . . ." He marveled further at Mount Sarandib, which he thought must be one of the highest peaks in the world, and said he had been able to see it nine days before the ship reached port. On a black rock of this mountain, he said, one could see the footprint of our venerable father Adam, eleven spans in length, which had been there since time immemorial.

When he left Ceylon the sultan gave him a string of jewels, but no sooner had he waved good-bye from the deck of a ship taking him to the Coromandel Coast than he was seized by pirates who took everything he owned, stripped him, and dumped him on the opposite side of the Indian peninsula without a rupee. If his adventures had not been documented, making allowances for gaps here and there, nobody would believe the story; reading what happened to him is like reading about Sinbad.

Well, off he went again to the Maldives, ingratiated himself as usual, and presently set out for Bengal to visit a notable saint. Then to Sumatra—or perhaps Java—where an old friend from Delhi introduced him at court and where he was astonished to see dancing horses. When he left this island, whichever it was, he had been presented with a fully equipped junk. After a boring sea voyage he landed in southern China and journeyed north to Peking. The Chinese concern for travelers impressed him; he found the country safe and well regulated. But the idolatry troubled him.

He started home to the land of true believers and endured his customary afflictions—getting lost at sea, storms, et cetera. Safe at last in the Moslem world he could not bypass Mecca, lodestone of his existence, and for the fourth time he paid his respects to the Prophet's birthplace.

From Alexandria he got a ship to Sardinia. From there he sailed to Algeria and continued overland to Morocco, arriving in November of 1349. He had been away twenty-four years.

After a few months he became restless. There was a war going on in Spain and he thought he would like to participate, or at least see it, so he crossed the Straits of Gibraltar, barely escaped being caught by Christian soldiers, and spent a while wandering around Andalusia.

Two years later the sultan of Morocco, who wished to know more about the empires in the south, instructed him to visit the kingdom of Mali. This trip took him as far into Africa as the Niger. He was in Timbuktu for seven months, in Gao for another month. He disliked that part of Africa, partly because the blacks were infidels, but also because they did not give him suitable presents. From the ruler of Mali he got "three cakes of bread, some beef fried in oil, and a calabash of sour curds." He had been expecting money, luxurious robes, and a title. But of course there were wondrous sights. Hippos bathing in the Niger dumfounded him; he had never seen such beasts and thought they must be elephants.

At Tagadda he received a message from his employer asking him to return to the sublime capital of Morocco. He seems reluctant to leave because of the extraordinary Tuareg women: "most perfect in beauty, most shapely in figure, of a pure white color and very stout." However, the sultan's wish was Ibn Batuta's command; obediently he joined a caravan that included 600 female slaves, and upon arriving at Fez he kissed the sultan's hand and "settled beneath the wing of his bounty." It was here that he dictated his book, modestly titled *Travels in Asia and Africa*, to Ibn Juzayy, the court secretary.

Altogether he must have gone at least 75,000 miles, most of it by land, which makes the journey of Marco Polo look like a stroll around the block. Nobody else, with the single exception of Magellan—who was aboard ship—traveled such a distance until the nineteenth century.

Africa has perhaps never welcomed two more disparate personalities than Ibn Batuta and Mary Kingsley. Everything imaginable separates them—religion, nationality, sex, race, cultural tradition, five centuries—yet you cannot help feeling that if their caravans had met they would have become great friends.

Kingsley, Bishop, Taylor, Marsden, North, and those other Victorian ladies—there is something improbable about them all. They are the most unlikely travelers the world has ever known. Halliburton astonishes us, yet he is not surprising; we can be amazed at his recklessness while admitting that reckless young men are nothing new. And although we cannot be sure of much about faraway individuals such as Pytheas, we are able to accept them. Or Hsüan-tsang—at least as remote to a twentieth-century Westerner—we cannot comprehend a medieval Chinese mystic riding through the Gobi and over the Himalayas, and we visualize him only approximately as he was in life, transfixed on the fanciful ocher and yellow background of an ancient Chinese painting in his sandals and silk robe and bamboo backpack. We cannot understand him, nevertheless we believe in him. He may be extraordinary, but he is not unreal. Or that most preposterous and indefatigable wanderer Ibn Batuta, charming one potentate after another, surviving typhoons, psychotic employers, wars and pirates, acquiring so many wives and concubines that you would think he was eating popcorn. He, too, is a storybook personality that we accept.

But the mind just cannot absorb Isabella Bird Bishop at the apex of her fame—shaped like a penguin, holding court in gold-embroidered slippers and a petticoat decorated with gold and silver Japanese wheels, with a royal ribbon and order across her shoulders which had been presented to her by the king of the Sandwich Islands. No, we say. No, no, I'll go along with Ibn Batuta or that Chinese whose name I can't remember, but this woman is too much.

Then there is May French Sheldon on the way to Kilimanjaro in a blonde wig, carrying a ceremonial sword, wearing a rhinestone-studded gown and a dozen Cleopatra bracelets. No. No, she must be the creation of a mad playwright.

They give the impression of being mildly batty, these upright, energetic, innocent, valorous, polite, intelligent, prim, and condescending British females in long skirts, carrying parasols, being conveyed across some of the roughest terrain on earth in wooden carts, stagecoaches, elephant howdahs, coal boats, dugouts, and not infrequently clinging like a huge black moth to the back of a coolie who must have thought he had been engaged by a creature from a different universe. "I am something like the famous Doge at the Court of Louis XIV," wrote Mary Crawford, "and may declare that I see no wonder in this shrubbery equal to seeing myself in it."

So we come upon Mary Kingsley: naturalist, ethnologist, sailor, scholar, guest of cannibals and champion of lost causes. Or, as she refers to herself: "the voyager."

She was born in 1862 and for thirty years lived in a state of suffocating restriction, tight even by Victorian norms. Then both of her parents died and all at once her life made no sense; suddenly she had nobody to care for. Her father had been an anthropologist who traveled quite a bit, but he had never gone to Africa; therefore, in accordance with the Byzantine laws of human behavior, Mary realized that she must go to Africa. At least that's how it appears underneath the green rust of time. But what seems mildly comic from a distance is very often not so at all, particularly to the people involved. Mary herself could hardly have been more despondent: "Dead tired and feeling no one had need of me any more," she wrote to a friend, ". . . I went down to West Africa to die."

However morbid her condition at this point, Mary Kingsley was much too energetic to expire like the pale heroine of a novel. She resolved to study the Africans, to collect zoological specimens, and come home to enlighten her countrymen about the Dark Continent.

Having decided it would be best to represent herself as a trader, she laid in a supply of tobacco, fishhooks, cloth, and such other British produce as might appeal to the locals, after which she embarked for the Congo on a Liverpool cargo boat.

Being unusually bright and observant, she quickly learned about navigation, about stowing cargo and how to manage a crew. Later, after more experience aboard other boats, she would be ready to argue seamanship with grizzled old mariners: "I say you can go across Forçados Bar drawing eighteen feet. . . . I have taken vessels of 2,000 tons across that Bar and up the Forçados creeks. . . ."

She landed at Saint Paul de Loana, visited the Fjort tribe along the Congo, then marched and paddled in a northerly direction until she emerged at the old city of Calabar. In order to reassure everybody when she materialized from the bush at some remote factory or trading post on the river she would call out: "It's only me!"

She returned to England with several crates of specimens, an ability to speak the traders' lingua franca, and enough anthropological knowledge to address the London Society of Medicine for Women. Her lecture was titled "Therapeutics from the point of view of an African witch doctor."

In December of 1894 she was off again, this time to southern Nigeria where she spent five months studying fish, plants, beasts, the native Bubis, and the immigrant Spaniards and Portuguese.

She liked mangrove swamps. She would paddle around for hours examining everything, stung by flies and threatened by crocodiles: "On one occasion a mighty Silurian, as the *Daily Telegraph* would call him, chose to get his front paws over the stern of my canoe and endeavoured to improve our acquaintance. I had to retire to the bows to keep the balance upright, and fetch him a clip on the snout with a paddle. . . ."

In the spring of 1895 she set out for the Ogowé River in the French Congo. The forest enchanted her. "It is as full of life and beauty and passion as any symphony Beethoven ever wrote: the parts are changing, interweaving, and returning . . . you hardly see anything but the vast column-like grey tree stems in their countless thousands around you, and the sparsely vegetated ground beneath. But day by day, as you get trained to your surroundings, you see more and more, and a whole world grows up gradually out of the gloom before your eyes."

To the north lay a belt of forest inhabited by the Fans, a tribe known to eat human flesh not merely on special occasions but rather often. She had met some of them, she admired their virility, and thought she should know more about them. So, in July, accompanied by an Igalwa interpreter and four nervous Ajumba armed with flintlocks, she started upriver to say hello to the cannibals.

They met the Fans on an island in Lake Ncovi: "I must say that never—even in a picture-book—have I seen such a set of wild wicked-looking savages as those we faced this night, and with whom it was touch-and-go for twenty of the longest minutes I have ever lived."

For whatever reason, Mary and her edible friends were invited to stay overnight at the village; and there, in a filthy hut, with a crude wooden bench for a bed, dressed in a long black English skirt, high-necked blouse, cummerbund, and closely fitted hat, surrounded by cannibals—having no doubt reassured them by exclaiming "It's only me!"—there she made herself at home and insisted on a cup of tea. Apparently she did not consider this unusual. Quite the opposite. "We each recognized we belonged to that same section of the human race with whom it is better to drink than to fight. We knew we would each have killed the other, if sufficient inducement were offered, and so we took a certain amount of care that the inducement should not arise."

The next afternoon while marching through the jungle she dropped into a game pit, the bottom of which had been furnished with sharpened stakes. "It is at these times," she observes, "you realize the blessing of a good thick skirt. Had I paid heed to the advice of many people in England, who ought to have known better, and did not do it themselves, and adopted masculine garments, I should have been spiked to the bone and done for."

After being hoisted out of the pit by her crew she continued along the trail. Suddenly one of the Ajumba dropped from view with a despairing shriek. He, in turn, was liberated and his wounds bound up with green leaves—"for he, not having a skirt, had got a good deal frayed at the edges on those spikes."

At the village of Efoua they were again welcomed and invited to stay over. During the night she awoke because of an odd stench and discovered a bag of curiosities: a shriveled human hand, a few toes, some eyes and some ears, all of which she emptied into her hat so as to lose none of them, and registered in her notebook the fact that these particular Fans kept mementos of their victims.

Approaching another village, she learned that the inhabitants were killing strangers immediately and inquiring about them afterward. For the first time she may have felt unequal to dealing with Africa. She led her men off the trail, intending to avoid the village, which she did, but ended up in a mangrove swamp. Just in time she realized that the swamp was tidal—a long arm of the Gaboon estuary—and the tide was rising. They all turned and scrambled frantically through the muck for more than an hour before escaping to a hillside.

After that things got easier. Oh, there were little inconveniences. Other swamps, for instance, through which they waded up to their chins in the reeking water: "we got horribly infested with leeches, having a frill of them round our necks like astrakhan collars, and our hands covered with them when we came out." But these were nothing compared to the rewards of travel.

She sailed down the Rembwé River in a canoe with a sail made from an old bed quilt—the canoe being the property of a trader named

Obanjo who preferred to be called "Captain Johnson"—and she would later commemorate this trip: "Much as I have enjoyed life in Africa, I do not think I ever enjoyed it to the full as I did on those nights dropping down the Rembwé. The great, black, winding river with a pathway in its midst of frosted silver where the moonlight struck it; on each side the ink-black mangrove walls, and above them the band of star and moonlit heavens that the walls of mangrove allowed us to see. Forward rose the form of our sail, idealized from bed-sheetdom to glory; and the little red glow of our cooking fire gave a single note of warm colour to the cold light of the moon. . . ."

Once more in civilization, sailing across Corisco Bay on a missionary's boat named the *Lafayette*, she sounds discontented by so much propriety: "I find I am expected to sit surrounded by a rim of alligator pears and bananas, as though I were some kind of joint garnished for table."

Homeward bound, she stopped in the Cameroons to climb West Africa's highest peak, Mungo Mah Lobeh, by its most difficult side. The rain was like a waterfall, there were rivers to ford, and always the mud and flies and thorns and more genuine threats; but Mary was determined to climb the mountain, although just as determined to do nothing unbefitting an English lady. With mud-caked skirts, scratched and bitten until her face and hands were bloody, she approached a trading station operated by a German; but instead of hurrying toward it she stopped to wash. After all, one should not appear untidy in front of a strange man. Even so, the German was appalled by what came marching out of the bush. He offered her a bath—an offer she declined because, as she asks rhetorically, how could she be expected to bathe in a house with inadequate shutters? Men! she laments. Men can be so trying!

And in London she refused to ride on a bus because it seemed improper. And she disapproved of the bicycle.

Her book, *Travels in West Africa*, was published in 1896, but it did not begin to tell the full story of her passionate affair with the Dark Continent. She omitted some of her most implausible adventures because she did not think anybody would believe what had happened, such as the time she found herself on a tight little island with a hippopotamus and finally persuaded the monster to leave by poking it with her umbrella. Or the time she traded several of her blouses to a naked Fan who wore "*nothing* else but red paint and a bunch of leopard tails." Or was saved from a gorilla's embrace by a lucky shot. And she almost neglected to tell about the leopard which she released from a trap because the animal was beating itself to death against the bars—and the creature, when it had been freed, stood looking at her in bewilderment until she stamped her foot and shouted, "Go home, you fool!"

And this same woman perceived, when British officialdom could not, that African society was as meticulously structured as European society; and that missionaries were doing more harm than good; and that traders were not villainous swindlers taking advantage of childlike natives; and that taxing a man's property, such as his hut, outraged the African's sense of justice. And being the woman she was, she let it be known what she thought. And the British government, being the government it then was, and is now—which is to say, a government not much different from others of that era, or of this—the British government debated her ideas and then, of course, did nothing. After all, a government is less easy to bestir than a hippopotamus.

The British Museum, though, welcomed her and studied the specimens she had collected and named three varieties of fish after her.

She was eager to return to Africa. There were so many swamps to be investigated, so many insects, lizards, turtles, crocodiles, and leopards to examine, so many cannibals to whom she had not yet introduced herself. You can almost see her emerging cheerfully from the bush. "Hello there! Hello? I say, is no one at home?"

She wanted very much to visit the river country near Lake Chad, but England had stumbled into the Boer War so she volunteered for nursing service. The government sent her to a place called Simonstown where there was an epidemic. Two months later she died of enteric fever. She was thirty-eight. The year was 1900, the year Richard Halliburton was born. And, like Halliburton, Mary Kingsley was buried at sea.

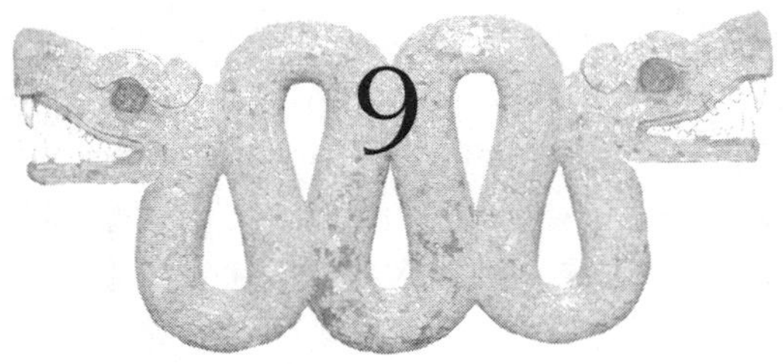

9

The Aztec Treasure House

Near the end of the nineteenth century a certain William Niven is known to have traveled through the Middle Balsas River region of Mexico, not far from the Pacific coast; and a diary he kept, dated 1896, now belongs to the American Museum of Natural History in New York. But more interesting than the diary is a baked clay figure somewhat less than six inches tall which Niven claimed to have bought in the vicinity of Zumpango del Rio and which, in 1903, he sold to the Peabody Museum of Harvard. This figure represents a seated personage—possibly a man, although it's hard to tell—wearing a skirt and a cape. At that time the figure did not seem to be related to any other ceramics discovered in the area, or to anything found anyplace else in Mexico. Because of this, or in spite of it, Mr. Niven's irregular artifact did not get much attention.

Seventy years later a few stone and ceramic items with similar characteristics, reputedly from the same area, were shown to an expert on pre-Columbian art, Carlo Gay, who concluded that they belonged to the Olmec tradition and that quite probably they were older than any previously known Olmec objects.

Now it should be explained that these people, whatever they may have called themselves, who have been labeled Olmecs—a term derived from an Aztec word *olméca*, meaning those from the land of rubber, from the southern Gulf coast where chico zapate trees provide the material for chewing gum—these Olmec people created the first high civilization of Mexico, dating so far back that the sixteenth-century Mayans encountered by Cortés seem almost as close to us in time as the Vietnam War. The Mayans, as just about everybody knows, developed one of the most sophisticated societies of the New World: they were accomplished architects, they studied the motions of the planets, they knew how to communicate ideas through picture writing, their calendar was quite accurate, and so forth. But what is not commonly known is that the Mayans inherited much of their culture from the Olmecs.

And what is utterly unknown at present, even to professional anthropologists, is where these people came from; because the great Olmec centers of La Venta, San Lorenzo, Cerro de las Mesas, and Tres Zapotes where the huge helmeted basalt heads were discovered, and the jade carvings, and the famous "wrestler" or "pelota player" which is now in the Mexico City museum—not one of these centers shows any sign of evolution. It is as though the Olmec culture arrived completely formed in the land of the chewing-gum tree, as though it had been magically transported from another country. Indeed there is speculation that it may have originated in the Orient and that these people crossed the Pacific several thousand years ago. There are reasons for thinking so.

The early Chinese, for example, painted their funerary jades red; so did some early Mexicans. Both observed the custom of placing a small object, frequently a jade bead, in the mouth of the corpse. Parcheesi, which originated in Asia, is almost identical to the Mexican game of patolli. Tripod bowls unearthed at Teotihuacán near Mexico City, although made of clay, can hardly be distinguished stylistically from ancient Chinese bronze vessels. The lotus motif, occurring throughout

Asia and Indochina, was used by the Mayans; furthermore, in both Asia and America the underground rootlike stem of the lotus, the rhizome, formed the basic element of this motif. The volador game—in which a man at the end of a long rope goes flying around a pole—this mad spectacle occurs on both sides of the Pacific. Then there are very similar conceptions of Hell and the punishments that await us. Alfresco mural painting. Lacquer. Identical musical instruments. Pineapple-shaped mace heads. The list of similarities goes on. How much can be attributed to coincidence?

Still, there are persuasive arguments against this theory, which is why the matter has not yet been decided.

As for myself, I once saw a Mexican woman who, if she had lived centuries earlier, might have been the model for one of those gigantic basalt Olmec heads. She must have been a descendant of those people, she could not have been anything else, and there was nothing Chinese about her. She looked like what she was, a Mexican Indian woman of Jalapa. So, as far as I am concerned, that woman by herself refutes the theory of Asiatic migrants disembarking on the Pacific coast of Mexico. Only now and then, usually while comparing ancient pottery or jade carvings, do I have doubts.

Most authorities, I am pleased to say, agree with me. That is, although they do not yet know where the Olmecs originated they reject the idea of a Pacific crossing. They suspect that the culture developed in one of two places, either in the swampy miasmic Gulf coast where it flourished and degenerated and disappeared, or 500 miles west among the ravines of Oaxaca and on the rocky Guerrero slopes.

Carlo Gay, accompanied by the curator of primitive art at Princeton, visited Guerrero in 1970. They went back twice the following year. As a result of their investigation it became known that several burial sites near the village of Xochipala had yielded a variety of stone and clay vessels and figurines which undoubtedly belong to the Olmec formative period. Ritual implements. Incised bowls. A frog. Ceramic rodents. The head of a serpent. A pyrite mirror. Earspools and other ornamental accessories. And, of course, representations of people. So far the Xochipala graves have given up more than 100 small baked clay figures of men, women, and children.

Tentatively, because these statuettes are unique and therefore disputable, they have been classified as Early, Middle, and Late Xochipala. The stylistic sequence moves from vivid naturalization to rigid formalism—a record of the course of their civilization. Of theirs, to be sure, just as it is a record of all civilizations.

The piece brought back by William Niven, the first example of Xochipala Olmec art to be identified, belongs to the earliest period—which probably is coincidence. At any event it reveals most of the characteristics: an assured portraitlike quality, perfect body rhythm, acute comprehension of anatomy, and a delicate heavy fleshiness which has not been vulgarized by exaggeration. The eyeballs are fully modeled, the pupils picked out. The hair has been parted in the center and carried over the ears. The hands and feet are finely worked. There can be no doubt that this was a person—not a god or goddess whose function and power we will never understand—not a symbol of humanity but a representative of it who lived in the area at that time, who sat cross-legged in the shade of a tree or in some thatched-roof hut while one of his neighbors manipulated the dark clay with a little stick, paused to stare, and tried again and then again in order to get the mouth just right, and the thrust of the nose, and the contour of the cheek, all for the sake of true expression.

Gradually, because the transition was not abrupt, nor even marked—indeed a "transition" exists merely because we say it does—Early gave way to Middle. Less attention is paid to anatomy. Symbolism begins to replace naturalism. The naked or almost naked people of a previous century now are fashionably clothed in ankle-length garments adorned with leaves; they wear kilts, necklaces, and meaningful discs; and sometimes a ritualistic uniform consisting of boots, loincloth, and helmet, which anthropologists think may have been the prescribed outfit for ballplayers. Then there are dancers, and grotesque two-faced people who must have been senators, and a variety of others. But none are individuals; they appear to be only the embodiment of a particular condition or activity.

Toward the end, like the late Etruscans, as if somehow they could sense the future, the Xochipala artists lose the creative impulse that carried their predecessors to such a high plateau. They resort to stereotypes. They do not dare to invent, they do not imagine. They produce coarse figures with few details, with conventionalized features: an oval welt instead of a mouth, flaplike ears, clumsily defined hair, the tool marks showing—as though they were exhausted or discouraged, and scrupulous craftsmanship was not worth the effort. Significantly, the hands quite often are closed, no longer receptive to the stimulus of life.

One of these Xochipala figurines, an early one, the careful portrait of an adolescent who looks rather Slavic, with a sensual mouth and meticulously combed hair ending in a queue, wearing a necklace and a loincloth, sits on top of my bookcase. Whether the figure is male or female, I don't know. At times the Olmecs ignored sexual features. Considered objectively—considering the resolute, authoritative pose—this calm determined personage suggests masculinity and therefore should be referred to as "he." But out of my own predilection, and because the model just might have been a girl, I think of it as female.

She has been atop my bookcase for three or four years, seated cross-legged in a dignified Olmec pose, her solid little hands balanced on her plump knees and her fine Tartar head slightly lifted, almost in the lotus position—reminding me once again that in spite of all objections there is something pervasively Oriental about the Olmecs. I look at her every now and then.

Once upon a time her hair must have been orange; the elaborate clay coiffure has a definite tint, and through a magnifying glass the color becomes obvious. Her body, too, could have been painted. I suspect it was. There seems to be a faint bluish white residue. Her right foot is missing, along with both thumbs and several fingertips. Her lower lip has been chipped, and her torso is afflicted with microscopic growths, stains, spidery cracks, and scratches. Then there are the calcium deposits, which Carlo Gay describes as typical of prehistoric ceramic sculpture found in this area. The figure must have been underground quite a while, judging by the condition of the surface, the calcium, and the root traces wandering like uncertain white worm trails in all directions.

Roots, provided they are large enough, given time enough, will crush whatever they grasp, which partly explains why most of the classic Greek statues are damaged. If roots can decapitate marble gods and pry temples apart, what they can do to a delicate clay bowl or a lady is not hard to imagine.

Innumerable root traces coil around the body of my Xochipala. Some are as thick as a string, which might not sound threatening, but the dealer from whom I bought the figure told me he was surprised that it had not been totally destroyed. Even so, the head and limbs were broken off. Now everything has been glued together in the original position; and all that's missing, except for a few flakes and chips, are the parts mentioned—thumbs, fingertips, and the right foot. Thumbs and fingertips would be easy to overlook, but I'm puzzled about the foot. How could it have been overlooked when the fragments were collected?

Anyway, that's how she appears these days with her coppery orange hair and absent foot—an undeniable presence with her slim, breastless torso on which two clearly raised little nipples cast tiny shadows, and her half-open hands resting on extraordinarily full thighs, sensuously round and thick, and her head just perceptibly lifted as though something or somebody, possibly myself, might be obstructing the view. She hasn't moved for quite a while, unless you count the infinitely slow dislocation caused by roots.

She must have been buried for at least a century, maybe two, when Queen Nefertiti was born. She had been buried more than a thousand years when Pericles ruled Athens. She was seated majestically in the rocky Guerrero soil, perhaps still upright, for 2,000 years when Charlemagne crossed the Pyrenees. Grasped by the tendrils of shrubs and trees that sprouted and grew and ultimately died and decayed and vanished, leaving no proof of their existence except lime white squiggles on the dark burnt clay, she had been there another eight centuries when Cortés led his clanking sweating glittering horsemen over the causeway into the shrill feathered pageantry of Tenochtitlán. And it is for this reason, I think, that whenever I pause at the bookcase to study her for a few moments I never say anything.

I described this little Xochipala figure to a sculptor. I mentioned the clay pellets that make up the necklace, I talked about the precise treatment of the eyes, the subtly raised brows, and the delineation of the coiffure. I thought he would be impressed by such a passion for detail and would want to look at the figure, but he seemed disinterested. He was not anxious to come look at it because exactitude is out of style, except as department-store art for the bourgeoisie. But I insisted, so he did, and was promptly seduced.

He marveled at things I had not even noticed. The breadth of the shoulders, for instance. He said she was like those Asiatic Indian dancers and courtesans on the twelfth-century temples of Khajuraho, men and women both, with unnaturally wide shoulders and a narrow tubular body, conceived by the artist with such harmony that one easily accepts their impossible proportions.

As for the detail—the striations of the hair and so on—having seen the figure for himself, he no longer objected. After all, what matters is not an artist's technique but his vision.

A neighborhood housewife also looked at the Xochipala figure. She asked what I had named it. Ramona? Jennifer? Gladys?

Then she asked why I had bought it.

Now, in order to understand this curious question it should be pointed out that I have a few Greek terra-cottas—Tanagras, so called for the site where these graceful dainty pre-Christian statuettes were first uncovered—but the woman who asked why I bought the Xochipala has never asked why I bought the Tanagras. The explanation is that, while Olmec art is unfamiliar, Tanagra statuary belongs to our Greco-Roman artistic heritage. We have seen Greek art as long as we can remember; museums are crammed with it, and the history books we read in school had pictures of Greek and Roman masterpieces. So, my neighbor reasoned, it would make sense to buy a Tanagra, but why would anyone want a prehistoric Mexican statue?

If, on the other hand, we knew nothing about Greek art but were familiar with Olmec concepts, then she would have asked why I bought the Tanagras. That is to say, how we react to something may depend less on what we perceive than on what we know, or think we know. Arthur Koestler tells a story about this. He noticed a Picasso drawing in the home of a friend named Brenda. The drawing had been a birthday present and she assumed it was a print so she hung it rather out of sight, beside the staircase. When Koestler visited her home the next time he saw Picasso hanging conspicuously in the front room. Brenda had learned it was not a print but an original.

Still, the longer I thought about my neighbor's question the more I wondered why I had in fact bought the Olmec. That it was supremely successful as a work of art, I had no doubt—which should be reason enough. But in addition to this Olmec piece I had bought quite a few other examples of ancient Mexican pottery: Jalisco, Michoacan, Colima, Maya, Chupícuaro, Nayarit, and so forth. Now this may not be as strange as collecting old dog collars or potato mashers or eighteenth-century epaulets; nevertheless I could see why people might regard it as peculiar.

Well then, why had I been acquiring such things? The Tanagras were explicable. But why these Mexican artifacts?

Unfamiliarity with an artistic tradition could not be the answer; if that were the case I might just as easily have picked up Eskimo or Tibetan antiquities. There must be a reason I had collected the work of these long-gone Mexican Indians, because our passions are never accidental. We do not by chance marry somebody with a particular way of walking or a certain kind of nose, or decide to specialize in epaulets.

For example, the scholar Henry Hart spent years researching and writing about fifteenth-century Portuguese explorers. It might not occur to us to ask why; after all, scholars do that sort of thing. But there was a reason. There always is. When Hart was a boy somebody gave him a book about those audacious men who opened up the world, among them da Gama. "I remember," he writes, "the picture of the ghost of Vasco da Gama fleeing in full armor through the air, pursued by his victims in full cry for vengeance—scantily clad men without hands, without arms, with gaping wounds and torture-stricken features, seeking to grasp and punish their mortal enemy.

"Still vivid are the gaudy double-page lithographs of his destruction of the Arab ship, his appearance before the Lord of Calicut, and all the other startling pictures illustrating his career."

Years after that book vanished—"in some unknown manner long ago in those far-off childhood days"—Hart found another copy of it. "Alas," he remarks,

> the disillusionment! Its pages are a crowded procession of inaccuracies and misstatements. Those beloved illustrations were stock cuts brought together from various sources and used in the subscription volume. Dom

> Vasco, discussing the chart of his projected voyage with Dom Manuel, is shown as a wild-eyed old man with a white spade beard. A few pages further on he is depicted as an Elizabethan gallant with an imperial beard, receiving the envoy of the King of Calicut; and in truth he was hardly thirty when he set out on his memorable voyage.
>
> But, though wiser and sadder for this seeing of the book after more than half a century, none the less I cherish it, for it first fired my imagination and interest in history and travel; and though I have visited and sojourned in many of the scenes in its pages, none of what my eyes have beheld in the flesh is as thrilling as those which I visited on its magic carpet, which annihilated time and space, and gilded all with the aura of the golden age of childhood.

And now, alas, after almost as many years, I have had that same experience. In a San Francisco flea market I came across a book with a brilliant tangerine binding, a book I recognized immediately and from a distance, long before I could make out the title. It was *The Aztec Treasure House* by Thomas Janvier, an adventure novel for boys. I recognized it because I had checked it out of the high school library at least four times.

In those days I was a heavy reader of Albert Payson Terhune's dog stories, and I could not get enough of Will James's noble horse Smoky galloping across the western landscape. And I had gone through most of the Hardy Boys thrillers despite the obvious ineptitude of their detective father, Fenton Hardy, who, so it seemed, had usually to be rescued by his teen-age sons. And I had read some Tom Swift. And there was a series about somebody who went to Yale. And, of course, *The Call of the Wild*. But as far as I was concerned, *The Aztec Treasure House* beat them all. I do not specifically remember telling my friends it was the best book in the world, but probably I said so. I do know that I recommended it. I was so impressed, in fact, that I memorized the name of the author.

And now after all these years here it was, the same edition, on a card table in a flea market.

After staring at the book for a while as though it were alive and conscious of me, perhaps the very copy I used to read—at last I picked it up and opened it, and saw penciled on the flyleaf the word *scarce*, followed by the price, $4.00, subsequently crossed out and reduced to $1.49.

My first thought was to buy it. Then I thought, No, I don't want to read it again, it's a boys' book. Besides, there are plenty of things I should read and haven't, and probably won't; it would be silly to waste two or three hours going through this again. It belongs to the past.

Then I thought, Well, if I don't buy it I'll never see it again.

So now I have the book, and just as I suspected I can't read it. The story is told in the first person by a young American archaeologist called "Don Tomas" by his fellow adventurers, these being a Franciscan monk, two Otomi Indians, a member of some gringo "engineering corps," two soldiers of fortune, and a barefoot Mexican boy named, inevitably, Pablo.

Don Tomas, by a great stroke of luck, comes upon a mortally wounded cacique who gives him a hieroglyphic map on a sheet of maguey paper. This map, as all good maps should, points the way to something fabulous, in this case the fabulous "walled city of Culhuacan."

Hurrah! Off we go to search for the walled city and the treasure of the last unconquered Aztecs. And a desperate tale it is, provided you are no older than twelve. If you happen to be more than that you cannot help noticing a number of implausibilities and inconsistencies floating past like ducks in a shooting gallery, so that reading what I once considered to be the world's greatest novel becomes a fearful chore.

I have tried several times to read it, but I cannot get very far. After a few pages I start to skip. Here is how it begins:

> My heart was light within me as I stood on the steamer's deck in the cool gray of an October morning, and saw out across the dark green sea and the dusky, brownish stretch of coast country the snow-crowned peak of Orizaba glinting in the first rays of the rising sun. And presently, as the sun rose higher, all the tropic region of the coast and the brown walls of Vera Cruz and of its outpost fort of San Juan de Ulua were flooded with brilliant light.
>
> And still lighter was my heart, a week later, when I found myself established in the beautiful city of Morelia, and ready to begin actively the work for which I had been preparing myself almost all my life long.
>
> Morelia, I had decided, was the best base for the operations that I was about to undertake. My main purpose was to search for the remnants of primitive civilization . . .

Skipping across half-remembered pages I come to these lines:

"'Hello, Professor!' Young called out, as he caught sight of me, 'have you given up antiquities . . . ?'"

No. No indeed, Mr. Young! I shout across the years, answering not for Don Tomas but for myself, surrounded as I am by cracked old Mexican pots and mutilated statuettes.

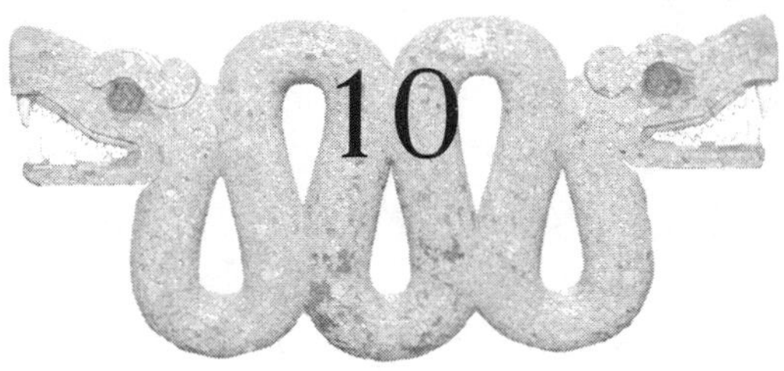

10

Aristokles' Atlantis

"I PROPOSE A CURIOUS EXCURSION," said Captain Nemo to Monsieur Aronnax.

And with that the intrepid submariners, having first put on their diving dresses, set foot on the bottom of the Atlantic at a depth of 150 fathoms. The waters were profoundly dark but Captain Nemo pointed out a reddish spot—a light shining with great brillance—perhaps two miles distant from the *Nautilus*. What this fire might be, what it could feed, why and how it illuminated the ocean depths, M. Aronnax could not say. Was it some electric effulgence? Could it be a natural phenomenon unknown to savants of the earth?

After half an hour's walk the floor of the ocean became stony, lit only by the phosphorescent gleam of medusae, microscopic crustacea, and pennatules. Captain Nemo advanced without hesitation; doubtless he had traveled this road before. M. Aronnax followed with unshaken confidence. But not until one in the morning did they approach a mountain from which the mysterious light seemed to emanate.

Before ascending the slope they were obliged to pass through a thicket of dead trees—yes, a copse of dead trees, all without leaves, without sap—trees petrified by the action of the water. Picture to yourself a forest in the Harz, M. Aronnax advises us, a forest encumbered with seaweed and fucus.

Fishes flew from branch to branch as the explorers pushed onward. Massive rocks were rent with impenetrable fractures, deep grottoes, and unfathomable caverns at the bottom of which formidable creatures could be heard moving. Millions of luminous dots glowed amidst the blackness; these were the eyes of giant crustacea crouched in their holes—monstrous crabs and lobsters setting themselves up like halberdiers, moving their claws with a clicking sound, and frightful poulps whose tentacles interwove like living nests of serpents. M. Aronnax felt his blood curdle.

Beyond this eerie copse lay vast ruins which betrayed not the hand of the Creator but that of man—the vague and shadowy forms of temples and castles over which had grown a thick mantle of vegetation. What was this ghostly portion of the globe which long ago had been swallowed by cataclysms? Who had placed these monumental stones like cromlechs of prehistoric times? Arronax would fain have inquired.

But Captain Nemo pressed forward.

Then, from the peak of the mountain, what a sight did the travelers behold! Under their eyes—ruined, destroyed—lay a city with its roofs open, its dwellings fallen, its arches dislocated, massive columns strewn about. Farther away, the remnants of a lengthy aqueduct. Still farther, an expanse of mossy sunken walls and broad deserted thoroughfares—a perfect Pompeii beneath the waters. And all was reddishly lit by a violent fulguration, for the mountain upon which the submariners stood was, in fact, a volcano. Yes, a volcano, from the crater of which vomited forth a rain of stones and scoriae, while fiery lava cascaded down the slope, illuminating the immense plain like a gigantic torch.

Aronnax could keep still no longer. Where they were, to what point Nemo had brought them, he must know at any cost.

With a gesture Captain Nemo bade him be still. And picking up a piece of chalky stone he advanced to a rock of black basalt upon which he traced the single word:

ATLANTIS

Atlantis! mused Aronnax. The ancient Meropis of Theopompus. The Atlantis of Plato. That continent denied by Origen, Jamblichus, D'Anville . . .

Monsieur Jules Verne quite obviously was not the first to write about the place. The first was a Greek wrestler, Aristokles, better known as Plato—the broad-shouldered one—and it seems likely that he named the doomed continent after the small island of Atalantë which was devastated by an earthquake and tidal wave in 426 B.C. Several quadrillion books and articles about Atlantis have risen and sunk since Plato's day, and a group of journalists, being asked to list the most significant stories they could imagine, put the reemergence of the lost continent fourth, well ahead of the Second Coming of Christ—which testifies to a ferocious grip on the psyche. That is to say, Atlantis ranks with buried treasure, monsters, ghosts, derelict ships, inexplicable footprints, and luminous objects streaking through the sky as topics that never fail to excite us.

The founding father described Atlantis in two of his philosophic dialogues, *Timaois* and *Kritias*. Beyond that we have absolutely no information.

The capital, he said, was a circular city such as we might expect: temples, parks, docks, bridges, racetracks, various public facilities, et cetera—enriched with gold, silver, ivory, and presumably whatever else the heart desires. Atlanteans lived the good life for a long time, but at last they succumbed to moral rot and the bottom dropped out. More specifically, although *Kritias* ends in midsentence, it appears that Zeus just got fed up with everybody and pulled the plug. Why Plato drowned his children instead of frying them forever in Hell is not known, except possibly to psychoanalysts, but it hardly matters. As for the location of Atlantis, he was indefinite, saying only that it lay outside the Pillars of Hercules.

Now, we always have coveted riches—silver and gold and sparkling stones—so you would think Plato's account might have inspired at least a few treasure hunters; but there seems to be no evidence that his fellow Athenians paid much attention to the story, perhaps because he was more adept at wrestling and philosophy than at fiction.

For whatever reason, Atlantis gave up no more than occasional bubbles until the first century B.C. when a certain Poseidonius, meditating upon the effects of earthquake and erosion, wrote that Plato's submerged continent might not have been altogether imaginary.

Another hundred years went by while the Greeks contemplated this, then Gaius Plinius Secundus—Pliny the Elder—very cautiously agreed. And, most cautiously, not eager to sound foolish, so did Plutarch. And then, in a less critical age, less sophisticated men began to argue for the continent's reality.

At this point the Age of Faith closed down like a fog, obliterating everything concerned with temporal matters, so that nobody thought much about Atlantis until the Renaissance. Even then, as though it were a distant reef, nobody considered Atlantis seriously. But when the New World had been discovered Plato's fable came floating up from the depths. The Spanish historian Gómara suggested that he could have heard rumors of these lands and founded an allegory upon them. The English wizard John Dee drew a map of the new continents and named one of them Atlantis. Sir Francis Bacon wrote *The New Atlantis*. A gentleman with the mellifluous name of John Swann carried it further in *Speculum Mundi*:

". . . this I may think may be supposed, that *America* was sometimes part of that great land which *Plato* calleth the Atlantick island, and that the Kings of that island had some intercourse between the people of *Europe* and *Africa*. . . ."

The celebrated naturalist Georges Leclerc, Comte de Buffon, did not find this idea unreasonable in the eighteenth century, nor did the explorer von Humboldt in the nineteenth. However, scraps of evidence had been piling up against such a theory, so that most advocates prudently demoted North and South America to the status of colonies, leaving the capital city on the ocean bed where only Captain Nemo could find it.

About this time along came The Honorable Ignatius T. T. Donnelly, who was not a fabrication of Gilbert and Sullivan but an erudite Philadelphia lawyer. He is now remembered as the author of the most wildly successful book on Atlantis ever written—leaving Plato far behind—a book that has been reprinted fifty or sixty times since it was published in 1882. But even before that *succès fou* Donnelly had made a name for himself. When he was very young he moved to Minnesota and with the help of a few other believers in the tremendous potential of that state he bought a tract of land near Saint Paul. They founded a city, which they named Nininger, and set about promoting it as the new metropolis of the Midwest. They formed a literary society and a musical society, and they opened a restaurant called Handyside House which developed quite a nice reputation, yet for some inexplicable reason Nininger refused to grow. Saint Paul grew and grew and grew. Nininger did not.

Donnelly turned to politics. At the age of twenty-eight he became lieutenant governor of Minnesota. Then he was elected to the U.S. House of Representatives, where he spent most of his time reading in the congressional library. He may have been the most educated man ever to serve in Washington.

In 1870 he retired to his Nininger mansion and there he commenced to write. His first book, *Atlantis: The Antediluvian World*, made him famous on both sides of the ocean.

He argued that civilization originated on a continent that had once existed in the Atlantic outside the mouth of the Mediterranean, and all other civilizations were its descendants. Egypt, for example, was an Atlantean colony. All of our myths and traditions are memories of Atlantis, he said. All gods and goddesses and their magical deeds are nothing but confused memories of historical events. Here lay the Garden of Eden, Olympus, the Elysian Fields, and so forth.

Now you might think these extravagant claims would be impossible to prove, but any book that is reissued fifty times has struck with overwhelming force. In other words, millions of people were convinced, among them Prime Minister Gladstone who asked the British cabinet to send out a ship in search of the sunken motherland.

Donnelly was long on facts, if short on logic; but whether he had the facts screwed on straight, and whether his deductions followed in a seemly fashion, is irrelevant. The point is that Ignatius T. T. Donnelly did more for Atlantis than Plato, Pliny the Elder, Plutarch, Sir Francis Bacon, Alexander von Humboldt, and several other preeminent gentlemen combined. It is possible that nobody else in history ever upstaged so many distinguished intellects.

His successor was Lewis Spence, a relatively moderate Scotsman who edited the *Atlantis Quarterly* and who offered his own version of the calamity in half a dozen books of steadily subsiding interest. Spence did not claim as much for the lost continent. He argued only that there had been a land mass where now there is none, which gradually evolved into two immense islands—Atlantis and Antillia. Atlantis lay outside Gibraltar, just where Plato said it was, and the West Indies are what remains of Antillia. These two vast islands did not disappear overnight; they sank slowly because of geological disturbances. Emigrants from Atlantis influenced later civilizations throughout the Mediterranean while emigrants from Antillia influenced the New World.

Spence is so much more plausible than Donnelly that it is easy to understand why he was never as popular, which might account for the crochety title of his last warning: *Will Europe Follow Atlantis?*

In any case, his theory appears to be substantiated by the existence of a submarine ridge running from Iceland to the South Atlantic. Along this ridge the average depth of the ocean is about one mile, compared to an average depth of three miles on either side, and occasionally—at Ascension island, the Azores, Tristan de Cunha—this ridge breaks the surface. But specialists in the deep-water business are of the opinion that Spence got it backward. The ridge is not what remains of a sunken land mass; instead, it was lifted from the ocean floor, probably by volcanic activity.

However, on the chance that Plato might have been correct, some oceanographers investigated the bed of the eastern Atlantic where the continent was supposed to be. They found an immensely thick deposit of pelagic red clay, consisting mostly of the shells of animal plankton. Now, it is known that this kind of sediment accumulates at the rate of three-tenths of an inch per millennium, and after various calculations it was learned that 500 million years must have been required to deposit all that clay on the supposed site of Atlantis, which is a bit much even for racial memories.

Well, then, where was Atlantis?

The moon has been proposed. Long ago Atlantis was sucked out of the ocean to become the moon. But professionals insist that if such a thing had occurred the Atlantic bed would be violently disturbed, which it is not.

Other candidates include Ceylon, Malta, Iceland, Palestine, the Canary Islands, Spitzbergen, and at least a dozen more.

In 1675 a Swedish scholar, having bent the facts into suitable shape, demonstrated that Plato's continent, fountainhead of civilization, could only have been Sweden, with its capital city located very near Upsala.

In 1952 a German pastor announced that the Atlantean capital lay six miles east of Heligoland on the floor of the North Sea, not far from the pastor's home.

More recently a British investigator suggested Bronze-Age Wessex.

So it goes. At first this predilection for situating Atlantis in one's own neighborhood seems strange, just as it seems strange that devout Christians always expect the Second Coming to take place somewhere nearby, perhaps in the backyard between the birdbath and the azaleas. But of course there's a reason. We like to be associated with significant events, past, present, or future. After all, one must listen respectfully to the person who shook Babe Ruth's hand, or heard the shot fired at Sarajevo, or whose progenitors raised the walls and battlements of the earliest civilization.

Consequently, Atlantis will be found near Upsala or Heligoland or Reykjavík, or in Britain or Jerusalem, or perhaps beneath the mud of the Guadalquivir between Cádiz and Seville—a site favored by Spanish partisans.

The Spanish have a good claim. Many researchers now think that Tartessus—the Biblical city of Tarshish, that storehouse of gold, silver, ivory, apes, and peacocks—settled majestically into the Guadalquivir mud; and if Plato should turn out to be not just a pamphleteer but a historian describing an actual city, this may be the one he had in mind.

There seems to be no doubt that an important city-state once existed in this area, visited often by Greek and Phoenician trading ships. Aristophanes speaks of the delectable eels of Tartessus—which is odd because Tartessus must have disappeared by his time—and various old chronicles mention the city. Silver was reputed to be so plentiful in Tartessus that hogs ate from silver troughs; and Phoenician businessmen, eager to carry away as much as possible, ordered the wood and lead anchors of their ships replaced with silver anchor stones.

What happened to the city has not been determined, but about the sixth century B.C. it was either destroyed or abandoned, perhaps as a result of the Carthaginian blockade, and the place where it stood has become Las Marismas, a vast marsh inhabited by herds of half-wild longhorned cattle. Archaeologists probing the marsh and other suspected sites in this region have found fragments of unique pottery, and copper and gold jewelry decorated with curious hemispherical knobs and rosettes. The most puzzling find was a ring with an unreadable inscription which appeared to be related to Etruscan and to Greek, and perhaps to the unclassifiable Basque language. Now this sort of thing naturally agitates archaeologists, but Las Marismas' high water table has prevented much digging, so that until now the legacy of Tartessus—if it was Tartessus—consists of these few perplexing items.

Despite the fact that the city has not been precisely located, and therefore a cloud of questions hangs overhead, the resemblances between it and Atlantis are significant. Both lay beyond the Pillars of Hercules at the mouth of a great river adjacent to an irrigated plain. Both were renowned for their wealth and trade, and both vanished.

Apart from Tartessus, the primary candidate seems to be not a city but a happening. That is, Plato's city may have been fictional, or derived from what he had heard of Carthage or Babylon or Syracuse, while the cataclysm he described was factual—the eruption of the volcanic island of Thera in the fifteenth century B.C., an explosion so violent that quite a few scientists believe it destroyed the Minoan Empire.

Sixty-six miles south of Thera on the island of Crete stood the palace of Knossos, omphalos of Minoan civilization. It is still there, ponderously reconstructed by Sir Arthur Evans in accordance with nineteenth-century taste, and if you visit Knossos you need not be an archaeologist to see that something terrible happened. Smoke stains on the walls tell you which way the wind was blowing on that unbelievable day 3,500 years ago.

The most thunderous explosion we know anything about was that of the volcano Krakatoa in the Sunda Strait between Java and Sumatra.

Krakatoa began to spout vapor and pumice during the summer of 1883, and dust from these eruptions was noticed as far away as Singapore. Then on August 26, about 2:00 P.M., the crew of a ship eighty miles distant saw a black cloud billowing upward to an estimated height of fifteen miles. Crewmen aboard another ship much closer to the volcano described this cloud as a huge pine tree with branches of lightning. White-hot lava was observed streaming down the southwest slope and a sinister rumbling could be heard all over Java.

By late afternoon, according to crew members of the ship *Charles Bal*, which at that time was twelve miles from Krakatoa, the air had become choking and sulfurous.

Booming eruptions continued all night, and early next morning Krakatoa annihilated itself with four stupendous explosions. The loudest was heard not only throughout the East Indies but in Vietnam, Ceylon, the Philippines, halfway across Australia, and on the island of Rodriguez 3,000 miles to the southwest. Atmospheric shock waves traveled around the earth three and a half times.

By noon it was over. Five cubic miles of volcanic material had been expelled from Krakatoa. The Sunda Strait was choked with floating pumice, the city of Batavia lay in smoky darkness, and a series of tidal waves had swept across hundreds of coastal villages drowning almost 40,000 people. The height of the largest tidal wave is not known exactly, but it is thought to have reached fifty feet. Ripples from these waves were measured at Cape Horn and probably accounted for a slight rise on tidal gauges in the English Channel.

The remnants of Thera and Krakatoa are in several respects very similar. Volcanic calderas are not always formed in the same way, but these two were. For this reason and for other reasons, the details of which excite nobody except geologists, a comparison can be made. The cauldron of Thera is about four times larger than that of Krakatoa. In other words, Thera threw up something like twenty cubic miles of stone and lava. And instead of Krakatoa's fifty-foot tidal wave the Aegean island of Anaphe shows evidence of a wave—unquestionably from Thera—that reached above two hundred feet. The wave might not have been much less than that when it struck the northern coast of Crete at a speed of perhaps 100 miles an hour.

How many people were washed away cannot even be estimated, because no records of that day have survived. But there are Egyptian references to some sort of catastrophe in the sea to the north, and it is believed that Solon heard about this when he visited Egypt in the sixth century B.C. And from Solon's report Plato may have gotten the idea for his cataclysmic deluge.

Whatever his sources—the end of Minoan civilization, the disappearance of Tartessus, the submergence of little Atalantë, some tale of Carthage—wherever he found his touchstone, Plato no doubt intended to write a meaningful allegory. Being dissatisfied with the behavior of his fellow citizens, he resolved to instruct them.

He tells us in *Kritias* that for many generations the Atlanteans obeyed the laws, revered the gods, and so on:

> . . . for they possessed true and in every way great spirits, uniting gentleness with wisdom in the various chances of life, and in their intercourse with one another. They despised everything but virtue, caring little for their present state of life, and thinking lightly of the possession of gold and other property, which seemed only a burden to them; neither were they intoxicated by luxury; nor did wealth deprive them of their self-control; but they were sober, and saw clearly that all these goods are increased by virtue and friendship with one another, whereas by too great regard and respect for them they are lost, and virtue with them. By such reflections and by the continuance in them of a divine nature, the qualities which we have described grew and increased among them; but when the divine portion began to fade slowly, and become diluted too often and too much with the mortal admixture, and the human nature got the upper hand, they then, being unable to bear their fortune, behaved unseemly, and to him who had an eye to see grew visibly debased, for they were losing the fairest of their precious gifts; but to those who had no eye to see the true happiness, they appeared glorious and blessed at the very time when they were becoming tainted with unrighteous ambition and power.

Zeus therefore pointed a finger and that was that.

Plato's allegory did not make much of an impression, so far as we know. Allegories seldom do. The Athenians did not feel especially rebuked by such criticism; it must have seemed as irrelevant to them as it does to us. Consequently, what endured was not Plato's didactic message but his lovely and terrible image of a drowned city, a city beneath the sea. We cannot stop looking for it.

The old wrestler would have been bitterly surprised.

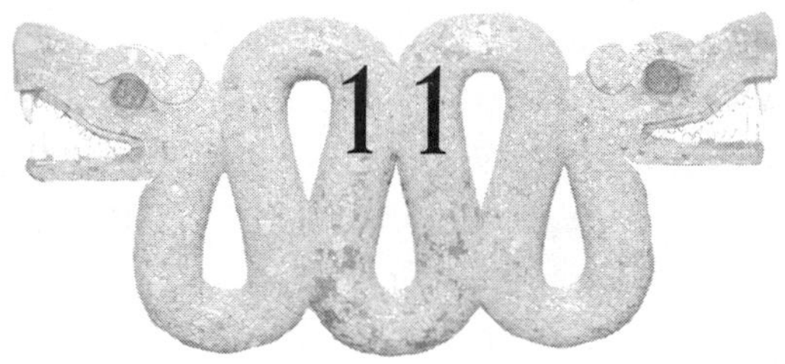

11

The Innocents' Crusade

EARLY IN THE SEVENTH century on Saint Mark's Day, April 25, while the bubonic plague boiled across Europe, Pope Gregory ordered the church altars draped in black and instructed priests to carry shrouded crosses through the streets. And because this ceremony would be repeated year after year Saint Mark's Day eventually came to be known as "Black Crosses." By the thirteenth century, however, it commemorated not only victims of the plague but all who had died in the struggle for Jerusalem and those who still were held captive by the Moslems.

Among the spectators when this grim procession wound through the streets of Chartres in the year 1212 was a shepherd boy named Stephen from the village of Cloyes. The unending prayers, the melancholy litanies, the parade of eerily nodding crosses, the frantic appeals to God for mercy, the screams and groans and seizures of penitents—all of this evidently excited the boy so much that he began talking wildly about his desire to see the Moslems expelled from the Holy Land.

A few days later some adult approached Stephen in the fields near Cloyes. Whoever he was, this man represented himself as a pilgrim returning from Jerusalem. Stephen offered him food and the stranger told stories of what he had seen and done. At last he revealed to the boy that in actuality he was not a simple pilgrim but Jesus Christ. He then commanded Stephen to lead the children of France on a new crusade, and gave him a letter addressed to King Philip Augustus.

Here the mysterious pilgrim vanishes, and nothing has been learned of him beyond what Stephen said. He might have been imaginary except that the illiterate shepherd boy did possess such a letter in the summer of 1212. Whether or not Stephen managed to deliver it to the king is disputed by historians. Steven Runciman thinks he did. Henry Treece agrees. George Zabriskie Gray, an earlier researcher, was unconvinced: "Whether he [King Philip] had received the letter which Stephen showed, we are not told."

Nor is the pilgrim's motive clear. According to one theory, a villager who had noticed the boy's excitement during Black Crosses decided to play a cruel joke. But most scholars believe it is more complex, perhaps related to the Albigensian heresy.

In the French town of Albi some Christians too wise for their own health had begun objecting to ecclesiastic corruption. They also spread the absurd idea that life is a struggle between the armies of Light and Darkness, and which force will prevail is altogether in doubt. Now, as we know, in the orthodox view Satan has no chance of defeating God. The Albigensian argument therefore was suicidal. Rigorous Christians could not permit such blasphemy to exist. Nor did they. Pope Innocent III butchered the Albigensians in one of the most sanguine spectacles you will come across anywhere.

"Slay them all," Innocent responded when asked how the heretics could be identified. "Slay them all. The Lord will recognize His own."

At least that is the hideous response attributed to Innocent. He may or may not have said it. One document suggests that a German monk contrived the story. The massacre of the Albigensians, though, cannot be doubted.

This slaughter was under way when Stephen met the pilgrim, but the Albigensians were not easy to exterminate. A few survivors would cling to their faith and perpetuate it until it outlasted Innocent himself; and papal curiosity about these repugnant ideas would finally beget that Un-Christian Activities Committee known as the Inquisition. However, the point is that an Albigensian priest may have decided to use the emotional young shepherd as a conduit to King Philip. Albigensian arguments could not reach the king directly, but deluded children sometimes work marvels.

Thus, historians theorize, the mysterious stranger may have been a Christian heretic. Not that his identity matters; what matters is the result.

Stephen, with the letter in his wallet, set out to visit the king—which sounds so improbable that it might be the opening of a fairy tale.

King Philip was spending the summer just north of Paris at Saint-Denis, burial place of Dionysius the martyr, one of seven apostles whose efforts converted Gaul to Christianity. Legend says that Dionysius' head was chopped off and his corpse thrown into the Seine, whereupon he emerged from the river with his head in his hands and walked to the place where he wished to be buried. Early in the eighteenth century when Ninon de l'Enclos was asked whether she thought the saint had carried his head such a great distance she replied that the distance wasn't important; what counted was the first step—which has nothing to do with Stephen but does add an ornamental detail.

At Saint-Denis, too, the kings of France had been buried ever since the time of Dagobert, last of the Merovingian rulers, and here the red flag of the Church and holy standard of the realm—the oriflamme—was kept. Because of these attractions Saint-Denis drew a good many pilgrims and tourists.

Stephen preached the crusade as he walked from Cloyes. It seems odd that anybody would listen to the exhortations of a twelve-year-old peasant displaying a letter of authorization from Christ, but then one remembers Jeanne d'Arc two centuries later who was just sixteen when she went to work. And in our own century people have knelt to be blessed and married by a four-year-old minister. So it should be no surprise that Stephen collected an audience wherever he stopped, and it is probable that by the time he reached Saint-Denis he already had picked up some followers.

Here, preaching day and night beside the martyr's shrine as well as in the public market, repeating familiar accounts of Christian suffering in the Holy Land, he became a noticeable figure. He emphasized the difference between the sepulcher of Dionysius, which was a scene of constant devotion, and that of Christ in Jerusalem, surrounded and scorned by Moslems. He asked his audience how they could tolerate this. He likened Jesus to a king banished from his heritage, Jerusalem to a captive queen. He is said to have cried out: "For the last time we have known defeat! Hereafter shall proud barons and mailed knights testify to the power of children commissioned by God!"

These words sound false because we cannot imagine a farm boy today, nor any boy—nor an adult—calling up such regal syntax. Yet what Stephen actually said might not have been very different from the speech attributed to him. As George Orwell points out, in ancient ballads the lord and the peasant speak the same language—which no doubt was poetic convention. Still, all of us who have grown up using English do sense that a long time ago we spoke with eloquence and strength. Maybe the people of every nation feel this. And it could be true: we might all have spoken a superior language in the past.

Stephen referred often to a dream he had in which the Mediterranean divided, allowing him and those who followed him to walk to Jerusalem, just as the Red Sea had opened for another shepherd.

And it is said by medieval historians that while at Saint-Denis he performed miracles.

To those who questioned his authority he showed the letter, telling again of his encounter with Jesus in the fields near Cloyes. He also told a curiously naïve story that has the cast of the Middle Ages on it. When he returned from Chartres, he said, after witnessing the procession of Black Crosses, his sheep had wandered into a field of grain. He was angered and began to beat them, whereupon they dropped to their knees and repented. By this sign, among others, he knew that he was destined for greatness.

People going home from Saint-Denis carried news of Stephen of Cloyes, and very soon the idea of a children's crusade spread throughout France and into Germany—although on this point modern historians disagree. Friedrich Heer states: "There is no discoverable connection between the two Children's Crusades, which started in the same year, 1212, one in the Rhineland, the other in the Loire valley."

Runciman, speaking for a majority, says that when reports of Stephen's preaching reached the Rhineland: "The children of Germany were not to be outdone. A few weeks after Stephen had started on his mission, a boy called Nicholas . . . began to preach the same message."

What is certain, though, is that news of Stephen's crusade did seep through France in an astonishingly short time.

Clerics were appalled, considering it sacrilege that the boy should liken himself to Moses, and denounced the crusade as an inspiration of Satan. However, Pope Innocent reputedly said: "The very children put us to shame."

They gathered like thistledown in a breeze, floating toward the place of assembly, Vendôme, justifying their cause with this passage: "Out of the mouth of babes and sucklings hast thou ordained strength because of thine enemies, that thou mightest still the enemy and the avenger."

They referred to Stephen as The Prophet and to themselves—some of them eight or nine years old—as minor prophets. Columns of boys and girls converged on Vendôme, following replicas of the oriflamme. Some of the children swung perfumed censers, others held crosses and burning candles. They sang hymns which they composed as they walked. They prayed and wept and appealed to God and beckoned ecstatically for other children to join them.

"Lord, restore Christendom!" they shouted. "Lord, restore to us the true and holy Cross!"

King Philip, when he realized that the shepherd boy actually was mustering an army, seems to have become confused. After all these centuries, and with such fragmentary documentation, it is hard to establish the truth; but at first he probably approved the idea. The pope had spoken in favor of it and Philip was not anxious to offend His Holiness.

But then the king's counselors advised him to suppress the movement. A horde of children would cause immense disorder. Many of them would die before reaching Palestine, others just as certainly would be killed there, and France could not afford the loss of these young people. Still, it might be awkward to suppress the crusade. Not only children but a number of adults were beginning to idolize Stephen. Then, too, there was a possibility that God did in fact wish it.

Philip turned for advice to the University of Paris, whose doors had recently opened. Those most learned men, the doctors of the university, should know how to resolve the problem.

According to Strayer and Munro: "They told him that the movement was unwise and he commanded the children to return home. They did so, and the children's crusade in France came to an end." But only the first half of this judgment can be supported. The university savants did advise against it, and King Philip did issue an edict ordering the children to go home. That much can be verified. What happened next is a different story.

The king's edict apparently was ignored. The children paid no attention and the adults charged with enforcing it did not do so with any vigor. Philip himself, rather strangely, seems to have stepped aside. Possibly he felt that by the issuance of a decree he had identified his position to the pope, which was the important thing.

Thus, with slight opposition, the children continued assembling at Vendôme. A few of them must have had permission to join the crusade; others simply disregarded their parents and ran away.

In Germany the crusade preached by Nicholas was similar, but not identical. Most of what we know about it comes from the account of a monk named Godfrey who was writing in Cologne between the years 1162 and 1237.

Nicholas must have been approximately the same age as Stephen, perhaps younger. And, like the French boy, he believed himself supernaturally ordained: a blazing cross appeared in the sky and he heard a voice. He may have been persuaded of these things by his father, described as a wicked man, who hoped to profit by his son's celebrity.

Nicholas copied Stephen's technique and established himself near a shrine. Cologne was the religious center of Germany and attracted thousands of pilgrims because the bones of the Magi were laid out in the old Byzantine cathedral, thanks to Archbishop Raynuldus who had accompanied Frederick Barbarossa to Italy and brought back three skeletons as part of his loot. During the nineteenth century, we are told by Gray, somebody discovered that one of the skulls was that of a child with milk teeth. But again, this should be considered an ornamental detail.

In Nicholas' day there they were, side by side, the undoubted bones of the wise men, adorned with jewels and gold trinkets, surrounded by votive offerings. He had only to point to them, just as Stephen could point to the sepulcher of Dionysius. Would true Christians permit the Savior's tomb to remain in the filthy grasp of Moslems while embellishing that of the Magi with precious gifts?

Appeals for the liberation of Palestine were familiar enough to adults who had heard it all their lives—the First Crusade having been launched more than a century earlier—but to children it sounded like an original idea. And there was, in fact, one singular difference. Nicholas, more so than Stephen, emphasized that this crusade would accomplish its purpose not by warfare but through conversion. Moslems, as soon as they had listened to the children of Germany, would gladly and without hesitation discard their faith like a worn-out cloak in order to put on the cross of Christianity. Therefore it would not be necessary to slaughter them.

Nicholas may or may not have considered meeting the French procession somewhere along the way, but his army was ready to march by the end of June and he understood that it must get moving. There was no alternative. His crusaders had almost no money and very little food. Traveling through the countryside they might forage enough to keep themselves alive, but they could not camp day after day in the streets of Cologne.

So, one fine morning about the first of July, he led 20,000 adolescents out of the city, leaving perhaps an equal number behind. Some authorities believe this exodus may be the origin of the Pied Piper legend, although how the rats got into the story is puzzling. Unless, of course, they represent the army of hungry children.

Nicholas' young crusaders wore a uniform—those who could afford it—the long gray cloak of a pilgrim with a cross sewn on the breast, and a broad-brimmed hat. Many of them carried a palmer's staff, symbolizing a visit to Palestine. Their average age, according to the Sicardi chronicle, was about twelve—slightly older than the children who gathered around Stephen. And for some reason the German crusade attracted more girls. A few adults went along: youthful priests, calculating merchants, stargazers, fanatics, whores, and idlers. In other words, a fair slice of humanity.

The chronicles do not explain why the Germans did not all march together, nor when the second army left Cologne, nor who its leader was.

Very little is known about this second army, which might possibly have started a few days earlier than Nicholas. It moved through central Switzerland, crossed the Alps at Saint Gotthard Pass, and like a swarm of dying locusts surged down the Italian coast through Ancona as far as Brindisi in the heel of the boot. Militant German emperors such as Barbarossa had not left the Italians with a great love for their blue-eyed northern neighbors, and the sins of the fathers fell heavily on these unfortunates. Those that survived the Alps, disease, starvation, wild animals, and human predators at last met their destiny in brothels, or, if they were lucky, as servants. According to the *Chronicon Rhythmicum*, which is thought to be the work of a contemporary, perhaps Benedictus Gentilotus: "Illi de Brundusio virgines stuprantur. Et in arcum pessimum passim venumdantur." At Brindisi the young girls were raped, sold to whoever wanted them.

The fortunes of Nicholas' army are better documented. He chose a course up the Rhine to Basle, through western Switzerland to Geneva, and crossed the Alps by the Mont Cenis Pass. At this point half of his army was gone. Some of the children deserted and tried to get home, but most of the absent troops were dead. Many of them starved. Others froze, or were murdered, or drowned while attempting to wade through mountain streams. Some were devoured by wolves.

Another 3,000 died before Nicholas arrived at the gates of Genoa on August 25.

He petitioned the Genoese senate, asking that his regiment be allowed to stay within the walls overnight, saying that next morning when the sea divided he would march on to Jerusalem.

The senators granted permission to remain a week. They assumed that the children would go back to Germany once they realized how foolish they had been, but after the long trip and the disappointment they would need a few days of rest. It is said that Nicholas and his captains accepted this offer derisively, they were so sure the Mediterranean would roll apart.

Within hours, though, after thousands of fanatical half-crazed children had pushed into Genoa, the senators rescinded this invitation. The army could stay overnight, but no longer.

From Genoa the crusaders marched to Pisa: it might be here, after all, that the sea was meant to divide. We have no record of how many died on the road to Pisa.

The Senones chronicle states that two shiploads of German children sailed from Pisa to the Holy Land. They never returned.

Nicholas's failing army turned inland. Small tattered sickly companies are known to have reached Florence, Arezzo, Perugia, and Siena, like the unraveling end of a rope. A few children walked to Rome, where Innocent granted the leaders an audience. "Moved by their piety but embarrassed by their folly," the pope told them to go home.

Nicholas himself may not have been invited to this audience. His prophecies had not turned out too well and he might have been deposed. He might possibly have been murdered. A thirteenth-century chronicle reports that later he fought bravely at Acre and at the siege of Damietta, returning unharmed; but this last seems very questionable because it is on record that when the people of Cologne learned what had happened to their children they hanged his father.

Stephen's army continued assembling at Vendôme for several weeks after the departure of the Germans and when he gave the order to march sometime in midsummer approximately 30,000 children followed him. Although they were not dressed as uniformly as their Teutonic cousins, each had a woolen cross sewn on the right shoulder.

Animals, birds, and butterflies are said to have joined the French crusade. Butterflies, bearers of the soul, were especially significant. Much later Jeanne d'Arc would be asked during her examination: "Is it true that you and your banner go into battle among a cloud of butterflies?"

Stephen chose a path southward through the rich heart of France, across the Loire to the Rhône at Lyons, through Valence and Avignon to Marseilles. It was a more hospitable route than that chosen by the Germans and Stephen traveled more comfortably than Nicholas, who had walked. He was looked upon as a saint, so he traveled in a chariot padded with carpets, with a decorated canopy to protect him from the August sun. Around his chariot rode the honor guard—a dozen boys from aristocratic families, armed with lances, mounted on the best horses available.

He often addressed the multitude, standing up in his cart, and it is said that many children were trampled to death during his speeches. Except for the lances it is probable that he, too, would have been buried by the reverent mob, so anxious were they to pluck a splinter from his vehicle, or a thread from his cloak, or a hair from the mane of one of the horses. Any of these items would almost sanctify the owner and could be sold or exchanged for food.

Whether Stephen was satisfied merely to address his disciples while trundling through the countryside in regal solitude, or whether he now and then helped himself to a few delirious bodies will never be determined; but Roger of Wendover, writing soon after the event, says that Stephen was "a child in years but accomplished in vice." So, lascivious or continent, reclining beneath a brightly painted canopy, he bumped along on wooden wheels toward Marseilles.

Both in France and Germany that summer was unusually hot and dry, which seemed to foretell the evaporation of the Mediterranean, but at the same time it resulted in a shortage of food. Stealing became the order of the day, fights erupted, corpses decayed beside the road, and because they had no idea where Jerusalem was they would ask, whenever a castle was sighted on a hill—ignoring the fact that they had not yet crossed the sea—if that could be the Holy City. And inevitably, when they found just another castle, the children grew more disenchanted and listened with less excitement to Stephen's exhortations.

About the end of August they reached the Mediterranean coast. Some had died or dropped out, but they had not been forced to cross the Alps, which decimated the Germans, and along the way they had picked up fresh recruits, so that almost as many children reached Marseilles as had left Vendôme.

The city elders responded very much as the Genoese had. They sympathized and wished to help, because they wished to see Palestine liberated; however, the sight of such a host was alarming. Stephen assured them that his army would remain only one night. In the morning when the waters parted they would be on their way.

It is gratifying to think that whenever a body of people has fallen upon hard times there always have been other people anxious to help them out. So it happened here. Two merchants of Marseilles appeared. The chronicles do not give their names in the French form; they are spoken of as Hugo Ferreus and William Porcus, which translates readily into Hugh the Iron and Will the Pig.

Seeing the children gathered disconsolately on the shore, these merchants volunteered to charter as many ships as necessary—*causa Dei, absque pretio*—for the sake of God, without price.

The waters of the Mediterranean, therefore, would indeed roll back, and all those who wished to continue would walk to Jerusalem as Stephen had prophesied.

Seven ships were chartered. The number of children who went aboard can only be estimated, but there must have been at least 5,000. We do not know the exact date the fleet sailed, nor much else about it. Almost certainly the departure was accompanied by the traditional hymn: "Veni Creator Spiritus."

A month or so later, when they should have had time to reach the Holy Land and news of their arrival should be spreading, those who came back from that part of the world—pilgrims, adult crusaders, merchants—were questioned. But the answer was always the same: no such fleet had dropped anchor at any port.

In 1215, three years after the children left Marseilles, John of England with very little grace drew his X on the Magna Carta. A year after that Pope Innocent died; Honorius became pontiff and immediately preached the Fifth Crusade. In 1222 the Mongols invaded eastern Europe. Philip Augustus died the following year. Saint Francis of Assisi died in 1226. Genghis Khan died a year later.

In 1230 a priest returned to Europe from Egypt and said that he had sailed with the children. At least four medieval chroniclers—Albericus, Belgicum, Roger Bacon, and Thomas de Champré—have preserved this priest's account of what happened.

Not many leagues southwest of Sardinia lay a bleak, deserted island called Accipitrum, which refers to the falcons that nest among the cliffs. On the third day out of Marseilles the fleet was close to Accipitrum when a storm drove two ships against it. They broke up and everyone aboard was drowned. The five ships that survived the storm did not sail around Sardinia and enter the straits of Sicily as had been expected, but veered south toward Africa and then followed the coast westward to the Moslem city of Bujeiah. Here the children were taken ashore and sold. Some remained in Bujeiah. Others were sent to Alexandria where the governor, Maschemuth, bought many of them for use in the fields. Some were taken to the Holy Land—past the city they had intended to liberate—to Damascus and Baghdad, where a number of them were decapitated, drowned, or shot by archers because they would not renounce the Christian faith. All the rest, about 700, including the priest who told this story, were bought by the sultan of Egypt, Malek Kamel, who took them to Cairo. Eighteen years later the priest was freed, although the chronicles do not say why. And by these accounts nobody else aboard the ships that left Marseilles ever returned to Europe.

Hugo Ferreus and William Porcus, after turning a nice profit, apparently skipped town. They had been in the business of selling Christians for a long time, although never on such a scale, and they might have become uneasy. News that they had sold 5,000 children could get back to France.

We hear of them once more but it sounds like an exemplary tale, perhaps a nineteenth-century addition. The emir of Sicily, Mirabel, employed them to kidnap or assassinate the German emperor, Frederick II. Things did not quite work out. Mirabel, his two sons, and the flesh merchants were caught—all five hanged on the same gallows.

As for Stephen, medieval historians do not mention him after his army reached Marseilles. Consequently we have no idea if he drowned in the surf at Accipitrum, or was beheaded at Damascus, or spent his life in the fields near Alexandria, or whether he declined to go aboard the Judas ships and started walking back to Cloyes.

In any case, when Pope Gregory IX heard the priest's story he decreed that a monument should be built to honor the children. Of the sites accessible to Christians it was felt that the most appropriate would be that island where two ships of the fleet had been wrecked. Many bodies had washed ashore during the storm and though most of them decayed a few were buried by fishermen. These remains were exhumed and placed inside a church which was built at the pope's direction. It was called the Church of the New Innocents, Ecclesia Novorum Innocentium, a reference to the murdered children of Bethlehem, and the pope endowed it so that twelve prebends could live on the tiny island and pray unendingly, day after day, year after year.

Accipitrum became a shrine. Boatloads of pilgrims arrived to worship the drowned children whose bodies—miraculously whole and uncorrupted, says Albericus—were on display.

But at last, during the sixteenth century, the church was abandoned and then forgotten.

In 1737 several Christians who had been held captive at Tabarca on the African coast managed to escape and sailed to the island. They settled there and founded the village of Carlo Forte. According to one account, not considered reliable, these fugitives happened upon the ruins of the church and felt surprised because they thought that except for an occasional fisherman they were the first people to have arrived. They could not imagine what it was or who had built it, so they avoided the place.

Near the ruins are two wells that supposedly were dug at the time the church was built, and there are some catacombs not far away. The site overlooks much of the island, which now is called San Pietro, and across the strait you can see the rocky outline of Sardinia.

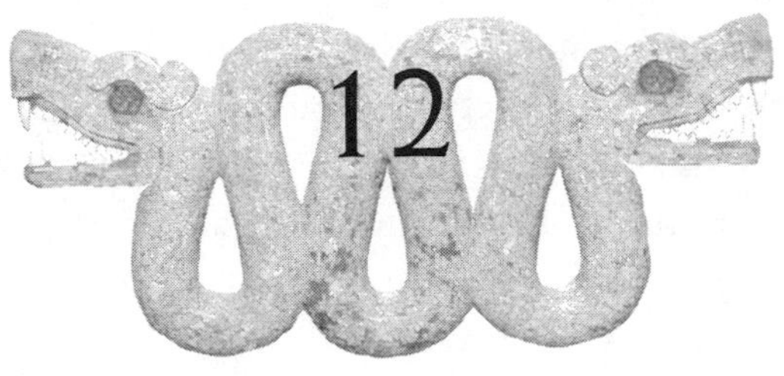

12

Prester John

HE LIVED IN ASIA, later in Africa, but first in the land of Pentexoria in a city called Susa, with the Great Khan's daughter as his wife. Twelve archbishops attended him, who themselves were mighty lords. His chamberlain was a king. His cupbearer was a king. His steward was a primate and king. His marshal was a king and archimandrite. His cook was an abbot and king. Beneath his banner lay seventy-two kingdoms whose monarchs, each utterly subservient, ruled several lesser kings—which ought to give you an idea of his importance. Nevertheless, as we know from his famous letter to Emperor Manuel Comnenus, he chose to be addressed simply as Presbyter Johannes.

Manuel Comnenus, a Greek, in that year of 1165 the most powerful Christian on earth, forwarded copies of Prester John's letter to Pope Alexander III and to the Holy Roman emperor, Frederick Barbarossa; and news of it roared like fire across Europe because the three acknowledged leaders of the Western world had been told they were insignificant.

This is what the letter said:

> I, Johannes the Presbyter, Lord of Lords, am superior in virtue, riches and might to all who walk under Heaven. Seventy-two kings pay tribute to Us. Our might prevails in the Three Indies. Our lands extend to the Farthest Indies where the body of St. Thomas the Apostle rests. . . . Our country is the home and dwelling-place of elephants, dromedaries, camels, metacollinarum, cametennus, panthers, tinserete, white bears, white merles, cicadas, mute gryphons, tigers, hyenas, wild horses, wild oxen and wild men, horned men, one-eyed men, centaurs, fauns, satyrs, pygmies, giants. . . . Thirty thousand people eat at Our table each day, apart from guests, and all receive gifts from Our stores. Our table is of emerald supported by four pillars of amethyst. . . . When We ride to war We are preceded by thirteen lofty crosses of gold ornamented with precious stones, and each is followed by ten thousand mounted soldiers and by one hundred thousand men on foot. . . . When We go forth on other occasions a plain wooden cross is borne before Us, that We may recall the passion of Our Lord Jesus Christ, and also a golden bowl filled with earth to remind Us that Our flesh must return to its original substance. But We carry also a silver bowl filled with gold, that everyone may recognize Us and render homage. Our magnificence surpasses the wealth of the world. . . . If thou canst count the stars of the sky and the sands of the sea, then shalt thou know how to judge the vastness of Our realm and Our power.

With these imperious words, and more, Prester John informed Europe of his existence, although for a long time there had been rumors of a Christian kingdom somewhere in the east beyond the Moslem empire.

In 1122 a Bishop John of India—by some accounts he was an archbishop—arrived to visit Pope Calixtus II. He stayed twelve months, delighting everybody with wonderful stories of Saint Thomas who had traveled to India after Christ's crucifixion to preach the gospel. Saint Thomas was well remembered throughout India, the bishop said, for he had converted many, and his martyrdom had not been forgotten. In fact, the saint's body still could be seen, unchanged and uncorrupted, on the day of the feast of Saint Thomas. The corpse stood erect within a precious silver shell: "The face shines like a star, having red hair hanging down almost to the shoulders, and a red beard, curly but not long, the entire appearance being beautiful to behold. The clothes are as firm and complete as when they were first put on."

In 1145 another high ecclesiastic emerged from the shadowy East. Hugh, Bishop of Antioch, came to the pope for help because Moslems were threatening the Christian enclaves in Syria. Hugh's visit was meticulously recorded by Otto of Freising, one of the most famous and reliable historians of the Middle Ages. According to Otto, the Syrian bishop told the pope about a certain priest-king in the Orient whose name was John, who was a Christian, and whose army had defeated the Medes and Persians after a three-day battle and occupied their capital city. Then the priest-king had marched to the aid of Jerusalem, but was stopped by the river Tigris. Unable to cross the river, King John led his army north because he had been told that sometimes the Tigris froze. He waited several years for this to happen; but finally, when it did not, be was obliged to return to the Orient.

Europe had no further news of this redoubtable Christian leader, nor of any Christian settlement in Asia, until the letter arrived.

Twelve years elapsed before the letter was answered. The probable explanation for this is that the letter was a fake, and the pope and both emperors realized it. The original copy has long since disappeared, but scholars have more or less reconstructed it by working backward from later versions. They suspect that the original did not include either a date or a place, which would be unlikely if it were authentic, and the bombastic tone rings untrue. Nor would any monarch announce himself to another with such conceit, not unless his object was war. Then too, the prose reeks more of literary craft than diplomatic craft. But the most convincing evidence of fraud is that many details in the letter can be found in books available to an educated European of the twelfth century. The writer borrowed from Marbod of Rennes, Isidore of Seville, from at least two books about Alexander the Great, and almost certainly paraphrased other medieval writers.

As to who wrote it—unquestionably somebody who had visited the East, perhaps a Crusader or a monk, or a European living in the Near East. He mentions Samarkand, which had been for centuries a trading center on the silk road to China. The Greeks and Romans knew about Samarkand, but Europeans of the Middle Ages did not, and there is no reference to Samarkand in any Latin document earlier than Prester John's letter, which suggests that the author had at least traveled through the fringes of the Orient. And he seems to be familiar with a ninth-century tale then unknown in Europe, *The Thousand and One Nights*.

As to why he wrote that letter, we can only speculate.

It was translated into Anglo-Norman by an English knight, Roau d'Arundel, who accompanied King Richard the Lion-Hearted on the Third Crusade. Roau picked up a copy of the Latin text in Constantinople, and prefaced his translation by saying that the letter offered an instructive view of Eastern miracles which one could either accept as truth or read for entertainment.

Modern analysts think it is more substantial than that. The letter may have been written to encourage the Crusaders by telling them about an invincible ally in the Orient; or it could have been a parable meant to embarrass the two emperors and the pope, because Prester John points out that in spite of immeasurable wealth and power he remains a humble priest in whose domain everything belongs to everyone—as opposed to Europe where leaders consider themselves divine, where the rich get richer while the poor get poorer, and justice is a foreign word.

In any case, on September 27, 1177, Pope Alexander III wrote to Prester John: "*Magnificus Rex Indorum, Sacerdotum sanctissimus*. . . ."

The pope went on to say that he had heard from various sources about John's good works and piety, but at the same time the Roman Catholic doctrine of papal authority over all Christians should be understood. In other words, there could be only one successor to the first pontiff, Saint Peter—namely himself, Alexander, in Rome. And because he had heard that Prester John was anxious for guidance he was sending his personal physician, Magister Philippus, to offer instruction.

Having pontifically signed and sealed this response, Alexander told Magister Philippus to deliver it.

Just why the pope answered a letter that he knew to be fictitious, especially a letter addressed not to himself but to Emperor Comnenus, is unclear. It is thought that the remarkable circulation of Prester John's letter throughout Europe at last compelled the pope to restate the guiding principles of Christianity. If so, the letter must have been intended as a social or moral tract.

Concerning Magister Philippus, be obediently marched off in the direction of Asia and right off the pages of history.

On Easter Sunday, 1245, a Franciscan monk named John de Piano Carpini climbed on a donkey and set out from Lyons, directed by Pope Innocent IV to assess the situation in windswept Asia and, if possible, to convert the king of the Tartars—whoever he was, and whatever he might be called. Brother Carpini was also told to keep an eye out for the spectral Christian monarch. Any information would be appreciated.

Innocent gave him some letters which might be useful along the way, and included a stern reproof to the Tartar king: "We find ourselves greatly surprised that you, as We have learned, have attacked and destroyed many countries belonging not only to Christian peoples but to others. . . . We wish all to live in peace and in fear of God, according to the Prince of Peace. Therefore We pray and earnestly beseech you to relinquish such undertakings, above all your persecution of Christians, and by suitable penance to appease the wrath of God which you surely have brought upon yourselves by reason of your many deeds of outrage."

Carpini, a former pupil of Saint Francis of Assisi, was sixty-two years old when he rode away from Lyons. It took him almost a year to reach Kiev, which had been practically obliterated by the Mongols. Here he got an escort. His Mongol guides did not waste time. They followed the imperial highway—extending from Kiev to Canton—and changed horses several times a day at relay stations. Carpini's journal reports that he was in the saddle from early morning until night, sometimes late at night. He had nothing to drink except melted snow, and his meals during the forty days of Lent while he was trotting across Asia consisted of boiled millet. On July 22, Mary Magdalene's Day, Brother Carpini was delivered to the court of Kuyuk—a grandson of Genghis Khan—just in time for Kuyuk's coronation festivities.

It must have been quite a show. The Russian Prince Yaroslav was there, along with various princes of the Kitai and the Solangs, and two sons of the king of Georgia. A sultan was there to represent the caliph of Baghdad, and Carpini was told by the imperial recorder that a number of other sultans were present. More than 4,000 ambassadors came to witness and to celebrate the ascension of Kuyuk.

In November the indestructible Franciscan started home. He traveled all winter, sometimes sleeping out: "When we awoke we often found ourselves covered with snow which the wind had blown over us. . . ."

A year later he entered Lyons and gave the pope a message from Kuyuk:

> You must come yourself at the head of all your kings and prove to Us your fealty and allegiance. If you disregard this Divine Commandment and fail to obey Us, thenceforth We must look upon you as Our enemy. Whoever recognizes and submits to the Son of God and Lord of the World, the Great Khan, will be saved. Whoever refuses will be annihilated. . . .

Kuyuk then asked:

> How do you know who is worthy in the sight of God to partake of His grace? We pray to God, and by His power We shall lay waste to the earth from east to west. If a man did not possess the strength of God how could he have done such things? When you say: "I am a Christian, I praise God and despise all others," how do you know whom God considers righteous and to whom He will show His mercy?

Just what effect this menacing soliloquy had on the pope, we can only guess, but he must have felt some disappointment because the Mongol's reply seemed to indicate that he did not, at least for the present, care to be baptized.

Nor did Brother Carpini have much news of Prester John, mentioning him only once. Carpini describes him as an Indian king, a black Saracen, who had once defeated a Mongol army.

William of Ruysbroek, a Flemish Franciscan, set out from Constantinople in May of 1253. His instructions were pretty much the same, to see what he could see, because bad news kept trickling out of Asia and it would be helpful to get in touch with Prester John—if there was a Prester John—or with his successor, if there happened to be any such. William, "a fat and sturdy man," was accompanied by another monk, Bartholomew of Cremona, about whom we know very little. Also in the party was an interpreter named Homo Dei, a slave boy named Nicolaus whom the monks bought in Constantinople, and somebody called Gosset.

They sailed across the Black Sea and landed at a Venetian trading post in the Crimea where quite possibly they met Niccolo and Maffeo Polo. This would have been just about the year Marco was born.

By oxcart and horse they rode into Mongol territory, encouraged by rumors of Christians somewhere ahead. At the court of Batu—another of Genghis Khan's grandsons—Nicolaus and Gosset were detained, although we aren't told why. So the two Franciscans and Homo Dei continued eastward, almost paralleling Carpini's route, until they were brought to the camp of Mangu Khan, who had been elected chairman after the death of Kuyuk.

On January 3, 1254, they were escorted to Mangu's house. And there at the end of the world, on the Great Khan's doorstep, wearing sandals and ragged brown cloaks, Brothers William and Bartholomew folded their hands and started to sing, because it was Christmastide in Asia as surely as it was in Europe:

A solis ortus cardine
et usque terrae limitem
Christum canamus principem
natum Maria virgine.

After they finished singing they were searched for knives. Then they were allowed into the presence of the khan. They saw a middle-aged, middle-sized, flat-nosed man lolling on a fur-covered bed beside his young wife. He had a daughter named Cirina by a Christian woman who was now dead. Cirina was seated on another bed with some babies, and to William's eyes she appeared "horribly ugly." The room, hung with gold cloth, was heated by a fire of wormwood, thorns, and cow dung.

"Fear not," said the khan.

"Had I been afraid," said William, "I would not have come."

Mangu invited them to drink: wine, mare's milk, rice wine, or mead. William declined with thanks, and presumably Bartholomew did the same; although out of respect William tasted the rice wine, which he found clear and aromatic. Homo Dei, the interpreter, accepted a cup without hesitation. Homo Dei then had another and another, so that before long the Franciscans could not understand what he was saying. The khan also got drunk. In fact, reports Brother William, during the four months they stayed at Mangu Khan's court this happened very often.

In April, at a final audience, the Mongol ruler told them:

"We believe there is only one God. By Him we live and by Him we die. Before Him we are righteous of heart. But just as God has given the hand a variety of fingers, so has He given mankind a variety of ways. To you He has given the Scriptures, yet you do not abide by them. . . . To us He has given soothsayers. We do what they say and we live in peace."

William and Homo Dei then started back, carrying a jeweled belt as a talisman against thunder and lightning. Brother Bartholomew remained at Karakorum, not because he wanted to but because he was sick, and that was the last anybody ever heard of him.

A year later William and Homo Dei reached the fortress of Acre, in what is now Israel. There William stopped to preach and to write a long account of his trip. His senses were acute, his memory exceptional, and unlike many servants of the Lord he did not restrict himself to ecclesiastic observations. He noted, for example, that the Caspian was an inland sea, not an arm of the ocean as geographers of the time maintained. He had watched the Tartars building and coloring their gigantic tents, which were transported on carts, twenty-two oxen drawing each cart. The oxen were yoked in two ranks, eleven abreast. And the shaft of the vehicle, he said, was as long as the mast of a ship.

He remembered that Orengai tribesmen were in the habit of fastening polished slats of bone to their feet so that they could glide across frozen snow and ice.

He described Mongolian money—bits of cotton paper, a handsbreadth square, "on which they print lines like those on Mangu's seal. They write with a brush such as artists use, and in one sign they combine letters to form a complete word."

He did not think the Asiatics could be converted. They appeared sympathetic to every religion, he said, but would submit to none. They were beyond understanding.

As for Christianity in that part of the world, he confirmed its existence, saying that on the thirtieth of November, Saint Andrew's Day, he and Brother Bartholomew entered a Nestorian church in the village of Cailac and "sang joyously, as loud as we could, *Salve regina*, it having been a long time since we last saw a church."

Nestorius, the fifth-century patriarch of Constantinople, had sent missionaries into Asia. Just how far they traveled will never be known, but they may have gone all the way through China, perhaps to the Pacific coast, because in the seventeenth century some undeniably hard evidence turned up. At Singanfu, capital of the province of Shen-si, laborers accidentally unearthed a stone tablet surmounted by a Nestorian cross embellished with flowers. This tablet, which measures eight feet by three feet, is covered with nearly 2,000 Chinese characters, followed by an inscription in Syriac. It repeats part of the Old and New Testament, and tells of a Bishop Adam, or A-lo-pen, who brought the Scriptures to Emperor Tai Tsung in the city of Singanfu. Tai Tsung, second emperor of the Tang dynasty, reigned from A.D. 627 to 649. According to the tablet, he approved of Christ's message and ordered it to be preached.

However, during religious persecutions of the late Tang era Christianity was prohibited and Christian churches were torn down. The huge tablet probably was buried at that time, at the direction of Nestorian priests, in order to save it from destruction. No other trace of Christianity has been found in this part of China, yet it is conceivable that a remote memory of Bishop A-lo-pen and his Chinese followers lasted until the Middle Ages. If so, he may have been the original Prester John.

In any event, Brother William had little use for Nestorians. Their polygamy troubled him, the amount of wine they drank, the beating of drums during Mass, and various other things:

"They say their offices, and have sacred books in Syriac, but they do not know the language, so they chant like those monks among us who do not know grammar, and they are absolutely depraved. . . . When they enter church they wash their lower parts like Saracens. They eat meat on Friday and have their feasts on that day in the Saracen fashion. A bishop rarely visits this place, hardly once in fifty years."

Concerning the elusive priest-king, he summarized what the Mongols had told him, but his account is a spider web of tales. Scholars say that he must have become confused by their half-truths, flights of memory, and luxurious fabrication. Still, fantasy is more persuasive than reality, and Brother William's rich narrative played dreamily upon the imagination of Europe:

Somewhere in Asia a powerful Christian monarch . . .

Marco Polo, like the Franciscans, listened for news of him.

After twenty-five years of travel Marco returned to Venice and reported that there had been a great Christian lord called Uang Khan, or King John, but he was killed in battle a long time ago.

Still the idea refused to wither. If Prester John could be found and his armies allied with those of Europe—as soon as that could be accomplished the Turks would be overwhelmed and Jerusalem set free.

During the fourteenth century Prester John moved to Africa.

He was now 200 years old, but very possibly he had access to that marvelous fountain "which hath within itself every kind of taste, for it changeth taste every hour by day and night, and is scarce three days' journey from Paradise." Whoever drank from this fountain three times, while fasting, would never again get sick and would remain thirty-two years old forever.

His first manifestation in Africa was vague—an Ethiopian patriarch who governed a vast number of archbishoprics, each of which contained many bishops. But then a peripatetic Dominican named Jordanus de Sévérac produced a book titled *Mirabilia Descripta*, regarding a number of countries he had visited and some he had not. About Ethiopia he wrote: "The lord of that land I believe to be more potent than any in the world. He is said to have under him fifty-two kings . . ." and so forth. Sévérac also announced that the people were Christian, which was partly true because there had been a Christian sect in Ethiopia ever since the fourth century.

A few years later an unknown Spanish friar wrote a book which unequivocally located the priest-king in Africa. Not only had he himself traveled through John's domain, said the friar, he had visited its capital city, Malsa. "From the time I came to Malsa, I saw and heard marvelous things every day. I inquired what the terrestrial paradise was like. . . ."

In Madrid are three manuscript versions of this friar's fabulous narrative. One of them has a drawing of John's imperial banner: a Latin cross between two shepherds' crooks.

Confronted by visible evidence, supported by personal testimony, who could doubt that the omnipotent monarch now reigned on the opposite bank of the Nile—for it was agreed during the Middle Ages that this river separated the two continents.

King João of Portugal, meditating upon Islamic power in Africa, ordered Affonso de Paiva and Pedro da Covilhão to find Prester John. João's command was not a death sentence, but it is probable that the emissaries told everybody good-bye with unusual affection.

Go find Prester John, said the king, so that we may combine our forces. And I would like to know more about India, what sort of goods we might buy and sell there. Also, find out whether the Indian Sea is surrounded by land, as Ptolemy taught, or whether it connects with the Ocean Sea. Let me know where Africa ends.

In May of 1487, with 400 golden cruzados and a briefcase full of credentials that might or might not provide insurance, Pedro and Affonso set out from Lisbon on horseback, charged by their sovereign "to discover and learn where Prete Janni dwelt, and whether his territories reached unto the sea; and where the pepper and cinnamon grow . . ."

At Barcelona they got a ship to Naples, and after a bit of difficulty sailed along to Rhodes. Here they were advised to continue the trip disguised as merchants, so they bought some honey to serve as merchandise and then proceeded to Alexandria, where they fell sick. While they were hors de combat their supply of honey disappeared. One scholar believes the thief must have been the sultan's chamberlain. Another says the governor of Alexandria confiscated the honey because he thought the Portuguese were about to die. No matter. They surprised the Egyptians by recovering and then managed to get paid for the stolen merchandise, which sounds incredible.

On to Cairo, where they joined a party of Moorish traders going to Aden in a dhow. And here they decided to carry out the king's orders by traveling in different directions. Affonso would look for Prester John in Africa while Pedro would continue to India. They would rendezvous at Cairo.

Covilhão sailed across the Arabian Sea to the Malabar Coast where he observed how business was influenced by the monsoon: ships from the west arrived in August or September and departed a few months later on the northeast monsoon—loaded with silk, porcelain, emeralds, rhubarb, ginger, frankincense, musk, cinnamon, amber, cloves, sandalwood, and other such exotic items.

Silks and jewels and intricate ivory carvings still are valuable, of course, but herbs and spices have become so common that we cannot imagine paying much for them. Five centuries ago things were different. Toast sprinkled with sugar and pepper was a rare delicacy, the delight of wealthy Portuguese. And enough pepper would kill the taste of spoiled meat. And bathing was not fashionable, so that anything —perfumes, aromatic herbs—anything that masked the odor of reeking flesh was bought eagerly. A citizen would often breathe through a perfume-drenched handkerchief when chatting with a neighbor who had not bathed for a couple of years. Covilhão's observation, therefore, was not that of an idle tourist. The king would be much interested in the kinds and quantities of Indian spices and knowing when the traders sailed.

He went next to Ormuz at the mouth of the Persian Gulf, and from there he caught a ship to the golden city of Sofala far down the coast of East Africa. Here he picked up information suggesting that Africa did come to an end somewhere below, which meant that King João's sea captains should be able to make it all the way. And with this important news Covilhão decided to start back. It was now the year 1490, about time to meet Affonso de Paiva in Cairo.

Affonso was not there.

Covilhão eventually learned that his associate had returned in very poor health and died without telling anybody where he had been.

For a while Covilhão seems to have hesitated, uncertain whether he should report to the king or continue the search for Prester John. He was about to start for Portugal when the king's secret service—a rabbi and a shoemaker—intercepted him. They said the king was most anxious to hear about Prester John. Covilhão obediently wrote an account of his trip for the shoemaker to take to Portugal; then he and the rabbi booked passage to Ormuz, because the rabbi had some sort of business there and did not like the idea of traveling alone.

At last, with the rabbi off his hands, Covilhão was free to resume the search. But instead—and nobody can quite explain this—he sailed past Ethiopia and disembarked at Jidda on the east bank of the Red Sea. From here he traveled to Mecca disguised as a Moslem pilgrim, dressed all in white, his head shaved. Apparently he wanted to take a look at the holiest of Moslem relics, the sacred meteorite. Very few unbelievers have been reckless enough to attempt this. Covilhão not only saw the stone, he got away without being discovered and decapitated.

Still he did not carry out the king's orders. He continued north to Sinai where he visited the monastery of Saint Catherine and heard Mass for the first time since leaving the Christian world four years earlier.

Only then did he sail down the Red Sea once more.

It was known that he got off at the port of Zeila, but there King João's secret agents lost track of him.

Five years later Vasco da Gama, en route to India, put in at Mozambique and inquired about Prester John: "We were told that Prester John resided not far from this place, that he held many cities along the coast. . . ."

But da Gama was told also that the domain of the great ruler could be reached only after a difficult journey on the backs of camels. It was beginning to sound familiar. Prester John was always just around the bend. Besides, if there should be a Christian king somewhere in this country, no matter what he might be called, he could not be the legendary monarch of the past. So, probably without much reflection, da Gama declined a camel ride and sailed off to India. Scholars think he may have picked up rumors of the ancient Zimbabwe Empire.

In 1520 a group of Portuguese reached the court of Lebna Dengel, the Christian ruler of Ethiopia, and it seemed that the priest-king had at last been found. That his name happened to be Lebna Dengel was unimportant. By the inscrutable laws of European logic he must be Prester John. Europe had heard about a Christian king of Ethiopia named Prester John. Here was a Christian king of Ethiopia. Ergo: Lebna Dengel must be Prester John.

His limitless realm, though, was terribly disappointing—a kingdom of mud huts.

As for his subjects: "They are a poor civil people with miserable clothes, and they come into the water uncovered, a black tall people with thick matted locks, which from their birth they neither cut nor comb, so that they wear their hair like a lump of wool, and they carry pointed oiled sticks with which they scratch the vermin which crawl beneath, because they cannot reach their scalps with their fingers, and scratching their heads is their sole occupation."

Lebna Dengel did not mind being called Prester John. He had a good many other titles and if the visitors were pleased to call him this—so be it. What did interest him about the Portuguese was their version of Christianity. The wafers used in Holy Communion, what were they like?—because in Ethiopia an ordinary roll served the purpose. Lebna Dengel was fascinated to learn that the Portuguese had an iron with which they imprinted a crucifix on each wafer.

What sort of garments did European priests wear?

Father Francisco Alvares, the expedition's chaplain, was obliged to get dressed up for Mass, meanwhile explaining the symbolism of each garment. Lebna Dengel was not satisfied; Father Alvares had to go through it a second time. "I brought to him the full vestments, the chalice, corporals, altar stone, and cruets. He saw all, piece by piece, and ordered me to take it and unsew the altar stone, which was sewn up in a clean cloth, and I unsewed half of it, and had it again covered up. . . ."

Lebna Dengel said that he understood there were two Churches in the Western World, one under the authority of Rome, the other of Constantinople. How could there be two?

Father Alvares explained the Roman Catholic position: although spiritual leadership of the Church had at one time emanated from Constantinople, this no longer was true. Lebna Dengel, whose Christianity derived from the Coptic Church of Egypt, did not argue with Alvares; he merely listened.

On Christmas Day the Portuguese assembled a little choir. Lebna Dengel did not attend the service, he remained out of sight; but each time they began anew he sent a messenger to ask what was being sung.

Ethiopian services were not favorably reviewed by Father Alvares. Ethiopian priests did nothing but dance and sing and jump, he said, and while jumping they touched their feet with their hands. Lebna Dengel asked if Portuguese priests danced like that. No, replied Father Alvares, they did not. "Upon this he sent to ask whether, as that was not our custom, we thought theirs bad. We sent word that the service of God, in whatever manner it was done, seemed to us good."

Another topic of mutual interest was the possibility of smashing Islam. Lebna Dengel thought the Portuguese should build a number of forts, for which he would gladly supply provisions and laborers. And Zeila should be captured in order to assure control of the Red Sea. After that, through the combined strength of Ethiopia and Portugal, the Moslem armies could be defeated and Mecca itself would fall.

"This seemed good to the Prester," Alvares wrote, "and he again said he would give the provisions, gold, and men, and all that was necessary."

During these discussions the interpreter was Pedro da Covilhão—now an old man but in good health, with a native wife and quite a few children. In Portugal it was thought that he had died many years ago, because there had been no word of him since he landed at Zeila. Alvares says nothing about the first encounter with Covilhão, which is strange, because they must have heard about his mission. Even if they had not known anything about him they must have been astonished to find a countryman at the court of the Ethiopian king.

Covilhão had not spoken Portuguese for such a long time that he had trouble telling his story. He had reached the Ethiopian court during the reign of Eskender, who was delighted to receive an envoy from a distant Christian monarch. Eskender promised to send Covilhão back to Portugal with a message of appreciation to King João, and with all sorts of gifts. Unfortunately he died and his brother, Na'od, inherited the throne. Na'od told Covilhão that foreigners were not permitted to leave the country.

Fourteen years later Na'od died and the crown passed to his son, Lebna Dengel. Covilhão tried again. Lebna Dengel said no.

According to Father Alvares, Covilhão was generally esteemed and had great influence over Prester John. His only problem was that he could not leave Ethiopia. When the other Portuguese left in 1521 he was still there.

Prester John would be heard from again. And again, and again, his majesty augmented by the invention of movable type. He began to reign over a kingdom of chapbooks—cheaply printed pamphlets illustrated with crude woodcuts and sold by street peddlers. Not many of these chapbooks have survived, for which we may be grateful; it is always embarrassing to come upon a hero in the marketplace.

In 1590 a forgotten traveler published *The Rare and Most Wonderful Thinges which Edward Webbe, an Englishman Borne, Hath Seen and Passed in His Troublesome Travailles in the Citties of Jerusalem, Damasko, Bathelem, and Gallely; and in the lands of Jewrie, Egipt, Grecia, Russia, and in the land of Prester John.* Webbe tells us that the Prester "keepeth very beautiful court" and "hath every day to serve him at his table, sixty kinges wearing leaden crowns on their heads, and those serve in the meat unto Prester John's table: and continually the first dish of meat set upon his table is a dead man's scull, cleane picked, and laid in black earth; putting him in mind that he is but earth, and that he must die, and shall become earth again."

Another Englishman borne, not a traveler but a poet of some repute, by name Wm. Shakespeare—or Shakspeare, or Shekespere, however you like it—this poet wrote his epitaph:

"I will go on the slightest errand now to the Antipodes that you can devise to send me on; I will fetch you a toothpicker now from the furthest inch of Asia; bring you the length of Prester John's foot; fetch you a hair off the Great Cham's beard . . ."

After that we don't hear much of him. When we do it is always faintly, and more faintly, like the distant tinkle of a camel's bell.

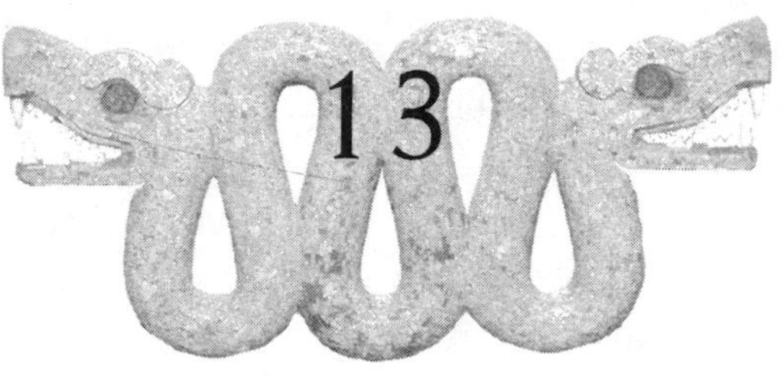

13

To the Indies

ENEA SILVIO PICCOLOMINI, whom you may know better as Pius II, declared in 1461 that just about everybody agreed on the spherical shape of the earth: *Mundi formam omnes fere consentiunt rotundam esse*. This conflicts with popular wisdom, which holds that nobody until Columbus truly understood the situation.

All the same, scholars insist that pre-Christian Greeks knew the earth was a globe, and they tell us that this knowledge was not lost during the Middle Ages—which sounds logical; consequently I am willing to go along with Enea Piccolomini.

What's curious, though, given this knowledge, is that until the fifteenth century there was no organized effort to find out what might be happening among the antipodes. Only a few people had crossed the horizon, and most of them went not because they were inquisitive but for some commonplace reason. The monks, naturally, to meditate and proselyte; the others to make money. There were very few pure tourists in the old days. Those who traveled merely for the satisfaction of wandering seem to have been oddities.

The one whose name is synonymous with visits to faraway places,

Marco Polo, accompanied his father and uncle on business, and the fact that we know where he went and what he experienced is simply a result of Marco's bad luck. Some time after their return, probably about 1296, during the war between Genoa and Venice, he was captured and spent a while counting his toes in a Genoese prison. There he met a professional storyteller named Rustichello and dictated to him that *sui generis* account of Eastern marvels. If he had not been imprisoned he might sooner or later have employed a scribe to record this unique trip, or he might not.

Anyway, Rustichello preserved Marco Polo's flamboyant narrative, which seeped gradually into the consciousness of Europe and crystallized, along with who knows how many other molecules of thought, until the Infante, Dom Henrique of Portugal—whom we call Prince Henry the Navigator—moved from Lisbon to Sagres and the earth we recognize yet never comprehend began to be unveiled.

Marco Polo's contribution to this can only be estimated, but it can be estimated more closely than you might suspect. For one thing, Henry's elder brother Pedro spent a while in Venice and was presented by the Signoria with a copy of Marco's travels. Henry must have examined this valuable gift and surely it affected the course of his explorations, though we will never know just how much because so many documents from those days were destroyed in the Lisbon earthquake of 1755.

We do know, however, that Columbus was influenced by Marco Polo because he took aboard the *Santa María* a Latin edition of this famous book. His personal copy now belongs to the Columbian Library in Seville and shows much use, its margins studded with notes in the admiral's handwriting. Especially significant is the fact that Marco located Japan far to the east of its actual position, thus bringing it much closer to the West, and his good student Columbus therefore underestimated the distance he would have to sail.

Still, unless you are mad you do not set off across an unknown ocean with no more than a book for guidance; and Columbus, however obsessed he may have been, was not mad. He had studied not only Marco Polo but everything else available, certainly the reports of Portuguese captains who went sailing uneasily down the African coast.

In 1412 the first attempt had been made to round Cape Bojador. It failed. So did the next attempt, and the next, and eleven more. If you look at a map you will see a minuscule extrusion of Africa just a fraction of an inch below the Canary Islands. It does not look in the least fearsome, but early mariners were terrified by the prospect of this cape which, in Arabic legend, marked the entrance to the Green Sea of Darkness. There a ship would stick fast in gelatinous slime, loathsome monsters hovered in the depths, and men turned black beneath a scorching sun.

Gil Eanes, one of the bravest men who ever lived, finally rounded this cape in a barca—a tiny ship with square sails—and to the amazement of everybody aboard, including himself, they saw open water to the south. As proof that he had succeeded, Gil Eanes brought home to his prince a flowering plant from Guinea.

In 1435 he again rounded the cape and went a little farther south, accompanied by Henry's "royal cupbearer," Affonso Baldaia. They rowed ashore to look around and saw footprints and camel tracks.

On the next trip Baldaia put two mounted knights ashore to reconnoiter. They rode into the desert until they were confronted by a group of citizens armed with assegais, at which point the knights wisely went galloping back to their ship.

A few years later Antão Gonçalves returned with ten captured Africans, some gold dust, an oxhide shield, and several ostrich eggs which were cooked and served to Dom Henrique. "And we may well presume," writes the royal chronicler Azurara, "that there was no other Christian prince in this part of Christendom who had such eggs upon his table." No doubt this was true. Henry must have enjoyed his eggs, which sounds like an innocent pleasure, but you may be sure there were those who bitterly objected. People might be out of work, yet there sat the prince scooping up an ostrich omelet.

Things began to change, though, because Captain Nuño Tristão brought back twenty-nine Africans. Then more captives arrived. People stopped criticizing Henry's expeditions.

"Their covetousness," writes Azurara, speaking of the Portuguese, "now began to wax greater. And, as they saw the houses of others full to overflowing of male and female slaves, and their property increasing, they thought about the whole matter and began to talk among themselves."

One of Henry's retainers, who called himself Lançarote—Lancelot—was awarded the first slave-hunting license. His caravels anchored at an island off the Guinea coast and raided a village: "And at last our Lord God, who rewards every noble act, willed that for the toil they had undergone in His service . . . they took captive of these Moors, what with men, women and children, 165, besides those that perished or were killed."

Lançarote eventually came home with 235 captives.

Henry, as sponsor, was entitled to a royal fifth, but he gave his share of the slaves to friends and courtiers. The successful voyage pleased him more than any profit, we are told, and he reflected "with great pleasure" upon the salvation of those souls which before were lost.

How remote it sounds, this medieval morality in which lives and bodies lay at the disposition of Christians. Azurara observes that the lot of Moorish slaves "was now quite the contrary of what it had been, since before they had lived in perdition of soul and body. . . . And now consider what a reward should be that of the Infante at the hands of the Lord God, for having thus given them the chance of salvation, and not only them, but many others whom he afterward acquired. . . . And so forthwith he made Lançarote a knight."

About this time Henry's endeavor received papal attention. In 1452 the bull *Dum Diversas* authorized Portugal to attack Saracens, pagans, and unbelievers, to capture and keep all their goods, and reduce the owners to slavery.

It sounds unreal and most un-Christian; but of course only the visage of morality changes. You recall the United States ambassador to Laos during the Vietnam War who explained that while we regretted the terrible suffering of the Laotian people it was better for them to die in the ruins of their country than for America to permit the advance of atheistic Communism. And the army officer who explained that in order to save a certain village it had to be destroyed. Plus ça change, plus c'est la même chose, say the French, who seldom deceive themselves about human nature.

The slave trade grew quickly, along with Portuguese knowledge of the African coast, and Henry seems always to have valued knowledge above profit. He demanded full reports from his captains.

Gonçalo Pacheco went raiding, but his landing party was ambushed. Seven Portuguese were killed and reportedly were eaten. Azurara, that faithful scribe, says the rumor was untrue; only their livers were eaten.

Nuño Tristão pushed on south with twenty-two men. He and nineteen of his crew were killed by poisoned arrows. The survivors were desperately wounded. Five ship's boys—all that remained of the company—managed to get the ship back to Portugal.

An Italian in Henry's service, Alvise da Ca' da Mosto—Cadamosto—explored as far as the Gambia, returning with news of palm wine, elephants, marriage customs, snake charmers, exotic foods, and so on. Everything interested him. He saw and described the hippopotamus, which he called the horse-fish, and he discussed the artificial elongation of women's breasts. The Renaissance was opening; life should be investigated.

He reported that while ashore in Gambia the natives would come to stare at him: "They were amazed no less at my clothing than at my white color . . . some touched my hands and arms, and rubbed me with saliva, to see if my whiteness was a dye or really flesh, and seeing that it was flesh, stood agape with wonder."

When some natives were aboard ship he told a sailor to play the bagpipe. The Gambians thought it must be a living animal until the sailor showed them how it worked; then they decided "God had made it with His own hands, that it sounded so sweetly, with so many different voices."

Cadamosto taught them to make candles, and they were delighted.

He traveled inland to visit a petty king named Budomel who had more wives than he could count. There were nine in the first village, each of whom kept five or six servant girls subject to the king's desire. All the same, Budomel was not happy and demanded of Cadamosto, "having been given to understand that Christians knew how to do many things, whether by chance I could give him the means to satisfy numerous women, for which he promised me a fine reward."

Farther south, Cadamosto's expedition was attacked by a fleet of fifteen canoes: "In each were eight to ten warriors, imposing figures in white cotton robes and white headdresses decorated with a wing on each side and a feather in the middle. . . . They all lifted their paddles up in the air and stared at us as if we were ghosts. Suddenly, without provocation, they took up their bows and shot a cluster of arrows at us." About this time the Portuguese sailors decided they had seen enough of Africa, so Cadamosto was obliged to turn around.

Prince Henry died in 1460, still dreaming of a route to the Indies.

A French scholar, Gilbert Renault, reflecting on this abstemious visionary—this devout ascetic who, in actual fact, slept on a bed of gravel and wore a hair shirt—wrote that twice a day the tides came sweeping toward the Sagres promontory as they had done for thousands of years, and to Henrique the waves seemed to beat, or sigh, or thunder, according to the humor of the ocean, these words: "Portugal! Portugal! Your destiny lies not among the mountains of the east, for all your glorious victories, but on my flowing plains whose infinite spaces I shall reveal to you . . . Portugal! Portugal!"

The prince himself wrote nothing; or, if he did, whatever he wrote has disappeared. We have no personal statement of what passed through his mind. And after death, for some inexplicable reason, he failed to decay; one Diogo Gomes, having been ordered to examine his body before it was reinterred at Batalha, found his corpse dry and intact—except the tip of the nose.

He was just the patron Columbus needed, but they missed each other by thirty years. It seems unfair, as though a cog slipped and the machinery of the world did not quite mesh.

Dom Henrique's insistent probe of the African coast may have seemed a trifle moonstruck to his contemporaries, but he had his reasons, only the first of which might be called impractical. He had a wish to know what lay beyond Cape Bojador, says Azurara, yet when his defeated captains returned again and again he listened courteously to their accounts and rewarded them as well as if they had fully executed his wishes.

Such tolerance might be attributed to a man's natural grace, but under the circumstances there has been speculation. For one thing, he never married and his captains all were surprisingly young. At the same time Portugal was exploring the Atlantic, yet the more experienced

Atlantic captains do not seem to have been treated with any lenience. As one historian delicately puts it, Henry's graciousness when confronted with failure after failure by his youthful Sea of Darkness adventurers is difficult to understand "except in terms of special relationships."

Apart from this he sounds pragmatic. He wanted commerce with other lands. He wanted to learn the extent of Moslem power. He was anxious to convert pagans. He hoped to find and join forces with that legendary Christian king of Asia, Prester John. So his young captains moved farther and farther south, uncertainly, but with rising confidence.

It's odd that nobody knew the shape of Africa. Egypto-Phoenician explorers during the reign of Necho II, about 600 B.C., had sailed completely around the continent: they went down the Red Sea, doubled the Cape of Good Hope, and entered the Mediterranean at Gibraltar. Herodotus summarized this voyage, so it's curious that the outline of Africa could be forgotten. Indeed, Necho's expedition may not have been the first; although evidence is meager, Egyptian mariners during the reign of Queen Hatshepsut—nine centuries before the Phoenicians —may have done the same thing.

One gets a feeling that some echo of these voyages survived until the time of Prince Henry, causing him to order his captains out again and again, as though he sensed that the hideous Green Sea of Darkness on Arabic charts already had been crossed.

In 1469 "a respected citizen of Lisbon" named Fernão Gomes was granted a five-year monopoly on the Guinea trade, provided be would explore 500 leagues to the south. His coat of arms was a silver shield with the heads of three Negroes, each wearing gold earrings, a gold nose ring, and a gold collar—which nicely illustrates what the Portuguese had in mind. His pilots reached the equator and were dismayed to find that the coast, which had been trending almost due east, as though they must be near the continent's end, now turned south again. Possibly it went south forever.

Diogo Cão sailed in 1482. He discovered a broad river which the natives called Nzadi, which the Portuguese corrupted to Zaire, which we call the Congo. He traveled some distance upstream before edging farther south, and when he returned to Portugal he was knighted by King João II.

A couple of years later he sailed again, venturing farther—almost four-fifths of the way to the bottom of the continent—but as far as he could tell it had no end.

Nothing else is heard of Diogo Cão, not even where and how he died; and because his name is written small in the logbook of explorers he is easy to forget. But he took with him on both trips some marble *padroes* which were set up at significant points—a *padrão* being a stone pillar surmounted by a cross. Until then each stage of a route had been marked with a wooden cross, or by carving on trees; but King João felt that the route to the Indies should be immortalized with something permanent. Cão set up four of these columns. All have been recovered, either in fragments or complete. On two of them the inscriptions still are legible. The last *padrão*, erected twenty-two degrees below the equator on Cape Cross, was found in 1893 and is now in Germany. It gives this information:

> 6685 YEARS HAD PASSED SINCE THE CREATION
> OF THE WORLD, 1485 SINCE THE BIRTH OF CHRIST,
> WHEN HIS MOST ILLUSTRIOUS AND SERENE
> HIGHNESS KING JOÃO OF PORTUGAL ORDERED THIS
> PILLAR TO BE ERECTED BY HIS KNIGHT DIOGO CÃO.

How many of us will bequeath to posterity such a dignified monument?

Bartolomeu Dias, being a larger name, was one you were expected to memorize in school, together with what he did; yet all that lingers is the melodic name. His tremendous accomplishment is meaningless now. He turned the corner of Africa, and did so without knowing it.

In August of 1487 two caravels and a supply ship started out, not on another coasting voyage but with the definite intention of rounding the southernmost cape—if there was a cape. Foul weather enveloped them; they ran before it with close-reefed sails day after day, and the sea grew cold. Out of the storm at last, far off course, Dias gave orders to steer eastward in search of land. Nothing appeared, so he altered course to the north. Mountains came over the horizon and in February of 1488 they dropped anchor at a pleasant bay. They went ashore to refill the water casks and then continued along the coast, wondering where they were. But the land bore steadily east, which told them what had happened, so Dias set up a *padrão*.

He was anxious to look further but supplies were short, the storm had been fearful, and his men wanted to go home. He wheedled three more days out of them, that was all. At the threshold of the Indian Ocean, just where the coast began curling north, they forced him to stop.

As they sailed back in the direction of Portugal, past the *padrão*, Dias acknowledged it "with as much sorrow and feeling as though he were taking his last leave of a son condemned to exile."

Again they doubled the cape, which he named Tormentoso because it was so stormy. King João renamed it the Cape of Good Hope, according to a sixteenth-century historian, "for that it promised the discovery of India that was so much wished for, and sought over so many years."

Dias would approach this cape one more time, in 1500, on his way to India with the fleet of Pedro Álvares Cabral. Almost within sight of the *padrão* a hurricane struck. Four ships were lost, one of them captained by Dias. The chronicler Galvão had this to say about him: "Q se pode dizer qvia terra da India, mas ña entrou nella, como Mouses ña terra de promissam." Even if you are not adept at sixteenth-century Portuguese the meaning is moderately clear; he saw India, but, like Moses and the Promised Land, he did not enter in.

However, that's looking ahead. His arrival at Lisbon after doubling the cape must have been very fine. What is more interesting, though, is that the ubiquitous and persistent Columbus somehow contrived to be present when Dias knelt before the king. On the margin of his copy of *Imago Mundi* Columbus wrote: "December of this year 1488 Bartholomaeus Didacus, commandant of three caravels which the King of Portugal had sent to Guinea to seek out the land, arrived in Lisbon. He reported that he had reached a promontory which he called Cabo de Boã Esperança. . . ."

Who actually named the cape Boã Esperança, Dias or King João, we do not know. It's unimportant, nevertheless such details ought to be preserved.

Cortés, Pizarro, Balboa, de Soto, Coronado, Ponce de León—however unique they may have been in life, as most assuredly each man was unique, they slant down the centuries in a group. So do those fabulous Elizabethans: Drake, Raleigh, Frobisher, Hawkins, and the rest. And the Portuguese: Magellan, da Gama, Eanes, Dias, Cão. But we never associate anybody with that blue-eyed red-haired mystic from the golden age of discovery: Columbus.

His mother was Susanna Fontanarossa. She must have been lovely, with such a name. His father, Domenico, was a weaver, a fact which embarrassed Columbus. His parents are not mentioned in any of his writings. Late in life, when he had become famous and could associate with kings, he would boast that he was not the first admiral of his family. And according to his son Ferdinand he declared: "Let them call me by what name they will. After all, David first tended sheep before becoming King of Jerusalem." And, like Shakespeare, he wangled a coat of arms. A coat of arms! The most celebrated explorer of all time and the most renowned dramatist. Surely it must be true, as somebody said, within the forehead of every man lies a world of streaming shadows.

He died at the age of fifty-five or so in Valladolid, half a day's travel northwest of Madrid. The old house is gone, except for part of one wall scarred by centuries of weather and overgrown with vines in which some officious sparrows have nested. Bolted to the wall is a blunt proclamation on a metal tablet:

AQUI MURIO COLON

Where the house once stood there is now a gloomy little museum which nobody visits. Valladolid is and has long been a cultural center, a university town, but it does not have much appeal for tourists. A few come to visit the Colegio de San Gregorio where there is a large and important collection of sixteenth-century painted wood sculpture—flamboyant, gilded, intensely religious works by Hernandez, Berruguete, Juan de Juni, and many others; but compared to the glamorous cities of Valencia and Seville and Granada and Toledo, Valladolid remains unknown. Architecturally it has developed like most cities, adding lifeless appendages of concrete and brick, while its heart beats on and on at the university, generation after generation. Now you see the dark-bearded dark-eyed boys in turtleneck sweaters jiggling pinball machines at their smoky hangouts, the girls with notebooks and lipstick and fashionable boots and jeans and long hair flowing. On the new walls, spray-painted here or there, today's graffiti: APALA LIBERTAD. F.E.I. LEGALIZACION. AMNISTIA TOTAL, Y AHORA! Demands that briefly mean so much.

Even the Casa de Colón, as the little museum is called, appears impatient with the past; it displays a TV antenna on the roof, perhaps because the elderly caretaker has not enough to do. Perhaps he is thinking about his favorite program, wondering who stole the diamonds or which team will win the soccer match, while he follows you around and gravely turns on a strand of weak yellow lightbulbs in one room after another.

Maps. Maps. All the maps you could possibly care about.

A nameless conquistador's sword and dented helmet. Did somebody drop the helmet or was it dented by an Aztec mace? One is tempted to ask, but that's not the sort of question the caretaker is prepared to answer.

Fragments of prehistoric clay sculpture from the New World—a disorganized offering of broken masks and pots.

Fourteen gold-framed representations of Columbus by various artists. All except two show the strong nose, the soft oval face, the incipient baldness. Those two exceptions present a lean, sinewy individual related to Don Quixote.

Then there is an eighteenth-century painting of the admiral on his deathbed, as white and calm as a saint. Diego kneels beside his father. Américo Vespucio, Judas-like, stands thoughtfully watching us. And a covey of brown-robed, hooded, candle-carrying Franciscans, obviously expectant, wait to ensure the Admiral's soul.

Thus you proceed through the solemn exhibit while the caretaker follows at a courteous distance, turning off the lights. There are no other visitors to the museum; there might be no more today, nor any tomorrow.

So much for all that. Maps and artifacts and etchings do not interpret what happened during the late fifteenth century, during those few years that affected the world more than anything else since the birth of Christ. Look at it this way: on a pedestal in front of the museum, a few steps from that ancient weather-pitted sparrow-infested wall, sits a black iron replica of the *Santa María* sailing firmly nowhere.

You might feel closer to him at one of Valladolid's sumptuous restaurants with leaded glass windows, heavy crimson drapes, and those ponderous hand-carved Spanish thrones called chairs. After enough brandy, seated like Ferdinand on one of those immovable chairs, you could imagine the admiral across the black oak table from you—except for the traffic noise outside. These days it's almost impossible to dream.

Well, in Valladolid on the twentieth of May, 1506, he died. This fact is useless, of course, unless you are preparing to take an examination; yet when we know a man's beginning we should know at least something about his end.

He was born and grew up in Genoa, as practically everybody agrees; but how he got from Genoa to Lisbon has been disputed. Probably as a seaman aboard an armed merchant ship that was attacked and sunk near Lagos. By some accounts he swam to shore while clutching a piece of wood from the ship.

Whatever happened, he reached Lisbon in 1476 and a year later he sailed to the British Isles. Near Galway he saw two corpses with bloated faces washed up on the beach. He described them as "men from Cathay." Presumably they were Lapps; if they were Chinese their bodies would have decomposed long before the boat drifted to Ireland. But their nationality isn't important; he thought they were Oriental, and nobody can even guess how much that misapprehension shaped the future of the world.

After several years in Lisbon he married the daughter of the first governor of Porto Santo, which is an island near Madeira. This, too, sounds unimportant, but one result of the marriage was that he inherited the old man's marine charts and documents. Bartolomé de las Casas tells us that this acquisition "pleased him much, and made his desire to study cosmography the more ardent. He thought more and more of this each day, and his imagination was set aflame."

In addition to bringing him all those maps and charts, his bride Felipa was related to the Portuguese royal family. Columbus seems to have been one of those men who are at the same time preoccupied and icily pragmatic. It seldom hurts to be related, however distantly, to a king.

They went to live on Porto Santo where he continued to nourish his fantastic idea. Here again, as though the gods had met and decided, corpses with Oriental features washed up on the beach. And branches of unfamiliar trees. And a plank carved with a strange design.

In 1484 he got an audience with the king. João de Barros, court historian, speaks of Columbus as

> . . . an eloquent man, a good Latin scholar, but much inflated with pride . . . Full of the dreams that came to him from his continual travels and the conversations he had had with men of our land well-known for past discoveries, he came to ask Dom João for ships to sail to Cypango through the Ocean Sea. . . . The King, seeing his stubbornness, sent him to Dom Diogo Ortiz, the bishop of Ceuta, to Master Rorigo and to Master Jozé, whose authority he customarily accepted in matters of geography and discovery, and they all considered Columbus' words to be vain, for all that he said was founded on imagination or on fictions such as the isle of Cypango in Marco Polo.

Then Felipa died. Las Casas writes with majestic ecclesiastic indifference: "It pleased God to take his wife from him, for it was proper that for his great enterprise he be freed of all cares."

After Felipa's death he left Portugal furtively, perhaps to escape some debts, and showed up at the Spanish court.

Ferdinand and Isabella listened to his wild proposal "with gracious countenance, and decided to submit the matter to a commission of learned men. . . ." Now, anybody who has been obliged to deal with a commission of learned men knows what to expect.

Columbus waited two years. Two years! What took so long? You would think a group of men could study the situation and report within a few days, or a couple of weeks. Two years! And still—after two years—they couldn't make a recommendation.

So he went back to Lisbon for another try at King João. And that was when Bartolomeu Dias arrived, home from Cabo de Boã Esperança with banners flying. King João of course was delighted. Columbus, we should assume, would be sick with dismay. Yet, judging from the marginal note on *Imago Mundi*, he seems to have been interested rather than depressed, as though he did not see how Dias' accomplishment might conflict with, or subvert, what he himself had in mind.

It's hard to imagine why Columbus did not quit when Dias returned. A sea route to the Indies had been found; that should have ended the matter. Instead, he traveled to Spain once more and renewed his petition.

Their Catholic Majesties could not make up their minds. They disliked the thought of Portugal establishing sea trade with the Indies and if Columbus could find a shorter route, excellent. Asia might be reached by sailing west, the royal cartographers admitted, yet they agreed that such a voyage would take three years. Under the circumstances should one gamble?

In the summer of 1491 Columbus again grew tired of waiting and decided to try his luck with Charles VIII of France, but hardly had he left court when Isabella sent for him. So he returned and waited some more. Then she said no.

He was riding away on a mule when he was overtaken by a captain of the guards. Isabella once again had changed her mind.

Why? An appeal to Spanish pride, according to some scholars. An unexpected offer of financial help, say others. Maybe both.

Personally, I like the story about Ferdinand playing chess. In this version the king busied himself with a game while Isabella gave Columbus the bad news. Hernando del Pulgar, the queen's secretary, was observing the game and noticed that unless the king made a particular move he would lose a rook. Hernando murmured to Isabella, who then whispered to her husband. Now this is dirty chess. And King Ferdinand —one cannot help feeling repelled—Ferdinand listened to the whispered advice and saved his rook. Consequently he won the game, which pleased him so much that he said to Isabella: "Oh, go ahead, give the Genoese whatever he wants!"

For this reason it came about that just before sunrise on the third of August in a year we all know, the *Niña*, *Pinta*, and *Santa María* slipped out of Palos harbor.

According to authorities who have studied this trip, and his later trips, Columbus was a superb dead-reckoning navigator. He was also dishonest. Like many a businessman today, he kept duplicate books: one for the facts, one for the public. His men were uneasy about this adventure, so the public log registered fewer leagues than they actually sailed. But in spite of the deception there was much grumbling and muttering while September faded, and by early October the unmistakable smell of mutiny emanated from his fleet.

On the seventh, after an argument with the *Niña*'s captain, Columbus altered course to the south. If he had not done this they would have landed in Florida near Cape Kennedy.

Signs of land floated by: green branches, plants, a carved stick. Overhead they saw migratory birds.

About ten o'clock on the night of October eleventh the admiral saw a light which he described as like a candle flame rising and falling. If he did see a light, what was it?

Fireworms spawning on the surface of the water? This is the theory of a British marine biologist. Indians fishing by torchlight? Luminous jellyfish? The Savior beckoning?

None of these, we are told by Samuel Eliot Morison, who explains that the natives of San Salvador often build fires outside their houses on October nights to drive away sand fleas. Morison arranged an experiment in 1959, duplicating as nearly as possible the conditions of 1492. He chose a night when the moon was in the same phase, and he looked toward San Salvador from the deck of a boat several miles offshore. The fire was visible, he said, flaring up each time his associate piled on more wood. So perhaps that was it. But still, crewmen aboard all three ships were gazing ahead, each hoping to claim the 10,000 maravedis offered by Ferdinand and Isabella to the first man who sighted land. The *Pinta*, in fact, was ahead of the *Santa María*, yet not until two in the morning did a sailor named Rodrigo aboard the *Pinta* sing out: "Tierra! Tierra!"

If those fires were occasionally replenished during the night why did nobody except Columbus see them?

All we know is that he claimed for himself, and got, the 10,000 maravedis, leaving the sailor with nothing—a fact one would as soon forget. However, that may be a twentieth-century bias. Las Casas speaks from a more godly age: "It was proper that the reward should go to that one man who had always kept the faith." Symbolically, philosophically, yes, all right, one can't argue. And Rodrigo's sharp eyesight at least guaranteed his corner in the history books: Juan Rodriguez Bermejo, "marinero de la *Pinta*," who was born in the village of Triana.

They anchored at sunrise. Then, very much as we have seen in popular paintings, the three commanders went ashore accompanied by the royal banner of Castile and by the standard of their patrons. They knelt to kiss the land, "thanking God who had requited them after a voyage so long and strange."

Columbus drew his sword, pointed at the sky, and claimed possession of everything in the name of his sovereigns, repeating as many of their titles as he could remember. He thought he had reached an island close to Cypango, the beginning of the Indies.

Morison, that indefatigable navigator, claims to have located the exact strip of beach where this bizarre Shakespearean prologue occurred. The site has been marked with a white cross.

Our heroes next took off for Cuba, stopping frequently, gathering beans, wild cotton, fruit, and other evidence, meanwhile trying to learn where all the gold was and where the Great Khan might be found. So the Arawaks, realizing that something was wanted and eager to be helpful, agreeably pointed ahead.

On Cuba, which he thought must be a Chinese peninsula, Columbus dispatched two ambassadors to the khan—Luis de Torres and Rodrigo de Xerez. They were well qualified. Torres spoke Arabic and Hebrew, therefore he should be able to converse with the Chinese. Xerez had once visited an African chief, so he knew how to approach royalty. The ambassadors started off with a porter, a guide, Latin passports, strings of glass beads, and a letter from Their Catholic Majesties addressed to Magnus Canus. It sounds like Gilbert and Sullivan.

Away they went, up an Indian trail through the Cacoyuguin valley to a settlement near the present town of Holguín. There they met an affable cacique who entertained them for the next four days. They lolled on ceremonial stools called *dujos*—"like some animal with short arms and legs, the tail lifted up to lean against, and a head at the other end, with golden eyes and ears"—while the villagers kissed their hands and feet, and the women explored their bodies to see if they were made of flesh like ordinary men.

Columbus wrote in his journal on the sixth of November that his messengers had seen natives carrying "some sort of cylinder in which sweetly smelling herbs were glowing. These they supposed were dried herb stalks covered by an equally dry but broader leaf. The people sucked the opposite end of the cylinder and, as it were, drank the smoke. Although this apparently intoxicated them it also seemed to protect them from fatigue. The natives called these cylinders *tabacos*."

On Christmas Eve while approaching Haiti the *Santa María* gently spiked herself on a coral reef and could not be saved. From her planks they built a little fort, called Navidad, and Columbus asked for volunteers to man the garrison until he returned. Most of the ship's crew volunteered, along with several men from the *Niña*. He instructed them to explore the land, to trade for gold, and to treat the people with respect.

Soon afterward he sailed for Europe aboard the *Niña*, carrying with him some kidnapped Arawaks.

"Let it not be said," he wrote about the natives, "that they give freely only that which is of little value, for they give away gold nuggets as willingly as they do a calabash of water; and it is easy to recognize when a thing is given from the heart. . . . These are most loving people, who do not covet. They love their neighbor as themselves."

Opposite the Azores in mid-February a gale blew up. He states in his log that the waves were fearsome, and during the night of the fourteenth he lost sight of the *Pinta*. Lots were drawn three times to see who would represent their ship by making a pilgrimage, assuming *Niña* survived the storm. Some chick-peas were shaken in a sailor's cap, one pea inscribed with a cross. And twice—twice out of three lotteries—Columbus himself drew the marked pea.

He must have been afraid the ship would go down, because he wrote an account of his discovery on a sheet of parchment which he wrapped in a piece of waxed cloth and addressed to the Spanish king and queen. The packet was placed in a small tightly caulked barrel and thrown overboard. It has never been found.

This undelivered message to Ferdinand and Isabella should be mentioned in the flat past tense, instead of implying that tomorrow or the next day somebody wandering across a deserted beach might notice the remnants of a fifteenth-century barrel with a waxed package inside. After all, it's been some time. However, the barrel might yet be recovered—though one should be cautious. In 1892, for instance, a London publisher claimed to have obtained it from a Welsh fisherman. This perhaps is conceivable, but the fact that the manuscript had been written in English would make most buyers suspicious.

And in Germany a facsimile edition entitled *My Secrete Log Boke* appeared on imitation vellum enhanced with authentic barnacles and authentic seaweed.

Well, in early March another storm drove the bedraggled *Niña* northward. Once again, gravely alarmed, they shook up the chick-peas in a sailor's cap and Columbus drew the marked pea. The odds against this are prohibitive.

At last they raised the European coast near Lisbon, and what should be riding at anchor in the Tagus but a great Portuguese man-of-war whose master was Bartolomeu Dias. The contrast between these two ships—and the coincidence of Columbus meeting Dias at this instant—is pure Hollywood.

Dias pulled over in a longboat with an armed escort and told Columbus to report aboard the warship. The admiral refused, but showed his credentials, which satisfied Dias who perhaps only wanted a closer look at the Indians. Then half of Lisbon came aboard to stare at them.

Columbus dropped anchor at Palos on March 15, having been gone thirty-two weeks. Ferdinand and Isabella were in Barcelona so he started overland to the peripatetic court. We are told that six Arawaks went with him. They wore gold nose rings, feathers, and guaycas—belts studded with gold and polished fishbone—and they carried cages of parrots. Las Casas, at that time a youth in Seville, remembered seeing this extraordinary procession.

But he had brought back ten Indians, not six. What happened to the other four?—those that didn't travel to Barcelona. Were they abandoned in Seville? Were they sold? Did they become a sideshow? So many flakes of paint are missing from the mural.

He must have ridden through Barcelona like Alexander through Persepolis. True, his caravels had not returned packed with silks and spices but the next trip should take care of that. Cypango could not be much farther.

News of his achievement spread slowly beyond the Mediterranean countries. In midsummer, months after he reached Lisbon, the *Nurem-*

berg Chronicle published "the events most worthy of notice from the beginning of the world to the calamity of our time," but failed to mention Columbus. And several days later a Nuremberg scientist urged the Portuguese king to seek a western route to the Indies. Northern Europe's ignorance seems very strange.

Before leaving on his second voyage Columbus traveled from Barcelona completely across Spain to the shrine of the Holy Virgin of Guadalupe in the mountains of Estremadura, fulfilling the promise he had made during the storm. It is almost certain that he passed through the village of Trujillo where another lad stared at him—an illiterate young swineherd named Francisco Pizarro.

He then returned to Seville by way of Medellín where Cortés, at that time eight years old, undoubtedly saw him.

Why such encounters should be interesting is something I can't explain, any more than it should be interesting that Las Casas watched Columbus pass through Seville. Yet the circumstances remain oddly fixed in the mind. During the Second World War, when I was a navy cadet at Pensacola, I was walking across the base one day and waited at an intersection for a black limousine to go by. Attached to its front fender was an admiral's flag. The limousine stopped at the corner, and because I had never seen an admiral I bent down and looked into the back seat. A gnarled old man with shaggy yellow eyebrows stared out at me. For two or three seconds we looked at each other, then the limousine drove off. I had been staring into the eyes of old "Bull" Halsey, scourge of the Pacific. I was fascinated. Pizarro, on a crooked dusty street in Trujillo, may have felt the same.

On September 25, 1493, Columbus sailed from Cádiz with a fleet of seventeen ships, under order to establish a permanent colony. He took along just about everything you need for settling in an unfamiliar world—sheep, horses, wheat seeds, grapevine cuttings, hundreds of ambitious young men, even a cavalry troop—just about everything except women. Presumably this was not an oversight.

He bore a little south of his previous track and had an easy crossing to Santo Domingo. Here he turned north and on Guadalupe—named for the Estremadura shrine—his ships frightened some Indians out of their village. The Spaniards went ashore to inspect it. The expedition's doctor wrote in a letter to the municipality of Seville:

> We inquired of the women who were prisoners of the inhabitants what sort of people these islanders were and they said Caribs. . . . They told us that the Carib men use them with such cruelty as would scarcely be believed; and that they eat the children which they bear them, only bringing up those whom they have by their native wives. Such of their male enemies as they can take alive they bring here to their homes to make a feast of them, and those who are killed in battle they eat up after the fighting is over. They declare that the flesh of man is so good to eat that nothing in the world can compare with it; and this is quite evident, for of the human bones we found in the houses, everything that could be gnawed had already been gnawed so that nothing remained but what was hard to eat. In one of the houses we found a man's neck cooking in a pot. . . . When the Caribs take boys as prisoners of war they remove their organs, fatten them until they grow up, and then, when they wish to make a great feast, they kill and eat them, for they say the flesh of women and youngsters is not good to eat. Three boys thus mutilated came running to us . . .

The fact that the fleet did not at once sail for Navidad indicates that Columbus was not worried about a cannibal attack.

When they did arrive they found Navidad destroyed—burned—the bodies of a dozen Spaniards nearby. But it had not been a Carib raid. Almost as soon as they were left alone the members of the garrison had begun to argue. Some went to demand gold from a village chief and then carried off several girls. The Indians retaliated by burning the fort, which was undefended because the hedonistic Spaniards were living separately in little huts, each with five or six women.

Columbus searched for the gold they must have accumulated. He even had the settlement's well dug up, thinking it might be concealed there.

Then the fleet moved on, looking for a more hospitable place.

Isabella was established on the north coast of Haiti a few miles east of Navidad, and like the first colony it soon began to disintegrate: sickness, putrid food, inexperience, a humid climate, hidalgos reluctant to soil their hands—and there stood an administrator who detested administration. "It was inevitable," Las Casas wrote, "that in the face of so many problems to resolve the Admiral should alienate everyone."

After several months at Isabella, bored and irritated and exhausted by his duties, he sailed away from his dissatisfied subjects. He wanted to find out if Cuba was an island or a promontory of China.

Bernáldez mentions something curious which happened on this excursion. A crossbowman who went ashore was surrounded by about thirty Indians, one of whom wore a long white tunic reaching to his feet. The Spaniard at first thought it must be the Trinitarian friar from the ship's company. Then two other light-complexioned Indians appeared in white tunics. The crossbowman was frightened and ran to the edge of the water calling for help.

Columbus, when told about this, must have concluded that he was indeed halfway around the world because three men in white tunics could only be disciples of the Christian king of the Orient, Prester John, whose realm lay close to the Great Wall of China. He tried for the next two days to find these priestly Indians, but scouting parties reported no men in white tunics, nor humans of any sort, only the tracks of some animals which might be griffons or lions.

Early in 1496 he returned to Spain, discouraged because of the problems at Isabella and because he had not located any gold mines. To punish himself, he put on the coarse brown dress of a Franciscan, and except when aboard ship he wore this gown the rest of his life.

Ferdinand and Isabella received him politely. They listened with interest and inspected a few gold nuggets he had brought, along with more Arawaks and various other tropical showpieces. Perhaps they were still enthusiastic, but two years elapsed before he got permission to try again.

This time he went farther south: "I wish to verify what Dom João claims, namely that there is a very large mainland toward the west."

The Portuguese may not have been the first to suspect the existence of South America, nor the first to reach it. Phoenician traders might have landed there, and medieval Africans almost certainly did. Pedro Martir, describing Balboa's trek across Panama, states that the explorers encountered black men whom they believed to have come from Ethiopia on piratical voyages, who were shipwrecked and so established themselves in the mountains of Panama: "The inhabitants of Caruaca have internal fights full of hatred with these Negroes. They enslave each other . . ."

Columbus himself spoke of having received *guanines* from the Indians on Haiti, or Española as he called it. They told him that black people from the south had visited the island and their spear points were made of this metal. *Guanin* is an African term referring to an alloy of copper and gold. The specimens acquired by Columbus on Haiti were assayed in Spain and contained the same proportion of copper to gold as specimens from Guinea, which might or might not be coincidence.

A few years ago I was talking to a dealer in pre-Columbian artifacts who mentioned that Venetian glass beads sometimes are found in Sinu tombs. He said he had seen lots of them in Colombia, but he did not buy any because they had no market value. I asked how he could be sure it was Venetian glass, and he replied that he knew those beads when he saw them because he used to live in Venice. Besides, Sinu Indians never made glass beads. All of which means very little, unless you know that Sinu tombs date from about the twelfth century.

How did the beads get there?—assuming, of course, that the dealer was not mistaken and that he was telling the truth. I believed him, mostly because he was not trying to sell me a string of beads. He had none to sell. He mentioned them in reference to something else and seemed bored by my questions. Beads, beads. There's no money in beads. Jade, yes. Ceramics, yes. Gold, yes. Beads, no.

Well, on his third voyage Columbus veered so far south that he sailed into the equatorial doldrums. Wine turned to vinegar, water to vapor, wheat to ashes. Lard and salted meat putrefied. But at last the wind came up and brought him to an island which, because of its three peaks, he named Trinidad. Next day his caravels entered the Gulf of Paria, fed by the many mouths of the Orinoco. Two weeks later, leaving this freshwater sea, he perceived the truth:

"If this river does not flow out from Paradise, it comes from an immense land to the south, whereof, until now, no one has had any knowledge."

Then he turned north to Haiti. And there, in September of 1500, the royal inquisitor Francisco de Bobadilla, who had come to reorganize the dreadful administration of the New World, threw Columbus in jail.

Las Casas writes: "When it came time to put the Admiral in irons none of those who were present dared to do the deed, out of respect for his person. But a lowly cook of his household who happened to be there put them on him, with an air of shameless impudence and as much self-assurance as if he were serving him some savory dish."

Columbus must have thought he was going to be executed, because the following dialogue took place when an equerry came to his cell:

"Vallejo, where are you taking me?"

"Sire, I am taking you to the ship that you are to board."

"Vallejo, is this the truth?"

"I swear it on Your Excellency's life that you are going aboard ship."

These words, according to Las Casas, brought him back to life.

When they were at sea, beyond the reach of Bobadilla, Vallejo offered to take off the chains. Columbus refused, saying he would permit them to be removed only at the command of his sovereigns. And in Spain, when they were taken off, he insisted on keeping them. His son Ferdinand remembered these chains; he said they occupied a place of honor in his father's house, and that his father left orders for the chains to be buried with him.

Aboard ship Columbus wrote a long self-justification. He appealed indirectly to Isabella, who had always favored him:

> The world has ever treated men ill. It has attacked me a thousand times; until this moment I have resisted all such attacks. Today it casts me down most cruelly; but the hope in Him who created all things sustains me, for His help has ever been at hand. Once before I was downcast and He said unto me: "Man of little faith, fear not, be comforted. I am with thee." . . . For nine years I have done deeds worthy of memory. They have counted for naught. Today even the lowliest of men revile me; only the virtuous do not consent so to do. If I had taken the Indies as booty and given them unto the Moors, I should not have been shown more hatred than in Spain. . . . If I have erred, it is not through evil intentions, and I believe that Their Majesties will so judge. I hold for certain that they will show me mercy, for my errors were committed unwillingly, as they will soon recognize, and will take account of my services, which will each day prove greater.

The ability to write with eloquence can be a useful art; he was freed and invited to present himself at court.

Las Casas tells us that the sovereigns received him graciously, assuring the admiral that his imprisonment had not been by their command, promising that all would be remedied and his privileges restored. Isabella seemed particularly anxious to console him.

Even so, it was late afternoon. Never again would he be trusted to administer a colony. Their Catholic Majesties might welcome him and listen with a show of attention to his monotonous lyric, but they were not anxious to finance another trip.

Eventually he wore them down: four caravels left Seville in the spring of 1502. It is generally thought that Ferdinand and Isabella authorized this last voyage in order to get rid of him. He might continue exploring, but they charged him to avoid Santo Domingo.

He still believed that Cuba was an extension of China and that below it he would find the Malay Peninsula. Accordingly, somewhere below Cuba there must be a strait leading to the Indian Ocean. Once through that strait he might encounter Vasco da Gama, who just then was en route to India for the second time via the Cabo de Boã Esperança. And should they meet on the underside of the world after having sailed in opposite directions, what a triumph that would be.

Ferdinand and Isabella thought it quite possible; they gave Columbus a letter of introduction to da Gama.

His route after he struck the Central American coast looks like a seismograph. Better than any written account it shows his desperate obsession. From Honduras south to Panama, as far as the Gulf of Darien, he beat against the shore like a bird fluttering at a window.

If only there had been a sea passage to the other side. If only there had been a passage, he would have emerged on the Pacific and sailed like a god to the Indies. He seems to have sensed how close he was.

Near the end, when the leaking caravels had been so devoured by worms that they resembled honeycombs, his fleet was almost sunk by a waterspout. As this terrifying phenomenon approached—a twisting column of water "the width of a cask"—Columbus unsheathed his sword. He traced a giant cross upon the sky and drew a protective circle around his ships. Then he opened the Bible and read to his men about the tempest on the Sea of Galilee, concluding: "It is I: be not afraid."

Eleven years later, as everybody except John Keats must know, Vasco

Núñez de Balboa stood silent upon a peak in Darien, after which he descended from the mountains and waded into the Pacific. We are told by the chronicler Ovalle that Balboa entered the water with a naked sword in his hand and took possession of it, with all its coasts and bays, for the crowns of Castile and León.

Gil Eanes, Diogo Cão, and others probed the African coast until Dias rounded the cape. Da Gama then sailed on to Calicut, opening an eastern sea route to the Indies.

Balboa saw the western route, though he did not live to exploit it; the governor of Darien ordered his head chopped off, which was very often the way things turned out in those ebullient days.

And it is commonly held that Columbus never reached the Indies. However, this depends on your interpretation. Describing the island of Haiti to his sovereigns, he wrote:

> In it there are many harbors on the coast of the sea, beyond comparison with others that I know in Christendom, and many rivers, good and large, which is marvelous. Its lands are high; and there are in it very many sierras and very lofty mountains, beyond comparison with the island of Teneriffe. All are most beautiful, of a thousand shapes, and all are accessible and filled with trees of a thousand kinds and tall, and they seem to touch the sky. I am told that they never lose their foliage, and this I can believe, for I saw them as green and lovely as they are in Spain in May, and some of them were flowering, some bearing fruit, and some at another stage, according to their nature. And the nightingale was singing, and other birds of a thousand kinds, in the month of November there where I went.

The Sea Must Have an Endynge

To find a Northwest Passage and sail through it, said Martin Frobisher four centuries ago, was "the only thing of the world that was left yet undone whereby a notable mind might be made famous and fortunate." Nor did he doubt that such a route existed, for it stood to reason that the world was a harmonious place, symmetrically balanced, with sea routes both north and south; and he, Frobisher, would accomplish what Christopher Columbus had not, and be first to drop anchor in the Orient.

Earlier explorers had probed those "icie seas." First came Irish monks. Brendan, who lived from 484 to 578, evidently reached Greenland where he beheld an iceberg or a glacier front and sailed serenely among its monstrous water-sculpted passages: "Run the boat now through an opening," he is reputed to have told the helmsman, "that we may get a closer view of the wonderful works of God."

Not long after Brendan's excursion we find documents by scribes whose names echo dustily down the corridors of forgotten college Lit courses: Adamnan, Dicuil, the Venerable Bede, et al. They write of Cormak seeking islands to the west, and of visitors from Thule where in summer the sun remains visible from one day to the next, so that, although it be midnight elsewhere, "a man may do whatever he wishes, even to picking the lice from his shirt."

Then came the Norse, scouring those upper latitudes, who forced the monks westward: "Iceland first was settled in the days of Harald the Fairhaired, son of Halfdan the Black. . . . At that time Iceland was covered with forests between mountains and seashore. And Christians whom the Norsemen call Papes were here; but afterwards they went away because they did not wish to live together with heathen men, and they left behind Irish books, bells, and croziers. . . ." Just how far west those touchy monks traveled is not known.

Norse settlers followed them. Eric, or Eirik, a red-bearded murderer expelled from Iceland, led a fleet of colonists to Greenland in 986. Many of them drowned en route, but it is thought that about 400 set up housekeeping along the southwest coast, and perhaps 10,000 Norse lived there during the prosperous years of the settlement. Eventually the colonies were abandoned because Europe did not care what became of them, Eskimos threatened them, and the climate got worse. So the last Vikings in the New World died of starvation and scurvy just about the time Columbus was getting organized; but during those five centuries they explored the northeastern fringe of the American mainland. Undoubtedly they put in at Newfoundland, almost certainly at Nova Scotia and New Brunswick, perhaps at Cape Cod, and how much farther south we can only guess. And it would be curious if these sea people did not investigate the northern waterways—which implies that some of them may have approached Alaska.

Various Bristol merchants also beat Columbus to America: there are records of six voyages to "Markland"—someplace on the east coast of Canada—before 1490. Columbus himself, prior to his famous trip, visited England and probably Iceland and took a careful look beyond, for there is an excerpt from a letter or diary that reads: "In the month of February, 1477, I sailed a hundred leagues beyond the island of Thule. . . ." The identity of his Thule has been argued, but most historians think he meant Iceland. And he refers to another island beyond this, which might have been Jan Mayen Island within the Arctic Circle; all of which indicates that Columbus thoroughly researched his project long before the *Santa María* hoisted anchor.

In 1497 a Venetian named Giovanni Caboto got Bristol financing for a voyage of exploration to the northwest. He reached Nova Scotia or Newfoundland, possibly very close to the ruins of Leif Eiriksson's settlement, and returned with news that he had found the Asiatic mainland. The report caused a sensation: "He is called the Great Admiral and vast honour is paid to him and he goes dressed in silk, and these English run after him like mad."

Caboto—John Cabot—thought he had indeed touched a projection of Asia, and that by coasting southwest he could reach Cypango. So certain was he, or so persuasive, that an Italian in London wrote to the Duke of Milan: "Perhaps amidst so many occupations of Your Excellency it will not be unwelcome to learn how His Majesty here has acquired a portion of Asia without a stroke of his sword. . . ." And His Majesty, Henry VII, known to be "wise and not prodigal," rewarded the explorer with ten English pounds.

Cabot set out again the following year as commander of five merchant ships. Very little is known about this expedition. One ship soon returned to England, the other four vanished. A contemporary account remarks that Cabot had found his new lands "only on the ocean's bottom."

His son, Sebastian, may have accompanied him on the first voyage, and in 1508 Sebastian himself may have led two ships northwest until they were blocked by ice. What Sebastian did after that is even more uncertain. He is said to have discovered the northwest passage and might have sailed through to Cathay, but his crew revolted; he is said to have sailed so far north that his crew froze to death in July; he is said to have explored as far south as Cuba. In other words, Sebastian is not unfamiliar; most of us have met him somewhere along the line. He pops up again in 1521, trying to raise money for a new expedition, whereupon Henry VIII asked some knowledgeable merchants what they thought of him. They answered that it would be a "sore aventour to joperd five shipps . . . uppon the singuler trust of one man, callyd as we understand, Sebastyan, whiche Sebastyan, as we heresay, was never in that land hym self, all if he makes reporte of many thinges as he hath heard his Father and other men speke in tymes past."

However, Sebastian landed on his feet like an acrobat; such charmers customarily do. Before bowing out he became a governor of the Muscovy Company and Grand Pilot of England.

Then for quite a few years almost nobody looked northwest. The excitement that followed Columbus' voyages seems to have faded, and trade with Russia appeared more lucrative than wild-eyed explorations of distant ice-clogged bays that might or might not lead to the Orient.

But along came Frobisher—lace ruff, doublet, sword, slippers, Vandyke beard, baggy pantaloons and all, with a horse pistol in his hand to prove that he meant what he said. And a northern route, quoth he, "was as plausible as the English channel."

Even so, it was not easy to raise money; the seas closer to home were alive with floating morsels, galleons wallowing in from the Caribbean glutted with silver and gold. But the Earl of Warwick listened, and a few other moneyed gentlemen, and on June 7, Anno Domini 1576, Captain Martin Frobisher aboard the *Gabriel* set out from Ratcliff. He was followed by the *Michael* and by a seven-ton pinnace. As they sailed down the Thames past Greenwich they saw Elizabeth waving from a palace window.

Before reaching Greenland they encountered such a storm that the pinnace sank, its four-man crew drowned. Then the *Michael*, "mistrusting the matter, privily made its way home," and the crew of the *Gabriel* implored their captain to do likewise. Frobisher said no.

Authorities on shipbuilding agree, contrary to what you might expect, that sixteenth-century English vessels were not as reliable as tenth-century Viking ships, and perhaps not as safe as a Mediterranean bireme of the fourth century B.C. In any event, the storm had sprung the *Gabriel*'s mainmast, her fore-topmast was blown away, and "water issued out of her and withal many things floated over the ship's sides." But Frobisher said no, no, he would not turn back. In fact, he told the dismayed members of his crew, be would "rather make a sacrifice unto God of his life than to return home without the discovery of Cathay." And besides, "the sea at length needs must have an endynge."

So they patched things up with glue and string and continued on their course.

After poking about in various Arctic bays the explorers anchored beside an island, went ashore, and climbed a hill. From there they could see two headlands with a broad opening between, which—because of the flooding tide—they judged to be the passage they had been looking for. Beyond those headlands must lie the beaches of India and Cathay.

They also noticed three houses covered with sealskin as well as "a number of small things fleeting in the Sea a farre off," which Frobisher at first took to be "Porposes, or Ceales, or some kind of a strange fishe," but which turned out to be Eskimos in kayaks, and it occurred to the English that maybe they should quit sightseeing and get back on their boat.

Presently quite a few Eskimos showed up "making signs of friendship."

Christopher Hall, master of the *Gabriel*, describes them thus: "They bee like Tartars, with long blacke haire, broad faces, and flatte noses, and tawnie in colour, wearing Seale skinnes, and so doe the women, not differing in the fashion, but the women are marked in the face with blewe streekes. . . ."

Alas for signs of friendship, or perhaps what occurred was Frobisher's fault. At any rate, when the *Gabriel* started home several days later five crewmen were missing and one kidnapped Eskimo was aboard.

Hall describes the attempt to find them: "We stoode in neere the shoare, and shotte off a fauconet, and sounded our trumpet, but we could heare nothing of our men: this sound we called the five mens sound, and plyed out of it, but ankered againe in thirtie fathome, and oaze: and riding there all night, in the morning, the snow lay a foote thicke upon our hatches."

As to the Eskimo: "Whereupon he found himself in captivity, for very choller and disdain be bit his tong in-twayne within his mouth; notwithstanding, he died not thereof, but lived until he came to Englande, and then he died, of colde which he had taken at Sea."

Along with this miserable captive Frobisher brought back a queer little black rock which he seems to have regarded as a curiosity, because he gave it to the entrepreneur responsible for financing his expedition—Michael Lok. And here the water becomes somewhat muddy. Mrs. Lok was said to have tossed this rock into a fire and then quenched it in vinegar, whereupon it "glistered with a bright marquesset of gold." As a result, the rock was tested by professional assayers, who agreed that it was quite promising.

Michael Lok admitted long afterward that he had contrived the story about his wife throwing the rock into the fire. He also had invented the assayers' verdict. As a matter of fact he did submit it to three assayers, all of whom agreed that it was worthless.

Why did Lok falsify the verdict? Because Frobisher's voyage had not been profitable and therefore Lok, who promoted it, was no longer welcome at the club. If Frobisher had discovered gold, though, every door would open.

Lok sounds like a total charlatan, which he could have been. But he wanted so desperately to believe in the gold-freckled rock that he may have convinced himself as thoroughly as any alchemist.

Whatever his motive, the scheme succeeded and within about fifteen minutes everybody from Dartmouth to Birmingham heard the news: Frobisher has found gold!

Lok then organized the Cathay Company, whose purpose was to scoop up the ore that littered the beaches of the New World. There was no shortage of investors. Elizabeth herself, with a long nose for gold, subscribed 1,000 pounds.

So, next year, Frobisher retraced his route, enjoined to proceed "onely for the searching of the ore, and to deferre the further discovery of the passage until another time." He now commanded one tall ship of Her Majesty's named the *Ayde*, as well as the much smaller *Gabriel* and *Michael*. They were comfortably provisioned with beer, brandy, wine, cheese, butter, oatmeal, salad oil, almonds, raisins, licorice, and barrels of honey.

It does sound good—almonds, licorice, et cetera—but the reality of shipboard life in those merry days may not have been so attractive. The interior of a sixteenth-century English ship was described by one voyager as "right evill and smouldring hote and stynkynge," furnished with rats, lice, roaches, and bilge water. The food and drink, too, no matter how appetizing it might appear on the menu, must have called for a robust stomach. Frobisher's men got seven gallons of beer a week because soon after leaving port the water would be covered with slime and anybody who drank much of it would feel his bowels turning to sludge. As to the weekly food ration—well, your able seaman got four pounds of brined beef known as salt horse, delicately flavored with maggots, and seven pounds of biscuit harder than limestone, called scouse, which was the home of many weevils. Indeed, we are told, sailors customarily began a meal by banging their food against the table in order to dislodge a certain number of bugs. Each man also received four sun-cured cod and a measure of plum duff—a mixture of hardtack, raisins, and drippings.

This bill of fare week after week naturally brought about swollen bleeding gums, loosened teeth, blisters, palpitations, aching joints, shortness of breath, exhaustion and—on long voyages—death.

Apart from that, one had to beware of ship's officers. The reward for profanity could be a marlinspike in the mouth. For more odious conduct, such as failing to attend religious services, a transgressor might be ducked from the yardarm or tied to the mizzen shrouds with iron weights slung around his neck and his hands full of nettles. Talk of mutiny brought out the cat-o'-nine-tails—a stick covered with red baize from which dangled a series of knotted cords. One victim, having lived through fifty lashes, compared his shirt to a butcher's apron.

Those were lusty days at sea or ashore, what with garbage hurled from the window, bubonic plague, witches howling and writhing at the stake, human heads displayed on pikes for public instruction, and convicts let down alive from the gallows so that they might be castrated or disemboweled while still quivering.

Frobisher is said to have been a fierce disciplinarian, which of course made him unpopular, but he was not likely the most malevolent of sixteenth-century captains. No doubt he ruled heavily, but he also was more intrepid and skillful than most. A muscular, vigorous man—who every so often would be arrested for piracy, scolded, and released—he seems also to have been by our standards extremely credulous, looking beyond Greenland's horrendous icebergs toward the silks, jewels, and spicy breezes of Cathay.

Anno Domini 1577 he set forth.

Elizabeth honored this second departure even more highly; she permitted Captain Frobisher to kiss her hand.

His squadron rolled through the usual weather:

"The 4. of July we came within the making of Frisland. From this shoare 10. or 12. leagues, we met great Islands of yce, of halfe a mile, some more, some less in compasse. . . . Here, in place of odoriferous and fragrant smels of sweete gums, & pleasant notes of musicall birdes, which other Countreys in more temperate Zones do yeeld, wee tasted the most boisterous Boreal blasts mixt with snow and haile. . . ."

And so onward to Eskimo land, where numerous citizens "shewed themselves leaping and dauncing, with strange shrikes and cries."

Master Dionese Settle speaks of other wondrous things: "On this West shore we found a dead fish floating, which had in his nose a horne streight and torquet, of length two yards lacking two ynches, being broken in the top, where we might perceive it hollow, into the which some of our sailors putting spiders they presently died. I saw not the triall hereof, but it was reported unto me of a trueth: by the vertue whereof we supposed it to be the sea Unicorne."

On an island near the mouth of what now is called Frobisher Bay some Eskimos insisted that three of those five Englishmen lost on the previous trip were still alive.

Frobisher wrote them a note: "In the name of God in whom we all believe, and who, I trust, hath preserved your bodyes and souls amongst these Infidels, I commend me unto you. I will be glad to seeke by all meanes you can devise for your deliverance, either with force or with any commodities within my Shippes, which I will not spare for your sakes, or anything else I can do for you. I have aboard of theirs a Man, a Woman, and a Childe, which I am contented to deliver for you. . . ." He also sent them a pen, paper, and ink so that they could reply.

Nothing was learned of these missing crewmen for almost three centuries. In 1861 the American explorer Charles Hall visited some Baffin Island Eskimos and was told by an old woman that long ago some white men—Kodlunas—had come there. Five of these white men were captured by her tribe, she said, and while trying to build a boat they froze to death.

Frobisher, after waiting several days, concluded that further delay would be useless. Obedient to his commission, he loaded 200 tons of glistering ore and returned straightaway to England. He lost just two men on this trip: "one in the way by Gods visitation, and the other homeward cast over borde with a surge of the sea."

He brought with him the man, woman, and child. The English seem to have been surprised at the propriety of the adult Eskimos, who were not a couple. Although obliged to share a bunk, nothing happened between them: "The man would never shift himselfe, except he had first caused the woman to depart out of his cabin, and they both were most shamefast, least anye of their privie parts should bee discovered. . . ." In England the trio drew great crowds, but they flourished no better than the previous exhibit; despite being fed raw meat all three died within a month.

As for the gold-bearing rock: it might be valuable or it might not. Opinions differed. Elizabeth had the ore locked up and guarded in Bristol Castle and the Tower of London.

Investors scrambled to finance a third voyage.

Early in 1578 he set out again, leading a fleet of fifteen ships. Elizabeth draped a gold chain around the neck of "her loving friend Martin Frobisher," and graciously allowed his captains to kiss her hand.

Approximately forty men died on this trip, which was not a lot, according to one chronicler, not if one considers how many ships there were.

They returned to England with 1,300 tons of ore, only to learn that during their absence the London assayers had concluded it was iron pyrite. Fool's gold. Now, what can you do with 1,300 tons of fool's gold? Frobisher dumped part of it in Dartford harbor, which must have been embarrassing. As to the rest, the stones "when neither gold nor silver nor any other metal could be extracted from them, we have seen cast forth to mend the highways."

That ended Frobisher's visits to the New World. The gold rush had not been his idea; nevertheless he was held responsible. Yet he seems to have been a lucky man, or a man whose quality lifted him like a cork to the surface no matter how far down he had been thrust. He joined the navy and was so quickly promoted that ten years later he was commanding one of Elizabeth's most potent warships when the Spaniards made their colossal mistake. And in 1594 when he died, still battling Spain, his popularity rivaled that of Sir Francis Drake.

"We have taken this fort," he wrote to the Queen's lord high admiral after he had been mortally hurt. "They defended it verie resolutelie. And never asked for mercie. So they were put all to the sword, saving five or six . . . I was shot in with a bullet at the battery alongst the huckle bone . . ."

Until his final breath he thought he had found the Northwest Passage, although in fact what he had seen was the entrance to Hudson Bay.

John Davis, solid and moderate as his name, was the next to go looking. Seven years after Frobisher's last voyage be sailed from Dartmouth aboard the *Sunneshine* accompanied by a four-piece orchestra, which was customary in those ornamental days, and by the *Mooneshine*. He pushed north along the west coast of Greenland, past the Viking ruins, and mentions a grave "with divers buried in it, only covered with seale skinnes, having a cross laid over them"—which must have been either the grave of some medieval Vikings or that of a Christianized Eskimo family.

Unable to find a passage in the north, Davis looked around in the south and then sailed back to England reasonably satisfied. After all, one step at a time. "The northwest passage is a matter nothing doubtfull," he wrote to Sir Francis Walsingham, "but at any tyme almost to be passed, the sea navigable, voyd of yse, the ayre tollerable, and the waters very depe."

Ready again, off he sailed with the *Sunneshine* and *Mooneshine*, followed now by the *Mermayd* and *North Starre*. What an engaging fleet: *Sunneshine*, *Mooneshine*, *Mermayd* and *North Starre*. Not only can you see it, you can all but hear the miniature orchestra.

This time he explored a bit farther, studied the climate and topography, did his best to make friends with the Eskimos, and encountered "a flie which is called Muskyto, for they did sting grievously." Frobisher, too, had met the muskyto, because Master Settle mentions "certaine stinging Gnattes, which bite so fiercely, that the place where they bite shortly after swelleth and itcheth very sore."

Once again Davis's backers were satisfied, though not completely.

They agreed to finance another voyage with three ships but insisted that the two larger vessels bring home some fish. Davis might use the small boat for sightseeing, gathering ferns, or whatever. And again John Davis came home unscratched, loaded with stockfish. And he wrote a correct, formal letter to his principal sponsor:

"Good M. Sanderson, with Gods great mercy I have made my safe returne in health, with all my company, and have sailed threescore leagues further then my determination at my departure. I have bene in 73 degrees, finding the sea all open, and forty leagues betweene land and land. The passage is most probable, the execution easie, as at my coming you shall fully know."

But Spanish warships soon would dot the English channel and everything else must wait a while.

Only one name fills the twenty-year gap between Davis and Henry Hudson. George Weymouth was commissioned by the East India Company to probe the strait found by Frobisher and confirmed by Davis, to see if indeed this could be a northern route to the Orient. His voyage is nicely documented and it is a pleasure to observe that among various expenses, including the sum of 120 pounds and 3 shillings for beer, a certain Mr. Seger was paid 6 pounds, 13 shillings and 4 pence "for writing her Majestie letters to the Emperor of China and Cathay."

Despite such preparations Weymouth never reached the gigantic bay. Storms, fog, and a fearful noise which they found to be "the noyse of a great quantity of ice, very loathsome to be heard" so frightened his men that they altered course while Weymouth was in his cabin. The leader of this revolt was the preacher, who had packed a new clerical gown in order to impress the Chinese—a detail that almost gives the squalid little affair some elegance. However, Weymouth got partly through the strait and saw no land ahead. The merchants at home were encouraged.

Then out of absolute obscurity stepped that strange figure gripped by a vision of sailing to China, not carefully through subpolar waterways, but right over the top of the world; for in those days it was commonly held that beyond the Arctic ice lay a mild and placid sea in whose center loomed a black rock—the Pole.

Those English businessmen listening to Hudson surely liked the tone of what they heard; here stood somebody who knew what could be done and was not afraid to do it, ice be damned. Of course he might get stuck up there, which meant one's investment would be lost. Still, it should be worth a try.

They gave him the *Hopewell*—a forty-ton relic that had not been new when it accompanied Frobisher twenty-nine years earlier—a crew of ten, and a cabin boy.

So, having been victualed and wished Godspeed, Henry Hudson weighed anchor and drove straight for the Pole. He got within 600 miles of it; nobody knows how, because the ship had been rotten when it left England.

On his way home, passing the Spitzbergen Islands, he noticed quite a few whales.

Next year, ready again, he persuaded the Muscovy Company that with a little help he could sail round Russia. He got to Novaya Zemlaya before ice and a doubtful crew stopped him. On this voyage a marvelous sight was noted: "One of our companie looking over boord saw a Mermaid, and calling up some of the companie to see her, one more came up, and by that time shee was come close to the ships side, looking earnestly on the men: a little after, a Sea came and overturned her: from the Navill upward, her backe and breasts were like a womans, (as they say that saw her) her body as big as one of us; her skin very white; and long haire hanging downe behind, of colour blacke: in her going downe they saw her tayle, which was like the tayle of a Porposse, and speckled like a Macrell."

Home again, deeply disappointed, Henry learned that his sponsors no longer were interested in a new route to the East. No indeed, not when there was a fortune to be made by sending whalers to the Spitzbergen Islands.

At this point most men would have quit the struggle and begun writing their memoirs, or have sued the Muscovy Company for a share of the whaling profits, or settled into a sympathetic pub until time ran out. Not Henry. Off he went to Amsterdam where he wrestled the burghers of the Dutch East India Company and emerged with a contract for one more attempt at Arctic Russia.

The smallest vessel the Dutch merchants could find that would not capsize outside the channel was the *Half Moon*, and the men they collected seem to have been waterfront dregs. Thus equipped, off went Henry once more, determined to circumnavigate Russia in a cockleshell. He zigged and zagged his way through the ice to Novaya Zemlaya and was still afloat when his sterling crew again revolted. They had seen enough of the Arctic. After some negotiation, however, they agreed to attempt a southerly route to Cathay, westward via the United States—for most geographers thought the North American continent must be divided by a waterway. So the *Half Moon* came about, laid a course to Newfoundland, and began inspecting the coast.

The passage could not be located, only that river we now call the Hudson, up which they traveled as far as the present site of Albany. No doubt much aggrieved, Henry sailed home a third time.

But instead of proceeding directly to the Netherlands he put in at Dartmouth, which was a mistake. English merchants complained about an English captain serving Dutch rivals and the authorities then announced that he had undertaken a voyage "to the detriment of his country." The ship and the Dutch crew were released. Henry himself was detained.

But he wrestled with this as he had wrestled for his rights before, and when the struggle ended he had been outfitted for his next odyssey by three affluent gentlemen: Smith, Digges, and Lord Wolstenholme. They rented George Weymouth's reliable old bark *Discovery* and hired twenty-two crewmen, including a defrocked priest named Abacuck Prickett. Prickett, who was the sponsors' watchdog, wrote the only surviving account of Hudson's last voyage. It is not a happy story.

They steered for a passage noted by John Davis and got through after a tremendous effort that lasted five weeks.

"Some of our men this day fell sicke," writes Prickett. "I will not say it was for feare, though I saw small signe of other griefe. . . . Our course was as the ice did lye."

Once inside—the first Europeans to enter that huge bay—they bore south, assuming they had reached the North Pacific. But the coast fell away southeast, not southwest as they anticipated, and in early September the *Discovery* sailed into a cul-de-sac. Winter approached, provisions were short, and their captain had led them not to the Spice Islands but into some grim bottle; the crew, most of whom never had liked this voyage, grew increasingly mutinous. There was no escape, though, not until spring. The carpenter built a little house and the men who were not disabled by scurvy went scrounging for food. Some willow ptarmigan were caught, and later "Swannes, Goose, Ducke, and Teal, but hard to come by." They began to eat frogs, moss, tamarack buds—anything that would nourish them "how vile soever."

As soon as the ice broke up they started north.

But Hudson had been suspected of concealing food, and on the morning of June 22, with the ship again stopped by ice, and only fourteen days' rations remaining, he was seized and bound. His son John, six crew members—five of them ill—and the captain himself were forced into the ship's tender. Just before they were abandoned the carpenter chose to join them rather than accompany the mutineers. With an iron pot, a fowling piece, and a handful of meal they were cut adrift. And because they died so miserably and unjustly we might at least preserve their names: Michel But, Sydrack Fenner, John King, Arnold Ladlo, Adam Moore, Philip Staffe, Thomas Woodhouse.

The mutineers sailed a short distance, took in the topsails, and began searching the hold for food. They found some butter and meal, half a bushel of peas, and twenty-seven slices of brined pork. Then the tender came into view, the castaways rowing after them, and in Prickett's words the mutineers "let falle the maine saile and out top sailes, and fly as from an enemy."

How long Hudson and his companions lived, or how they died, has never been determined. Some historians believe they made it to an island in James Bay and subsequently reached the Canadian mainland where they might have survived for several months, possibly years.

The *Discovery* got back to England with eight or nine men aboard, the rest having died en route. Four are said to have been killed by Eskimos and one starved to death. The survivors were arrested and imprisoned, though later freed. The official inquiry reads in part:

"They all charge Master Hudson to have stolen the victuals by means of a scuttle or hatch cut between his cabin and the hold; and it appears that he fed his favourites, such as the surgeon, etc. and kept the others at only ordinary allowance, which led those who were not so favoured to make the attempt and to perform it so violently."

One of the mutineers, Robert Bylot, accompanied the next expedition under Captain Thomas Button, whose purpose was to verify the good news that a northwest passage had been found, for it was still believed that Hudson bad reached the Pacific. But the expedition had a second purpose: to attempt his rescue. The mutineers, dancing frantically before the tribunal, had stressed the idea that Hudson just might be living comfortably somewhere around James Bay. However, the farther he got from England and the gallows, the more did Bylot disparage this idea. Consequently they did not retrace Hudson's route; once inside the bay, instead of turning south to look for him, they continued west in the direction of China.

And when Captain Button at last saw land dead ahead he named the region Hopes Check'd. He veered south, but found no great flood tide welling in from the Pacific. He turned north, still optimistic, but finally realized the truth. The fact that he has been almost forgotten is rather unjust because it was he who deduced that Hudson Bay was an impasse; and therefore the Northwest Passage, if such a thing existed, must lie elsewhere. The reason he has been forgotten is that his employers suppressed the details of his survey; they did not want any commercial rivals to make use of it.

Bylot sailed again in 1616 as captain— which sounds odd considering his part in the Hudson debacle. William Baffin was pilot-navigator, and on this voyage they discovered the true passage, Lancaster Sound, although neither guessed what it was. Baffin charted it as an ice-clogged inlet. Having charted it as such, and finding no other passage, they steered for Greenland to collect some scurvy grass because the crew was falling sick. Then they sailed home.

At this point Bylot disappears from history. He died unnoticed. Baffin's exit was spectacular. He got a job with the omnipresent East India Company and in 1622 he took part in an Anglo-Persian assault on the Portuguese fort of Kishm in the Persian Gulf. According to Samuel Purchas: "Master Baffin went on shoare with his Geometricall Instruments, for the taking the height and distance of the castle wall;

but as he was about the same, he received a small shot from the Castle into his belly, wherewith he gave three leapes, by report, and died immediately."

Two Danish ships under the command of Jens Munck, the *Unicorn* and *Lamprey*, entered Hudson Bay in 1619. They fetched up on the bleak west coast and the expedition turned into a horror story—though a student of Gothic drama would not be surprised because there had been numerous omens. First, a sailor jumped overboard. Next, the *Lamprey* sprang a leak off southern Norway and when Munck put in at Karmsund he saw that the carpenters had left three bolt-holes open. Another crew member died before they left Karmsund. So it went. Munck took a shot at some birds: the gun exploded and tore away the brim of his hat. The anchors of the *Lamprey* were crushed by ice. Two days later the rudder head of the *Unicorn* was smashed.

Sickness and starvation picked off the crew. On February 20, says Munck, the priest died. On the eighth of March died Oluf Boye, who had been ill nine weeks. Next day died Anders the cooper, ill since Christmas. On the twenty-first died Povel Pederson and the surgeon, both ill since almost Christmas. "Now, and afterwards, the sickness raged more violently. . . . I was then like a wild and lonely bird."

Sixty-four men had left Norway. Munck and two others eventually got back. They had not found the passage.

In 1631 two British expeditions sailed within a few days of each other, both persuaded that it must empty into Hudson Bay. Luke Foxe deftly mapped the northern coast and returned to England before winter. Thomas James had some problems:

> October 7th it snowed all day, so that we were fain to clear it off the decks with shovels; and it blew a very storm withal. It continued snowing and very cold weather, and it did so freeze that all the bows of the ship, with her beak-head, was all ice. Afterwards the sun did shine very clear, and we tore the top-sails out of the tops, which were hard frozen in them into a lump, so that there they hung a-sunning in a very lump, the sun not having power to thaw one drop of them. . . . The land was all deep covered with snow, the cold did multiply, and the thick snow water did increase; and what would become of us, our most merciful God and preserver only knew.

James spent the winter on Charlton Island—where Hudson may have died—and probably surprised himself by getting out alive. His trip is said to have inspired "The Rime of the Ancient Mariner."

After Foxe and James the bay was taken over by traders; a quick profit in furs was what excited European merchants. The fugitive passage was ignored, with one exception, until the British Admiralty dispatched Sir John Ross in 1818.

That exception was the attempt by James Knight, a longtime employee of the Company of Gentlemen Adventurers Trading into Hudson's Bay—later known as the Hudson's Bay Company. Knight often had asked permission to explore the northwest, but not until he was almost eighty years old did the adventurous London gentlemen who controlled the purse strings cautiously acquiesce. They let him use the *Albany Frigate* and a sloop called *Discovery*.

Knight left Gravesend in 1719, expecting to return that fall. He did not show up. Nor did he come back the next year.

In 1721 the sloop *Whale-Bone* was ordered to look for him, but as it was a bit late in the season the search did not get under way until 1722. The *Whale-Bone*'s master then reported nothing significant, so everybody assumed that Captain Knight had discovered the Northwest Passage and very probably was loitering in China or California.

Forty-five years later a boat passing Marble Island off the west coast of Hudson Bay noticed the ruins of a house. In five fathoms of water lay what was left of Captain Knight's ships. Some very old Eskimos in the area were questioned. They said that at the beginning of the third winter no English were still alive. The last two, the Eskimos said, lived much longer than the rest and often climbed to the top of a large rock where they spent a long time looking to the east, after which they sat down together and wept.

Sir John Ross sought the passage farther north, in the region where two centuries earlier Baffin had stopped. Ross entered Lancaster Sound and sailed about fifty miles until he saw a chain of mountains ahead, which caused him to turn back. Several of his subordinates, including Edward Parry, were unable to see any mountains and thought he should have continued.

In 1819 Parry led an expedition through the sound as far as Melville

Island—halfway to Alaska—before being halted by ice. Yet even then Parry failed to recognize the truth. Twice more he probed the area without trying Lancaster Sound again.

The next assault, led by George Back, was planned as a variation on a familiar theme. Instead of going all the way by sea they would sail up Hudson Strait to the neck of the Melville Peninsula, drag some boats overland, and proceed by the next waterway. So the sturdy ship *Terror* was refurbished and in 1836 they set out.

Very soon they were caught by Hudson Bay ice. Since there was no escape until spring, Back ordered the upper masts dismantled, housing erected, and the decks banked with snow. Stoves were set up and a system of pipes carried off vapors. From a distance the *Terror* resembled a factory. After about a month the ice began drifting eastward. Lashed by gales, compressed and twisted by masses of ice, the *Terror* almost collapsed. The captain's door split, reinforcements thrown up by the carpenter were squeezed out of position, and "beads of turpentine started from every seam." Back preached a sermon to which his crew listened "with the most profound and serious attention."

Ten months later the ship was released somewhat closer to home. That is, farther from their goal. Back was understandably embarrassed about having traveled the wrong direction and might have attacked the Arctic again, but his ship had been ruined. Nobody knew if it would stay afloat until they reached England.

They set a course for Stromness. After one more gale, however, Back drove straight at the Irish coast and deliberately ran aground on the first sandy beach. Next day at low tide they inspected the hull and "there was not one on board who did not express astonishment that we had ever floated across the Atlantic."

The British Admiralty was quite put out by this. One must expect failures but it was now well into the nineteenth century. Four centuries of failure seemed a bit much.

So they decided to launch an elite expedition commanded by the veteran Sir John Franklin. They provided him with a good ship, the *Erebus*, and the reconditioned *Terror*. Both had been meticulously overhauled. The masts were painted white, the superstructures yellow, the hulls black. Sheet iron covered the bows. Twenty-horsepower railway engines were installed along with an apparatus that would lift the propellers if they were threatened by ice. An ingenious hot-water system warmed the cabins.

Twelve months should be sufficient to negotiate the passage—wherever it might be—but *Erebus* and *Terror* were provisioned for three years. Besides vast quantities of fuel and food, each ship carried all sorts of agreeable accessories: solid Victorian silver, handsomely cut glass, decorative china, et cetera. Each carried a hand organ that would play fifty tunes, and each had a library of 1,200 books—everything from Dickens to manuals on steam engines to the latest issues of *Punch*.

The 129 crew members were selected for experience, initiative, and physical condition. None of your Elizabethan wharf rats.

Everyone understood that Franklin would succeed; no question about it. No previous expedition had been so liberally endowed or so thoughtfully planned.

A photograph of him taken for the occasion shows a relaxed, portly gentleman in late middle age, jowls awash. He wears a somewhat rumpled coat with a twin row of brass buttons and fringed epaulets, and one of those preposterous commodore hats, and he holds a collapsible telescope.

The Admiralty at first had been dubious. Said the First Lord: "I might find a good excuse for not letting you go, Sir John, in the rumour that tells me you are sixty years of age."

Franklin replied: "No, no, My Lord, I am only fifty-nine."

His two captains, Crozier and Fitzjames, look amiable enough, though not especially forceful. The sort of men you meet in a pub.

All the officers in the group photo have assumed those calcified nineteenth-century poses—gazing beyond the camera or pensively aside, arms folded. Only one man looks alert: Lieutenant Graham Gore. There is something rakish about him in the tilt of his cap and his faint, dark, sardonic smile. He resembles one or two of the cavalrymen in the last photograph of Custer's doomed squadron.

Erebus and *Terror* sailed in May of 1845. On July 26 they were becalmed near a whaling ship in Baffin Bay. Franklin asked the whaler's captain to supper, but during the afternoon a breeze came up and the expedition sailed westward. That was the last time anybody saw them.

Five years later some clues were found: shattered bottles, ropes, a rock cairn, meat canisters, bird bones, a scrap of paper. Then the embankment of a house, washtubs, coal bags, clothing, and the graves of three men.

In 1859 a search party under the command of Leopold McClintock, financed by Lady Franklin, met some Eskimos and bought from them six silver spoons and forks, a medal, a length of gold chain, several buttons, and some knives fashioned out of iron and wood from one of the ships. McClintock's party subsequently came upon a partly clothed skeleton lying face down in the snow and concluded that the man must have been either a steward or an officer's servant because of his blue double-breasted jacket with slashed sleeves and braided edging, and because his neckerchief had been tied with a loose bowknot—a style not used by seamen. Near the skeleton they found a pocket comb and a clothes brush.

Not long after that they saw a boat mounted on a sledge—a total weight of 1,400 pounds. In this boat lay two skeletons. One had been torn apart, perhaps by wolves. The other skeleton was dressed in furs. Beside them lay five pocket watches, two loaded guns, remnants of a pair of handworked slippers, and half a dozen books including The *Vicar of Wakefield* and a devotional manual inscribed by Sir George Back to Graham Gore. Nor was that all. McClintock reported "an amazing quantity of clothing" such as silk handkerchiefs and eight pairs of boots, towels, sponges, soap, toothbrushes, bayonet scabbards, nails, saws, files, two rolls of sheet lead, and twenty-six pieces of silver plate—eight of them bearing Franklin's crest.

On King William Island a cairn was discovered in which there was a rusty tin box containing a note. It told of Franklin's death, the deaths of nine officers and fifteen enlisted men, and of abandoning the ships on April 22, 1848. This information had been scribbled by Fitzjames on the margin of a bureaucratic form that gave precise directions in six languages:

> WHOEVER finds this paper is requested to forward it to the Secretary of the Admiralty, London, with a note of the time and place at which it was found: or, if more convenient, to deliver it for that purpose to the British Consul at the nearest Port.

> QUINCONQUE trouvera ce papier est prié d'y marquer le tems et lieu ou il l'aura trouvé, et de le faire parvenir au plutot au Secretaire . . .
> CUALQUIERA que hallare este Papel, se le suplica de enviarlo al Secretario del Almirantazgo, en Londrés . . .
> EEN ieder die dit Papier mogt vinden, wordt hiermede verzogt . . .
> FINDEREN af dette Papiir ombedes, naar Leilighed . . .
> WER diesen Zettel findet . . .

Lieutenant Frederick Schwatka of the U.S. Army came across more relics and bones in 1879. He also heard from Eskimos that a group of about thirty white men had died in a remote cove and that their bodies, when the Eskimos saw them, had been surrounded by papers. But not until 1923 did anyone visit this cove, at which time the bones were still visible, although no trace of the documents remained.

Schwatka's party discovered a few other things: the graves of two Englishmen, scraps of red and blue cloth, tin cans, blankets, sledge harness, copper kettles, a two-gallon jug, cookstoves, a brush with the name H. Wilks, various iron and brass implements, an empty grave, human bones scattered in the snow, and a silver medal—a prize for mathematics that had been awarded by the Royal Naval College in 1830 to John Irving, third officer of the *Terror*. Schwatka also picked up a fragment of paper on which there was a drawing of a hand with the index finger pointing, but the paper had rotted, so that whatever message might have accompanied the hand had disappeared.

In 1929 a Canadian surveyor talked with two ancient Eskimos who said that when they were young they had come upon several wooden cases on a small island. Inside these cases were containers filled with white powder. They could not imagine what the powder was, so they and their families tossed it up into the air to watch it blow away.

Other commonplace articles, now curiously poignant, have been recovered: wine bottles labeled BRISTOL GLASS WORKS, a barrel-shaped wooden canteen, an ax, part of a backgammon board presented to the *Erebus* by Lady Franklin, a pewter medal commemorating the 1843 launching of the steamer *Great Britain*, a George IV silver half crown dated 1820, and one snowshoe marked MR. STANLEY.

In 1931 several more skeletons were found, and since then other bones, but altogether only about half of Franklin's men have been accounted for.

A footnote in W. H. Markham's *Life of Sir John Franklin* tells us something else. About 700 preserved meat tins "filled with gravel" were found at the expedition's winter quarters on Beechey Island. A great many more of these tins lay nearby. They had been supplied under directions from the Admiralty, and it seems that another consignment which was delivered to the British navy at home had turned out to be putrid. Because such a quantity of meat as these empty tins were calculated to hold could not possibly have been eaten by Franklin's party during that first winter, Markham notes, "it is supposed that the defective condition of the contents of the tins was discovered, and a survey of them ordered. If this surmise be a correct one, the loss of so large a proportion of what would be considered fresh, in contradistinction to salt, provisions would be most serious. . . ."

You can almost see the faces of Franklin's men while those tins of putrid meat were being opened. Most serious. Indeed.

What happened, as closely as it can be reconstructed from Eskimo oral history and from the remains, is that Franklin died—probably of heart failure—on June 11, 1847. At just about this time Lord Egerton was writing in the London *Quarterly Review*: "With interest which accumulates by the hour do we watch for the return of these two vessels which are perhaps even now working their way through the Bering Strait into the Pacific. Should the happiness be yet allowed us of witnessing that return, we are of the opinion that *Erebus* and *Terror* should be moored henceforth on either side of the *Victory*, floating monuments of what the Nelsons of discovery can do, at the call of their country in the service of the world."

Several months after Franklin's death one of the ships was crushed by ice and probably sank. The other stayed afloat, although trapped, and the surviving explorers—perhaps 100—built sledges and tried to walk to a Hudson Bay post.

What became of *Erebus* and *Terror* is not altogether certain. Some investigators believe that both ships may have drifted until 1849, or possibly longer, with a few men still aboard.

In mid-April of 1851 an extraordinary spectacle was noted by the crew of the English brig *Renovation* en route from Limerick to Quebec. Just off the Newfoundland banks an officer of the watch, Robert

Simpson, observed two ships resting on a large ice floe. Their hulls were painted black and both vessels corresponded in size and appearance to *Erebus* and *Terror*. Simpson reported this apparition to the captain, who,

> being very ill at the time, did not notice at first what I said. I again repeated the circumstance, and asked him what he intended to do, but he only groaned out, "Never mind", or something to that effect. . . . I was anxious to get up on deck again, but before I went up called Mr. Lynch (a passenger), who immediately jumped up and looked at the vessels. . . . The largest one was lying on her beam-ends, with her head to the eastward, and nothing standing but her three lower masts and bowsprit; the smaller one, which was sitting nearly upright, with her head to the southward, with her three masts, top-masts on end, and top-sail and lower yards across, and to all appearance having been properly stripped and abandoned.

The ships remained in sight for approximately an hour, at a distance of about three miles, and were studied through a telescope by several members of the *Renovation*'s crew. Her captain, though, did not wish to be bothered.

Later, during an Admiralty investigation, the captain testified that he got out of his sickbed in order to look at the ships. He stated that he considered them to be mere wrecks, and being pressed for time, with bad weather imminent, he concluded that they were not worth examining. The captain's testimony is regarded as suspect. It is thought that he may have lied in order to conceal the fact that he had passed close by *Erebus* and *Terror* without doing anything.

Regardless of what the *Renovation*'s captain did or did not see, there are various eyewitness accounts. J. S. Lynch, the passenger, wrote to his uncle—a Mr. Creilly—in Limerick soon after the brig docked in Quebec:

> We arrived here on yesterday. . . . The icebergs we met with were frightful in size, as the basis of some of them would cover three times over the area of Limerick; and I do not at all exaggerate when I say that the steeple of the cathedral would have appeared but a small pinnacle, and a dark one, compared to the lofty and gorgeously-tinted spires that were

> on some of them; and more to be regretted is that we met, or rather saw at a distance, one with two ships on it, which I am almost sure belonged to Franklin's exploring squadron, as from the latitude and longitude we met them in they were drifting from the direction of Davis's Straits. Was there but a single one, it might have been a deserted whaler, but two so near each other, they must have been consorts. . . .

And there is a splendid letter from crew member James Silk to his brother John:

> . . . On the 14th day in the morning wee saw a very large hice Burgh to whindward of ous, and 12 o'clock 14th, wee saw as many as 6 hice Burg. . . . Apon one of the very large burghs in which wee see there was 2 large ships on them, 1 laying Apon her broad broad side, and the other were A laying as comfortable as if she was in the dock fast to her moreings. The wether was very fine and the wather very smouth, but the captain being laid up at the same time it was not reported to him untell 8 o'clock, and we out of sight of them, so, dear friends, I canot tell you whether there was any living sould there are not.

Rupert Gould, an inquisitive and versatile historian who loves such occurrences, sifted just about everything turned up by the Admiralty investigation and concluded that the ships on the floe were, indeed, *Erebus* and *Terror*. Gould adds, however, that his judgment "may be due simply to a subconscious prejudice in favor of the marvellous." He also points out that his friend Mr. R. J. Cyriax, who is perhaps the leading authority on the Franklin disaster, does not share his opinion.

No matter what happened to Franklin's ships, the course of the men on land is clear. Some turned back toward *Erebus* and *Terror*, obviously planning to reboard them. Others who were too sick or weak to travel simply camped and waited. Others continued marching, dragging sleds piled with necessities and with luxuries—dying as they marched. No doubt some of them encountered Eskimos, but the English did not understand, or refused to admit, that their only chance of survival was to emulate the natives. Instead, they went on towing the crested silver plate, the wine goblets, the boxes of nails, the sheet lead, the silk handkerchiefs, the soap, the medals, the backgammon board, the bayonet scabbards, and the cookstoves, and bottles, and brushes, and *The Vicar of Wakefield* until they fell down exhausted in the snow. At this point they were longitudinally just about halfway between Alaska and Greenland, approximately 2,000 miles north of Nebraska.

The saws they had carried did become useful. At the end, collapsing from stupidity, scurvy, and starvation, some of the explorers lopped off the skulls of dead companions in order to get at the brains. This bit of gastronomic news when it reached the British public was most unpalatable. One could not bear to think that men from good families would turn savage, so it was agreed that Eskimos must have been responsible.

The Franklin catastrophe chilled England's perennial search for a northwest passage. Enough was enough.

In 1903 a brash young Norwegian named Roald Amundsen set off in a seventy-foot fishing boat, the *Gjoa*, after having reinforced the hull and installed a thirteen-horsepower engine. Six other young men went with him. They sailed on a foggy night to escape a creditor. After paralleling Baffin's route up the Greenland coast they bore west into Lancaster Sound and followed Franklin's presumed course south toward the Canadian mainland. For almost two years they stayed on King William Island, catching plenty of fish and game, although this was the area in which Franklin's men starved to death.

In August of 1905 they were able to push through the ice, and on the morning of the twenty-sixth Amundsen was awakened by his second-in-command, who told him there was a vessel in sight—the *Charles Hanson*, a Bering Sea whaler out of San Francisco.

They spent that winter locked in by ice and one crew member died of pneumonia. Next summer they were on the Pacific, six presumptuous Scandinavians in a herring boat.

If Amundsen was the first man to sail the Northwest Passage—and as far as anybody knows, he was—his *Gjoa* might not have been the first ship to make it through. There is a story about the merchantman *Octavius* which is so bizarre that one cannot help feeling suspicious. Yet it may be true. If not, never mind: it's marvelous.

On the morning of August 11, 1775, the *Herald*, a whaler under the command of a Captain Warren, was just west of Greenland when the lookout reported a vessel ahead. At first the hull could not be seen, only her masts protruding above an iceberg, but when she drifted into view

Captain Warren looked through his telescope. The vessel glistened with ice. There seemed to be nobody aboard.

Accompanied by four crew members, be pulled over in a longboat. They went aboard and found the entrance to the forecastle blocked by snow, but after this had been cleared away they were able to open the door. A musty stench poured out. In the forecastle twenty-eight dead seamen were lying on their bunks, each man wrapped up as though he had tried to protect himself against the cold.

The same musty odor poured out of the master's cabin. They found the master slumped in a chair with his hands resting on a table. A faint green mold obscured his features and veiled his eyes, but his body had not putrefied. The log was open, a quill pen beside it.

Captain Warren gave the log to one of his men and they entered the adjoining cabin. They discovered a woman lying in a bunk, covered with blankets, her head on her elbow as though she had been watching something when she died. A sailor with a flint in one hand and a piece of steel in the other was sitting cross-legged on the deck. Some wood shavings had been heaped together on the deck in front of him. Nearby lay the sailor's jacket. Under it was the body of a small boy.

Captain Warren inspected the galley, which had no provisions. He wanted to inspect the hold but his men refused and threatened to pull away in the longboat, so they returned to the *Herald* and watched the *Octavius* drift out of sight.

When Captain Warren asked for the logbook the sailor who had been carrying it handed over the binding and four pages. The book had come apart while the sailor was getting into the longboat and most of it had dropped into the water.

This log is now said to be in the archives of the London Registrar of Shipping. The first two pages list the ship's company, including the captain's wife and ten-year-old son, and disclose that the *Octavius* left England bound east on the China trade on September 10, 1761. The next page carries the earliest entries, mentioning fair weather, good headway, and sighting the Canary Islands. The last page contains what must have been the final entry. It is dated November 11, 1762, and obviously was written by a crewman. It gives an approximate position—Longitude 160 W., Latitude 75 N.—and states that the ship has been enclosed by ice for seventeen days. After noting that the master has unsuccessfully attempted to kindle a fire, the entry concludes: "The master's son died this morning and his wife says she no longer feels the terrible cold. The rest of us seem to have no relief from the agony."

Longitude 160 W., Latitude 75 N. is in the Arctic Ocean high above Point Barrow. The log's missing pages might have explained why the *Octavius* was so far north, but without them we can only speculate. On his return voyage, instead of charting a course around the Cape of Good Hope, the ship's captain must have yielded to some desperate urge. He must have thought he could accomplish what Frobisher and so many others had not, and be the first to navigate a northwest passage.

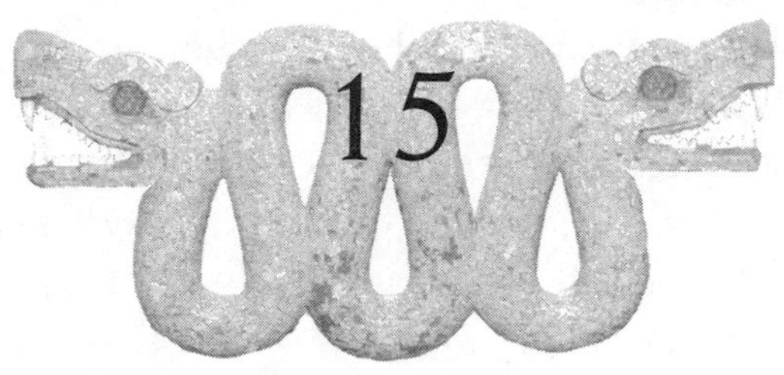

15

El Dorado

If you go to Bogotá and visit the Banco de la República you will see, in the bank's Museo del Oro, nearly 10,000 pre-Columbian gold artifacts: labrets, nose rings, brooches, masks, spoons, pincers, receptacles, representations of birds, snakes, crocodiles, people, animals. You walk down a corridor lined on both sides with display cases, each case packed with these opulent creations. You turn right, walk down another corridor past more of the same. Then more. And more. Finally, instead of going out, you are led into a dark room. After you have been there awhile the lights begin rising so gradually that you expect to hear violins, and you find yourself absolutely surrounded by gold. If all of Tut's gold were added to this accumulation, together with everything Schliemann plucked from Mycenae and Hissarlik, you could scarcely tell the difference.

Quite a lot of it is Muisca, a name that may not mean anything unless you happen to be an anthropologist, or a collector, or at least a Colombian. The Muisca Indians were one of the Chibcha tribes living in the highlands around Bogotá. They were sedentary farmers with no great authority or influence; but for a number of years, nobody knows just how long, until they were deprived of their independence by some Chibcha cousins, they observed a ritual unlike any other in the world.

Guatavitá was their principal village. High above it at an altitude of about two miles is a small circular lake which was formed several thousand years ago when a meteorite plunged into the earth. People were living in the Andean cordilleras at that time and a memory of the phenomenon must have survived, because Chibcha mythology relates how a golden god dropped from the sky to make his home at the bottom of Lake Guatavitá.

Whenever a new Muisca chieftain was elected—or perhaps each year on a certain day—he gave thanks to this radiant underwater deity. After first being anointed with sticky balsam gum, he was sprayed with gold dust through cane tubes until he became a glittering living statue. Then he walked from the temple to the lake shore, accompanied by priests wearing black cotton robes and by the Muisca men whose bodies were painted red. At the shore he stepped aboard a raft and was paddled to the center of the lake where—possibly at dawn, just as sunlight illuminated the water—he dove in and washed away the gold. Then the people who had followed him, who now stood all around the perimeter of the lake, hurled emeralds and golden trinkets into the water.

The last performance of this ceremony seems to have taken place about 1480, but when the Europeans arrived they heard stories of a gilded man; and after they had told the stories to each other often enough the Muisca chief became an omnipotent king who ruled a golden empire. Not only did the king himself go about his daily affairs dressed in a golden crust, so did the nobles of his realm; and because it was uncomfortable to sleep in a golden suit they washed it off every night, gilding themselves afresh in the morning. And the warriors wore golden armor. And the buildings were sheathed in gold. That is to say, practically everything in this kingdom except food either was made of gold or was sheathed in gold.

The first European to go looking for it was a young German, Ambrosius Dalfinger—some say Ehinger—who had been appointed governor of Venezuela as the result of a little hanky-panky in the Old World. After Maximilian of Habsburg died, three rulers competed for the title of Holy Roman Emperor: Henry VIII, Francis I, and Charles I of Spain. Who was to receive this crown would depend on the Electors; and, as the Spaniards say, Don Dinero speaks with a loud voice. Charles borrowed a wagonload of ducats from two German banking families, Welser and Fugger, in order to bribe the Electors. Dalfinger was related to some Welser officials, Charles owned Venezuela, et cetera.

Thus, in 1529 young Ambrosius landed at Coro, a settlement of several dozen thatched huts. He was expected to infuse the colony with a more businesslike spirit and speed up the exports—the most profitable being a substance derived from the bark of the guaiac tree which reputedly cured the so-called French disease, morbus gallicus. But the German bankers had misjudged their deputy because Ambrosius Dalfinger-Ehinger-Einguer-Lespinger-Alfinger went marching into the jungle with about 200 soldiers and several hundred reluctant Indian porters to see what he could see. How much he knew of a golden man at this point is uncertain; perhaps not much because the El Dorado legend was just taking shape, although he probably had seen and handled a few seductive ornaments in Coro.

On this march he acquired some gold. Nothing comparable to what Cortés had earlier found at Tenochtitlán, but by force or by trade he did pick up a number of high-carat gold pins, nose rings, diadems, and bracelets. More significant than these gold ornaments, however, was the fact that Venezuelan Indians had not made them. The workmanship was beyond their ability. They came from a place called Xerirá, which was renowned also for emeralds. In Xerirá one could trade seashells and cotton for emeralds and gold.

Dalfinger spent ten months in the jungle searching for this wonderful kingdom and when he got back to Coro he learned that during his long absence a new governor had been appointed. The Welser home office, believing that Ambrosius and all his men must have marched into eternity, sent forth a replacement—Hans Sinserhoffer, or Seissenhoffer, accompanied by one Nikolaus Federmann. It was a bit awkward, having two governors, but Sinserhoffer graciously resolved the problem by dying.

For a while then Dalfinger attended to gubernatorial business, at the same time accumulating supplies and soldiers for another attempt. And he became convinced that the way to locate Xerirá was to terrorize the natives. Sooner or later, he reasoned, they would stop being evasive and lead him straight to it.

In June of 1531 he started off again.

Even by conquistadorial standards he seems to have been unusually brutal and myopic. Indians who welcomed him with gifts and music were stabbed or shot. Rebellious captives were burnt alive. He had linked his porters together by a neck chain and when one died of exhaustion it was at first thought necessary to unshackle them all to get rid of the corpse; then Dalfinger realized it was simpler to decapitate the body, or, in some cases, a living porter who was unable to carry his load.

Meanwhile they were collecting gold. The expedition's accountant listed a great quantity of earrings, brooches, brassards, labrets, and so forth, along with more interesting items such as gold replicas of eagles and humans. Dalfinger loaded it all on a string of Indians and dispatched them to Coro with a guard of soldiers. One man, Francisco Martín, survived. Either he staggered into Coro several weeks later half dead of starvation, or he was adopted by a tribe and told his story long afterward. Historians disagree. In either case, it appears that the convoy got lost, and when food ran out the Europeans began eating Venezuelans before being eaten themselves by predators and scavengers. As for the treasure, Martín said they had buried it at the foot of a ceiba tree. Thus, unless some Indians happened to be watching and later dug it up, which seems unlikely, there must still be approximately 100 kilos of gold ornaments at the foot of a ceiba tree somewhere in the jungle.

A little over two years after leaving Coro thirty-five exhausted ragged men tottered back into town. Governor Dalfinger, who had stopped a poisoned arrow with his throat, was not among them. They brought very little gold, but of harrowing stories they had more than enough. Vampire bats. Malaria. Yellow fever, accompanied by black vomit and death. A fever called verruga, transmitted by flies, which disfigured the body with abscesses. Crocodiles, jaguars, a climate where everything rotted, to say nothing of invisible enemies—one torment after another. And as for the soldiers who exercised themselves with native women, they had syphilis.

Those who listened to the grim recital and looked at the survivors grew more than ever convinced that someplace in the jungle a kingdom of inconceivable splendor must exist. As proof, a sizable treasure already had been found, though regrettably lost. Then too, if such a kingdom did not exist why would God create so many obstacles to its discovery? Therefore it must be.

Oveido, an early historian, was equally persuaded. Having asked some experienced conquistadors why the elusive prince should be called *dorado*, he was told that, according to the Indians, this great lord walked about coated with gold as finely pulverized as salt. Oveido continues with blunt practicality that he would rather have the chamber broom of this prince than the gold smelters of Peru, adding that if what he had been told was indeed so, and the great cacique gilded himself afresh each morning, it must follow that he owned some exceptionally rich mines.

After Dalfinger came Gonzalo Jiménez de Quesada, or Ximenes de Casada, an attorney who saw little future in the gloomy Andalusian courts. He sold everything and embarked for Santa Marta on the Colombian coast.

In 1536 he was sent upriver with approximately 900 men to look for a passage to the South Sea. Charles wanted a short route to the Spice Islands, so those were Quesada's marching orders—although everybody in the expedition and everybody in Santa Marta understood that he would be looking for the gilded man.

Quesada's troops hacked their way through some of the most unpleasant territory on earth. Ants, hornets, snakes, ticks, bats, mosquitos, fevers, and tropical rain made their days memorable, with a quick flight of arrows now and then for emphasis. Stragglers caught by Indians were cooked and eaten. Juan Serrano was taken from his hammock by a jaguar, as easily as a cat runs off with a mouse. Others, including the good swimmer Juan Lorenzo, were swallowed by alligators. Graves decorated the trail. Germán Arciniegas reports that sometimes the hand of a buried corpse remained visible, as though waving good-bye to those who struggled on toward the land of gold.

When there was no decent food they scrambled for lizards, rats, insects, bats, and whatever else might sustain them a few hours longer; they gnawed leather shields and the hides of dead horses.

Next came the mountains. They climbed and shivered, chewed on raw corn, and dragged the surviving horses upward.

At last they looked down on a vast cultivated plain. Everything appeared green and peaceful. This was the plateau of Cudinamarca, land of the condor, home of the Chibcha Indians. A year had passed since Quesada left Santa Marta. Three-fourths of his men were dead.

Indifferent now to danger, they descended from the mountain like a company of insects—swarming on whatever opposed them—and invaded the city of Tunja, where thin sheets of beaten gold dangled from almost every hut, tinkling faintly and shimmering in the sunlight. They found one of the three Chibcha rulers inside a wooden palace. He was very old and fat and was seated on a throne or stool encrusted with emeralds. Quesada, remembering the lesson taught by Cortés and Pizarro, seized the fat old man and never once let go. The city of Tunja quickly surrendered.

It was late afternoon when the Spaniards arrived. Now, after the conquest, they rushed around by torchlight ripping sheets of gold from the huts, filling bags with emeralds and gold dust.

Their next prize was a temple full of royal mummies with parrot-feather headdresses, emerald eyes, and golden ornaments. The temple caught fire while they were stripping the mummies, but the treasure was salvaged.

Still they had not found what they were looking for: el hombre dorado.

They were shown the lake above Guatavitá and were told that here the story of a golden man had originated. Here, it was explained to them, the Muisca used to anoint and gild their chief. But that was a long time ago. Now there was no such man. El Dorado no longer existed.

The Spaniards refused to believe it.

Quesada and his men remained on the plateau for two years, relentlessly seeking hidden treasure and gold mines. What they discovered was unquestionably worth stealing in the name of the Spanish crown, but it did not compare with the wealth of Mexico or Peru. So there must be more, Quesada reasoned. Much more. But there was not. The Chibcha had no treasuries, no secret mines. Most of their gold came from trade with Ecuador.

At last, somewhat frustrated because he had expected to rival or surpass Cortés and Pizarro, Quesada began to think about returning to Spain to publicize his conquest and ask for a suitable reward—the governorship of this territory, which he had chosen to call New Granada.

Just then he learned that another expedition led by one of Pizarro's captains, Sebastián de Belalcázar, was on the road to Cudinamarca.

This man's name, in fact, may have been Garcia, but he has ridden down the centuries as Sebastián from Belalcázar. He was a blue-eyed son of Estremadura, home of many conquistadors, and he governed the northern sector of the Inca realm, which we now call Ecuador. Such an office would satisfy most men, but not Belalcázar. Everything in Quito appeared orderly, which is to say boring, and nobody knew what might be disclosed in the lands beyond. On one of those plateaus, it was said, lay a kingdom of gold. He therefore appointed a lieutenant to run the business and, without notifying Pizarro, started off in a northerly direction. If no rich kingdom existed—well, should that be the case one could always plant the seeds of future cities. For this purpose Belalcázar took along a multitude of pigs, cattle, dogs, extra horses, and whatever else seemed appropriate, including fine silver for his table. And if the grand column could proceed no faster than its slowest members—ay, so be it.

Quesada, awaiting his arrival, grew a bit nervous. He had been told that the invader wore silk clothes and was accompanied by well-equipped soldiers dressed in coats of mail. Quesada's own army was now seriously weakened; his men had very little powder for the harquebuses, few bolts for the crossbows, and their armor was falling apart.

Soon after Quesada got his first report of Belalcázar's host he learned that still another army was approaching. This was led by the red-bearded Nikolaus Federmann, Capitán Barba Roja, who had landed at Coro with Governor Sinserhoffer.

Federmann had no idea that Quesada was firmly planted on the Chibcha plateau, nor did Belalcázar. Nor had Quesada any previous warning that his New Granada would be saturated with armed guests.

So three armies met in the Colombian wilderness. Quesada had come down almost 1,000 miles from the north, Federmann about that same distance from the northeast, and Belalcázar had marched up from the southwest. On a map their routes loosely resemble a Y tilted to the right, converging on the Chibcha realm, for all three—though they knew nothing of one another—all three had heard of El Dorado.

Belalcázar and Federmann arrived at nearly the same time. As fiction it would be impossible, nobody would believe it, yet there they were. Belalcázar with his pigs, soft silk shirts, and well-fed Peruvian conquistadors in plumed steel helmets. Quesada, gone native, his men in Chibcha cotton. And Federmann's skeletal column, his soldiers racked by fever and dressed partly in animal skins; they had been battling the jungle and the mountains for many months.

Who was most surprised? It's hard to say. Federmann, no doubt, was dismayed. Reaching the goal after such hardship, only to learn you are not the first. As for Belalcázar, he could afford to be philosophic; he would not have minded more gold and glory, but his pockets already were as full as his stomach.

And Quesada? He must have been dumfounded. Not one threat, but two.

Although owning the plateau by virtue of squatter's rights, Quesada understood that he was some distance from the courts of Spain and was confronted on one flank by a famished red-bearded German, on the other by an experienced conquistador. Rather than thumping the tub, he decided, it would be wiser to negotiate.

He seems to have approached Federmann first, which is odd. Evidently he considered his countryman, Belalcázar, the greater threat. He gave Federmann a substantial present of gold and emeralds and in exchange was allowed to recruit some of the German's army, which then gave him a military advantage over Belalcázar. That being so, Belalcázar was even less inclined to fight. Besides, he too received a present.

Quesada next put on his advocate's gown. He persuaded the other two that all three captains should return to Spain where the matter of ownership might be legally resolved.

There is disagreement about whether Quesada had formally taken possession of the land in 1538 before an audience of mystified Indians, or in 1539 when Belalcázar and Federmann were present. Either way, it must have been a grand occasion governed by dignified ritual, reminiscent of Balboa wading majestically into the Pacific. Quesada rode into the middle of a field, dismounted, pulled up a handful of grass, and set one foot on the bare earth. He then proclaimed that everything belonged to Charles V. This fact having been established, Quesada got back on his horse, drew his sword, and challenged anybody to dispute his authority. There was no challenge, so he sheathed the sword and again dismounted.

Father Domingo de Las Casas now took charge. The conquistadors knelt in prayer while Las Casas communicated with the ultimate sovereign.

Quesada then marked off the site of a town, specifying twelve huts in honor of the twelve apostles, and the business was concluded.

Bogotá had been founded, named after the reigning chief.

A few weeks later, or perhaps quite a bit later, Captains Quesada, Federmann, and Belalcázar traveled together to Cartagena and from there to Santa Marta, planning to continue as a triumvirate to Europe, each to ask Charles if he might have New Granada.

They landed together at Málaga, but the Spanish wheel of fortune ticked inexorably past them all.

Federmann was accused by his employers—those ever watchful German bankers—of pocketing some gold and emeralds. He died in Valladolid in 1541, vainly waiting for the emperor to help him out.

Belalcázar at first had better luck. He returned to the New World as governor of the northern realm and everything seemed propitious for the foundation of an empire. Accordingly, he was very much surprised to find himself challenged by a longtime comrade, Jorge Robledo. Belalcázar either hanged or beheaded him, executed his followers, and burned down the house containing their bodies. He almost got away with it. Robledo's widow, Doña María, seems to have been the only one seriously troubled by the incident—although it is said that Robledo did have friends at the Spanish court. No matter who was responsible, Belalcázar was ordered back to Spain, but at Cartagena he fell sick and died. Some member of the party bought a length of Rouen muslin for one peso and two reales. Another peso went to the woman who cut his shroud, and twenty pesos to the church that conducted his funeral. Twenty-two pesos, two reales.

Quesada, after depositing in Seville the Royal Fifth—572 emeralds and a respectable quantity of Chibcha gold—believed that, like Pizarro and Cortés, he would be made governor of the territory he had conquered. But intrigue at court persuaded Charles to reward the financier behind Quesada. Thus the financier's son, who had nothing to do with the discovery and conquest of New Granada, became its governor. Quesada returned to Colombia ten years later with a coat of arms, the meaningless title of marshal, and 2,000 ducats annually. Even then, at the age of fifty, he continued to dream. Having actually found El Dorado—or at least the legend's origin—and found it less than he expected, be thought it must be somewhere else.

He was afflicted with leprosy during his last years, we are told by Flórez de Ocariz, and spent much time in the desert near Tocaima where there was a sulphurous river, "and he rested amid its fumes." He died without a peso, owing 600,000 ducats, in the city of Mariquita in 1579.

His younger brother Hernán, who had been left in charge while the three great conquistadors went to Spain, looked at Lake Guatavitá more intently during their absence. If the legend were true, if Muisca Indians had indeed showered the lake with golden knickknacks, it should be possible to collect some treasure. Hernán therefore lined up a company of Indians, issued empty calabashes, and ordered them to start dipping. An Indian at the edge of the lake would fill a calabash and hand it to his neighbor, who handed it to his neighbor, and so on until the calabash appeared at the rim of the surrounding hill. There it would be emptied and the calabash would start back down the line.

After this had gone on for several months Hernán was able to inspect part of the lake bed and he picked up a few gold offerings—though in fact they were not gold but gilded copper. The pure gold objects, being heavier, had skidded down the muddy slope toward the middle. Nevertheless, these offerings confirmed what the Indians said. Now you would think that after studying these artifacts Hernán would lash his water brigade into furious action until Lake Guatavitá had been reduced to a muddy puddle. Not so. Hernán Quesada had not traveled all the way from Spain to superintend the draining of a lake. Surely this miserable pond, despite a few trinkets in the mud, could not be all there was to El Dorado.

Quite naturally, therefore, he marched away to find it. Several thousand Indians accompanied him, and about 260 Spaniards. Fewer than 100 soldiers got back, all of them afoot, having been obliged to cook their horses. This baroque expedition destroyed Hernán Quesada physically and financially; and soon afterward, while playing cards on a boat on the Río Magdalena during a thunderstorm he got in the way of a lightning bolt. He was by now very shaggy, reports the chronicler Ocariz, and the lightning burned up his beard, his clothes, and all the hair on his body, leaving him naked and as black as a Negro.

Pizarro's youngest brother, Gonzalo, set out from Quito—at that time called San Francisco—in 1541, four years after Belalcázar. He, too, had heard rumors. From a tortured Indian he learned that El Dorado actually was to be found in a region known as the Guianas. But before reaching the Guianas, he was told, one comes to the land of cinnamon trees —La Canela.

Now, in those days cinnamon was expensive, and a sixteenth-century physician, Nicholas Monardes, spoke well of American cinnamon in his famous book, *Joyfull Newes out of the Newe Founde Worlde:* "it hath the same pleasantness of taste as the same Cinnamon hath, which they bring from the India of Portugal. . . ."

America thus far had provided no spiceries such as the East Indies had given Portugal; perhaps in La Canela they might be found.

Gonzalo recruited 4,000 Ecuadorians, a considerable menagerie of pigs, llamas, horses and dogs, and quite a few Spanish soldiers. According to Garcilaso de la Vega there were 340 Spaniards. Cieza de León says 220. Either way it was a menacing little army.

They struggled across the Andes where dozens of half-dressed Indian porters froze to death. Then at the base of the eastern slope they plunged into a jungle so choked and darkened by frenzied growth that they had no idea where they were going. In this poisonous green twilight, stumbling down a path chopped by macheteros, the expedition began to rot.

At one point, searching for La Canela, Pizarro left his army and went off with seventy men "in the direction of sunrise." They came across a few cinnamon trees. Pizarro thought there must be more, although the natives of that territory said they knew of no others. And where did El Dorado live? Nobody could say. "I took measures to inform myself," Gonzalo later wrote to Charles V, by which he meant that he stretched some Indians on cane racks, roasted them, and threw them to his dogs.

"They decided to return by the way they came," one early historian remarks laconically, "and see if they could not find another track. . . ."

At last the demoralized army stopped beside a tributary of the Amazon, which they named the Coca. Here they constructed a brigantine, caulking the seams with their own ragged clothes. Then for two months Pizarro led his bewildered troops alongside the Coca while the brig *San Pedro*, commanded by Francisco Orellana, carried the heaviest cargo and those who were too sick to walk or ride horseback.

Things got worse until at last Orellana with about sixty men continued downstream in the brig and several canoes, the plan being that when they discovered food they would load up the *San Pedro* and return. It was an interesting plan because Orellana could not possibly sail upriver against the current. Nevertheless, away he went. Long afterward he summarized this departure with a line that might have been written by Cervantes: "After boiling our boots in herbs we set off for the kingdom of gold."

Pizarro's army waited and waited beside the Coca, meanwhile enjoying such delicacies as toasted stirrup leather and dogflesh simmered with tree leaves.

A scouting party turned up a plantation abandoned by Indians. It held a crop of *yuca*—little more than roots—which the starving adventurers ate without bothering to wash away the dirt. They began cooking it to make bread. Several men stuffed themselves so full of root bread that they died; others became bloated and had to be roped to their saddles.

The army was now in a bad state, declares Cieza de León: "They all went with bare feet and legs, for they had nothing in the way of shoes, except that a few made a sort of sandal from the leather of the saddles. The road was all through forest and full of prickly trees; so that their feet got scratched all over, and their legs were constantly pierced by the many thorns. In this condition they went on, nearly dead with hunger, naked and barefooted, covered with sores, opening the road with their swords. . . ."

At last, their clothes ripped and moldering, they understood what lay ahead.

Two years after he had left Quito, Pizarro returned with seventy-nine men, several of whom soon died because they could not stop eating. How many Indians got back is unknown; by most accounts all 4,000 died. Near the end of this journey Pizarro had a dream in which a dragon plucked out his heart.

Six years later in Peru, after another debacle, Gonzalo Pizarro was beheaded.

A priest who accompanied the Orellana detachment, Father Gaspar de Carvajal, kept a journal and by his reckoning the clumsy brig traveled as much as ninety miles a day. It sounds like a perfectly splendid tour, if you disregard the menu. Foragers saw nothing edible, so that before long they were chewing not only their boots but their belts and leather sword scabbards. Sometimes they crawled ashore—unable to stand erect—and grubbed for roots.

Eventually they saw a village, staggered into it, and gobbled up everything while the Indians fled.

At the next village, not quite so hungry, they built another brig, the *Victoria*, because the *San Pedro* was unseaworthy and before long they would reach the ocean. Then both brigs swept on down the Amazon. There was no thought of returning to Pizarro.

After eight months on the world's most powerful river, with blankets for sails and vines for rigging, they arrived at the estuary. It is said that one island in this estuary is larger than Switzerland, and so strong is the current that fresh water can be found 100 miles offshore.

Orellana's men followed the coast up to Nueva Cadíz on the island of Cubagua near Trinidad, and from there they reached Santo Domingo. Orellana then returned to Spain where Charles—entranced by his adventures—commissioned him to colonize the florid river basin. It sounds peculiar. You would expect Orellana to be hanged for deserting Pizarro. He must have told his story with great skill.

His triumphant return started badly. An epidemic struck before they left the Canary Islands. Then three of his captains and a number of soldiers objected to crossing the Atlantic, some because they were ill, others because they sensed disaster. At sea the drinking water gave out and had it not been for a rainstorm everybody would have died. On the Amazon they were hit by arrows, toppled by fever, bitten by snakes, spiders, bugs, crocodiles, et cetera. Orellana died aboard ship. A few of his wretched colonists turned around and got to Margarita Island, their lives indirectly ruined by the Gilded Man.

It would be hard to devise a campaign more star-crossed than Gonzalo Pizarro's, but there was one. The Viceroy of Peru, Don Andreas Hurtado de Mendoza, nobody's fool, having observed that El Dorado hunters invariably were out of town quite a while and frequently never did come back, concluded that searching for the elusive prince might be just the way to get rid of certain redneck soldiers at least temporarily and, with luck, permanently. He therefore encouraged the quest, and no doubt helped to decide who should go, because there were plenty of volunteers.

So it happened that a great butcher of Indians, Pedro de Urzúa, started toward the promised land in 1560 with a regiment of seasoned cutthroats. Like Belalcázar, Urzúa believed that one should dine adequately and travel comfortably while battling the Andes. He took along a swarm of pigs, dogs, cattle, and horses, as well as that most valuable commodity, women, notably his mistress—the beautiful young widow Iñes de Atienza.

Deep in the Amazon basin an officer was murdered. Urzúa's response was to execute everybody he suspected. Yet even before this thoughtful display of leadership the expedition had begun to putrefy. And on New Year's Day, in the evening, Pedro de Urzúa was stabbed to death while dozing in a hammock. His lieutenant was skewered with such violence that the sword protruded from his back and wounded a conspirator standing behind him. Cristóbal de Acuña, whose chronicle appeared in 1641, says that Doña Iñes and a mutineer, "thinking they had a favorable occasion to satisfy their Lust and Ambition together," organized the revolt. Other historians doubt this.

In any case, one Fernando de Guzmán now ascended the steamy throne.

The cardinal manipulating Guzmán was a middle-aged gallows bird named Lope de Aguirre who seems to have been a bona fide psychopath. He was small, ugly, about fifty years old, with a black beard and malevolent eyes. What is curious about him is that he never believed in El Dorado. The maddest of a demented lot, he could not be tricked by a luminous phantom in the jungle. He proposed returning to Peru.

Because of the current they would have to float all the way down the Amazon to the Atlantic, sail north around Guiana and Venezuela, march across the isthmus of Panama, then walk or sail down the Pacific coast. En route they would attack settlements, kill the administrators, and recruit more men for an invasion of Peru. There, after overthrowing the Spanish government, they would divide the kingdom's enormous wealth.

According to Walker Chapman there are certain men "so shaped by birth and breeding that they dedicate themselves to a nihilistic demolition of all human institutions." Now this may be argued; but if it's true, Aguirre was such a man.

Garcilaso de la Vega relates that in 1548, at Potosí, Aguirre received 200 lashes for mistreating Indians, after which he vowed to kill the judge, Esquivel. This threat so alarmed Esquivel that he gave up his post and fled to Lima, but within two weeks Aguirre found him. Esquivel fled to Quito. Twenty days later Aguirre arrived. Esquivel fled to Cuzco, but presently Aguirre arrived, "having traveled on foot and without shoes, saying that a whipped man had no business to ride a horse." For three years and four months Esquivel tried to escape. Aguirre followed him, and caught up with him in Cuzco at noon on a Monday, asleep over his books, and stabbed him.

This was the brain behind Guzmán, the expedition's new commander.

Somewhere along the way Aguirre learned from Indians that it was possible to switch rivers. That is, move entirely by water from the Amazon to the Orinoco because of a stream called the Casiquiare which empties into them both. The Orinoco would deliver them close to a settlement on Margarita Island.

While they were in the midst of this transition the bed of Doña Iñes caused trouble. After Urzúa's death she had become the mistress of one Salduendo, who now rearranged things on the boat for their mutual comfort—which included an extra mattress. The second mattress infuriated Aguirre; he killed Salduendo and then had Doña Iñes murdered.

The woman's death was especially bloody and unexpected, but there had been others; and Don Fernando de Guzmán, reflecting upon his subordinate's temper, began to think it might be wise to kill Aguirre before Aguirre hollowed out everybody on the boat. However, he was slow getting organized and Aguirre heard about the plot. As a result, Don Fernando with three of his associates quickly joined their ancestors.

Aguirre now proclaimed himself "General of the Marañón," the Marañón being a tributary of the Amazon, and promised his followers victory in Peru.

They devastated Margarita Island—slaughtering, raping, burning, and looting. The governor and several other officials, having been assured by Aguirre that he meant them no harm, were strangled at midnight in the fortress. Anybody who displeased him was garroted, shot, or stabbed.

Told of a conspiracy against him, he butchered the supposed ringleader and then summoned a longtime friend, Antón Llamoso.

"They also tell me that thou wert one of the party," Aguirre said to Llamoso. "How was this? Was this friendship? And dost thou hold so lightly the love I feel for thee?"

According to Padre Simón, Llamoso was terrified by Aguirre's words. He fell upon the body of the dead conspirator, shouting: "Curse this traitor, who wished to commit so great a crime! I will drink his blood!" And putting his mouth over a horrible wound in the head, he began sucking the blood and brains, swallowing what he sucked "as if he were a famished dog."

Before leaving the island Aguirre murdered two priests, various citizens who got in the way, and several of his own men. Then he embarked for Venezuela in three ships flying a black flag with crossed red swords. At the moment of departure he killed his admiral, Alonso Rodríguez, who had suggested that Aguirre go below decks to avoid being splashed by the waves.

He now had approximately 150 insurgents, although when they stepped ashore this number was reduced by one; he shot a Portuguese named Farias who asked whether they were landing on another island or the mainland.

They seized the port of Burburata, and here the touchy general declared war on Philip II. Their next stop was Valencia, a short distance up the coast, where he wrote an irrational vituperative letter to the Spanish king, concluding: "I am a rebel against thee until death." This letter was carried by a priest to Santo Domingo and from there it reached Spain. Whether Philip saw it is not known; probably no one dared show it to him.

After executing a few more of his revolutionaries who did not sound enthusiastic enough Aguirre marched on Barquisimeto, which he found deserted. But the hour had come. Government troops besieged him, his little army melted away, and at last, as wild as Hitler, he stabbed his adolescent half-breed daughter Elvira who had accompanied him all the way from Peru. "Commend thyself to God," he told her, "for I am about to kill thee; that thou mayest not be pointed at with scorn, nor be in the power of anyone who may call thee the daughter of a traitor."

He was shot by two of his own men. His head was then cut off and exhibited in an iron cage. His body was quartered, the pieces tossed into the street like dog food. And in faraway Peru the house in which he had lived was demolished and salt was sprinkled over the earth where it stood so that nothing of him would remain. All of which, provided your mind has a skeptical slope, may cause you to reflect on the nature of madness.

Still, Lope de Aguirre has not been forgotten. Today—or tonight—if a flickering phosphorescence plays above the Venezuelan marshes, a prudent traveler considers it wise to cross himself: he has observed Aguirre's soul fleeing the approach of man.

Such a repugnant tale ought to conclude the saga of El Dorado, but gold exudes a deadly charm. Only a few years later two roving bands of conquistadors met head on in the jungle and mauled one another for three days in order to decide which group owned the territory. Survivors of this engagement were picked off by Chuncho Indians.

By now it was agreed among El Dorado experts that the fabulous kingdom must be somewhere in Guiana—the name given by Spaniards to the great unmapped basin of the Orinoco. And of those who went hunting for El Dorado in Guiana the most businesslike was Don Antonio de Berrio, who found himself more or less sucked into it.

Berrio was a captain of the guards living comfortably in Granada when his wife's uncle died, leaving the estate to her. Now it happened that Doña Berrio's uncle had been Gonzalo Jiménez de Quesada, and it appeared that after all these years Tío Gonzalo's property in the New World was producing 14,000 ducats annually. Therefore, in 1580, Berrio, his wife, their six daughters and two sons sailed off to the Antilles. Life perhaps could be agreeable in the New World, even more pleasant than Granada, considering those ducats.

However, Tío Gonzalo had left a stipulation in his will that the heir to his estate must use part of that income to look for El Dorado. Thus, instead of relaxing on a colonial patio, the middle-aged captain of the guards found himself once again on horseback leading a bunch of grubby provincial troops. But before setting out on this distasteful trip he studied the problem: he read the accounts of previous explorers and talked to some who had actually fought their way through the jungle.

And at last, as it had seeped into the blood of earlier men, the legend obsessed him. He spent fifteen years looking for El Dorado. He led three expeditions across the territory, established trading posts, and quarreled with everybody. He knew the kingdom could not be far away. After all, if so many men had destroyed themselves searching—well then, only a fool would claim El Dorado did not exist. Besides, as he explained in a letter to King Philip, the Indians he questioned invariably agreed that in the mountains there was a vast lake and on its far side were cities with many people who had gold and precious stones.

While Berrio was marching back and forth a wild figure emerged from the jungle—Juan Martín de Albujar, last survivor of an expedition that had vanished ten years earlier. Depending on your source,

Albujar spoke "perfect Spanish," or he had almost forgotten his native language. Such minuscule discrepancies aren't important, but they are exasperating; one wants to know precisely what happened. Anyway, he was first noticed in or near the Margarita church, dressed like an Indian, and Berrio later talked with him. He said that after being held captive for a long time by Caribs he was taken to see the Gilded Man. He had been led through the jungle blindfolded, and when the blindfold was removed he found himself at the edge of a city which the Indians called Manoa, beside a lake called Parima. This city was so large, said Albujar, that it had taken a full day to walk to the palace. The streets were lined with stone houses, not thatched huts, and in the palace he saw with his own eyes the man they had been looking for, El Dorado, resplendent as the sun.

He stayed seven months in Manoa and was questioned by the Gilded Man about the customs of Spaniards. Then the great ruler presented him with some gold and jewels, after which he was again blindfolded and led into the jungle. Finally the Indians released him and pointed the way to the coast.

Unfortunately, he said, El Dorado's gift had been stolen by some other Indians he met. That's how it is. Something always happens to the treasure. Yet Albujar did have, in fact, a calabash filled with gold beads; and he offered to swear on a Bible that every word he spoke was true—a pledge not lightly regarded in those days. And when he lay dying of fever in Puerto Rico he continued to insist he had told the truth.

Apart from what Albujar saw, or thought he saw, his story reinforced Berrio's conviction that El Dorado must be close by. As a result, though be was no longer young, Don Antonio began to make preparations for one more trip.

But just then—in the spring of 1595—four strange ships dropped anchor at Icacos Point, the southwest corner of Trinidad. A roving English gentleman of fortune had arrived, by name Sir Walter Raleigh, carrying a royal patent from Elizabeth to "offend and enfeeble the King of Spain, and to discover and subdue heathen lands. . . ."

Raleigh, like Berrio, had done his homework. He had talked with the captains of vessels that traded in the Caribbean and with men who had spent time ashore. He had read everything he could find on the subject of South America and he claimed to be familiar with the details of twenty-three expeditions that had searched for El Dorado.

"Guiana is a countrey that hath yet her maydenhead," he wrote, "never sackt, turned, nor wrought, the face of the earth hath not bene torne, nor the vertue and salt of the soyle spent by manurance, the graves have not bene opened for golde, the mines not broken with sledges, nor their Images puld downe out of their temples. . . ."

His presence quickly was reported to Berrio—who had been named governor of Guiana and El Dorado, evidently because of his persistence. Berrio dispatched some soldiers to find out what the English pirate wanted. They were assured that the English had stopped at Trinidad only for refreshment.

Berrio mistrusted this. He dispatched a larger party.

Raleigh invited these emissaries aboard. Four Spaniards accepted. And there, beneath Raleigh's flag—five silver lozenges on a blue field—the Englishmen and the Spaniards sat around drinking wine and pretending to be friends, meanwhile subtly pumping each other for information.

Raleigh learned from an Indian that there were less than eighty soldiers on the island. That being so, the hour was ripe. He sent a boatload of food and wine to the Spaniards who had remained ashore and when they settled down to enjoy English hospitality a landing party slaughtered them. Raleigh then murdered his four guests. It might be observed, if one wishes to pick at cause and effect, that during the previous year eight Englishmen who visited Trinidad intending to hunt for meat had been captured by Spanish soldiers who trussed them up like pigs and slit their throats.

Now that the preliminaries were over, Raleigh's men set out for San José. They marched all night and arrived at dawn. The attack was a great success; practically the entire garrison was killed and Berrio was captured. The English then looted the town, set it afire, and marched back to their ships.

Raleigh began to interrogate his prisoner courteously because they both came from good families.

Berrio pretended to be senile. He answered vaguely, talked about how difficult it was to travel up the Orinoco, there were all sorts of wild animals, Indians with poisoned arrows, and so forth. Nobody could reach the land of gold.

But Sir Walter had not crossed the Atlantic for amusement. We regard him as one of Elizabeth's seagoing knights, so it is a surprise to learn that he detested water travel and when aboard ship he usually got sick. John Aubrey remarks that, in order to cross the Thames, Raleigh would "go round about over London Bridge" rather than take the convenient wherry boat.

In any case, now that he had put up with the unpleasant voyage he did not intend to be duped by an elderly Spaniard's nonsense. With Berrio as his prisoner he entered the mouth of the Orinoco—that is to say, one of the mouths—and got lost. The Orinoco delta, 150 miles wide, has fifteen or twenty channels which loop and divide and braid together in such confusion that there are places where the current flows the wrong direction.

Raleigh sounds dismayed:

"We might have wandred a whole yeere in that laborinth of rivers ere we had found any way, either out or in, especiallie after we passed the ebbing and flowing. . . ."

Fifteen days after entering the delta they managed to get into the mainstream, which astounded them by its size—four miles across. They rowed upriver, sometimes helped by the wind, and occasionally met native fishermen in dugouts from whom they got not only fresh fish but gourds full of the local palm toddy. Raleigh was smarter than most of the Spaniards when dealing with Indians; he insisted that they not be robbed or abused, with the result that he and his men often were invited to the villages. So well liked was he that he was given a strange little beast "which they call Cassacam, which seemeth to be all barred over with small plates somewhat like a Renocero." The tail of this creature, he noted in his diary, if powdered and blown into the ear would cure deafness. But for all the exchange of gifts and pleasantries he had not forgotten his purpose. By means of Arawak interpreters he asked about a lake called Parima. And did they know of a city or a land called Manoa? A chief who covered himself with gold?

Oh yes! the Indians replied. Yes indeed! Oh yes! Through the jungle. Beyond the mountains.

Raleigh decided he had gone far enough. The directions sounded familiar. Besides, the river was flooding, which made progress more difficult, and there were hints of a Spanish flotilla approaching. But before turning downstream he left behind, 300 miles up the Orinoco, two volunteers named Hugh Goodwin and Frances Sparrey or Sparrow. According to the plan, Raleigh would return someday to pick them up. Until that day Goodwin was to live with the Indians and learn their language. Sparrey's assignment was to find out what truth there might be to the legend of the Gilded Man. With native guides he would proceed through the jungle to the mountains, cross the mountains, locate the city—if it did exist—then draw sketches of its fortifications and otherwise prepare a guidebook on ways and means of capturing it. Then he would return to the Orinoco. If Raleigh was nowhere in sight he would walk to the coast, attract the notice of the first English ship he saw, and thus return to England.

So, having bade his secret agents good-bye, Sir Walter weighed anchor and started home, accompanied by all the debris of the giant river in flood—entire trees now and again roiling past the ship like battering rams. The level of the water rose ominously. In his diary he wrote: "The fury of the Orenoque beganne daily to threaten us with daungers in our return, for no half day passed, but the river began to rage and overflow very fearfully, and the raines came down in terribel showers, and gusts in great abundance: and withall: our men beganne to cry out. . . ."

What became of his two benighted emissaries is in wondrous accord with everything else. Goodwin ingratiated himself so thoroughly with the Indians that when a posse of Spaniards came looking for him the Indians declared that he had been eaten by a jaguar. This was good news. The Spaniards therefore went away and for the next twenty-two years Goodwin worked on his assignment. Raleigh located him in 1617, by which time he could hardly speak English.

Sparrey, poking around the jungle, was ambushed by Spaniards. After questioning him they shipped him to Spain where he spent six years observing his fingernails in prison. English authorities eventually negotiated his release on the assumption that he must have learned all about the mysterious city, but Sparrey did not have much news.

Raleigh himself—escaping "the Orenoque's terribel daungers"—

returned to his base at Trinidad. There, after failing to obtain any ransom for his distinguished captive, he exchanged Don Antonio for an English prisoner and sailed away to England.

He did not bring back much—some tobacco, a few gold trinkets, specimens of ore, and additional rumors concerning the whereabouts of the ephemeral golden kingdom:

"I have been assured by such of the Spanyardes as have seene Manoa, the emperiall Citie of Guiana, which the Spanyardes call El Dorado, that for the greatness, for the riches, and for the excellent seate, it farre exceedeth any of the world, at least of so much of the world as is known to the Spanish nation; it is founded upon a lake of salt water 200 leagues long. . . ."

Raleigh's sponsors, having put up quite a lot of money, were not pleased with the meager result. His enemies, though, were delighted; they claimed that the voyage never took place and said that for seven months he had been skulking off the English coast.

He thereupon wrote his magnificent, preposterous account of what he had seen, as well as much that he had not, entitled *The Discoverie of the Large, Rich, and Bewtiful Empyre of Guiana, with a Relation of the Great and Golden Citie of Manoa (which the Spanyards call El Dorado)*.

This is less than the complete title, but it is the important part, even though untrue: Raleigh had discovered nothing that was not already known to the Spaniards. But his narrative was widely accepted and reprinted many times, and his huge saltwater lake began to appear on maps—very like a grotesque insect—between the Orinoco and the Amazon. Cartographers faithfully drew Lake Parima on every map of South America until 1800 when Alexander von Humboldt drained it with a single word: "imaginary."

Sir Walter quite naturally included in his *Discoverie* the legend of a chief "anoynted all over with a kind of white balsamum" and coated with gold dust until he stood forth "al shining from the foote to the head." He included, too, some fairly bizarre creatures such as the topless giants reported by Sir John Mandeville in other parts of the world. These existed, in a sense. One of the Orinoco tribes made enormous ceremonial masks which fitted over their heads and shoulders so that, as Raleigh claimed, their mouths opened in the middle of their breasts. The moral, obviously, is that we should not be too skeptical.

On March 24, 1603, Queen Elizabeth died and a few days later Raleigh woke up in the Tower of London under sentence of death. The charge was old, and it sounds unfair: he had been guilty of negligence in failing to report treasonous talk, which was serious enough, but hardly deserving execution. In any event, he seems to have reasoned that his last hope of emerging from the Tower was Guiana—golden Guiana. If he could lead one more expedition, and if all went well, he would be restored. He may still have believed in the legend of a golden king, or he may have thought only that the mineral wealth of Guiana would save him. Or perhaps he was just pretending.

"It is a journey of honnor and riches I offer you; an enterprise fesible and certayne," he suggested to Viscount Haddington, who might possibly intercede on his behalf. And he went on to say that if he could not lead an expedition to a Guiana mountain alight with silver and gold, "let the commander have commissione to cut of my head ther."

To King James he wrote: "I do therefore, on the knees of my hart, beseich your Majesty to take councell from your own sweet and mercifull disposition, and to remember that I have loved your Majesty now twenty yeares, for which your Majestie hath yett geven me no reward. And it is fitter that I should be indebted to my soverayne Lord, then the King to his poore vassall. Save me, therefore, most mercifull Prince. . . ."

And, all hope gone, to his wife:

> You shall receave, deare wief, my last words in these my last lynes. My love I send you, that you may keepe it when I am dead; and my councell, that you may remember it when I am noe more. . . . I trust my bloud will quench their mallice that desire my slaughter; and that they will not alsoe seeke to kill you and yours with extreame poverty. To what frind to direct thee I knowe not, for all mine have left mee in the true tyme of triall: and I plainly perceive that my death was determyned from the first day. Most sorry I am (as God Knoweth) that, being thus surprised with death, I can leave you noe better estate. . . . I cannot wright much. God knowes howe hardlie I stole this tyme, when all sleep; and it is tyme to separate my thoughts from the world. Begg my dead body, which living was denyed you; and either lay itt at Sherborne if the land continue, or in Exiter church, by my father and mother.

In March of 1616 he was released from the Tower for one last attempt.

Twenty-one years had elapsed since his first voyage. Thirteen of those years he had spent locked in the Tower. He had not been treated badly: he was allowed to walk through the garden, he had visitors such as Ben Jonson, all the books he needed, and paper and ink because he was working on his ambitious *History of the World*. He was nearly as well off as some of our imprisoned politicians. He was permitted to set up an alchemical laboratory where he tinkered about, and when not otherwise occupied he tutored the heir apparent, Prince Henry. His wife shared his bed and his son Carew was born in that sinister place.

Still, despite these comforts, Raleigh had been in prison for thirteen years. He was troubled by headaches, fever, and persistent abscesses on his body, and he walked with a limp. An "ould and Sorroeworn Man," he said of himself, "whom death would shortlye deliver." He was sixty-four.

If the gods had been indifferent to his first voyage, they now looked down with disapproval. The expedition had a spectral quality. It started four months later than planned, fights erupted among the crew, supplies were inadequate, the weather turned uncommonly bad, scurvy broke out.

"Gualtero Rale has set forth . . ." wrote the Spanish ambassador, Count Gondomar, to Philip III on June 26, 1617.

Before his flagship *Destiny* reached South America forty-two crewmen were dead. Raleigh himself lay ill with malaria, and so appointed Captain Keymis to take charge of the trip upriver—a disastrous excursion that resulted in a battle with Spaniards, the death of Raleigh's elder son Wat, and Keymis's clumsy suicide.

"I never knewe what sorrow meant till nowe," he said in a letter to his wife; ". . . my braynes are broken, and it is a torment for mee to write, and espetially of misery."

The ships of his fleet returned one by one to England, until only the *Destiny* remained in South America. At last he, too, had no choice but to return. In England again he was called a pirate and doomed, the victim of changing times, reaccused of treason.

On October 29, 1618, about eight o'clock in the morning, he was conducted to the palace yard of Westminster.

Because this was a particular occasion, Raleigh dressed with meticulous care: beneath his black velvet cloak he wore a velvet waistcoat, satin doublet, black taffeta breeches, and ash-colored silk stockings.

En route he paused to chat with a bald-headed old man, then took off a lace nightcap he had been wearing under his hat and gave it to the old gentleman, saying, "Thou hast more need of it now than I."

On the scaffold he delivered his final speech, which lasted half an hour. He then shook hands with the Earl of Arundel and embraced him. "I have a long journey to go," Raleigh said, "and therefore will take my leave."

After having removed his cloak and doublet he asked to see the ax. "This is sharp medicine," he observed while feeling the blade, "but it is a physician that will cure all my diseases."

He knelt on the boards, but faced the wrong direction. Somebody pointed this out.

"So the heart be right," he responded, "it is no great matter which way the head lieth."

These epigrams, instantaneously composed by a man arranging himself for execution, flash across the centuries with such brilliance that average people stand bewildered. Who can explain a quicksilver tongue?

The executioner struck twice and picked up Raleigh's head by the bloody gray hair in order to display it—"with great applause of the beholders." Raleigh's eyes were open.

The head was presented to his wife, who had it embalmed and kept it in a red leather bag.

He left a slim estate: not much money, a sample of ore, two gold ingots, some rough maps of Guiana, and a diamond ring given him by Elizabeth "which he weareth on his finger."

He left also a misty heritage drifting through the Guianas. There is a letter from an English physician, Edward Bancroft, written while traveling on the Río Demerary. It is addressed to Bancroft's brother and is dated October 25, 1766:

> The Carribbee Indians are at perpetual variance with the Spaniards, and frequently commit hostilities on their settlements at the River Oronoque. They retain a tradition of an English Chief, who many years

> since landed amongst them, and encouraged them to persevere in enmity to the Spaniards, promising to return and settle amongst them, and afford them assistance; and it is said that they still preserve an English Jack, which he left them, that they might distinguish his countrymen. This was undoubtedly Sir Walter Raleigh, who, in the year 1595, made a descent on the Coast of Guiana, in search of the fabulous Golden City of Manoa del Dorado . . .

Today in Bogotá's Museo del Oro among those ancient Muisca treasures you will discover a gold raft on which a tiny gold king is riding, no doubt toward the middle of Lake Guatavitá. And should your mind have a certain cast—if, let's say, you believe yourself related to Sir Walter Raleigh, or de Berrio, or Quesada, or Dalfinger, or those others—well then, as you contemplate this miniature tableau it might occur to you that South America is huge, much of it has yet to be explored, and those first adventurers may not have had the right information. And in the archives, as everybody knows, are innumerable musty old documents, some of which should contain new directions.

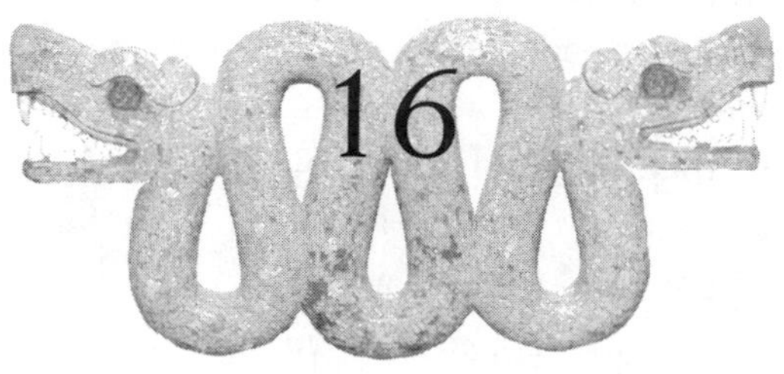

16

Seven Cities

IN A.D. 711 THE BERBER GENERAL Tariq crossed into Spain by way of a rock that carries his name—Jebal al-Tariq, the mountain of Tariq, Gibraltar. On the shore of Lake Janda he was challenged by the Spanish king Rodrigo in what has become known mistakenly, through a misreading of Arabic chronicles, as the battle of Guadalete. Rodrigo was defeated and Tariq's army carved a bloody path across the Iberian Peninsula, scattering terrified Christians in every direction. Some of these refugees boarded ship at Oporto, hoping to find safety on Madeira or the Canary Islands which at that time were vaguely known.

From this exodus arose a legend that seven Portuguese bishops, fearing the end of Christianity, set sail for the mysterious island of Antillia —*ante-ilha*, opposite island—somewhere in the Western Ocean; and there, in order to preserve Christianity until the Moors should be expelled, they burnt their ships and founded seven cities.

Years passed without word from these prudent bishops. Centuries went by. Nevertheless the legend persisted, and sailors far out in the

Atlantic kept watch for an island with seven cities. Or, as it sometimes was told, seven islands, each with a Christian community.

In 1447, according to the Portuguese scholar Galvão, a caravel bound for Lisbon under the command of Captain Antonio Leone was disabled by a storm and driven off course to the west. Eventually a flat crescent-shaped island was sighted where Captain Leone made port—an island inhabited by people "who spake Portuguese and inquired if the Moors did yet trouble Spain." Furthermore, it had seven communities, each with a rude basalt cathedral; and when Captain Leone and his crew attended Mass they saw gold candlesticks and crucifixes and a gold-embroidered altar cloth.

They spent several weeks on this island while repairing their ship, and when they sailed for Portugal they took along a quantity of sand from the beach, which was good for scouring decks. In Lisbon they found out that the sand was streaked with gold.

Now you might think Captain Leone returned at once, either because of the gold or because he had discovered the seven cities; but if he did we have no record of it.

The Dominican priest Las Casas mentions that in Columbus' notebooks he came across an account of this voyage. Las Casas does not say so explicitly, but Columbus could only have been referring to Captain Leone because the story is almost identical: a storm-driven vessel anchors at an island where the people speak Portuguese and the sand is flecked with gold. In this version, however, Prince Henry heard about it, scolded the captain for failing to learn more, and ordered him to return; but the sailors were afraid and refused. We are not told anything else about Captain Leone, nor what happened to the sailors who defied their prince.

Columbus very possibly believed in the medieval legend. One reason for thinking so is that he corresponded with the famous cosmographer Toscanelli—probably on this subject—via the Portuguese court. Toscanelli had included Antillia on his charts, suggesting it as a port of call en route to Japan: "From the island of Antillia, which you call the Isle of Seven Cities . . . to the most noble island of Cipangu is fifty degrees of longitude . . ."

Soon after this a Fleming whose name is given as Fernão Dulmo was authorized by King João II to locate and govern "a large island, islands, or mainland, beyond our shores, presumed to be the island of the Seven Cities." Dulmo went into partnership with a wealthy gentleman from Madeira named Estreito, each of them to provide a caravel. Some historians believe they sailed in March of 1487; others think the caravels were delayed by foul weather and never put to sea. In either event, Dulmo & Estreito are not heard from again.

In 1498 a Spanish ambassador to England, Pedro de Ayala, informed Ferdinand and Isabella that the people of Bristol "fitted out every year, two, three, or four caravels in search of . . . the Seven Cities."

By the early sixteenth century they were thought to be on the American mainland. Why? Nothing could be more obvious. These cities existed—obviously they existed, otherwise men would not be searching for them; consequently, if they did not exist in the Atlantic they must be someplace else, and beyond the Atlantic lay America.

A map in the British Museum, which probably was drawn about 1508, locates them on the eastern seaboard. Who set them there, and why, is unknown.

But they could not be found on the littoral, which meant they must be inland. This brings us to one of history's classic bunglers—a most unpleasant personage even among odious companions, the conquistador Pánfilo de Narváez. Bernal Díaz tells us that he was very brave, a good horseman, tall and strong, with a red beard, and a voice so deep that it seemed to come from a vault. "He was a captain in the island of Cuba, and a rich man, though reputed to be very mean."

He arrived in Mexico with authority from the governor of Cuba to arrest Cortés. The reasons for this are irrelevant; more interesting is the fact that when it was all over Narváez had lost his soldiers, one of his eyes, and his personal liberty—spending the next three years as Cortés' prisoner.

Cortés at last let him go and Narváez returned to Spain, where he managed to become appointed governor of Florida, which at that time was almost entirely unexplored. Ponce de León had been there, along with a few others, but the peninsula had been so lightly touched that it was still thought to be an island.

Narváez landed on the west side of Tampa Bay in April of 1528, authorized by Charles V "to conquer and govern the provinces which should be encountered from the River of Palms to the cape of Florida." He had 42 horses and about 600 men, but not for long. First he divided his forces, ordering his ships to proceed up the coast. Then he led his cavalry and infantry into the swamps. Accidents, alligators, snakes, dysentery, malaria, hunger, and misanthropic Indians began to pick them off. Nevertheless he kept going, encouraged by traces of gold in some of the Indian huts, until the remnants of his cavalry threatened to desert.

Cabeza de Vaca, the expedition's treasurer, later wrote that a third of their force had fallen sick: "We felt certain that we would all be stricken, with death the one foreseeable way out."

Unable to locate their supply ships, the Spaniards tried to escape from this labyrinth of lagoons, salt marshes and mangrove-tangled islets by constructing some boats.

"We knew not how to build them, nor had we either the tools, irons, forges, tow, tar, or rigging; nor, in short, a single one of the many things required, nor anyone capable of directing the work, and above all, no food to eat whilst they were being built."

The alternative, though, was to go on plunging through the swamp.

One soldier contrived some deerskin bellows in order to melt just about everything metallic—armor, lances, stirrups, buckles, spurs, conchos—because metal would be needed for nails, axes, and saws. Another soldier had been a carpenter. So it went.

They built five barges, each about thirty feet long, caulked with palmetto oakum and tarred with pine pitch. Sails were made out of shirts. Ropes were braided from horsehair and palmetto husks. Stones served as anchors. Meanwhile they were eating the horses and trying to fashion water bottles out of their hides.

At last they piled aboard, hoping to drift or sail west along the coast to Mexico, which they thought could not be far away. There were nearly fifty men on each barge. The gunwales rode just a few inches above the surface.

Eleven years later Hernando de Soto would be told by captured Indians that other Spaniards had come through the land and had built boats on which they escaped. The Indians did not know what had become of these Spaniards. De Soto found a tree that had been chopped down near Saint Marks Bay. The tree had been cut into rude planks and nearby were the bleached skulls of several horses.

It took the Narváez castaways a month to reach the vicinity of Pensacola. The horsehide bottles were rotting, and their food—supplemented by raiding an occasional thatched-roof village—was almost gone. Why they were unable to catch fish, although they had observed the Indians fishing, has not been explained.

Farther west the miserable flotilla became separated, but de Vaca managed to catch up with Narváez and asked him what they should do. Narváez replied that this was no time for one man to be giving orders to another, each should do as he thought best to save himself; and having offered such good advice, the commandant told his boatmen to pull away. Since he had chosen the healthiest men for his crew he quickly left de Vaca behind. Not long after this, and no doubt because of it, the gods blew Narváez out to sea.

De Vaca says that just five men in his group were strong enough to stand. "At nightfall only the navigator and I remained able to tend the barge. Two hours after dark he told me I should take over; he believed he was about to die."

Next morning a wave hurled them onto an island—possibly San Luis island near Galveston—and when they tried to shove off they capsized. Three men drowned. The survivors crawled ashore naked because they had stowed their clothing on the barge before attempting to launch it.

A few more castaways turned up and they spent that winter as uneasy guests of some exceptionally large Indians who billeted them in various huts. Most of the Spaniards starved to death. Some not only ate the flesh of dead companions but apparently tried to preserve it for future snacks. In one hut de Vaca came across bits of four Spaniards and the untouched corpse of a fifth "whom nobody was left alive to eat."

The Indians too were dying, not from hunger but from disease—perhaps cholera, or perhaps they had become infected by the Spaniards' dysentery. And either because of the cannibalism or because of this epidemic they began to look upon the Spaniards not as guests but as slaves.

In the spring only about two dozen conquistadors remained alive, sixteen on the island and a few others scattered along the Texas coast, all of them expecting death at any hour. De Vaca himself had become an indentured servant of a tribe he called the Capoques, being shuttled to the mainland whenever his services were required for semiskilled labor: "In addition to much other work, I had to grub roots in the water or from underground in the canebrakes. My fingers got so raw that if a straw touched them they would bleed. The broken canes often slashed my flesh . . ."

Life improved during the next five years, although not much. Consequently, in September of 1534, he and three other men struck out for Mexico. The season was late and the prickly pears upon which they depended for food were nearly gone, but they thought they could get by on acorns. Regardless of what lay ahead, they had resolved "not to live this life, so savage and so divorced from the service of God and all good reason."

The fugitives, in addition to Álvar Núñez Cabeza de Vaca, were Alonzo del Castillo Maldonado, Andrés Dorantes de Carranca, and Dorantes' remarkable Moorish slave, Estebán. Their names are worth recording because, out of hundreds, only these four were obstinate enough to survive.

De Vaca seems to have been the organizer, the demonic spirit, the brightest and most determined. Also, he was the only one who thought enough of their odyssey to write about it. And because he had such an odd name—head-of-a-cow—perhaps this should be explained. One of his ancestors, a shepherd named Martin Alhaja, guided King Sancho VII of Navarre through the Sierra Morena north of Seville, marking the pass with a cow's skull, which enabled the Spanish army to cross over and defeat the Moors at the battle of Las Navas de Tolosa. The shepherd's reward was nobility of a sort, and his descendants were entitled to the honorary name.

The route of this naked, starving quartet after they left the Gulf resembles the track of an undecided snail: northwest through the middle of Texas to the Pecos River, which they followed up into New Mexico, south to El Paso, and west to the Gila River in Arizona. At this point they were well over 1,000 air miles from Mexico City, much farther from their destination than when they started. Evidently they thought they were paralleling the coast.

We have the usual scholarly argument about their route; they may not have gotten quite that far north, but it hardly matters.

Along the way they practiced medicine. De Vaca sounds embarrassed: "Our method . . . was to bless the sick, breathe upon them, recite a Pater Noster and Ave Maria, and pray earnestly to God our Lord for their recovery."

This curious treatment seems to have worked more often than might be expected, thanks to the beneficence of God and the strength of suggestion, so that the travelers' reputation began to precede them. As they advanced from one Indian territory to the next they were heralded, followed, and presented with ceremonial arrows, beads, gourds, little bags of mica, deer tallow, dried herbs, spiders, worms, and quail—the native menu varied considerably—as well as cowhides, feathers, blankets, copper trinkets, and whatever else their hosts thought valuable. This must have been awkward, but the Spaniards were shrewd enough to continue the charade, touching and blessing the sick and injured, even attempting minor surgery when the chances of success looked good. And instead of speaking directly to the Indians they made Estebán their intermediary:

"He was constantly in conversation, finding out about routes, towns, and other matters we wished to know."

From the Gila they turned south, and somewhere below what is now the Mexican border they saw an Indian wearing a strange ornament around his neck: a buckle from a sword belt. Where had this come from? From Heaven, replied the Indian. But who had brought it from Heaven? Bearded men on horses with lances and swords.

In March of 1536, guided by other fragments of evidence and by rumors, they caught sight of several Spanish horsemen who had been out raking the provinces for Indians to enslave. So, once again among their own, the weary travelers were escorted southward. They rode into Mexico City on July 24, and were welcomed by the Viceroy.

Eight years had passed since Narváez's expedition began falling apart in the Florida swamps.

The viceroy, Don Antonio de Mendoza, listened to their stories. They had wandered through wretched blistered territory and had met no Indians of any consequence, none whose civilization even remotely approached that of the Aztecs. Still, they had seen copper, iron, a few bits of gold, and other metals, and they were convinced that "pearls and great riches" could be found on the Gulf of California, which de Vaca called the South Sea.

Wild rumors swept Mexico City. The travelers had forded streams whose beds were solid gold. They had seen Indian children playing with rubies and diamonds and emeralds and pearls the size of hen eggs. They had walked past a mountain so studded with jewels that they dared not look at it in bright sunlight for fear of being blinded.

Mendoza, a cautious man, did not want to be held responsible for ordering a disastrous expedition into the unknown north. On the other hand he might be just as much at fault if he neglected an opportunity to benefit the Spanish crown. It was unlikely, yet just possible, that somewhere to the north lay another Aztec treasure house. Pizarro had discovered and captured the incredible wealth of the Incas to the south; there might conceivably be a wealthy nation in higher latitudes.

An Indian called Tejo who belonged to Nuño de Guzmán, governor of the northern provinces, insisted that there were seven flourishing towns up there. He had seen them, he said, when he was a child and went with his father on a long trip. These towns were perhaps as big as Mexico City, their streets crowded with silversmiths and goldsmiths.

The number seven also occurred in Aztec legend. Ancestors of the Aztecs had emigrated to Mexico from seven caves somewhere to the north.

Mendoza probably had little faith in the medieval European story, but nevertheless it was curious that the number *seven* should reappear; so he decided to send a Franciscan, Marcos de Niza, to look around and take possession of whatever might be worth possessing. Estebán could be his guide. Whether or not an expedition should be organized would depend on the Franciscan's report, because he was thought to be a trustworthy man, "reliable, of approved virtue, and fine religious zeal . . . skilled in cosmography and the arts of the sea, as well as in theology." If the stories told by de Vaca and his companions were fanciful—well, not much would be lost.

Mendoza's marching instructions cautioned the friar also to obtain information about the coast "because the land may narrow and in the country beyond some arm of the sea may enter." That is to say, the Northwest Passage might be discovered.

Fray Marcos and Estebán set out in the spring of 1539.

The farther they traveled the more impatient Estebán became. During the long walk from Texas he had been an important figure, treated with respect by the Indians they had met along the way, admired for his black color and his medical knowledge; but upon entering Mexico he was once again nothing but Dorantes' slave. He was therefore anxious to get out of Mexico and into those northern lands where he had been regally welcomed.

Fray Marcos at last gave him permission to go ahead, with instructions to send back word of his findings by an Indian runner. If he should come upon something noteworthy he should send back a wooden cross the width of his hand. If he came upon something unusual, say a very large town, the cross should be twice that size.

Estebán traveled in style, carried on a litter and accompanied by a pair of greyhounds which may have been given to him by Coronado—the recently appointed governor of New Galicia. His legs and arms were decorated with clusters of brilliant feathers and jingling copper bells. Necklaces of turquoise and coral adorned his chest. He was a big, bearded, powerful man, and he wore plumes to accentuate his height.

Packed among his considerable baggage, which included a tent and plenty of comfortable bedding, were four green pottery dishes on which he was ceremoniously served every meal. Nobody else could use those dishes. He also brought along a sacred medicine rattle made from a gourd; it is said to have been embellished with strands of tiny bells and with two feathers, one white and one red.

Four days after Marcos permitted Estebán to go ahead by himself some Indian runners arrived carrying a cross as tall as a man. They said Estebán had reached people who knew of important cities in the north—seven cities ruled by a lord whose house was several stories high. The first city was called Cíbola. Its buildings were made of stone mortared with lime, the doors abundantly decorated with turquoise, and the people were richly clothed. Beyond Cíbola lay other lands with cities still larger, more influential, and more wealthy.

"So many marvels was I told," Marcos reported, "that I postponed believing them until I could see for myself, or have further verification."

He pushed ahead rapidly, and as he walked he received confirmation of the wonderful news. Pima Indians told him that the houses of Cíbola were indeed very large, and beyond Cíbola lay at least three kingdoms: Marata, Acus, and Totonteac.

A second huge cross arrived from Estebán, urging him to hurry. Then a third great cross.

And while passing through the Sonora valley Fray Marcos met an old man who claimed to be a native of Cíbola, who insisted that despite its wealth, which was very great, the kingdom of Totonteac was the largest, richest, and most populous in the world.

Marcos hurried forward, but it was difficult to catch up with Estebán.

Then another messenger arrived, this time with very different news. Estebán had approached Cíbola at sunset, demanding gifts of turquoise and women. He had not been allowed to enter the city. He and his escort had been confined to huts outside the walls. Next morning, said the messenger, he himself had gone to a nearby stream for a drink and when he looked around he saw Estebán and the others being pursued by the men of Cíbola, who killed them with arrows.

Marcos concluded that he must go forward to find out if what the messenger said was true; and presently he met two other members of Estebán's entourage, both covered with blood. They said the Moor was dead.

Why Estebán was murdered is not known, although his demand for women and turquoise undoubtedly angered the Indians. Perhaps they thought he was a spy from some nation planning to invade their territory. Or the medicine rattle might have alarmed them.

Medicine rattles, unless they came from a tribe hundreds of miles distant, could be identified by the symbols carved or painted on them, by their shape and size, by the feathers or bells or claws or other fetishes attached to them, and sometimes by the gourd alone. The rattle carried by Estebán was picked up in Texas by the traveling quartet; almost certainly it was Comanche or Apache. Whatever it signified, wherever it came from, he miscalculated when he sent it ahead to announce his arrival. The cacique to whom it was offered "flung the gourd to the earth with much wrath" and ordered the emissary to leave.

Estebán, being informed of his ambassador's reception, did not take the hint. He is said to have laughed and remarked that there was nothing to fear. He had been greeted like this before, he said, while traveling with de Vaca.

After Estebán had been killed, to prove that he was mortal and not a man from the sky, the Indians cut his body into very small pieces. Bits of his flesh, bones, and skin were dried and distributed among neighboring tribes as tokens, perhaps to indicate what should be done if any more strangers arrived. The greyhounds and the green dinner plates were confiscated. The rattle was either thrown away or smashed.

So perished the flamboyant sensual overconfident Moorish slave; captured in Morocco, he died in New Mexico during a horizontal rain of arrows without knowing why.

Marcos got close enough to Cíbola to have a look at it. At least that was his claim. He described it as larger than Mexico City and extremely beautiful: "I was tempted to go to it, knowing that I risked only my life . . . [however,] if I should die there would be no account of this land, which, in my opinion, is the greatest and best of all those discovered."

Accordingly, at a prudent distance, he ordered a cairn to be built and surmounted with a cross. Then, after having claimed possession for the king of Spain in the name of Don Antonio de Mendoza, not only of the Seven Cities but of the kingdoms of Totonteac, Marata, and Acus, he started back to safety, "traveling with all possible speed until I came upon the people I had left."

Whether he approached Cíbola is debatable. Most historians doubt it, and the stories he told after his return to Mexico City caused one of them to call him the Baron Munchausen of America.

The fabulous city of Cíbola was, in fact, the pueblo of Hawaiku, now a heap of ruins near Zuñi on the New Mexican plateau. Its name may have been invented by Estebán, but *Cíbola* probably comes from the Zuñi word *Shi'wona*, which refers to their tribal range.

Regardless of Fray Marcos' veracity, he became man of the hour when he got back to civilization. He was elevated to father provincial of his order and everybody repeated what he said. Bishop Zumárraga wrote to a friend: "There are partridges and cows which the father says he saw, and he heard a story of camels and dromedaries and other cities. . . ."

The people of Cíbola wear leather shoes and buskins, another priest wrote to somebody in Burgos, and many wear silk clothing. "Of the richness of this country I do not write you because it is said to be so great that it does not seem possible. The friar himself told me this, that he saw a temple of their idols the walls of which, inside and outside, were covered with precious stones; I think he said they were emeralds. They also say that in the country beyond there are camels and elephants."

Marcos, a generous man, did not hoard such nuggets of information. He told his barber that in Cíbola the women wore strings of gold beads. The men wore girdles of gold and white wool gowns. They had sheep, cattle, slaughterhouses, iron forges, and so on.

Mendoza was not a credulous man, but the friar's report plainly demanded further exploration. He commissioned Francisco Vásquez, better known as Coronado.

The expedition assembled at Compostela northwest of Mexico City and started north in February of 1540—a most noble and distinguished assembly, according to the chronicler Pedro de Casteñada.

No doubt the most visible was Coronado, wearing gilded armor and a gilded helmet with a plume, a new manifestation of El Dorado, the legendary gilded man. Behind him rode 225 horsemen, some dressed in chain mail, a few in full armor, others in native buckskin armor, all of them carrying lances and swords. Next came 60 foot soldiers: pikemen, crossbowmen, harquebusiers. Then a swarm of Indian servants and Negro slaves driving the sheep, swine, cattle, and pack animals, and dragging six bronze swivel guns called pedreros. Finally came a horde of about 1,300 Indians wearing fantastically colored parrot-feather headdresses, carrying slings, bows, and obsidian-edged maces, their flesh smeared with black and ocher warpaint.

Ahead of this army walked four Franciscans, including Marcos.

They followed the prehistoric trade route out of Compostela, through scrub thickets to the coastal plain. Progress was slow because they could not get very far ahead of the livestock. It took a month to reach Culiacán. Here, impatient to behold the gleaming northern cities, Coronado split his force; he advanced with a squadron of about seventy horsemen, twenty-five or thirty foot soldiers, the artillery, the priests, and a host of Indians. They carried rations for eighty days.

From Culiacán they marched north, this wild and wonderful procession, bearing gradually inland until they crossed what is now the border between Mexico and Arizona. "There are no trees without spines," wrote Casteñada, "nor any fruit. . . ."

The monotonous Arizona desert was littered with dry thickets of mesquite, saguaro, gray sage, and the green prickly pear that de Vaca in his extremity had learned to eat. All day the sun reflected from the helmets and shields and breastplates of the armored soldiers. Their swords became too hot to touch. Horses lurched and fell. The desiccated earth shimmered in waves of heat. But ahead of them, they believed, lay Cíbola, first of the Seven Cities. And beyond that? Anything was possible.

Five months later they reached Cíbola—a poor, sun-baked, adobe pueblo on a low bluff overlooking dusty fields. And when at last the soldiers understood that nothing else was to be seen, "such were the curses hurled at Fray Marcos," wrote Casteñada, "that I pray God may protect him from them."

However, they had no choice but to attack the wretched place; otherwise they would starve. Some of the soldiers already were so weak they could barely lift their weapons, yet Cíbola was captured without much of a fight. Later the subjugated Zuñis said it had been foretold that men such as the Spaniards would arrive from the south to conquer the land. Were the Zuñis revising the myth of Quetzalcoatl? Had they heard rumors of Columbus?

When the job was done Coronado dispatched a letter to Mendoza:

"The Seven Cities are seven little villages . . . within a space of four leagues. Taken together they are called the Kingdom of Cévola. Each has its own name, and no single one is called Cévola, but collectively they have this designation. This one where I am now lodged and which I have called a city, I have named Granada, both because it has similarity to the place, and in honor of your Lordship."

Mendoza was a native of Granada.

The Spaniards saw neither gold nor precious jewels in the adobe pueblos. "Some little broken stones, rather poor, which approach the color of garnet, were found in a paper under some stone crystals."

Coronado knew the viceroy would be interested in native crafts, so he made up a nice collection: "I am sending you twelve small mantas such as the people of this country ordinarily wear, a fabric which seems to me to be very well made. . . . I am sending also two canvases showing the animals they have in this country, although, as I have said, the painting is poorly done." And he included fifteen combs, a cowhide, two wicker baskets, a mallet, a shield, a bow and several arrows, and "two pads such as the women customarily wear on their heads when they carry water from the spring, just as they do in Spain. . . . God knows I wish I had better news to write to your Lordship."

Viceroy Mendoza would not be greatly pleased and Coronado could only hope that having the first of the Seven Cities renamed Granada might placate him. "I have decided to send men throughout the surrounding regions to find out if there is anything worthwhile. . . ."

These search parties returned one after another to report such interesting but useless things as the Grand Canyon, the Hopi nation, the Rio Grande, and the sky city of Ácoma. It was all very depressing.

Captain Cardenas' sidetrip to the Grand Canyon has been detailed by Casteñada, who says they spent three days trying to find some way to the river "which from above appeared to be only a fathom wide." At last Captain Melgosa and two agile soldiers started down. Late that afternoon they returned. They had descended about a third of the way and from there the river looked very large, just as the Indians had said. The soldiers who stayed on top had estimated that some rocks jutting from a shelf in the gorge must be approximately the height of a man; but when Melgosa and his companions got back they said these rocks "were taller than the great tower of Seville," by which they meant the Giralda, the cathedral tower, 295 feet high. That was remarkable, to be sure, but not likely to excite Viceroy Mendoza or King Charles I.

Good news, however, arrived from Captain Alvarado on the Río Grande. He had picked up a singular individual wearing a sort of turban, for which reason the Spaniards called him El Turco. The Turk had been captured by one of the Pueblo chiefs along the eastern border of their domain and obviously he knew something about those vast plains to the east.

The Turk "by signs and in the Mexican tongue of which he understood a little" protested that he knew nothing about the region to the east, and urged Captain Alvarado to march northeast because in that direction lay a country called Quivira—very rich in gold, silver, and fabrics. He also said he had a gold bracelet from Quivira, which the Pueblo chief had stolen from him. The chief denied this, insisting he had no knowledge of any such bracelet. Alvarado therefore dressed them both in chains and sent word to the general.

Coronado arrived before long, having left a garrison at Cíbola, and questioned the Turk. One gold bracelet was unimportant; what mattered was the territory ahead.

Quivira, said the Turk, contained a river two leagues wide in which there were fish the size of horses. The name of the gray-bearded king of Quivira was Tatarrax—a Wichita word meaning "chief"—and he prayed to the image of a lady who was the goddess of Heaven. As for gold? Each afternoon he rested beneath a tree hung with tiny golden bells that lulled him to sleep with their music. Every jug in his palace was made of gold, every platter. Even the oarlocks of his canoes were golden. That was how much gold could be found in Quivira. If the Spaniards intended to visit King Tatarrax they should bring many carts to carry away all the gold he would distribute. Furthermore, beyond his kingdom lay the lands of Arache and Guas whose wealth put the wealth of Quivira to shame.

"All this," says the chronicler Jaramillo, "moved us to go in search of that country. . . ."

Coronado's army prepared to march as soon as the snow began melting; and so persuasive was El Turco that nobody wanted to stay behind.

Before leaving the Río Grande valley they picked up two more Pueblo captives. One was named Xabe, a Pawnee, who said yes, yes, there was gold in Quivira, though not quite as much as El Turco claimed. The other captive disagreed; he said the Turk was a liar. His name is given as Sopete, or Ysopete, and he must have been a Wichita because he is described as having tattoos encircling his eyes—which gave the Wichita their tribal name of Kidi Kidesh, Raccoon Eyes.

It is now impossible to follow Coronado's trail with much precision across eastern New Mexico and the Texas panhandle because of the flatness of the country. There are almost no landmarks. Even the Indians who lived there often got lost. Coronado later wrote that they could not see a stone, no rising ground, not a tree, not a shrub. Since there was nothing to guide them, each morning they looked at the rising sun, then an archer shot an arrow in the direction they wished to take, and before coming to it another arrow was shot to extend the line; and by this method they were able to avoid marching in a curve.

They seem to have been mystified by the expanse, by the insignificance of their expedition. Casteñada wrote: "Who could believe that 1,000 horses and 500 of our cows and more than 5,000 rams and ewes and more than 1,500 friendly Indians and servants, in traveling over these plains, would leave no more trace where they had passed than if nothing had been there—nothing—so that it was necessary to make piles of bones and cow dung now and then to enable the rear guard to follow the army. . . . The country is like a bowl, so that when a man sits down the horizon surrounds him. . . ."

Somewhere in this region Coronado once again decided to ride ahead of the main force. It was now the end of May, their stock of corn had been exhausted, the horses were bony, soldiers were getting sick from eating only meat, and Coronado was troubled by Sopete's insistence that they would find nothing in Quivira except thatched huts.

With thirty horsemen, half a dozen foot soldiers, and several guides, including Sopete and the Turk, he angled northeast across the Oklahoma panhandle and entered Kansas near the town of Liberal. Beyond the Cimarron lay the Arkansas—Río de Pedro y Pablo, so named because they came to it on the feast day of Saints Peter and Paul—which they followed for a while and then continued northeast until they could not have been much more than fifty miles from the exact geographical center of the United States. That was early in July, 1541.

At this point Coronado met some buffalo hunters. Sopete was delighted and the Turk was dismayed, because the wretched appearance of these hunters confirmed what Sopete had been saying about Quivira and belied everything the Turk had said. After being interrogated again the Turk confessed that he had lured the Spaniards onto these plains hoping they would die of hunger. He said he had been encouraged in this idea by the Pueblo people who were anxious to see the last of their unwelcome guests. He had planned to slip away from the army when it approached Pawnee territory; he had not expected to be traveling in chains. Now, like an animal that all at once quits fighting for its life, he appeared indifferent to his fate. As for gold, there was none in Quivira.

In spite of the Turk's confession Coronado refused to give up. It seemed to him that the story of King Tatarrax might be true: possibly some member of the Narváez expedition, other than de Vaca and his companions, had survived and moved inland and now reigned over a wealthy tribe. There is another possibility. Coronado may have beard rumors of Hernando de Soto, who just then was only a few hundred miles southeast, although neither of them knew it.

In any event, he wrote a letter in magniloquent Castilian to the graybearded Christian monarch Tatarrax—just as Pope Alexander III had written to the legendary Christian monarch Prester John four centuries earlier. The pope entrusted that letter to his personal physician, Magister Philippus. Coronado, too, had a reliable envoy; he gave his letter to the honorable Sopete, instructing him to deliver it to King Tatarrax somewhere in America. Sopete started off at once, and like Magister Philippus he was never heard of again.

Coronado's army then pushed forward and soon came across six or seven villages where the houses looked like grass and dirt beehives. They saw no canoes with golden oarlocks, no Christian king taking his siesta beneath a tree hung with golden bells. No golden platters or jugs, only drab clay water jars.

Still they could not give up the dream. This might not be the kingdom of Tatarrax, maybe it lay just a little farther.

They marched on, demanding that their guides lead them to other villages, until at last they came to a miserable settlement beside a river—probably the Kansas—which their guides said was the end of Quivira. Upon being asked if there was anything beyond, "they said there was nothing more of Quivira, but there was Harahey, and it was the same sort of place."

By Coronado's order the Turk was strangled; and late that summer, anxious to avoid being caught by snow on these desolate plains, the army marched southwest.

But before leaving they raised a cross, "at the foot of which some letters were cut with a chisel saying that Francisco Vásquez de Coronado, general of the army, had reached this place." No doubt the cross has vanished, being made of wood; but the inscription—because we are told it had been chiseled—almost certainly was cut in stone and might still be there, someplace in the middle of Kansas.

In this area, too, links of sixteenth-century chain-mail armor have been found, and shards of Pueblo pottery.

That second winter they spent in familiar territory and the general addressed a letter to his sovereign, Charles V: "I have done all that I possibly could to serve Your Majesty and to discover a country where God our Lord might be served and the royal patrimony of Your Majesty increased, as your loyal servant and vassal. For since I have reached the province of Cíbola, to which the viceroy of New Spain sent me in the name of Your Majesty, seeing that there were none of the things there of which Friar Marcos had told, I have managed to explore this country for two hundred leagues and more around Cíbola, and the best place I have found is this river of Tiguex where I am now, and the settlements here."

On All Fools' Day, 1542, began the long march home.

That autumn Coronado led what remained of his army across the deserts and mountains into Sinaloa where, at Culiacán, it was disbanded. The army consisted of about ninety men dressed in animal hides and rusty, dented mail. Later, during a period of several weeks, a few more soldiers straggled in. Those who were present to observe this ignominious spectacle have reported that the feeling in Mexico was not of bitterness but of disappointment.

Casteñada, musing on the adventure, reflects that so long as we have a thing we take it for granted, and the longer we have it the less we value it. But once we have lost it we begin to suffer, and look for ways of getting it back again. This is what happened, he writes,

> to all or most of those who went on the expedition which, in the year 1540 of Our Saviour Jesus Christ, Francisco Vásquez de Coronado led in search of the Seven Cities. Granted that they did not find the riches of which they had been told, they found a place in which to search for them, and the beginning of a good country to settle in, from which they could go on further. Since they returned from the country which they conquered and abandoned, time has given them a chance to understand

> the direction and locality in which they were, and the borders of the good country they had in their hands, and their hearts weep for having lost so favourable an opportunity.

Coronado himself was broken by the experience, although he was just thirty-two years old. He had been injured in New Mexico when a saddle girth broke during a race, and he never quite recovered from this; but the failure of his exploration seems to have weakened him more than the accident. He resumed his post as governor of New Galicia but handled the job carelessly and before long the king's auditor filed thirty-four charges against him, including neglect of duty, short accounts, accepting bribes, favoritism in appointments, and inhumane treatment of the natives. Although absolved of some of these charges he was arrested, fined 600 gold pesos, and removed from the governorship. Ten years later he died, and with his death the legend began to fade.

In 1571 the renowned cartographer Ortelius noted Sept Cités in the ocean, thus continuing the tradition that they would be found on an island.

They reappeared on the American mainland when Hakluyt published the *Relation of Henry Hawks, merchant, who lived for five years in Nova Hispania*. This is the testimony of merchant Hawks: "The Spanyards have notice of Seven Cities, which old men of the Indians show them should lie toward the North-east from Mexico. They have used and use daily much diligence in seeking of them, but they cannot find any one of them. They say that the witchcraft of the Indians is such that when they come upon these townes' they cast a mist upon them, so that they cannot see them. . . ."

A few years later Mercator's map returned them to the ocean.

And in 1639 a party of Franciscan monks arriving in Lisbon swore that while en route from Madeira they were blown off course by a storm and had been saved by the miraculous appearance of an unfamiliar island. They said in their deposition, which strangely echoes the fifteenth-century tale of Captain Leone, that on this island was a city with very few inhabitants, with no sign of a priest or a monk. They were greeted by people who spoke Portuguese, who escorted them to a circular palace with a lighthouse rising above it, where they saw paintings of battles between Portuguese and Moors, and statues of many kings, and a chapel guarded by lions in which they beheld a statue of the Virgin holding a sword. They thought the island was not far from Madeira, no more than a day's sail, although because of the storm they were not sure in which direction. But it is said that nobody believed their statement.

The myth was fading, gradually losing color, retaining only its texture and dignity, like those stiff frayed tapestries from the Middle Ages that now and again we meet in the corridors of great museums.

17

Gold! Gold! Gold!

ATAHUALPA, AFTER BEING CAPTURED by the Spaniards, tried to buy his freedom. Through an interpreter he said to Pizarro, meanwhile indicating the apartment in which they stood, that he would cover the floor with gold. Pizarro did not respond immediately; he and the other Spaniards who were present when Atahualpa made this offer merely listened with incredulous smiles.

Then the Inca, misinterpreting their silence, thinking they wanted more, said that if they would release him he would fill the room with gold as high as he could reach. And standing on tiptoe, he touched the wall.

Pizarro accepted. He had not planned to release the hostage so his reasoning can only be surmised, but the Spaniards had heard tremendous rumors—Atahualpa himself had described Cuzco, where the temple roofs were plated with gold and the floors were inlaid with golden tiles. It is thought that Pizarro reasoned simply: There might be truth to these rumors, let us see. Atahualpa remains my captive. If he delivers all this gold, so much the better.

Pizarro ordered a line to be drawn around the room at the height

Atahualpa had indicated, and the terms of the proposal to be recorded. The gold need not be melted into bars, it might retain the form into which it had been cast. But the Inca should, in addition, twice fill a small adjoining room with silver.

The dimensions of the principal room are given differently by various chroniclers. According to the notary Xerez, who was Pizarro's secretary, the room measured twenty-two by seventeen feet. Hernando Pizarro, Francisco's half-brother, said it was seventeen or eighteen by thirty-five. Another contemporary account gives it as fifteen by twenty-five. Whatever the true dimensions it was no closet, and trying to imagine such a room filled with gold is difficult.

As to the depth of this treasure, again there is some discrepancy. Prescott, a most respected historian, says the mark on the wall was nine feet above the floor. Yet how could Atahualpa, who probably stood not much more than five feet, have reached that high? Hernando Pizarro states that the ceiling was nine feet above the floor, which makes more sense. By the account of some anonymous conquistador this room was to be filled up to a white line "which a tall man could not reach." Jonathan Leonard says that the stone-walled room where the offer was made can still be seen in Cajamarca, and the line—which has been renewed—"is about four inches below the level that a six-foot man can reach."

No matter. Atahualpa promised something like 3,000 cubic feet of gold, not to mention the silver. Quite a lot even by Inca standards. The job would take a couple of months, he explained, because it would have to be brought from all over the empire.

Pizarro agreed to this.

Couriers went out.

The empire was not wide, but from north to south it covered thirty-six degrees of latitude, from what is now Colombia to the middle of Chile. A highway ran the length of the realm, almost 3,300 miles, which would take you from Maine to California and beyond.

Soon the treasure began to arrive, some of it in the form of solid gold slabs weighing twenty pounds. We hear no more about incredulous smiles. Incredulity, perhaps, but neither a sixteenth-century Spaniard nor anybody else would respond with amusement to what was being deposited in that room.

Pizarro had Atahualpa strangled while the gold was still pouring into Cajamarca, but that's another story. As to the amount delivered, we know exactly, because Xerez was a meticulous accountant: 1,326,539 pesos of gold and 51,610 silver marks.

In those days a peso de oro was not currency but a unit of measurement, equal in weight to the coin known as a castellano. There were about six castellanos to an ounce, though numbers do not suggest the value of the Inca's ransom. It was, of course, millions of dollars—perhaps sixty million on the basis of today's gold price. And more was on the road. Much more. We will never know how much more.

If you want to evaluate what was delivered not in terms of weight, as though it were cotton or beans, but as high-carat gold artworks to be priced accordingly and marketed at posh galleries in New York, London, Geneva, and Paris—well, on that basis an apartment stuffed with fifteenth- and sixteenth-century Inca treasure could save a middle-sized nation from bankruptcy.

Look at it like this: the famous hammered gold masks, et cetera, that Schliemann dug from the ruins of Mycenae weighed, altogether, thirty-three pounds.

There never has been a collection of gold artwork, with perhaps one exception, remotely equal to that brought to Cajamarca by the Inca's command. And Pizarro, impatient to get on with the conquest, did not even let him finish. All told—which is to say, Atahualpa's ransom in addition to the rest of the gold the Spaniards carted off during this burglary—altogether it is thought to have totaled about nine tons. Nine tons of gold. Schliemann's thirty-three pounds made him an international celebrity.

The exception could be the treasure hauled away from Persepolis by Alexander. We are told that 5,000 camels and 10,000 pairs of mules were required, but we have no idea how much of this was gold. Alexander might have loaded the beasts with rolls of silk, carpets, embroidered shawls, and pistachio nuts.

And besides, the Inca's treasure train may have equaled or surpassed

Alexander's. "We hold it to be very certain," wrote Cieza de León, "that neither in Jerusalem, nor in Rome, nor in Persia, nor in any other part of the world, by any state or kings of this earth, was such wealth of gold and silver and precious stones collected. . . ."

As to what the Spaniards missed, S. K. Lothrop says there is a Peruvian tradition that 11,000 llama loads of gold dust were buried near Jauja. Another 500 loads of silver and gold are said to be buried in the Casma valley. And 4,000 loads in a vault beneath the plain that faces the Sacsahuaman fortress. Now, whether such tales are true we can't be sure, but there is no doubt that prodigious quantities of gold and silver were hidden as soon as word got around the countryside that Atahualpa had been strangled.

Among the fantastic creations reported on the imperial highway was a gold chain about 800 feet long—either a chain or a multicolored rope embellished with gold plates—which was so heavy that 200 Indians carried it. This chain, or rope, was held by dancers during important festivals, and is said to have been cast into a lake just south of Cuzco. But a thing like that, how could you throw it into a lake? How far could 200 men throw it? My own opinion is that it was buried.

Unfortunately the Incas left no written records, which might tell us where to start digging; they communicated information by means of a knotted string, the quipu, and although a good many of these strings have survived, nobody knows how to decode them. But tomorrow, perhaps, or the next day, after enough rain or a landslide in the high Andes, a Peruvian farmer crossing the imperial road might pause to look at a gleaming oval in the mud.

Such things happen. A while ago in the Mimbres Mountains of New Mexico a sheepherder who sat down to rest beneath a cottonwood tree saw a length of metal protruding from the roots. He dug it out and found it was the hilt of a Spanish sword inlaid with gold. It must have lain there since 1540 when Coronado passed that way.

And the Bolivian mines at Potosí—the most fabulous source of silver the world had known—Potosí, too, was discovered by chance. An Indian pursuing a llama on a mountainside caught hold of a bush, the earth crumbled, and the Indian suddenly held in his hand a bush festooned with silver nuggets. It sounds implausible, like cheap fiction, yet that seems to be what occurred.

Now, what became of Atahualpa's stupendous ransom?

"Según Dios Nuestro Señor le diere á entender teniendo su conciencia y para lo mejor hazer pedir el ayuda de Dios Nuestro Señor. . . ." In other words, Francisco Pizarro with the fear of God in his eyes invoked the assistance of Heaven to do the work before him conscientiously and justly.

Thus fearing God, Pizarro took for himself 57,222 gold pesos, the Inca's gold throne which was valued at 25,000 pesos, and a hefty slice of silver.

His captains drew less; even so they were at once transmogrified into Peruvian millionaires. And it is said, with perhaps a little exaggeration, that ordinary foot soldiers grew as rich as Spanish dukes.

What happened next was inevitable.

At that time in Castile you could buy several acres of choice land for ten gold pesos. What could you buy in the New World for that?—a few sheets of writing paper. Did a conquistador want a bottle of wine?—the price would be sixty gold pesos. A warm cloak?—one hundred pesos. Or say he wanted to buy a horse. Provided the owner could be talked into selling, a horse would cost thousands.

Debtors, followed by Indian slaves wearing preposterous necklaces of gold—gold pots, gold plates, gold urns, gold statuettes—debtors visited their creditors in the hope of settling accounts, but would be told that the debt was not due. Or the creditor would hide so that he would not be obliged to accept any more gold.

As for silver, in Peru during the sixteenth century they shod horses with silver. They used it to mortar the walls, which explains why the Spaniards tore apart so many walls. They had no tapestries, wrote Garcilaso de la Vega, because they decorated the interior walls with gold and silver. And listen to this: in one palace the Spaniards saw three rooms filled with gold furnishings, five rooms furnished with silver, and 100,000 gold ingots—each ingot weighing five pounds.

Pedro Pizarro says that while looking for something to eat he wandered into a native hut and found ten silver slabs. Each slab was twenty feet long—twenty feet!—and one foot wide, and three fingers thick. The Indians were carrying these slabs to Trugillo where they meant to build a shrine for their idol, Chimo.

And in Cuzco there was a massive gold image the size of a ten-year-old boy.

There was even a stack of firewood reproduced in gold.

And the priest who officiated at important ceremonies wore an immense headdress with a golden replica of the sun on his forehead, with a silver moon beneath his chin, and he was crowned with macaw plumes.

But where is it now?

Those conquistadors, being practical men, decided to ship it to Spain in the form of ingots. All the baroque shapes—goblets, salvers, ewers, masks, birds, serpents, crickets—such things would be difficult to pack into the hold of a galleon. Only a few of the most remarkable specimens would be preserved and delivered to Charles V so that he might obtain some idea of native ingenuity.

Very often the objects were demolished by the same artists who had conceived them. "They toiled day and night, but such was the quantity to be recast, that it consumed a full month." And when the job was finished the gold and silver ingots weighed several tons.

Pizarro, contrary to what you might expect, made sure that Charles was not swindled: "He would often rise from his seat while watching the melting down of the gold and silver to retrieve a small piece of the king's share, which had fallen to one side as it was being broken down, and in so doing he remarked that he would pick up the king's property with his mouth if need be."

On January 9, 1534, the galleon *Santa María del Campo*, carrying Hernando Pizarro and an incomprehensible load of treasure, sailed heavily up the Guadalquivir to Seville. Pizarro was escorting one consignment of the royal fifth.

Albrecht Dürer did not live quite long enough to see what was aboard the *Santa María del Campo*, but he did see the Aztec goldwork that Moctezuma had sent to Charles thirteen years earlier and he described it in his diary: "all sorts of marvelous objects for human use which are much more beautiful to behold than things spoken of in fairy tales. These things were all so precious that one has appraised them worth one hundred thousand guilders. And in all the days of my life I have seen nothing which so rejoiced my heart as these things. For I saw among them wondrous artful things and I marveled over the subtle genius of these men in strange countries. And I know not how to relate all of what I saw there before me."

The court historian, Peter Martyr, if less emotional than Dürer, also enjoyed the Moctezuma exhibit: "I do not marvel at gold and precious stones, but am in a manner astonished to see the workmanship excel the substance. . . . I never saw anything whose beauty might so allure the eye of man."

Charles, however, was unimpressed by native ingenuity. An imperial *cédula* published in 1535 directs that all gold and silver objects from Peru shall be melted in the royal mints at Seville, Toledo, and Segovia. Thus we have only the chronicles to describe what we shall never see:

Replicas of Indian corn, each gold ear sheathed in silver, with tassels of silver thread. Innumerable gold goblets. Sculpted gold spiders, gold beetles, gold lobsters, gold lizards. A gold fountain that emitted a sparkling jet of gold while gold animals and gold birds played around it. Twelve splendid representations of women, all in fine gold, as lovely and complete as though they were alive. And the sandals, or slippers, that women like—these also were reproduced in gold. The Inca's throne, which Pizarro claimed.

The list goes on and on, as Dürer said, until one can hardly relate all of what was there. Nevertheless, after the death of Atahualpa, some Inca nobles poured a bucket of corn in front of the Spaniards, and one of them picked up a grain and said, "This is the gold he gave you." And then, pointing to the heap on the ground: "This much he has kept."

But the most spectacular agglutination of wealth seen by the Spaniards was at Cuzco, 600 miles south, when they entered the Coricancha—the Golden Enclosure. This temple complex occupied the site where according to legend the first building of the empire had been erected by Manco Capac, the first Inca.

A Dominican monastery now occupies this site, although some of the original Inca masonry peeps through. The entrance was by a side door of the present church, and around the inner patio stood thatched-roof chapels consecrated to various plenipotentiaries.

The most important shrine was that of the sun. Just what it held is a matter for scholarly dispute because sixteenth-century writers describe it differently. Garcilaso de la Vega mentions an altar on which there was an image of the sun fashioned from pure gold: "The face of the god was adorned with flames, extending from one wall to the next, in the same way that our painters often represent the Sun. The whole temple contained just this one idol, since the Incas have but one god, the Sun. On both sides of the Sun were ranged the mummified bodies of the Inca kings, so artfully embalmed that they seemed to be alive. They were seated on golden thrones. . . ."

Another report has the mummies seated on stone benches encrusted with emeralds.

In addition to the central image of the sun there seems to have been a representative disc on the western wall "looking forth from amidst innumerable rays of light which emanated from it in every direction." According to Cieza de León, the sun's face was engraved on a gold plate thickly powdered with jewels: "muy primamente engastonada en muchas piedras ricas." This plate was so situated that through the east portal the rising sun illuminated it like a shimmering cymbal, reflecting upon a variety of silver and gold ornaments, warming and filling the shrine with an unearthly effulgence. Twelve immense silver vases were supposed to have been discovered in this chapel, each taller than a good lance—"mas altos que una buena pica"—and of such circumference that two men with outstretched arms could scarcely reach around one.

In the shrine dedicated to the moon, mother of the Incas, the moon was personified just as the sun was personified, except that the disc was larger: a great silver platter nearly hid the wall. And every object in this room had been fashioned from silver, which best complements the pallid lunar light.

Other shrines were dedicated to the rainbow, to the stars, and to thunder and lightning—ministers of vengeance.

Sarmiento writes that in the Coricancha every utensil, every ornament—everything—was either silver or gold: religious censers, ewers that held sacrificial water, the pipes that conducted water through subterranean channels, even the agricultural implements used in the temple gardens.

And at the heart of this spectacle, surrounded by the various shrines, stood a perfect replica of a field of maize, each stalk carefully contrived of gold and planted among golden clods. Here, too, on good authority, stood at least twenty-three life-size llamas with their young, all made of gold, with life-size Indian shepherds to guard them, each shepherd fashioned from gold, each with a golden sling and a golden crook. Miguel de Estete, an inspector for Charles V, was present and his account has survived. After summarizing what he saw he tells us that if he were to recount everything that the Incas had made of gold his story would never end.

Now the Coricancha has disappeared, except for a few plastered walls, replaced by the church of Santo Domingo. Prescott puts it like this: "Fields of maize and lucerne now bloom on the spot which glowed with the golden gardens of the temple; and the friar chants his orisons within the consecrated precincts once occupied by the Children of the Sun."

Gone, too, is Atahualpa's throne. Pizarro undoubtedly seated himself on it, at least once. After that? Probably it was melted.

And the massive gold lid of the sun-god's chicha basin, what happened to that? It was awarded to the redoubtable conquistador Mansio Serra de Leguizano, who lost it the same night in a game of dobladilla. The proverb "Juega el sol antes que amanezca"—gamble the sun before dawn—is thought to have originated with this conquistador's bad luck. But we do not know who won it, nor what the winner did with his prize. We assume it was melted.

Then what became of the ingots?

Most of them reached Spain where they were melted again and cast into coins, although many bars of Peruvian and Mexican gold settled on the bed of the Atlantic.

In 1622, for example, nine ships stuffed with bullion from the New World went down in a hurricane near Fort Pierce, Florida. Hundreds of Spaniards drowned, along with an undetermined number of Indians and Negroes whose deaths were not listed on the casualty report. As for the value of the cargo, it cannot even be estimated, but according to documents in the Archiva General de Indias in Seville, one galleon—*Nuestra Señora de Atocha*—had been loaded with 250,000 freshly minted silver coins, 901 silver ingots, and 161 bars of gold, in addition to an unknown amount of contraband.

The wreck of the *Atocha* has been found and much that is valuable brought to the surface: silver coins, a gold chalice, a bronze astrolabe, a gold boatswain's-whistle, small gold bars. But if all of her cargo could be recovered the *Atocha* would be one of the world's richest prizes.

In 1702 a fleet of twenty-three heavily loaded galleons escorted by French men-of-war sailed from Havana toward Cádiz. News of this wallowing treasury reached England, and Sir Cloudisley Shovell—for that was his name—set out to capture them, because the War of the Spanish Succession had just begun. However, news of the English force got back to Spain and a friendly Genoese vessel sailing from Cádiz to Portugal warned the approaching galleons. The Spanish commander therefore changed course and arrived safely at Vigo in northern Spain. But here the bureaucrats took charge. Cádiz did not want the treasure unloaded at Vigo; being destined for Cádiz, it should be delivered to Cádiz.

And while this point was being argued the English learned where the galleons were hiding.

When the Spanish admiral Don Manuel de Velasco realized that his French protectors were being defeated, he ordered the treasure thrown overboard; and then, to save the ships themselves from capture, he ordered them scuttled. He gave this order almost in time. The English seized only three galleons. The two smaller ones—*Santa Cruz* and *Tauro*—eventually got to England "with a mighty freight of bullion," but the largest, which held as much as the other two combined, struck a submerged rock and went down just outside Vigo Bay.

"We do not, as yet, exactly know the amount of booty taken at Vigo," says a contemporary English account. "We are sure that they have taken a value of 1,200,000 pounds Sterling in silver, with a great quantity of gold ingots. . . ."

Whatever it came to, this was the produce of two unimportant ships plus a certain amount collected ashore. Twenty-one galleons, including the largest, went down.

All the same, it was a great victory and the English government celebrated by issuing coins minted from this New World wealth—gold guineas and silver crowns with VIGO stamped below the portrait of Queen Anne. The procedure was supervised by Sir Isaac Newton, master of the mint, and today the very least of these silver crowns is a treasure by itself.

As for the remaining gold and silver, worth an incalculable fortune, it rests in fifty feet of mud at the bottom of Vigo Bay.

In 1715 a much smaller fleet set sail from Havana, but was annihilated by a hurricane off the east coast of Florida not far from where the *Atocha* sank. More than 1,000 men drowned. Of eleven ships in this fleet, ten were lost. Aboard were 2,290 chests packed with freshly minted silver and gold coins from Vera Cruz and a cargo of emeralds, pearls, and gem-studded jewelry from Cartagena. Don Juan del Hoyo Solórzano, sergeant major of Havana, was assigned to salvage whatever he could.

After having located several of the wrecks, Solórzano camped on the beach and put his Indian divers to work. It is said that about a third of them died, but that was unimportant; the rest brought up four million pesos of silver which the honest sergeant major dispatched to Havana.

Word of this got around and an English privateer named Jennings led two brigantines and three luggers from Port Royal to Florida where he lay offshore, observing things through a spyglass, until the Spaniards accumulated another heap of pesos. Then, as we learn from *A General History of the Robberies and Murders of the Most Notorious Pyrates*: "The rovers came directly upon the place, bringing their little fleet to anchor, and landing 300 men, they attacked the guard who immediately ran away; and thus they seized the treasure which they carried off, making the best of their way to Jamaica."

Solórzano did what he could for the crown, despite several such interruptions, and it is thought that altogether he retrieved about six million pesos, leaving another eight million in the shallow sandy water. Very little of this has been recovered.

At the beginning of the nineteenth century a surveyor picked up hundreds of escudos and doubloons on the beach near Fort Pierce inlet.

And there was an old man who had been postmaster in the nearby town of Sebastian who kept a cigar box full of Spanish coins; but one night he was murdered and the coins were stolen.

And there was said to be another man who found a strangely heavy brick in the surf, which he used when he built a fireplace, and the brick melted.

But these stories may have been discolored by time, or by the long human dream of treasure.

Much more recently, just a few years ago, a building contractor who was walking along this beach picked up a copper maravedi dated 1649. He then borrowed a metal detector and began finding silver pieces of eight, so many that he melted a number of them to make bracelets for neighborhood children.

Later, having read about attempts to salvage the 1715 treasure fleet, the contractor located Solórzano's camp. Here he dug up some cannonballs, a pair of cutlasses, broken porcelain, a gold ring set with a diamond, and thirteen more pieces of eight.

Next he decided to look offshore, and while paddling around on a surfboard he saw five ship's cannon and a huge old anchor. In the shallow water nearby he found a cluster of coins as big as his fist. The shape of this cluster indicated that the coins had originally been in a pouch.

He organized a company and very soon his divers were bringing up hundreds of blackened silver coins, some of which had undergone a sea change—fused by the water into rocklike greenish black clumps. One clump was so large that a diver sat on it, using it for a stool while he probed the sand.

And the treasure multiplied, as though the sea were a great alchemist. They scooped up handmade silver forks, plates, buckles, a pewter jewel box, and more.

While inspecting the beach after a storm they came upon a superb gold chain glittering in the sand—a chain eleven feet long—with more than 2,000 flower-shaped links. It had a dragon pendant, a whistle, which served also as a gentleman's grooming tool: a toothpick swiveled out of the dragon's belly, and the dragon's tail was a tiny spoon which aristocratic Spaniards used for cleaning their ears.

One day the divers brought up a clump of coins that weighed seventy pounds. Then five more clumps.

Twenty-eight valuable K'ang Hsi ceramic pieces were found unbroken, packed in clay for shipment. And another gold chain, although not as elaborate as the first. And two gold discs, each weighing seven pounds. And a gold doubloon dated 1698.

Something else they found was a pocketknife with this inscription: SIBO A MI DUEÑO Y SR. DON DIEGO PENALOSA Y PICAZO. Don Diego himself disintegrated; but that trusty uncomplaining servant, his knife, remained to honor him.

In another place the divers blasted a trench through the sand and were almost blinded by a sudden gleam. The trench appeared to be paved with gold. It is said that they swam to the surface with their hands full of gold doubloons, spilling fifty or sixty at a time on the deck of their boat.

Ten discs eighteen inches in diameter—an alloy of gold, copper, platinum, and silver—ten such discs were recovered at one site. Then eight more, along with several thick bars and wedges of solid silver. So much wealth had been flung across the bed of the sea that after a while they swam above loose coins, pausing only to collect the discs and clusters.

They saw a black wooden chest. Its top had rotted away, but the interior had been lined with lead and was filled to the brim with Spanish silver and gold.

Now, have you heard enough? Or do you want more? Because what I've described represents only a fraction of the cargo. For example, vacationers walking along the nearby beach after a storm sometimes pick up coins from that doomed fleet, flung ashore by General Juan Estéban de Ubilla, the drowned commander.

We hear of such things—sunken galleons, the Inca's golden enclosure, a mountain veined with silver. We hear about these luminous treasures, or read about them, just as we learn that somebody somewhere has won the Irish Sweepstakes. Then for a moment we feel vaguely baffled and resentful, wondering why the ponderous wheel of fortune has once again ticked slowly past us. Why, we ask, should our good luck be limited to picking up a nickel on the pavement?

One evening several years ago a professional treasure hunter knocked at my door—a pleasant, brown-bearded man with rather stagnant breath. He said he had been told by mutual friends that I was interested in antique objects such as coins and manuscripts and prehistoric pottery, and he wanted to show me something. I invited him in and gave him a glass of wine and listened while he talked about his adventures, and then he took out of his shirt pocket a triangular gold lump—three Spanish doubloons which had been in the sea for so many years that they could not be separated.

I weighed this curious object in my palm, this heavy warm triangle as smooth as velvet. I turned it over and over between my fingers and stared at the royal lettering.

I asked what he planned to do with it.

He said he knew of a galleon that had never been explored and he meant to sell this gold piece along with some others he had found in order to finance the expedition. This was what he always did. He cared very little about treasure; what excited him was the search.

At last he dropped the gold triangle into his pocket as though it had no more significance than a cigarette lighter. He stood up, shook hands, thanked me for the wine, and slipped away into the night. I've not seen him since. He told me where he found that lump of doubloons, but I've forgotten—someplace in the Caribbean. Maybe Bermuda.

Now that I've had several years to think about our conversation, I believe that everything he told me was true. If I had made an appropriate offer he would have sold the piece. Undoubtedly he had a sale in mind when he came to visit; but I made no suggestion, so he took back his treasure and disappeared.

Once in a while I dream of finding coins, although I doubt if the gold he showed me was responsible because in my dream—which never varies—the coins are silver. I have two Spanish pieces of eight, which might possibly explain a dream like that, yet I don't think they account for it either.

I bought these pieces of eight at an auction. One is counterfeit, the other authentic. The authentic coin, blackened and worn, carries a portrait of Ferdinand VII and is dated 1820. The fake looked very much the same at first, but then it began turning yellow. It never did ring as sweetly when I dropped it on the table and its surface is pocked. The inscription—CAROLUS IIII DEI GRATIA 1791—looks irregular when compared to Ferdinand's inscription, and the milled edges are not well delineated. Some previous owner, frankly suspicious, had drilled a tiny hole beneath the king's chin. I inspected this hole through a jeweler's glass and the metal appears to be lead.

I doubt if they have anything to do with my persistent dream because, if I remember correctly, it began sometime after I had read about Potosí. The symbolic image of an Indian pulling up a shrub spangled and trembling with silver nuggets—that image must be the origin of this recurrent dream because I always see the coins among bushes or on dusty ground. I become aware of myself floating toward them with the splendid buoyancy we all have experienced while we sleep. I float toward them with the intention of picking them up. But just then the dream concludes.

My most sensuous dream of money—and it has materialized only once—concerned ordinary American paper dollars. It began while I was infinitely high in the air, floating gently downward, weightless as a mote of dust. I remember floating down beside a tree where bunches of dollars grew in the forks like cabbages or heads of lettuce. I remember myself wrenching these tough, crisp, fat bunches out of the tree. I seized them with both hands. I twisted them and wrenched them loose, these bundles of dollars, one after another, but I don't know what became of them.

Then I was rising swiftly upward as though I had touched the earth and bounded hundreds of feet into the air, because in a little while I came floating down again, pausing once more at this tree among trees where I promptly resumed harvesting those excellent leafy green tufts. I remember being surprised at the silence. The dollars were fresh and crisp, yet when I wrenched them out of the tree they made not a sound. However, I could be wrong about that. Maybe it was sometime later when I felt surprised by the silence. Perhaps, too, the dollars weren't green, for it is said that men seldom are conscious of color in their dreams. I might have added the green later, I can't be sure. As to what became of these handsome cabbages, I have no idea; the instant I caught them they vanished. This didn't bother me. I was always reaching for the next fine bunch.

Every so often when I feel sleep approaching I remind myself of that dream because it was pleasant, to say the least, and I wouldn't mind dreaming it again. But of course the inner being who directs our lives pays no attention to what we want.

The contemplation of money usually leads me to think about my father, who worked industriously for sixty years to accumulate as much of it as possible. In this respect I suppose he wasn't unusual; he differed from most men only in that he put together a larger packet. More than enough to feed the family. Now, any man who has gotten himself into that situation must figure out what to do with the surplus—which is not as much fun as you might think. After the sensible investments and a few luxuries, if there still remains a little extra, what do you do? My father used it to become a millionaire. He was a millionaire for several weeks. He told me how this happened a long time ago, when I was a child. It was during the Depression. He and some friends who also had a bit of extra money decided to finance an Oklahoma oil prospector.

Well, sometime after they had done this they got a telegram.

There are things I would ask my father now, but it's too late. I would ask how they behaved when they got the news, whether he and his friends pounded each other on the back and roared and danced a little jig. I suppose they did. I would ask, too, why he told me this amazing story only once; I should think he would have told it again and again, until my mother and my sister and I were unspeakably bored.

It's too late, as I say, and all I know is that they chartered a railroad car for the trip to Oklahoma and they sat up all night drinking champagne. And my father said that when they reached Tulsa they were driven out to a field where they had to put on rubber boots and raincoats and rubber hats because in those days it was difficult to cap a gusher and the air was saturated with oil. Everything everywhere was oily, he said. You couldn't touch anything without getting oil on your hands. The entire field was soaked. They walked through pools of oil up to their ankles. "Great Lord!" my father said to me, wagging his head as he remembered. "Great Lord, I never saw anything like it!"

So all at once they became grotesquely rich, the prospector and his middle-class financiers. Then the Oklahoma legislature cooked up some sort of a bill to prevent the money from leaving the state.

My father sold his share and I believe he said his partners did the same. They made money, quite a lot for those days, but nothing like the million or two or three or five or ten or twenty that each man expected would be his.

As he told me this story I thought about the black mist in the air, the dangerous black column of spouting oil, and the pools in the field. I don't remember thinking about anything else. Nor do I recall what questions I asked. Maybe I asked if he had to take a bath afterward, or if they were still drinking champagne, or whether anybody slipped and fell. But now, if I had the chance, I would ask what went through his mind when he learned that the Oklahoma legislature had seized his fortune. Although, because he was my father and I knew him so well, I think I could answer for him. He would have been angry. He would have felt that he was being cheated.

At first I would have felt the same, I suppose. And yet, unlike my father, I would have decided very soon that what occurred was inevitable. I doubt if we are meant to get our hands on unreasonable wealth.

For instance, now and then an orange comes floating down a certain river in the Sierra Madre of Mexico, and each time this happens the people who live along the banks of the river stop whatever they are doing and look upstream because they know that the orange has come from El Naranjal.

Not much has been learned about this fabulous mine, except that it is in the country of the Tepehuane Indians, probably in Sinaloa near the Durango border, and that during the seventeenth century, according to church records in Guadalajara, it produced millions of dollars worth of gold and silver. Then, around 1810, the Tepehuane laborers revolted, killed their Spanish overseers, destroyed the haciendas, and concealed the entrances to the huge mine which had been the cause of their suffering. Since that time nobody has been able to locate El Naranjal—whose name means "the orange grove"—although a great many men have spent years searching the archives for clues, and others have lost their lives exploring the tremendous barrancas of the Sierra Madre.

It is thought that some of the Indians who live in that country know the location of the mine, but even today they are not anxious for it to reopen.

The historian J. Frank Dobie states that in Mazatlán he once met a German assayer who showed him a reproduction of an eighteenth-century road sign. The sign had been carved on the face of a rock. This is what it said:

DEPARTEMENTO
DE
CAMINOS
CAMINO A LAS MINAS
DE ARCO
Y
NARANJAL

The sign, therefore, was inscribed by the department of roads to indicate the way to the mines of Arco and Naranjal.

One gringo prospector may actually have seen El Naranjal. A white-haired old man who lived in the mountains pointed out a trail to him. The prospector traveled for several days and then came to a precipice. Looking down thousands of feet he was able to make out a river, the white ruins of a hacienda, and some bright green foliage unlike any other growth on the canyon floor, which could only have been the orange grove. He was unable to find a path down the cliff and on the way back be almost starved. He reported that there must have been a trail to the canyon floor, but probably some act of nature had annihilated it. Whether or not anyone could descend from someplace farther along the cliff, he did not know.

Seventy or eighty years have passed since then, perhaps more. The prospector is long dead, and of course everything may have happened in his imagination. Nevertheless, an orange occasionally does come floating down the river from somewhere in the mountains and orange trees do not grow by chance in the Sierra Madre. Thus, if it were possible to identify the tributary that empties into this river—if you could do that, my friend, you might be able to locate El Naranjal. But each tributary is fed by smaller tributaries, and each of these by lesser ones. Look at the problem this way: given a gigantic tree, could you find a particular leaf if you began at the trunk and followed one limb after another upward and outward, each smaller than the last, returning again and again to your starting point?

In other words, asleep or awake we dream of treasure, we search for it in numberless directions, and perhaps for an instant we see it from a distance, as blindingly white as the ruins of a hacienda, as green as the foliage of an orange grove. We might even touch it, just as I held three gold doubloons from the bed of the sea. Or, as my father did during the Great Depression, we may slosh ankle-deep through spreading pools of oil. But ultimately some power intervenes.

It may be that treasure exists for the purpose of tantalizing us. If so, how strange. Why should something we passionately desire be subtly withheld?

18

Philippus Theophrastus Aureolus Bombastus ab Hohenheim & Co.

During the Middle Ages it was held that God bestowed a knowledge of alchemy upon Adam, who passed along this wisdom to Abraham, who gave it to Moses, who gave it to Job—who septupled his assets before handing over the secrets to certain illustrious disciples. Other legends concerning the origin of alchemy are more appealing, such as the belief that Nature's ineffable mysteries were betrayed by angels who fell in love with earthly women. But no matter how this art originated, the goal of almost every alchemist was to equal or surpass the accomplishment of Job.

It is true that many of those who spent their lives diddling with retorts and alembics considered the search twofold, philosophic as well as material. That is, they hoped to realize not just the transmutation of common metals but some method by which unhappy Man could shed his greatcoat of imperfections. "False alchemists seek only to make gold," wrote Becher, "whereas true philosophers desire knowledge. The former produce mere tinctures, sophistries, ineptitudes; the latter enquire after the principles of things." Even so, the initial objective from which all subsequent iridescence came streaming was the pot at the rainbow's end: a crucible bubbling thickly with gold.

How was this to be achieved? By the discovery or development of an elusive substance known by various names—stone of Egypt, elixir of quintessence, tincture of gold, powder of projection—but which most often was called simply the philosophers' stone. As to its appearance, whether in fact it was a stone, a liquid, or a powder, every alchemist had his opinion. In short, nothing could be said with certainty about this vital substance except that it represented potential gold, which meant that its color should be red, deep orange, or possibly yellow.

Raymond Lully described it as a small coal, or carbuncle, glowing like fire; though he says that, like a coal, it might first be black, then red, and finally yellow before reaching a state of whiteness. It might even turn green, if necessary. Indeed, the stone might take on any color of the universe, yet it could never be mistaken for anything else because it shone like the eyes of fishes.

Berigard of Pisa, who taught physics during the seventeenth century, said it had the color of a wild poppy and gave off an odor of scorched salt.

Jean-Baptiste van Helmont claimed to have seen the stone and handled it frequently. He said it had the color of saffron, "yet weighty and shining like unto powdered glass."

As to just how this substance was to be concocted, distilled, or perfected—"Poor idiot!" exclaims the alchemist called Artephius. "Could you be so simple-minded as to believe that we would teach you clearly and openly the greatest and most important secrets?"

So the ingredients, their proportions, and the intricate alchemical procedures were expressed vaguely, or in cabalistic language. We are told by Rhazes: "Take of some unknown thing any quantity that you wish." And according to Morenius: "From several things make 2, 3 and 3, 1, 1 with 3 is 4 . . ."

Even when you unscramble alchemical directions they don't make sense. M. *the azothi aoefth epuhiloqosophersa lisati ptheiruri imeracurerty* sounds like Etruscan, but can be restructured to read "The azoth of the philosophers is their mercury." Wonderful. We seem to be making progress. Now what is "azoth"? It comes from the Arabic *al-zāūq*, meaning "quicksilver," which, as everybody knows, is another word for mercury. All right, what have we? The mercury of the philosophers is mercury. So is a rose a rose.

However, nobody said making a pot of gold would be easy. Quite the opposite; the alchemist flings as many obstacles as possible in front of us. The German monk who called himself Basil Valentine took the trouble to write "Visitetis Interiora Terrae, Rectificando Invenietis Occultum Lapidem" in order to avoid writing "vitriol." And once you have translated his Latin you find yourself no nearer the fabulous stone. It's someplace in the bowels of the earth. Good luck.

At times the alchemist refuses even to title his manuscript because the title might provide a clue. Everything must be masked. Everything. Still, there was more than militant perversity in these fantastic circumlocutions: a good many alchemists were murdered—strangled in their sleep—because word got around that they had achieved the miraculous transmutation, and not only would heaps of gold be found in the laboratory but also the recipe. And perhaps a bit of the stone itself. So there was a degree of logic, a not wholly unnatural desire to avoid being strangled, that encouraged him to clothe his works in the rich brocade of allegory and symbol.

Nor were manuscripts the only textbooks: medieval paintings and tapestries are not necessarily what they seem. The diabolic visions of Bosch, for instance, are alchemically precise; and in Paris, in the Cluny museum, you will find a tapestry called "The Lady and the Unicorn," which has to do only incidentally with the relationship between a lady and a unicorn.

In this same museum, bolted to the wall beside a staircase, is the tombstone of Nicolas Flamel who knew how to change lead into silver and mercury into gold. His tombstone, by the way, is not as cold as you might expect; it is oddly warm. I've touched it.

Flamel probably was born at Pontoise, the birthplace of François Villon, just north of Paris, about the year 1330. He received education enough to set himself up as a notary or public scribe in Paris, and is known to have worked in a small wooden booth near the church of Saint-Jacques-la-Boucherie. He lived close by, in a house called At the Sign of the Fleur de Lys, where he gave calligraphy lessons and where he and several assistants produced illuminated manuscripts. His reputation was sufficient to attract ladies and gentlemen of the court who wanted to learn how to write their names. He died March 22, 1417, and was buried in the church, most of which was demolished soon after the French Revolution. At this point Flamel's tombstone disappeared, but turned up years later in the shop of an herbalist on the Rue des Arcis. The shopkeeper was using the smooth back side of Flamel's tombstone as a chopping block for dried herbs. A petshop owner, Monsieur Guérard, then got hold of it, expecting to make a profit, and consigned the stone to a Monsieur Signol who sold antiques. Some years after this the Cluny museum bought it for 120 francs. All of which may seem irrelevant, but is required to prove the existence of Monsieur Flamel.

Our hero displayed no interest in alchemy until he purchased, for two florins, "a guilded Booke, very old and large," whose leaves were made of bark or papyrus instead of parchment. The text was beautifully inscribed with an iron point in clear Latin, supplemented on every seventh leaf with symbolic paintings. Flamel then discovered that he had bought an important book, the *Asch Mezareph* of Rabbi Abraham, which Jewish cabalists thought had been lost forever; and from a converted Jew known as Maître Canches he learned enough to interpret some of it. The book revealed to Jews the art of transmuting ordinary metals into gold so that they could pay the tribute demanded by Roman emperors.

Flamel began a series of experiments that went on for three years and at last believed he had produced the catalytic substance. On January 17, 1382, with his wife Pernelle as witness, he melted half a pound of lead and added to it the white elixir he had devised. The lead promptly turned to silver.

On April twenty-fifth, about five o'clock in the evening, again with

Pernelle as witness, "I made projection of the Red Stone upon the like quantity of Mercurie . . . which I transmuted truely into almost as much pure Gold."

Flamel achieved only three more transmutations—or perhaps three altogether—yet he acquired gold enough to build three chapels, to endow fourteen hospitals, and to make substantial gifts to various churches not only in Paris but in Boulogne, where scholars think his wife was born. According to Jacques Sadoul, "some forty deeds have been found, legally drawn up, showing evidence of the considerable gifts made by the one-time humble Public Scrivener." And apparently it is a fact that Flamel's wealth caused Charles VI to send his chief tax inspector, the Sire de Cramoisy, to investigate. How this investigation ended is unclear, but Monsieur de Cramoisy may have been bribed.

Even so, the size of Flamel's fortune has been disputed. The provisions of his will totaled only about 800 pounds and much less than that was found in his house, an amount not to be kicked aside, but hardly what his heirs expected. And whether he was just a frugal scribe, or whether he actually distilled the philosophers' stone, is another matter not yet settled. We are free, therefore, to believe or disbelieve.

In the spring of 1602 a wealthy Scot named Alexander Seton, who was touring the Continent, got into an argument with a professor of medicine at Freiburg, Johann Wolfgang Dienheim. The two men were on a boat going from Zürich to Basle. Dienheim scoffed at the possibility of alchemical changes and Seton replied by offering to give a demonstration, saying there should be an additional witness, preferably a skeptic. In Basle a test was arranged with several slabs of lead, a crucible borrowed from a jeweler, and some sulfur bought at a shop. Seton, who did not touch either the materials or the apparatus, ordered the lead and sulfur put into the crucible and the crucible placed over a fire. Fifteen minutes later he took out of his pocket a small paper in which there were a few grains of heavy, greasy, lemon-colored powder. He told Dienheim to throw this into the crucible, which was done. Then the lid was put back on. About fifteen minutes later Seton ordered the fire quenched, and when the lid was lifted it was found that the lead had turned to gold. The jeweler attested to its purity. The witness, Dr. Jakob Zwinger, from a prominent Swiss family, wrote a letter to Professor

Emmanuel König in Basle supporting the incident in every detail. Zwinger's letter also states that Seton performed another transmutation before resuming his tour of the Continent, this time for the goldsmith André Bletz.

Seton next appeared in Strasbourg during the summer of 1603, where he worked his magic at the shop of a goldsmith named Gustenheover. Not long afterward he concocted gold in Offenbach, then in Cologne, then in Hamburg, always in front of witnesses, some of whom were given gold souvenirs. However, he made the mistake of demonstrating his art before the Duke of Saxony, Christian II, who had him imprisoned and tortured in an attempt to get the secret. Although he was smuggled out of prison by a sympathizer, Michael Sendivogius, he had been so brutalized that he soon died.

Johann Friedrich Schweitzer was born in Köthen in the duchy of Anhalt in 1625 and became a famous doctor, personal physician to the Prince of Orange. He is better known as Helvetius. Professor E. J. Holmyard has this to say about him: "A man of culture, education, and discernment, he can scarcely be suspected of having lied, or wilfully misreporting the remarkable events he describes."

Helvetius reports that in December of 1666 "came a Stranger to my house in the Hague, in a plebian habit, honest Gravity, and serious authority; of a mean Stature, a little long face, with a few small pock holes. . . ." After discussing transmutation the homely stranger displayed three lumps of the philosophers' stone "each about the bigness of a small walnut, transparent, of a pale brimstone colour." Helvetius asked for a piece and was given a crumb. The visitor then promised to return the next morning to demonstrate how it should be used. At half past nine a message arrived saying he would be there at three in the afternoon "but [he] never came, nor have I heard of him since; whereupon I began to doubt the whole matter."

Nevertheless, being urged by his wife to attempt a transmutation, he cut a small amount of lead which he melted in a crucible. Then the crumb, wrapped in wax, was added to the pot. The mixture began to hiss and bubble and "within a quarter of an hour all the mass of lead was totally transmuted into the best and finest gold, which made us all amazed as planet-struck . . . Truly I, and all standing about me, were exceedingly startled, and did run with this aurified lead (being yet hot) unto the goldsmith, who wondered at the fineness, and after a short trial of touch, he judg'd it the most excellent gold in the whole world, and offered to give me most willingly fifty florins for every ounce of it."

Helvetius refused to sell the gold, and word soon got around The Hague. Master Porelius, controller of the Dutch office of assay, came to see him, inspected the hermetic gold, and demanded that it be tested in a government laboratory. Under his personal supervision it was subjected to the usual tests, after which Master Porelius declared that it was indeed gold of very high quality.

Helvetius then took it to a silversmith named Brechtel who melted it, mixed it with silver, and finally separated the two components. During this process some of the silver turned to gold. The philosopher Spinoza was in The Hague at about that time, and in March of 1667 he wrote to a friend:

> When I spoke to Voss about the Helvetius affair, he made fun of me, and said he was surprised to find me interested in that sort of nonsense. To make sure of my facts, I went to see Brechtel, the man who did the assay. He told me that while it was being melted, the gold had actually increased in weight when they dropped some silver into the pot. . . . Not only Brechtel, but other people who were present when the tests were made have told me that this is a true account of what occurred. After that I went to see Helvetius himself, who showed me the gold and the crucible, that still had some traces of gold on the inner surface. He told me that he had used a piece of the Philosopher's Stone about a quarter the size of a grain of wheat in the melted lead, and he added that he was going to tell everyone in the world about it.

A Swedish general named Paykull, convicted of treason and sentenced to death, offered Charles XII one million crowns a year in exchange for his life, saying that he could make gold artificially. He had learned the secret, he said, from a Polish officer named Lubinski. Charles agreed to a test, supervised by an independent observer, General Hamilton of the British Royal Artillery. All of the materials were examined and every precaution taken against fraud; nevertheless, General Paykull created a lump of gold which subsequently was coined into 147 ducats. A medal was struck to commemorate the event. It is inscribed: O.A. VON PAYKULL CAST THIS GOLD BY CHEMICAL ART AT STOCKHOLM, 1706.

What should we think of such implausible stories?

One might suggest that they be accepted verbatim; after all, not many of us dispute the Christian miracles. But if this answer seems unsatisfactory then we must say that in many cases of "transmutation," probably in most, the miracle was accomplished by sleight of hand. A certain Geoffrey the Elder wrote in 1722: "They often used double-bottomed crucibles or culpels, lining the bottom with oxides of gold or silver, then covering it with an appropriate paste. They also sometimes made a hole in a lump of coal and poured gold or silver into it; or sometimes they soaked coals with solutions of these metals and pulverized them before projecting them on the substances to be transmuted. . . . They stirred fused substances with wands or little wooden batons; these had been hollowed out at one end, filled with gold or silver filings, and then stopped up again. . . ."

Apart from fraud, what explanations could there be?

Self-deceit? At times, yes.

Credulity? Yes.

Ignorance? Of course. In this enlightened age, for example, we know all sorts of things our predecessors did not, such as the fact that many copper ores contain gold. You see what might happen. The alchemist, unaware that gold had been present from the start, deduced incorrectly when he found a trace clinging to the sides of the pot that his own efforts were responsible.

So it's hard to be sure after six centuries just what took place on the seventeenth of January, 1382, in Paris. Or on that day in Stockholm when a treacherous general supposedly coined a lump worth 147 ducats. And Helvetius? One feels a bit uncomfortable discrediting such a man. Even more uncomfortable when it comes time to laugh at Sir Isaac Newton—for Newton, that supreme scientist, thought transmutation was quite possible. His annotated copy of a famous alchemical text, *The Open Door*, is now in the British Museum. As a matter of fact, he and the chemist Robert Boyle were so convinced of alchemical truths that they urged Parliament to prohibit disclosure of the process for fear the gold market would collapse.

Today, plucking details from brittle documents, how do we isolate the truth? What good is Newton's opinion? Who cares that Helvetius was honorable and distinguished? Nor does a medal in a Swedish museum reveal much, no more than Flamel's tombstone or Spinoza's letter.

We do know there were plenty of charlatans, just as engaging and industrious as their descendants. We know they gulled the public, the nobles, and the kings because some were a trifle heavy-handed, and if you care to muck about in the archives you can find out what happened to many of those who were caught. And follow the paths, at least for a while, of some who were caught but contrived to escape. How slippery they were in the good old days.

Our own masters of deceit—presidents, congressmen, generals, industrialists—seem merely vulgar when compared to the Comte de Saint-Germain, alias the Marquis de Montferrat, alias Prince Rakoczi, and so on. Or to Giuseppe Balsamo, who might not have gone far with his own name but did very well as Comte Alessandro di Cagliostro. Or to Jean de Gallans, alias the Baron of Pezerolles, who took the bona fide Duke of Anjou for 120,000 pounds—although, sad to say, Monsieur Jean bowed out of the ducal presence a moment too soon and concluded his performance by imitating a tap dancer high above the ground.

Then there was that slick Neapolitan, Domenico Manuel Caetano. Born in the provinces, he was apprenticed to a goldsmith but seems also to have studied the art of legerdemain, an ominous mixture. Before long he was demonstrating his alchemical skill by producing gold from dross, saying he had learned the science from an old manuscript. And so spectacular were these conversions that he was invited to perform in Brussels before Maximilian Emmanuel, governor of the Spanish Netherlands. Domenico's act must have been impressive because he received 60,000 gulden, either to perfect his art or to arrange a massive transmutation. With this honorarium in his pocket he tried to skip town, but not being as fast with his feet as with his hands he spent the next six years in prison.

Somehow he escaped and popped up in Vienna where he dazzled Emperor Leopold.

Next he appeared in Berlin, conducting a successful experiment before Frederick I and promising to make a generous supply of the philosophers' stone. Frederick, against the advice of suspicious counselors, rewarded him with a variety of gifts and "lucrative offices"; but after a couple of months when the magic stone was not forthcoming the king grew peevish and Domenico decided to visit Hamburg—which he did without bidding his imperial host good-bye. Frederick found out where he was, though, and abruptly changed his address to the Kostrzyn fortress. Domenico, aggrieved at such rude treatment, complained that nobody could make gold in these drafty quarters, so he was escorted back to Berlin. However, he once again chose to leave in the middle of the night. He was caught at Frankfort and returned to Kostrzyn; and Frederick, having mulled things over, decided that the Neapolitan was less than impeccably honest. On August 23, 1709, therefore, dressed in a cloak glittering with tinsel, Domenico Manuel Caetano was suspended from a gilded gallows.

So much for swindlers. They come and go, parasitic, imaginative, voracious as locusts, otherwise meaningless.

Most alchemists, like a fair majority in any age, were not crooked; however unlikely their goal and however peculiar their approach to it, concealing hollow secrets behind a screen of cryptic nonsense, they seem to have been passionately sincere—although at times they wandered sincerely down questionable paths.

For instance, Rudolph von Habsburg, that indecisive, dreamy, optimistic ruler of the Holy Roman Empire. Being convinced that not only his private troubles but all the world's problems could be solved alchemically, Rudolph ordered a large silver coin to be struck which portrayed him with mysterious symbols attached to his coat, and he began assembling a team of highly regarded alchemists at his court in Prague. He built each of them a little house—living quarters and a smelter. These houses, nearly 200 munchkin houses, were situated within the outer wall of the palace, convenient to Prague's apothecary shops, and all day and all night alchemists scurried back and forth, each persuaded that at the appointed time his crucible would yield the magic stone.

Rudolph himself did a certain amount of experimenting and is said to have become engrossed in the work while his authority as emperor was being subverted by his brother, Archduke Mathias. This erosion of power did not trouble him until too late. Then, in a frantic effort to blunt the challenge, he attempted to blend alchemy with sorcery. Hans Holzer states that a Jesuit, Father Damiano, left a diary describing an event that took place in the cellar of the Belvedere adjacent to Hradshin Palace:

> I was summoned by His Majesty to help him with the preparation for the magical invocation His Majesty had in mind in relation to the attacks directed towards him by the Archduke Mathias. I was to secure a small dog which would form part of the experiment.
>
> I did not know what use the animal was going to be put to. . . . His Majesty, dressed in his long cloak and wearing the five-pointed silver star around his neck, seemed unusually grim that evening. Promptly at the stroke of midnight, another man joined us in the enterprise. This was the alchemist Christopher Hauser, lately arrived from Regensburg. . . . Hauser brought with him certain tools, which I recognized as being a brazier, a short knife, a salt cellar, a silver candlestick, and a vial of oil. In addition, I noticed a leather whip, a tool I had never seen before in any of His Majesty's magical evocations.
>
> After His Majesty had consecrated the magical circle in the usual manner with his Spanish sword, and sprinkled salt, then water into the four corners of the room, carried the candle aloft and the brazier around the circle, setting them all down again on a small table in the center which served as altar, His Majesty sat back and allowed Christopher Hauser to take the center of the circle.

Hauser began to invoke the powers of light, at which point, says Father Damiano, the little dog grew frightened and started howling and pulling at the leash. Hauser led it to the center of the circle, touched its head, and the animal sat down, moaning, but otherwise strangely silent.

Hauser then said: "In the name of the Holy Trinity, and in the name of that which is above and also below, I hereby baptize thee, O creature, to the name of Mathias." He sprinkled a few drops of oil on the dog's head, which caused it to let out a dismal howl.

Rudolph stood to one side, ignoring the procedure, gazing straight ahead.

Hauser then began beating the dog with a leather whip. Father

Damiano says that he himself could hardly endure this and wanted to leave, but was afraid of angering Rudolph. So, instead of leaving, the priest "sent thoughts of a pleading nature to His Majesty. . . ."

After having beaten the dog for several minutes, during which time he referred to it as Mathias, Hauser picked up a knife and cut off its head.

So much for the wretched dog, so much for Rudolph. Archduke Mathias soon controlled the Holy Roman Empire.

It should be noted that this crossbreeding of alchemy with black magic was rare; the adept usually was closer in spirit to the mystic than to the sorcerer. In fact there were some who looked down not only on wizards and mountebanks but upon all those who devoted themselves to fabricating gold, calling them "puffers" because of the bellows they used to fan the fire. And of these alchemists one in particular emerges with archetypal clarity—that quasi-genius who proclaimed himself Philippus Theophrastus Aureolus Bombastus ab Hohenheim.

Few recognize him by that grandiloquent title, but as Paracelsus he may sound familiar.

"Many have said of alchemy," he wrote, "that it is for making gold and silver. For me such is not the aim, but to consider only what virtue and power may lie in medicines." And he continues: "The art of medicine is rooted in the heart. If your heart is just, you will also be a true physician . . . one for whom the ultimate instance is man's distress. Privilege and lineage pale to nothingness, only distress has meaning."

All of which is a long way from decapitating a dog or relieving a simpleminded countess of her gold florins. It is equally distant from those curious "transmutations" effected by Flamel, Seton, Helvetius, Paykull, and nobody knows how many others. In those cases the subject was unashamedly material; Philippus Theophrastus focused on Man.

His medical philosophy grew from the belief that astral influences determine sickness and health, and these influences must be countered by secret alchemical prescriptions. Treatment was intended to restore harmony between the private "astrum" of the patient and the heavenly astrum, implying that the essence of a remedy should be celestial. That is to say, the medicine itself would be earthly stuff but its nature should be celestial. A physician, therefore, must acquaint himself with the stars.

For example, he recommended a drink made from black hellebore to patients over fifty years of age, advising them to gather the plant under a full moon. Now you may not think such a brew would do much for a fifty-year-old who feels poorly, but it happens that the dose he prescribed is just right to alleviate certain symptoms of arteriosclerosis. And eventually we may discover that he also happened to be right about the full moon. In short, how do you evaluate this man?

It may or may not help to know what he looked like and where he came from. Several portraits of him exist. He resembles Immanuel Kant, with the skull deformation characteristic of rickets—from which Kant also suffered—but in Paracelsus' case it was the result of desperate poverty, although the Hohenheims once had been rich. His grandfather, in fact, had been a commander of the Teutonic Knights and lord of Hohenheim castle near Stuttgart but lost the estate after a serious political miscalculation.

So Paracelsus grew up poor and sickly. And it is thought, although this cannot be verified, that he was a eunuch. There are at least two stories of how this came about, if it did. In one version he was attacked by a wild boar; in the other, which sounds curiously plausible, a group of drunken soldiers decided to operate on him. In any event, he never associated with women; and he advocated continence, insisting it was better to be a castrate than an adulterer. Nor is there an authentic portrait of him with a beard, which doesn't prove anything—and yet it does, so to speak, fit the picture. He made enemies enough, who salted him with just about every imaginable vice, but he never was accused of lechery. Still, he grew bald, which eunuchs seldom do. Anyway, what we see is an intelligent, somber, middle-aged man with troubled eyes sunk in a huge, domed head.

From the beginning he had been restless. His mother drowned herself in the Siehl River when he was nine, but how this affected him we have no idea. His father then moved to a Tyrol mining community where the boy was put to work in the metallurgy shops, but at fourteen he left home to become a traveling student—drifting from school to school, wearing the traditional velvet hat and yellow scarf.

In Heidelberg, he said, the students devoted themselves more to pleasure than to knowledge. Freiburg he labeled "a house of indecency." Nor did Ingolstadt please him; the lessons were unimaginative. At Cologne the instruction was obscure.

In 1509, aged sixteen, he enrolled at the University of Vienna where he lasted two years, studying the high arts of the time: arithmetic, geometry, music, and astrology. But he grew impatient. "At all German schools," he wrote, "you cannot learn as much as at the Frankfort Fair."

He resumed wandering. The great teachers were known to be in Italy, so he went to Ferrara but his studies were interrupted by war. He fled south and became an army surgeon. It was customary to dress wounds with a poultice of feathers, dung, snake fat, and whatever else looked appropriate. The result usually was gangrene. Paracelsus, with nothing to support his heretical opinion, refused to apply these poultices and to everybody's amazement quite a few of his patients recovered. Though he did on occasion use frog's eggs as a disinfectant, without knowing that they contained iodine. At the same time he thought frost blisters should be treated with children's hair boiled by a red-headed person.

On his way home, tired of army life, he stopped at Würzburg to visit the famous alchemist Johannes Heidenberg, known as Trithemius, whom he seems to have revered all the rest of his life. Yet not even Trithemius could satisfy his deep hunger for knowledge, and in 1517, as Martin Luther nailed that reverberating document to the church door in Wittenberg, Paracelsus set out again:

"No man becomes master while he stays at home, nor finds a teacher behind the stove. . . . I traveled on to Granada and Lisbon through Spain, England, Brandenburg, Prussia, Lithuania, Poland, Hungary, Walachia, Transylvania, Croatia. . . ."

It is now impossible to trace much of this obsessive circuitous journey, but beyond doubt he traveled thousands of miles, staying nowhere very long, telling himself that the next town or the next school or the next master might hold the key to enlightenment.

He turned up in Sweden, then in Russia where he was captured by Tartars. A Tartar prince took him to Constantinople where he either escaped or was freed, because he appears next in Egypt, amazed and alarmed by the sight of "Monsters so fearful you would jump right back into your mother's womb"—presumably hippos and crocodiles.

In 1524 he was home again, at his father's house in Villach, and somewhere he had acquired the huge sword that he carried for the rest of his life and slept with every night. People said that in the hollow pommel of the sword he kept a devil, though it was more likely a supply of his greatest treasure, the drug laudanum.

After a while he moved to Salzburg, but got involved in a peasant rebellion and just escaped the gallows, leaving town with such speed that he did not even pack his belongings. An actuary's inventory at the time lists one compass, one magnetic needle, a portrait of his father, several Oriental garments, fur-lined coats, and a variety of medical unguents.

On the road again, peddling drugs, promising health and long life, he met the duke of Bavaria, who was interested in the possibility of manufacturing gold. The duke already had an alchemist named Kilian on his payroll, but he hired Paracelsus and the two of them went to work in the basement of the duke's castle. Their laboratory was adjacent to the wine cellar, which evokes some images; but after a few months, despite the proximity of the wine, Paracelsus moved along—arguing, belittling, boasting, studying.

He became a citizen of Strasbourg where he promptly entangled himself in a debate with the celebrated surgeon Dr. Vendelinus Hock. Hock knew anatomy, a subject Paracelsus hated and knew nothing about. The result was inevitable. Humiliated and ridiculed, he was driven from the lecture room.

Such a brutal exposure ought to have ruined him; but the great publisher Froben, lying ill in Basle with an infected leg, sent for him. Froben's doctors were ready to amputate, which in those days very often meant the end of the patient. Paracelsus contrived to save the publisher's leg, probably by intuition rather than by knowledge, and at the same time met Erasmus who was living on the upper floor of Froben's house.

The contrast between Erasmus and Paracelsus could hardly be more graphic. As Henry Pachter, a biographer of the alchemist, puts it: "One was the most refined Latinist, the other sought to make his coarse Swiss dialect a language of science. One was fastidiously neat; the other wore an alchemist's smeared apron. One was a master of innuendo, the other given to outspoken abuse. One was the most balanced mind of his time, scrupulously weighing each word, the other a mystic, rash of judgment and fond of speculation. The one lived with books, the other considered life the only book of value."

Several letters between them have been preserved. The two did not care much for each other, yet there was mutual respect; and when Erasmus did not feel well he wrote to Paracelus for advice. "I cannot offer thee a reward equal to thy art and knowledge—I surely offer thee a grateful soul. Thou hast recalled from the shades Frobenius who is my other half: if thou restorest me also thou restorest each through the other."

What doctor could resist such a gracious, elegant patient?

Paracelsus diagnosed the ailment and prescribed a cure.

Erasmus responded courteously, thanking him, but declined the treatment: "At present I have no time for a cure, indeed I have no time either to be sick or to die, for I am engaged in exacting studies. . . ."

Paracelsus stayed in Basle longer than he had anticipated, forcing himself like a splinter into its midst. When he was appointed municipal doctor and given a university professor's office a new quarrel blossomed, which he encouraged by being rude not only to his antagonists but to his friends. He was told that, although he might be a professor, no lecture halls were available. He retaliated by scheduling class off campus, and appeared for his first lecture dressed in the traditional academic robe; then with a melodramatic gesture he tore off the robe to reveal his sooty old alchemist's apron. The students, of course, loved it.

So he went about his affairs in Basle, seeing patients, writing outrageous pamphlets, experimenting with drugs and herbs and distillations, lecturing, drinking prodigiously, insulting everybody.

To a citizen who offended him, his reply began: "So then, you wormy and lousy Sophist . . ."

According to one Johannes Herbst, who worked for Paracelsus:

> The two years I passed in his company he spent in drinking and gluttony, day and night. . . . Nevertheless, when he was most drunk and came home to dictate to me, he was so consistent and logical that a sober man could not have improved upon his manuscripts. . . . Often he would come home tipsy, after midnight, throw himself on his bed in his clothes wearing his sword which he said he had obtained from a hangman. He had hardly time to fall asleep when he rose, drew his sword like a mad-

> man, threw it on the ground or against the wall, so that sometimes I was afraid he would kill me. . . . He was a spendthrift, so that sometimes he had not a penny left, yet the next day would show me a full purse. I often wondered where he got it. . . . He did not care for women and I believe he never had doings with any. In the beginning he was very modest, so that up to his twenty-fifth year, I believe he never touched wine. Later on he learned to drink and even challenged an inn full of peasants to drink with him and drank them under the table, now and then putting his finger in his mouth like a swine.

"He is said to have received the philosophers' stone during his 28th year," wrote Jöcher in the *Scholar's Dictionary*, "and knew how to go about making gold, which is why he spent money like hay, often not having a penny left at night but loaded with bags of money next morning. . . . The rumor is, he made a pact with the devil."

On Saint John's Day, June 24, 1527, Paracelsus surpassed himself. Into the traditional campus bonfire went the accumulated rubbish of a year, whatever the students did not need or like. And into the fire this year—at his command—went a gigantic book, the greatest of all medieval medical books, the *Canon* of Avicenna. It was too big to be carried; it had to be dragged to the ceremonial fire.

"There is more wisdom in my shoelaces," said Paracelsus, "than in such books."

He, and he alone, Philippus Theophrastus Aureolus Bombastus, henceforth should be regarded as the supreme authority.

"I am a rough man, born in a rough country," he wrote later. "I have been brought up among pines, and I may have inherited some knots."

The Basle establishment was of that same opinion. After he publicly accused the clergy and magistrates of corruption, they decided the best way to silence the knotty professor was to imprison him. Some friends at last convinced him of the danger and he left Basle in the middle of the night, hours ahead of the police.

He fled to Neuenburg, then to Colmar in Alsace where he was given a temporary resident's permit. But his permit was not renewed; he had become too controversial.

He moved to a village in Württemburg where he resumed studying astronomy; years later the house where he had lived was renovated and the chimney and roof were found to be covered with astrological signs.

Nuremberg was the next stop. Sebastian Franck in *Chronica of Our Times* wrote: "Item Dr. Theophrastus ab Hohenheim, a physician and astronomer. Anno 1529, said doctor came to our town; a peculiar and wondrous man . . ."

Here, as usual, he antagonized influential citizens, especially the doctors, and once more was obliged to flee. It had become the pattern of his life. He would arrive, impress himself with overpowering strength on a community, challenge its authorities, alienate those whose support he needed, and be expelled. "They drove me out of Lithuania and Prussia," he complains, "and from Poland, and still it was not enough for them. The Dutch did not like me either, nor the schools, neither Jews nor monks . . ."

But constant rejection, instead of depressing him as it does most men, seems to have stimulated him. One observer, struck by his furious energy, noted that he seldom slept: "he never undresses, throws himself on his bed with boots and spurs, rests for three hours, then gets up and continues to write."

What he was writing about were matters never before discussed—"invisible diseases"—leading toward modern concepts of gynecology and human psychology: "I am not embarrassed to be the first who dares to write on the diseases of women. . . ." Martin Luther, whose name always has outshone that of Paracelsus fifty times over, was commenting at about the same time: "If women die in childbed, that does no harm. It is what they were made for."

And he understood, as perhaps no one else did, that the cause of erratic behavior might not be a devil but an emotional crisis. In the sixteenth century he was explaining that weak personalities could be shaken by the force of their instincts. Such people should not be condemned, he argued; instead, they deserved treatment.

He wrote of faith healers: "It is not the curse or the blessing that works, but the idea. The imagination produces the effect." Man's imagination, he said, "is like the sun, whose light cannot be touched and yet may set a house on fire. It guides man's life."

"As we desire things in our hearts," he said, "so they appear to us in dreams."

The name he suggested for the disease we call Saint Vitus' dance was "chorea lascivia," indicating that he realized its sexual origin.

Yet his cures might include camphor and mandrake mixed with "quintessence of gold"—medieval remedies prescribed by a man whose intellect was centuries ahead of his time.

Germany in 1532 was disrupted by religious disputes; and Paracelsus, congenitally unstable, resumed wandering, almost aimlessly, always searching. But he has changed; now he worries about personal salvation: "The time of geometry has come to an end, the time of art is over, the time of philosophy has come to an end. The snow of my misery has thawed. The time of growing has ended. Summer is here and I do not know whence it came. It is here. Now is the time to write of many things on which I have ruminated for years, namely of blessed life. . . ."

Then he continues: "The world cannot be gained by astronomy, which has little value except for its own sake, nor by medicine, which lacks power over all diseases, nor by philosophy, which is held in contempt. . . . Where I had seen flowers in alchemy, there is but grass."

The deterioration of belief so affected him that not only his temperament but his appearance changed. He paid little attention to insults, he fasted, he began to give away his clothes and money, and he abandoned alchemical experiments. He meditated, tried to help the poor, preached, wrote incoherent moralistic tracts. Dramatic conversions are not unusual but they are always unexpected, and in this case the resemblance to Leo Tolstoy is startling.

He decided there were two kinds of wisdom, one eternal, the other mortal. "I started out in the Light of Nature . . . and finished in the Light of Eternity."

He subsisted by begging, complained about those who would not give him a bowl of soup, and found himself an outcast. Wherever he went, the door slammed.

"I have sickness in me, my poverty and piety."

And, of course, the more he was ignored or abused the more desperate became his message. If the wealthy and powerful would not listen to him they must ultimately hear the message of the Apocalypse.

And lo!—it arrived.

Plague.

The town of Sterzing was struck. Most of its citizens fled, leaving sick relatives and friends to rot. Paracelsus, indifferent to his own safety, hurried to Sterzing where he helped care for the victims. Yet as soon as the plague subsided the town burghers ordered him to leave. So he left, meanwhile bestowing a fresh title on himself: Professor of Theology. And, very much like his old self, he addressed a letter to the authorities of Sterzing, denouncing them for bigotry, stupidity, and hypocrisy, railing especially against the Catholic priests whom he considered responsible for his eviction. He scorned all ecclesiastics. Luther and the pope, he said, were two whores discussing chastity.

From Sterzing to the village of Merano, where he seems to have been treated with respect; but his private crucifixion forced him to leave. He moved to Saint-Moritz, but once again was unable to find a home.

He returned to the Tyrolean metallurgy shops where he had worked as a boy, and the result of this visit was the first essay ever written on an occupational disease: *Von der Bergsucht*, concerning respiratory infections suffered by miners. Tradition ascribed such sickness to the displeasure of mountain spirits who guarded the veins of ore; Paracelsus attributed the problem to metallic vapors.

In 1536 he published a book on surgery. Ambroise Paré usually gets credit for being the first to emphasize cleanliness after surgery; but Paracelsus, a generation earlier, offered the same advice.

Other books followed. *Occult Philosophy*. *Explanation of Universal Astronomy*. And his masterpiece: *Sagacious Philosophy of the Great and Small World*, which considers man, salvation, geometry, the healing power of stones, meteorology, phrenology, witches, ghosts, sorcerers, and just about everything else. Someday, he prophesies, the human voice will be carried long distances "by the aid of pipes and crystals." He speculates on mirrors to project images across mountains, or even into the future. "Man possesses the capability of seeing his friends and how they live, though they are 1,000 miles away."

He reveals his formula for creating the homunculus:

"If the sperm, enclosed in a hermetically sealed glass, is buried in horse manure for about forty days and properly 'magnetized', it begins to live and to move. After such a time it bears the form and resemblance of a human being, but it will be transparent and without a corpus. . . ."

While he wandered across Europe his father died. Paracelsus

returned to Villach to claim the estate but the townspeople did not think he was a reputable successor. He departed meekly, without his inheritance. Then the prince bishop of Salzburg offered him asylum, so there he went and there he lived until his death the following year. He was forty-eight. The cause of his death is not known. Enemies said he was killed during a tavern brawl; friends believed he died from an overdose of that great elixir he carried in the pommel of his sword.

He left very little: ten guilders to one of his mother's relatives, twelve guilders to the executors, some surgical instruments and ointments to the Salzburg barbers, and several boxes of manuscripts. He did not bequeath his manuscripts to anybody; he did not think anybody deserved them.

"I have traveled throughout the land," he wrote, "and was a pilgrim all my life, alone and a stranger feeling alien. Then Thou hast made grow in me Thine art under the breath of the terrible storm in me."

Not long after his death a legend began to take shape, that of man's infinite desire for knowledge—and Dr. Faustus was born.

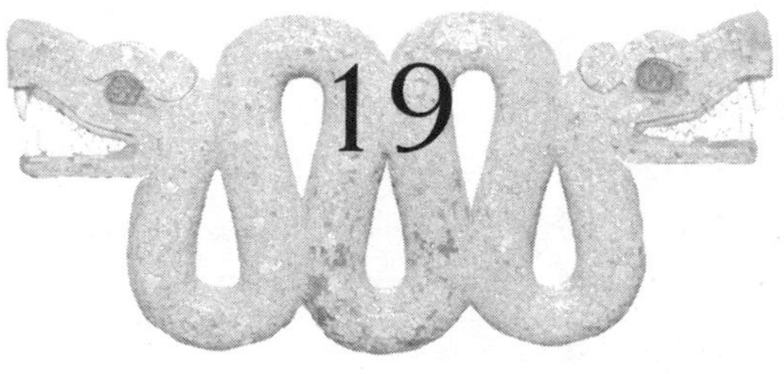

19

Mesa Verde

IN JULY OF 1776, TWO THOUSAND miles southwest of Philadelphia, Fathers Francisco Atanasio Domínguez and Silvestre Vélez de Escalante left Santa Fé to enlighten savages and establish a route to the California presidio at Monterey. With these Franciscans went a retired artillery officer and cartographer, Captain Don Bernardo Miera y Pacheco, and seven other men including a native interpreter who had been given the name Andrés Muñíz.

Two years earlier Escalante had served as pastor of Nuestra Señora de Guadalupe de Zuñi, and while there he visited the land of the Moqui Indians in what is now Arizona. From the Moquis he learned about an impassable gorge farther west, and he heard rumors of cannibals. Escalante therefore concluded that a safer route to California must be found—possibly by traveling north through the land of the Yutas. In his journal he wrote that the expedition hoped to reach California "without noise of arms" and without profiteering at the expense of such Indians as they might encounter.

On the twenty-ninth, having implored the protection of their most holy patrons and received the Eucharist, they started up the juniper-covered ridge north of Santa Fé, followed by pack animals and a herd of cattle which they intended to butcher as required. On their right lay the Sangre de Cristo range, on their left the Río Grande. They rode past the Indian pueblos of Tesuque, Nambé, Pojoaque, and San Ildefonso, crossed the river and paused that night at the mission of Santa Clara, having made nine leagues.

Next day they rode up the Chama River valley to the mission of Santa Rosa de Abiquiú, beyond which lay no Spanish settlement. On August 1, after celebrating Holy Mass, they proceeded northwest toward the land of the Yutas. Father Escalante writes that a good shower fell upon them and they traveled seven leagues.

August 2. They lost track of four animals in a dense grove of oaks. Luckily, these animals were recovered; and after emerging from the oak trees they came to an agreeable little plain alive with flowers resembling carnations. Here also were trees bearing a red fruit the size of blackthorn which tasted like lemon.

Continuing northwest, they entered what is now Colorado.

There is much rain, Escalante writes. All feel the cold. Father Domínguez suffers from rheumatic fever.

August 13. They remained encamped beside the Río Dolores so that Captain Miera could employ the astrolabe to determine their latitude, but also with the hope that Father Domínguez might improve. Escalante considers the land. There is adequate pasturage, plenty of timber, the soil could be irrigated. He climbs to the summit of a hill where in ancient times there must have been a tiny village of Indians—crumbled walls, the earth littered with broken pottery. And from this hilltop Escalante could not help seeing Mesa Verde on the southern horizon; but the immensely long green mesa did not interest him enough to mention it in his journal. Father Domínguez being somewhat better, Escalante writes, they will resume their journey the next day.

Some leagues farther north they are overtaken by Juan Domingo and Felipe, two men from Abiquiú of mixed blood, for which reason Escalante refers to them as a *genízaro* and a *coyote*. They had fled Abiquiú without permission in order to accompany the explorers. To send them back might create mischief, so they are allowed to stay.

Mid-September found the expedition in Utah. Captain Miera fixed their latitude by the polestar at 41° 19', near the present town of Jensen. Six large black cottonwoods grew in pairs at this site, and there was another growing by itself on whose trunk Don Joaquín Laín cut a rectangular space with an adz so that he might chisel the year: 1776. Don Joaquín then added his name—LAÍN—in very big letters, with crosses to either side.

The travelers continued westward almost to Great Salt Lake, about which they were told by Laguna Indians. At this point they decided to turn south before venturing again toward California.

September 29. They met a very old Indian living by himself in a hut like the hermits of Europe. He had a long thick beard. By means of the interpreter, this old man told them about a river they would come to and described the country they must cross, directing them to a pleasant meadow where they camped, which they named Santa Ysabel. Here, by the polestar, Captain Miera fixed their latitude at 39° 4'.

Next morning twenty strange Indians arrived, all wrapped in blankets made from rabbit skins. They had much heavier beards than the Lagunas and through the cartilage of their noses they wore polished bone ornaments. By their features they might almost be Spanish. Andrés Muñíz explained to them the unity of God, the necessity of Holy Baptism. They listened with great docility, saying they would do whatever they were taught if only the Fathers would return. And when the expedition departed, they wept copiously. From a long distance one could hear the lament of these miserable little lambs of Christ who had strayed merely for lack of teaching. This place was named Llano Salado because so many seashells covered the ground that it looked white as salt.

October 5. Misfortune. The Laguna called José María disappeared, leaving them without a guide. Two men went forward to look for some way across the western sierra. After dark they returned, saying they had found no pass whatever. Thus, Escalante writes, since they were unable to take this direction, which offered the best hope of reaching Monterey, it was resolved to continue south. But for several days a fierce wind has blown out of the south; now the peaks and plains are mantled with snow.

In the morning when they awake it is snowing. All day the snow falls. They dare not move. They implore the intercession of their Mother and Patroness, reciting in chorus the three parts of her Rosary and of all the saints, singing the litanies. At nine o'clock that night God willed that the snow should stop.

Because of excessive cold and snow they are unable to leave on the next day, and the day after that with great difficulty they travel just over three leagues.

According to Captain Miera, their latitude is not far above Monterey, but they have advanced only 136 leagues toward the west. Because of this, and the terrible cold, and the fact that Indians they have met know nothing about any Spanish colony—because of all this Fathers Escalante and Domínguez begin to reconsider. The sierra as far as can be seen is white with snow. There is not much food. If they go on searching for a route to Monterey it is possible they will subject themselves to death by starvation, if not from cold. It would be wiser to proceed south to the Río Colorado and from there turn eastward through the land of the Moquis and Zuñis. By doing so, with the help of God they might reach Santa Fé.

When the Franciscans came to this decision they were some three hundred miles west of Mesa Verde, but still very far from California, less than halfway from Santa Fé to the Pacific.

Their decision did not please Captain Miera, or Don Joaquín Laín, or the interpreter Muñíz. The reasons for returning to Santa Fé were explained, but instead of appreciating the force of the argument they opposed it with their own views and grew insubordinate. These three talked of how fruitless the journey would be. What previously had been discovered—a vast region inhabited by untutored people willing to attach themselves to the Lord's vineyard—seemed of no value. And then, because Captain Miera had gorged their simple heads with nonsense, the servants began to object and say it was but another week to Monterey.

Fathers Domínguez and Escalante chose to absolve themselves of responsibility by casting lots. If God willed that they should proceed toward Monterey, that would they do; if He willed that they should return to Santa Fé, that would they do. But if the lot fell to Monterey there should be no one to direct their course save Captain Miera, since he thought it so near. Then, the insurgents having said the third part of the Rosary and other petitions, Fathers Escalante and Domínguez having said the penitential psalms and the litanies that follow—this being concluded, the lot was cast. It fell to Santa Fé.

Next day the explorers overtook some badly frightened Indian women who had been gathering seeds. Father Escalante notes that they wear only a few scraps of buckskin hanging from the waist—which scarcely covers what cannot be looked at without peril. According to these women, there are people farther south who wear blue clothes, but it is impossible to learn what this means.

By mid-October the expedition is in northwestern Arizona. They have almost no food. Captain Miera is sick. They resolve to take the life of a horse in order that they might not lose their own.

October 23. Tortuous canyons, mesas scored by stony arroyos—this land is inhospitable. They encounter a few wretched Indians to whom they preach, but the Indians will not sell them any food. Although members of the party carry guns, Domínguez and Escalante will not authorize force, so they are obliged to eat roots, seeds, whatever they can swallow. Father Domínguez suffers from pain in the rectum.

Three weeks later, starving, they name one campsite in honor of the porcupine they have caught. Its flesh seems delicious compared with what they ate the previous night, a patch of toasted horsehide. Yet, when distributed among so many people, the taste of porcupine only makes them hungrier.

Finally they begin to see the ranchos of Cosnina Indians, then Moqui cattle herds, and at nightfall on November 24 they come to the Zuñi mission where Escalante had served as pastor.

December 28. They reach the mission of San Francisco Javier de Albuquerque.

January 2. Completing a ragged circle, they arrive in Santa Fé.

Captain Miera's report of this journey, addressed to the King of Spain, opens with a protestation of his desire to spread the Holy Faith and to serve His Sacred Royal Catholic Majesty. Miera then speaks of traveling through vast areas and visiting many tribes named in the journal of Father Escalante and shown on a map which he, Miera, has drawn. The journal and the map are enclosed by order of Don Pedro Fermín de Mendinueta, governor of New Mexico.

There is no doubt, Miera explains, that many unenlightened tribes long for baptism, since with tears in their eyes they have manifested such a desire. But in order to harvest these souls it will be necessary to overcome certain obstacles, not only the great distance which separates them from Santa Fé, but also the barbaric Apaches whose warriors terrorize neighboring tribes. Also the Moquis—who inhabit a sterile region of steep red cliffs near a tremendous canyon of the Río Colorado—these Indians must be brought down by force from their cliffs, since even though they do not make war they are obnoxious. And to accomplish this it would be advisable to establish three presidios with adjacent settlements. By such means will a door be opened to colonization with all attendant benefits, thus recompensing the royal treasury.

The second of the presidios that Captain Miera wished to establish lay at the junction of the rivers Animas and Nabajóo—now called the San Juan—just southeast of Mesa Verde. And he informed his king that in this territory there yet could be found vestiges of irrigation ditches together with the ruins of ancient pueblos.

Captain Miera's report is dated October 26, 1777.

In 1824 an American trader and trapper, William Becknell, wrote to Governor Bartolomé Baca requesting a license to pursue his business in Spanish territory. When this license was granted, Becknell replied courteously: "I shal Cum an see you when I Cum in from the Woods the winter is approchin."

Becknell's party left Santa Cruz de la Cañada, just above Santa Fé, on November 5. Their exact route is not known, nor is the location of their winter quarters, but they must have set up camp very close to Mesa Verde, possibly within the boundaries of the present national park. They noticed broken pottery, well baked and nicely decorated, together with the remains of little stone houses, some of which had been constructed partly underground.

Becknell was no tenderfoot; nevertheless he underestimated the Colorado winter. Snow piled up to such a depth and the cold grew so intense that trapping became almost impossible. He and his men retreated as soon as they could, which was not until the beginning of April, and reached the comparative warmth of New Mexico with very few pelts to exchange.

An intrepid young lawyer named Orville Pratt traveled through the

Dolores valley en route to the west coast in September of 1848. He may have camped near Father Escalante's hill, or perhaps a few miles farther south, quite literally in the shadow of the mesa. In either event, he failed to mention this conspicuous landmark; nor did he think much of the environment, which he described as less than desirable. Whether he, like Becknell and Escalante, wandered through the detrius of earlier lives is a matter for speculation.

Eleven years later the San Juan Exploring Expedition set out from Santa Fé under the leadership of Captain J. N. Macomb to survey the uncharted region of Utah. With Macomb went a geologist, Professor John Newberry, and when the expedition approached Mesa Verde he climbed the north rim to get a better view of the Colorado plateau. Presumably he looked all around, and having noted that the sandstone formation belonged to the Cretaceous period, Professor Newberry rejoined his party. From the rim, he said, all was terra incognita.

In 1861 another trapper or trader or solitary adventurer climbed the mesa and carved that date after his name on the wall of a disintegrating cliff house: T. Stangl. How long this man stayed, who he was, and what other ruins he visited have not been learned.

In 1873 a group of prospectors led by one John Moss settled just north of Mesa Verde. They remained for several years, ranching and mining. Moss and a few companions explored Mancos Canyon where they noticed apartments stuck to the cliffs high above, but they had come looking for gold or silver so they did not investigate.

At this same time photographer William Henry Jackson was at work with a government territorial survey in the San Juan Mountains, and there he chanced to meet an old friend from Omaha named Cooper who had gone prospecting with Moss. Cooper thought Jackson might like to take pictures of some old cliff houses in a Mesa Verde Canyon. Jackson would indeed, so Cooper directed him to John Moss. Oh yes, said Moss, the ruins were there, all right. On September 9, 1874, Jackson and five associates started out, guided by Moss. They got back three weeks later, having circled the mesa. Jackson wrote in his 1876 report of the Hayden Survey that it was rough country, a jungle of dense grass interlaced with grapevines as tough as wire, on a thick mat of undergrowth. The banks of the Mancos River were perpendicular and the bottom muddy, making it exceedingly difficult to cross. He suspected there might be other cliff dwellings in the deep branch canyons.

This was Ute Indian territory and the Utes did not like these explorations. At first they did nothing because they were distracted by traditional enemies to the south—Hopis and Navajos. Besides, these Bearded Mouths did not stay very long and some of them, such as John Moss, gave presents. But still the whites kept coming. More and more settled in the Mancos valley where they built cabins, planted fields, and looked for gold. After a while the Utes began to retaliate; a settler's cow, for instance, might be found with its tongue cut out. The Bearded Mouths took to carrying rifles.

Among these immigrants was a peripatetic Pennsylvania Quaker named B. K. Wetherill, who arrived in 1880 with his wife and their five sons and one daughter. Just northeast of Mesa Verde he built a shingle-roofed log cabin. Things went pretty well. B.K. and his sons got along with the suspicious Utes. The old Quaker had not packed a gun during his travels through Oklahoma Territory, nor did he show a gun in Colorado, and no doubt the Utes observed this. Whatever the reason, they allowed his cattle to winter in Mancos Canyon and in the Mesa Verde branch canyons. Because the Utes tolerated him, Wetherill's Alamo Ranch expanded—corrals, barns, a reservoir, enclosed pastures. The *Mancos Times* called it "one of the most beautiful and fertile mountain farms in the West."

Richard Wetherill, the eldest son, built a cabin in Mancos Canyon so that somebody could winter near the herd, and one day an old Ute named Acowitz appeared. Richard knew him. Acowitz lived not far away. Their conversation turned to a canyon on the opposite side of the river. Acowitz said that near the head of this canyon were houses built by the ancient ones—those who have vanished. He, Acowitz, and other Utes had seen these houses, although they had not gone inside because the abandoned houses were sacred. Richard asked how to find them, but Acowitz would say nothing else.

Sometime after this, in December of 1888, Richard and his brother-in-law Charles Mason were hunting stray cattle on the mesa. They dismounted to rest their horses and walked out on a rocky point. Through falling snow Richard saw a deep recess in the cliff facing them half a mile away. Among the shadows he could see the outline of an enormous apartment house with a high round tower. Stray cattle could wait. The ranchers descended to the canyon floor and then made their way up to the ruin. They wandered through one room after another, leaving boot tracks in dust that had been accumulating for centuries. Almost everywhere they looked they saw painted clay mugs, bowls, water jars, and other household objects, as though the people who had lived here would return at any moment. It occurred to them that the inhabitants might have fled during an attack, an idea substantiated by the discovery of three skeletons. Conquistadors looking for the gold of Cíbola might have been responsible. In any case, afternoon was drawing down and they were anxious to see what else the canyon held. After collecting a few pots they decided to go exploring separately. Charles Mason found nothing significant, but Richard Wetherill saw another cliff house through a fringe of spruce trees. The implications were profound.

Many years later an ex-government surveyor, Chapman Ballard, claimed that he and members of his party discovered the huge apartment house—which Richard Wetherill named Cliff Palace—during the summer of 1875. Ballard had come west to enlist in the U.S. Army at Fort Garland, but at the last moment he changed his mind. He said the Seventh Cavalry was then stationed at Fort Garland and had he done as he planned he might have died with Custer. Mr. Ballard's account seems questionable to some extent because the Seventh Cavalry was then stationed not at Fort Garland but at Fort Lincoln, Dakota Territory, hundreds of miles away. Whatever the facts, he said the government surveying party to which he belonged was fixing the north boundary of the Ute reservation when somebody saw Cliff Palace. There were ten or eleven men in the group, and from where they were at work on the opposite side of the canyon it was very plain to see. They went over to investigate, he said, and found lots of broken pottery. Whether or not this discovery had been mentioned in the government report, he didn't know.

"I was alone the day I first got a glimpse of the Cliff Palace," Richard Wetherill's brother Al wrote in 1945. "But I was too tired to do anything about it—and that is why there has been some confusion over its discovery."

Al, Richard, and a visitor from Fort Lewis, Dr. George Comfort, had gone prospecting for ruins one summer day in 1887. Richard and Dr. Comfort rode horseback up Johnson Canyon, but Al decided to walk through Cliff Canyon. Along the way he saw an apartment and climbed up the slope only to find that it had been nearly demolished by the trappers or miners who sometimes came down from the La Plata range. Those people, he wrote, were just like government surveyors—pot hunters who would wreck a cliff house in the hope of finding something to sell. Deeper in the canyon he saw Cliff Palace through an opening in the trees. He would have climbed up for a look if he had realized how big it was. Instead, after meeting Richard and Dr. Comfort, he told them what he had seen. By this time it was late in the day, so they returned to the ranch. Not until December of the following year did Richard Wetherill and Charles Mason walk out on the rocky point that Al had described.

Regardless of who first saw Cliff Palace—trapper, miner, surveyor, cowboy—he had better things to do than shuffle through a collapsing prehistoric apartment house. For the Wetherill family and Charles Mason this meant tending cattle at Alamo Ranch, so there they worked; but whenever possible they continued to search, and as more ruins were found their collection of artifacts increased.

They thought the people of Durango would be interested, so in the spring of 1889 the Wetherill collection went on display. Several hundred citizens visited the exhibit and there was talk of buying the relics, but nothing happened; Durango cared less for Mesa Verde's past than for Durango's future.

The Wetherills took their antique cooking pots, ladles, broken mugs, axes, arrowheads, and everything else across the San Juan range to Pueblo. The citizens of Pueblo, being more sophisticated, ought to be interested. Not at all. The collection was ridiculed.

On to Denver. Surely the cosmopolitan people of Denver would understand. Again it was rejected.

Meanwhile, back at the ranch—which is to say, not very far from Alamo Ranch—Mason and the fourth Wetherill brother, Clayt, had found a mummified child, which they shipped to Denver. Well! This was more like it. As if by magic the crowd increased. And having feasted its eyes on this wrinkled brown child, the public began to look more attentively at old pots, axes, and mugs; and among those visiting the exhibit was a representative of the Denver Historical Society who thought that if a fair price could be arranged, the Society would purchase the lot. Richard consulted his brothers. Three thousand dollars seemed a fair price, so the collection moved to the Denver Chamber of Commerce building.

In December of 1889 the Wetherill brothers and Mason began to search the canyons more systematically, and by the following spring they had located almost two hundred cliff houses. Quite obviously Mesa Verde was a site that deserved professional attention. Richard Wetherill wrote to the Peabody Museum at Harvard and to the Smithsonian, asking if they would sponsor the work, or if not, whether they might assign somebody to supervise it. Neither organization chose to get involved, although the Smithsonian did say that if the Wetherills wished to contribute some artifacts the institute might be willing to accept them. Al commented years later that it would have been difficult to satisfy the Smithsonian requirements because Alamo Ranch was the Wetherills' first responsibility. Assembling a first-rate collection would be expensive, and like most ranchers they had their hands full just trying to meet the mortgage payments.

Consequently, the five brothers and Mason went on excavating and collecting without professional guidance.

John Wetherill wrote about breaking into one room that had a concealed entrance. After leveling a section of wall he began to shovel out the debris. Burial matting turned up, remnants of a three-colored belt or cinch—red, white, black—and a complete arrow with an agate point. He called Mason. Together they dug into the earth. A few more shovels of dirt exposed a large basket. Then they struck an important burial: five bodies in a row, separated by four ceramic bowls. Not far from this group lay a man with a hunting bow at his side who wore nothing but a pair of moccasins, and next to him were the skeletons of three babies. Underneath was a mat covering the entire floor. The ranchers pulled it up. They found the skeleton of a man who could have been a sorcerer, buried with his ceremonial stick and two pouches made from prairie dog skin.

Life had ended abruptly in another apartment: a family of four had been murdered, their skulls smashed by a stone ax. The man lay on his back in a curious position, arms outflung, his legs thrust up the ventilating shaft. A little boy, presumably his son, sprawled across one of his arms. Nearby lay a woman with her baby. Someone, perhaps the killer, had thrown a mat over the man's body. The ax was still there. Richard was able to fit the blade into the fractures.

News of such prehistoric dramas brought a great many visitors to Alamo Ranch, and the Wetherills profited by escorting tourists through the ruins. Al estimated that between 1889 and 1901 they had perhaps one thousand sightseers. Among them was a boy who eighty years later could recall how he had entered the dusty rooms only after the guide tossed a quarter-stick of dynamite inside to scare away rattlesnakes. Nor had he forgotten the discovery of four skeletal Mesa Verdeans leaning against a wall.

Another visitor was a prosperous Connecticut druggist with a taste for mountaineering, Frederick Chapin. Unlike most, he declined to go pot hunting; he seemed content to sketch and photograph, and upon returning to Connecticut he wrote a paper for the Appalachian Mountain Club. After a second visit in 1890 he wrote *The Land of the Cliff-Dwellers*, which included photographs and data from both excursions. In style and outlook Chapin was very much a nineteenth-century Romantic. While the traveler meditates, "his horse's hoofs clink among broken pottery, and, if he will but bend from his saddle, he will see in profusion the fragments of the ware of the prehistoric tribes. . . . Crowning the cliffs, and built upon the cañon's brink, he will catch sight of the picturesque towers, from whose walls the primitive sentinels watched and guarded the approaches to peaceful valleys below." He explores a canyon named for Acowitz: "No sounds were heard to disturb the scene but the croaking of ravens."

In the summer of 1891 a young Swede named Gustaf Nordenskiöld came visiting. He had contracted tuberculosis on a voyage to Spitsbergen, and after three months at a German clinic he toured Italy with the idea that his health might improve. From there he sailed to America. He saw the Wetherill collection while he was in Denver and decided to spend a week at Alamo Ranch. A letter to his family, dated

June 27, mentions that he has safely reached Colorado and has bought a ticket to Durango: "I am going there to look at the cliff dwellers; on my way I shall visit Pikes Peak and many other places."

Late one evening, after a thirty-mile buggy ride from the Durango railroad station, he drove into the yard of Alamo Ranch, told the Wetherills who he was, and asked if they would show him around Mesa Verde.

Of course! They were delighted to do so after the indifference and ridicule they had endured, and they were further delighted because Nordenskiöld came from a scientific family, all the way back to his great-great-grandfather who had been director general of saltpeter boileries in Finland. Gustaf's father, Adolf Erik, chief of the mineralogical department at the Swedish Royal Academy, was an honorary member of various scientific organizations and had been granted the title of baron by King Oscar II after successfully navigating the Northeast Passage. The Wetherills had heard about Baron Nordenskiöld's famous voyage. So they were more than simply pleased to welcome young Gustaf, and they soon realized that despite his youth he understood better than any of them how to excavate these fragile buildings.

Gustaf wrote to his parents that on his first trip with Richard and Al they rode twenty-four miles down the Mancos valley to a place called "Blowout" because of a volcanic extrusion. Next day, from atop the mesa they entered a cliff house by descending steps cut into the rock by people who had lived there centuries before. On the following day they studied petroglyphs, several of which Gustaf copied.

When he returned to Alamo Ranch after a week at the cliff dwellings he was obsessed. He wrote his parents that he meant to stay at least a month, possibly two. Al Wetherill's memoirs state that the young man's enthusiam "had increased almost beyond his control." He wanted to find out who these people were, where they had gone, and why; he wanted to know everything about them. Financial support was needed. He proposed making a collection of antiquities which could be displayed in Stockholm, and he was anxious to get started. He thought Long House in Navajo Canyon would produce what they wanted.

Such exuberance sounds naïve, especially when one reflects that Gustaf had no formal training in archaeology and that he was just twenty-three, but a high order of intelligence accompanied this excitement: "Before I determined upon the more extensive researches and excavations required to gain a thorough knowledge of the cliff villages and their former inhabitants, I wished to undertake some preliminary work on a smaller scale." This he did, helped by Richard and Al. Together they rummaged through dusty debris and pulled out scraps of cloth, fragments of animal hide, bone implements, sandals, ears of corn—all perfectly preserved.

In one letter to his father, Gustaf mentions that, apart from their Denver collection, the Wetherills had accumulated a great deal more, which they would sell for $8,000. Could this material be purchased for public display in Sweden? And with the inquiry Gustaf enclosed a catalogue: mummy of child with fine brown hair, bones of another child wrapped in feather cloth, mummy of woman found in rock tomb five hundred feet above canyon bed, skeleton of man dressed in fringed suit of tanned skins with bow and arrow at his side, skull of cliff dweller with brown whiskers. Then there were less disconcerting antiquities such as cedar-bark headbands, a baby board cushioned with corn tassels, toy animals, turkey-bone awls, corn husks filled with salt, grinding stones. jet ornaments, a goatskin suit, a jar of walnuts—altogether some five thousand specimens. And in that same letter Gustaf comments that no photographs exist of these astonishing ruins. He wonders if his camera might be shipped to Colorado, along with a barometer.

Adolf Erik Nordenskiöld shipped the barometer and camera, but replied that funds to purchase this collection were unavailable. Gustaf went home in the spring of 1892, and like Frederick Chapin he at once began to write about his experience. He concluded by saying: "It is reserved for future research to carry out a careful investigation of the numerous archaeological remains."

The artifacts he wanted to buy eventually were displayed at a Minneapolis industrial exposition. Later they became part of the Wetherill exhibit at the 1893 Chicago World's Fair—housed not so aesthetically in a fake cliff dwelling at the end of an artificial canyon—where they competed with Egyptian belly dancers, cotton-candy booths, a Ferris wheel, and other midway attractions. Richard supervised the exhibit, answering the same questions again and again. Evidently he wanted to look inconspicuous, because he wore a conservative suit and a white shirt bought just for the occasion, but his frontier mustache and the wind wrinkles around his eyes belonged to a man from somewhere else.

In 1908 the Department of the Interior asked a prominent ethnologist, Dr. Jesse Fewkes, to direct the preservation of ruins at Mesa Verde; and with his arrival began that era of scientific investigation predicated by Gustaf Nordenskiöld. Dr. Fewkes had been digging through the Southwest for twenty years, notably in Arizona, where he had turned up a number of elegant prehistoric Hopi bowls. So meaningful and expressive were these bowls that the celebrated potter Nampeyo, who lived not far away, came by to watch Dr. Fewkes at work. One day Nampeyo borrowed a pencil and paper in order to copy some designs; and ever afterward, Fewkes observed, her pottery was decorated with modified prehistoric symbols. "The extent of her work, for which there was a large demand, may be judged by the great numbers of Hopi bowls displayed in every Harvey store from New Mexico to California." These clever imitations, though, he warned the prospective buyer, were not so fine as the originals; hence a collector should be cautious.

A photograph of Dr. Fewkes taken at Mesa Verde in 1908 or soon thereafter shows a scholarly little gentleman wearing a baggy suit and a necktie. For some reason he has taken off his hat, probably because the brim would shade his face. He has a white Vandyke beard and a sun-darkened bald head, and from his expression it is obvious that he enjoys his work. He is standing outside Mesa Verde's first museum, essentially a log cabin, next to a table piled high with ancient pots and human bones.

What cannot be deduced from this picture of Dr. Fewkes is a streak of mysticism. An unpublished manuscript in the Smithsonian archives recounts a ghostly experience at the so-called Sun Temple, where he lingered one afternoon. There appeared "an influence," which gradually assumed the form of a gigantic bird much like an eagle, and Dr. Fewkes realized that the sun had returned to its abode in order to deliver a message. This apparition identified itself as the archaic god of fire and said that it was followed by the Kachinas, its children, who would communicate their thoughts to him. From a nearby grove of cedars came a rustling noise. Various shadowy personages emerged. First, according to

Dr. Fewkes, was an old man wearing the kilt of a Pueblo priest who declared that he inhabited Aztec ruin, forty miles away. This spectral figure said Aztec was being excavated, as Dr. Fewkes knew quite well, because archaeologist Earl Morris was working there. The apparition went on to say that Morris was doing a good job: "I rejoice exceedingly that the life of my people is being revealed by archaeology and my pueblo repaired and preserved for all time for students and visitors."

The Kachinas spoke up. They too applauded all this scientific investigation, specifically praising the National Geographic Society for sponsoring a project in Chaco Canyon some distance south of Mesa Verde. "The last visitor disappeared as noiselessly as the others," Fewkes wrote, "and as the darkness increased I followed the trail on foot back to my camp, pondering on the visitation."

Dr. Fewkes has been criticized by later archaeologists, not so much for his engaging fantasies as for inadequate field notes and inaccurate maps. Also, while attempting to protect several early sites he poured concrete over the walls. This would prevent water seepage, he thought, although in fact the concrete soon cracked and further destabilized the walls.

Fewkes' penchant for communing with ectoplasm implies a less-than-rigorous mind, but it is understandable because there always has been an aura of mystery about these cliff houses. A century ago Frederick Chapin speculated and struggled mightily to visualize ages past, wondering if a deserted apartment might not become a museum "filled with relics of the lost people." So did the Wetherills, those hard-boiled Colorado ranchers. Al, the most imaginative, addressed poems to the ancients, and in his memoirs he wrote that while excavating ruins he and his brothers could almost see men at work in the fields, see women busy at their looms or grinding corn, could almost hear dogs barking, turkeys calling.

Alfred Kidder, who would become the dean of southwestern archaeology, worked at Mesa Verde as an apprentice in 1907. One morning he descended to a pool of rainwater below Cliff Palace and as he knelt for a drink he looked straight into the eye sockets of a skull. Rain had washed out the grave of a large man, carrying most of the skeleton over the edge of a cliff, but Kidder located his jawbone, part of his pelvis, and a shoulder blade. After climbing back up to Cliff Palace with this treasure he fitted the jaw to the skull and then paused for lunch. Many years later he remembered the experience with great clarity. How had this cliff dweller come to his end? Was he born here? If so, in which apartment did he live? How long ago?

In 1917 the peak of romantic fancy was scaled by a Denver woman, Virginia McClurg, when she and her Cliff Dwellings Association staged a pageant titled "The Marriage of the Dawn and the Moon" amid the ruins of Spruce Tree House. Afterward the audience settled down to Mrs. McClurg's idea of a prehistoric banquet: roast calf, baked ears of maize, and peaches. According to present evidence, however, this is not exactly what the Indians ate. During winter it was apt to be cornbread, beans, and dried meat—fox, deer, coyote, mountain sheep, rabbit—week after week. Spring brought cornbread and beans, as usual, along with juniper berries, wild onions, edible roots, fresh meat, tansy mustard, beeweed, and a fungus-like growth called puff ball. Then came squash, more beans, more cornbread, maybe piñon nuts.

The menu, relevant as it may be to a scientific reconstruction of prehistoric life, does not interest Mesa Verde visitors quite as much as the inherent mystery of empty rooms. Where did these people come from? When did they build these apartments? Why did they leave? Where did they go?

Dr. Fewkes, for one, might be disappointed that not much mystery remains. A century of research has established the presence of nomadic hunters on southwestern mesas and valleys and deserts for thousands of years. By the beginning of the Christian era there were temporary villages, and somewhat later the nomads perceived that raising crops was easier than chasing animals. High country holds little water, but Mesa Verde provided enough for several hundred people, so they dug pit houses and then built slab-sided homes above ground. Why they abandoned these in favor of cliff dwellings is one of the few imperfectly answered questions. No doubt it was warmer in the caves, secluded from wind sweeping the mesa top, and nearly all of the caves in which they built their apartments opened to the south. Or there might have been some religious or psychological motivation. Or the move could have been defensive. Kidder thought it obvious that the people were afraid.

Afraid of what? Of whom? He would not speculate. In any event, during the eleventh century they began to move from the mesa top to the cliffs.

An astronomer at the University of Arizona, Dr. A. E. Douglass, who had been studying the relationship between sunspots and the earth's climate, inadvertently created a science—dendrochronology—which dated these ruins. Astronomers for a long time had noticed sunspots. A Chinese sky-watcher reported them in 28 B.C. and Galileo saw a good many through his telescope in 1611—an observation that almost cost him his life, because the Church taught that celestial bodies were eternal and unblemished. Later astronomers had found that temperature changes on earth coincided with sunspot activity; and because tree growth is affected by climate, Douglass reasoned, a pattern of solar activity should be reflected by a pattern of tree rings.

Accordingly, he asked several archaeologists working in the Southwest to send him core samples of logs from ancient pueblos. His work culminated in 1929 with a tree-ring calendar, which proceeded further and further backward from logs known to have been cut at a certain date. And out of this came proof that the Cliff Palace discovered by Richard Wetherill and Charles Mason was under construction in the year 1073. Spruce Tree House was built and/or reconstructed between 1216 and 1262. Earliest and latest dates for the Balcony House apartments were 1190 and 1206. Earl Morris sent core samples from Aztec, forty miles southeast of Mesa Verde, which Douglass fitted into the years 1110 to 1121. So it went.

This concept of tree-ring dating was not original. Gustaf Nordenskiöld had tried to count the rings of a tree growing through masonry of a cliff house and concluded that the house was at least two hundred years old. Four centuries earlier Leonardo da Vinci had studied the idea, and no doubt there were perceptive men before Leonardo who suspected a correlation, but Douglass turned surmise into science.

The last date from Mesa Verde was 1273. In some areas the canyons are almost inaccessible, which means that other ruins could be found and might give dates after 1273, but this seems unlikely.

Why did these people quit building? Pollen analysis, in conjunction with tree-ring charts, suggests a definite change in climate. From the beginning of the ninth century until the middle of the eleventh, the Mesa Verde region was colder than it is now, with about as much rain—not very much. For the next century it was a little warmer. Then a long period of dry cold ensued, with less and less rain or snow, and the narrow tree rings speak of extreme drought from 1276 to 1299. These cliff dwellers were accustomed to dry years, several in a row; but according to Douglass' record, which covered many centuries, there never had been anything like twenty-three consecutive years of drought. So it is believed that one family or clan after another left the mesa in search of water and warmth, and perhaps by the close of the thirteenth century all were gone.

Harold Gladwin, director of Gila Pueblo Museum in Arizona during the 1930s, mistrusted tree-ring charts and pointed out that a narrow ring does not necessarily indicate deficient moisture. Also, the growth of a tree depends mostly on winter precipitation, not summer rainfall; annual rings are thus an unreliable index of summer crop conditions. Then too, it was known that Mesa Verde people were moving south at least fifty years before the long drought. Gladwin proposed a different and far more dramatic explanation—a wave of aggressive newcomers sweeping down the east slope of the Rockies: "As the Athabascan horde increased . . . it split, and some bands who were to become the Navajo turned to the west, attracted by the prosperous and exposed settlements in Chaco Canyon and on Mesa Verde. The remainder, later to be known as Apaches, continued south to the Upper Gila, to raid the Mimbres, Cíbola, and Mogollon villages."

These northern predators first plundered outlying farms in what is now New Mexico, and by the year 1250, having ravaged southwestern Colorado, they began to attack Mesa Verde's fortified apartment houses. As the frequency of such raids increased, the cliff dwellers began to leave, and of course each departure left those who remained more vulnerable. Gladwin thought it was all over by the year 1280: "A few of the fortresses to the west may have lasted a few years longer, but they were picked off one by one." By the end of the century no Mesa Verde people were left alive north of the San Juan River.

Archaeologist Neil Judd reported in 1964 that throughout the high country one could hear tales of ancestral warriors who defeated the cliff dwellers and set fire to their houses; and according to Dr. Fewkes, Ute Indians had a tradition that their ancestors killed many of the ancients.

Charles Mason wrote in 1917: "The final tragedy of the cliff dwellers probably occurred at Cliff Palace. There is scarcely room to doubt that the place withstood an extended siege."

When Mason and Richard Wetherill first entered this ruin they discovered that nearly all of the wood had been removed. Only two timbers were still in place. Even the slender willow joists used to support the mud roofs were gone. Mason thought the wood must have been used as fuel. Also, a great many valuable objects were smeared with clay—perhaps an attempt to hide them from enemies. Furthermore, disconnected human bones suggested massacre. "It seems to me that there can be no doubt that the Cliff Dwellers were exterminated by their more savage and warlike neighbors, the men being killed and the women being adopted into the tribe of the conquerors."

This brutal scenario has been modified by later archaeologists and ethnologists. Contemporary wisdom holds that the Utes, Apaches, and Navajos were nibbling at the edges of a civilization already crippled by climatic change. And if this were not enough, the cliff dwellers might have deforested the mesa, leaving very little to put in the fireplace. They might have killed off most of the game, or depleted the soil through excessive farming, and a rudimentary social system could not respond to unusual stress. If there were priests, which is the usual state of affairs, their authority may have been weakened by ominous black spots crawling across the sun, by diminishing rain, by the hardship of lengthening winters. Thus, if the emptiness cannot be specifically explained, neither is it inexplicable.

Whatever the primary cause, whatever its tributaries, these people felt compelled to move; yet they left behind so many possessions that some of them must have expected to return. A strangeness hangs over all.

Joyce Kayser, who interviewed an old woman of the Southern Ute tribe, reported that when this woman was very young she was told by an old man that as a youth he had watched the ancients construct one of their buildings at Mesa Verde—or maybe it was Aztec. The old woman no longer was sure, it had happened so long before. The old man who was then a youth had said that men and women worked together carrying stones and sand and water, and that they dressed alike—the men and the women—which surprised him. They looked like ants, they were so little. Much later he went back to the place and saw the house was finished, but those who built it were gone. He thought they had gone to the south or southeast. He never saw them again.

Another old Ute reported that his great-grandfathers used to hunt in Mancos Canyon where they saw cliff dwellers who were like phantoms that disappeared into the piñon if a Ute came near. They spoke a language that the Utes could almost understand.

What became of these people? Again, it is less mysterious than one might think. A noticeable increase in the size of Río Grande pueblos, as well as of several pueblos farther west, toward the end of the thirteenth century suggests an influx of Mesa Verde emigrants. And it is considered very possible that some of these northern San Juan people moved into Arizona, where they at first joined and later intermarried with the Hopis—the Moquis visited by Fathers Domínguez and Escalante.

The two Franciscans on their historic journey had marched around a civilization, but knew no more of it than scattered potsherds on a piñon-covered hill.

20

Messages on a Sandstone Bluff

CAPTAIN GASPAR PÉREZ DE VILLAGRÁ relates in *Historia de la Nueva Mexico* that he expected his miserable life to end at any moment when—famished and burning with thirst—he discovered a pool of water at the base of some lofty cliffs. The year was 1598, and the sandstone bluff where he found water faces the Zuñi Mountains in western New Mexico. Spanish explorers of the next century would call it El Morro, a name perhaps derived from *morra*, a Basque word meaning the crown of the head. Nineteenth-century Americans would call it Inscription Rock, because a gallery of prehistoric pictographs mingled with Spanish and English names and messages for several hundred yards along the base.

Capt. Villagrá belonged to the colonizing expedition of Don Juan de Oñate. Just why Villagrá was alone in this arid land is not entirely clear; but he had lost his horse, which plunged into a pit dug by Indians, and he was almost dead when three of Oñate's soldiers accidentally found him. His sword and dagger were missing, his feet were swollen so badly that he was unable to walk; according to Oñate's journal, the captain had eaten nothing for several days.

Seven years later Oñate would camp beside the pool of water where Captain Villagrá nearly died, and he would leave this announcement on the cliff:

> Paso por aquí el adelantado Don
> Juan de Oñate del descubrimient de
> la mar del sur a 16 de Abril de 1605.

That is, he passed by this place after discovering the Sea of the South—the Pacific. Oñate had marched some 600 miles to the Gulf of California 15 years before the Pilgrims touched Plymouth Rock.

Paso por aquí . . . appears again and again.

Along came a certain captain-general of the provinces of New Mexico, assumed to be Gov. Don Juan de Eulate, whose 1620 message on El Morro stated that he had subdued the Zuñi pueblo with clemency, zeal, and prudence, being a great gentleman and gallant soldier not apt to be forgotten. Somebody in the party thought less of his character because *gran caballero* was scratched out, almost obliterated.

Spanish efforts to Christianize the Zuñi and Hopi were at times nominally successful; more often the result was sullen compliance, deceit, or hostility. Fray Francisco Letrado became the first martyr, killed at Zuñi pueblo on February 22, 1632, a week or so after his arrival. Father Letrado may have antagonized the natives by insisting that they attend mass on a day that was important to their own religion. Whatever the cause, soldiers left Santa Fe to avenge his death. One member of this company carved an ominous warning on the rock:

> Se passaron a 23 de Marzo de 1632
> años a la venganza de muerte del
> Padre Letrado.

In 1680 the pueblo natives revolted, butchering 400 settlers, officials, and priests. Those who escaped the massacre fled south along the Río Grande to El Paso, and for the next twelve years the Indians lived as they had always lived. Then came a Spanish army led by the redoubtable Diego José de Vargas Zapata y Lujan Ponce de León y Contreras, who quickly reconquered New Mexico. On the cliff his name is abbreviated:

> Aqui estubo el General Don Diego
> de Vargas, quien conquisto . . .

Gen. Juan Paez Hurtado passed this way on a tour of inspection, July 14, 1736. Beneath the general's name is another, carved with less authority, probably in haste, by a corporal who lagged behind to immortalize himself: *y en su compania el Cabo, Joseph Truxillo*.

One year later the most illustrious Bishop of Durango, Don Martín de Elizacochea, paused at El Morro. Two inscriptions a few yards apart, but cut in the same style, suggest that both were done by his secretary, *el Bachiller Don Juan Ignacio de Arrassain*—a bachelor of law or of the arts.

Many travelers who camped by the pool, or at least stopped to drink, are unknown. *Por aqui paso Andres Romero*. Who was he? Where was he going? The inscription dates from 1774. Beyond that, scholars have learned nothing.

Then came the Americans:

> Lt. J.H. Simpson USA & R.H. Kern
> Artist, visited and copied these
> inscriptions, September 17th 18th 1849.

Simpson was an army engineer. His report begins: "The incidents of to-day have been peculiarly interesting. . . ." Interesting, too, is a slight mistake. Instead of "inscriptions," it is "insciptions"—with a tiny proofreader's mark below the word pointing to a tiny "r" above.

Simpson describes El Morro as quadrangular, about 250 feet high, "of a pearly whitish aspect." The natural buttresses reminded him of heavy Egyptian architecture. That night he and Kern talked about what they had seen—"the grim visage of the stupendous mass behind us occasionally fastening our attention by the sublimity of its appearance in the dim twilight." Simpson had trouble sleeping; he ascribes this to the hard ground, excitement, and howling wolves.

More and more Anglo names decorated the rock as the nation pushed westward.

Lt. Edward Fitzgerald Beale, formerly of the U.S. Navy, subsequently employed by the Department of Indian Affairs, arrived in 1857 at the head of a camel caravan. This may sound implausible, but the desert Southwest had to be crossed. What better vehicle than the famous ship of the desert? Accordingly, the government bought some camels in Syria, Turkey, and/or Egypt. By one account, the beasts were assembled at Smyrna and shipped to Indianola, Texas, for training. In any event, twenty-five camels under the command of Lt. Beale, assisted by a Virginia Military Institute graduate named P. Gilmer "Peachy" Breckinridge, plodded out of Texas toward the West Coast. This remarkable column included a Syrian camel driver known as Hi Jolly because he saluted one and all with the Levantine greeting: "Hadj Ali!"

Lt. Beale & Co. reached El Morro on August 23, 1857. His animals undoubtedly drank quite a bit of the pool. From El Morro they proceeded at a dignified pace, eventually reaching California.

Beale and Breckinridge returned two years later, adding their names to the roster. *Lieut. Beale*—on the wall of a shallow cave—is difficult to see. Breckinridge, less introverted, carved his name where the sun would shine on it, using stately capitals in the so-called tombstone style. He was killed fighting for the Confederacy at Kennon's Landing, Virginia, in 1863.

Not long after Beale's 1857 visit an emigrant train stopped for water. It was led by a Baptist preacher from Missouri named John Udell, and trailed by a herd of cattle. Quite a few members of this party scratched their names on the cliff. Udell noted his age, 63, and *First Emigrant*—with the letter "n" reversed—just under the inscription by Gen. de Vargas. From El Morro these wagons followed the camel route, but on the east bank of the Colorado River there was trouble with Mohave Indians. Eight emigrants were killed, others wounded, and Mohaves stole most of the livestock. California suddenly had become an impossible dream, so the party turned around and walked back to New Mexico.

Ten years after Udell's tragic journey a crew of Union Pacific surveyors visited the historic rock, which explains why several names are accompanied by UPR, as though they were fraternity brothers.

In 1906, Teddy Roosevelt declared El Morro a national monument.

A tract of 160 acres was set aside. The proclamation warned all persons "not to appropriate, excavate, injure or destroy said monument. . . ."

Eighty miles west of Albuquerque a two-lane blacktop loops south from Interstate 40 and climbs through scrub evergreens to the Zuñi reservation. Except for the narrow road, this high desert probably looks very much as it did when the earliest hunters arrived. Weathered sandstone mesas, dusty slopes, juniper, piñon, cactus. At 7,800 feet one rolls across the Continental Divide and presently turns left to the ranger station.

Inside, a museum displays just about what one expects: artifacts, pottery, written summaries, illustrative scenes. Unexpectedly, though not illogically, there is the tarnished steel helmet, breastplate, and long sword of a conquistador.

Outside, everything becomes subordinate to the cliff. One hears the wind like a distant river, maybe the croak of a raven. Otherwise the silence is that of all ancient, uninhabited places. Nothing overshadows the cliff, nothing approaches.

The writer Mary Austin visited El Morro in 1923. Presumably she drank from the pool because she describes the water as "sweet," blue, and amber-shadowed. Today it is murky green and looks poisonous, with some ugly little amphibians called mud puppies nosing through the bulrushes and spiders skating on the surface. Unless you are as thirsty as Capt. Villagrá, you probably will not stoop to drink. Although decades have passed since Austin's visit, she would find the pictographs unchanged: mountain sheep, lightning bolts, votive hands, stick-figures, geometric forms, parrots—brought by traders from old Mexico en route to Chaco—snakes, deer, and one creature that must be a lizard but resembles a crocodile. High above, indifferent to human concerns, migratory swallows have plastered the vertical palisade with hundreds of mud nests.

Finally, around the north face where the sun rarely shines, a path leads to the a summit. Here the wind sings as it has from the beginning, and if you are subject to vertigo you do not stand close to the edge because the big ponderosa pines are far below.

Here, mostly underground, are the remnants of two A'ts'ina pueblos—a Zuñi word that means writing-on-rock. Both were built during the late thirteenth century, but were abandoned after sixty or seventy years. Why? Drought? Enemies? There is no water on the summit unless it rains, so why did the Old Ones settle on top? They might have been afraid to live below where they were vulnerable. Or perhaps they liked the view.

The small ruin has not been touched, and the National Park Service has excavated only one corner of the large pueblo. Two ceremonial rooms, *kivas*, are exposed. One is round, the other square. Round *kivas* were built by the Anasazi people of the northern Four Corners area: Utah–Colorado–Arizona–New Mexico. Square *kivas* were built by the Mogollon people of southern Arizona and New Mexico. On top of El Morro these cultures met. What brought them together? If the day is pleasant, you might see a couple of butterflies playing tag in the wind above the ruins. Maybe it's that simple.

Mary Austin fell in love so deeply with El Morro that she wanted to be buried on the cliff. This could not be done—her ashes are cemented into a boulder of the Sangre de Cristo range overlooking Santa Fe—but she expressed her great love in *The Land of Journey's Ending:* "You, of a hundred years from now, if when you visit the Rock, you see the cupped silken wings of the argemone burst and float apart when there is no wind; or if, when all around is still, a sudden stir in the short-leaved pines, or fresh eagle feathers blown upon the shrine, that will be I . . ."

BIBLIOGRAPHY

Alter, Dinsmore. *Pictorial Astronomy*. Los Angeles, 1948.

Anton, Ferdinand, and Frederick J. Dockstader. *Pre-Columbian Art*. New York, no date.

Arbman, Holger. *The Vikings*. Translated by Alan Binns. New York, 1961.

Arciniegas, Germán. *The Knight of El Dorado*. Translated by Mildred Adams. New York, 1942.

Ardrey, Robert. *African Genesis*. New York, 1967.

Armitage, Angus. *The World of Copernicus*. New York, 1947.

Arrhenius, Olaf W. *Stones Speak and Waters Sing*. Mesa Verde National Park, 1984.

Ashe, Geoffrey. *The Quest for America*. New York, 1971.

———. *Land to the West*. New York, 1962.

Bakeless, John. *The Eyes of Discovery*. Philadelphia, 1950.

Banti, Luisa. *The Etruscan Cities and Their Culture*. Translated by Erika Bizzarri. Berkeley, Calif., 1973.

Baring-Gould, Sabine. *Curious Myths of the Middle Ages*. Boston, 1904.

Basham, A. L. *The Wonder That Was India*. London, 1954.

Berenguer, Magín. *Prehistoric Man and His Art*. Translated by Michael Heron. Park Ridge, N.J., 1973.

Berlitz, Charles. *Mysteries from Forgotten Worlds*. New York, 1972.

Berrill, N. J. *Journey into Wonder*. New York, 1952.
Bickel, Lennard. *Mawson's Will*. New York, 1977.
Blindheim, Joan. *Vinland the Good*. Oslo, 1970.
Bloch, Raymond. *Etruscan Art*. Greenwich, Conn., 1965.
———. *Etruscans*. New York, 1958.
Boland, Charles M. *They All Discovered America*. New York, 1963.
Bolton, H. E. *Pageant in the Wilderness*, 1950.
———. *Coronado*. *Albuquerque*, N.M., 1949.
Brace, C. Loring. *The Stages of Human Evolution*. Englewood Cliffs, N.J., 1967.
Brandon, S. G. F., ed. *Ancient Empires*. New York, 1973.
Brebner, John Bartlett. *The Explorers of North America*. New York, 1937.
Brent, Peter. *Captain Scott*. New York, 1974.
Briggs, Walter. *Without Noise of Arms*. Flagstaff, 1976.
Brodrick, James. *Galileo*. New York, 1964.
Brown, Peter Lancaster. *Comets, Meteorites & Men*. New York, 1973.
Brundage, B. C. *Empire of the Inca*. Norman, Okla., 1963.
Brunhouse, Robert. *In Search of the Maya*. New York, 1974.
Bureau of Land Management. *Domínguez and Escalante Ruins*. Dolores, Colorado, 1988.
Burgess, Robert. *Sinkings, Salvages & Shipwrecks*. New York, 1970.
Bushnell, G. H. S. *Ancient Arts of the Americas*. New York, 1967.

Calvin, Ross. *Sky Determines*. Albuquerque, N.M., 1948.
Cameron, Ian. *Antarctica*. Boston, 1974.
de Camp, L. Sprague. *Lost Continents*. New York, 1975.
de Camp, L. Sprague, and Catherine de Camp. *Citadels of Mystery*. New York, 1973.
Carlson, Kathy Nielsen. *Gustaf Nordenskiöld*. Swedish-American Historical Quarterly, Vol. XLIV, 1993.
Caron, M., and S. Hutin. *The Alchemists*. Translated by Helen R. Lane. New York, 1961.
Cary, Max. *Ancient Explorers*. London, 1963.
Casson, Lionel. *The Ancient Mariners*. New York, 1959.
Ceram, C. W. *The First American*. Translated by Richard and Clara Winston. New York, 1971.
———. *The March of Archaeology*. Translated by Richard and Clara Winston. New York, 1970.
———. *Gods, Graves, and Scholars*. Translated by E. B. Garside and Sophie Wilkins. New York, 1967.
Cerquone, Joseph. *The Domínguez and Escalante Expedition of 1776*. Denver, 1976.
Chapin, Frederick. *Land of the Cliff Dwellers*. Tucson, 1988.

Chapman, Walker. *The Golden Dream*. New York, 1967.
———. *The Loneliest Continent*. Greenwich, Conn., 1964.
Christensen, Erwin O. *Primitive Art?* New York, 1955.
Clark, Wilfrid Le Gros. *Man-Apes or Ape-Men*. New York, 1973.
Cleator, P. E. *Lost Languages*. New York, 1962.
Cles-Reden, Sibylle von. *The Buried People*. Translated by C. M. Woodhouse. New York, 1955.
Clissold, Stephen. *The Seven Cities of Cíbola*. London, 1961.
Coe, Michael. *The Maya*. New York, 1966.
Cohen, Daniel. *Mysterious Places*. New York, 1969.
Columbus, Christopher. *Journal*. Translated by Cecil Jane. New York, 1960.
Constable, George. *The Neanderthals*. New York, 1973.
Cottrell, Leonard. *Lost Worlds*. New York, 1964.
———. *Wonders of Antiquity*. London, 1964.
Cousteau, Jacques. *Diving for Sunken Treasure*. Translated by J. F. Bernard. New York, 1971.
Crone, G. R. *The Explorers*. New York, 1962.
Crow, John A. *The Epic of Latin America*. New York, 1971.

Daniel, Glvn. *Man Discovers His Past*. New York, 1968.
———. *Myth or Legend?* New York, 1968.
Dart, Raymond A. *Adventures with the Missing Link*. New York, 1959.
Day, Arthur Grove. *Coronado's Quest*. Berkeley, Calif., 1940.
Debenham, Frank. *Antarctica*. New York, 1961.
———. *Discovery and Exploration*. Garden City, N.Y., 1960.
Descola, Jean. *The Conquistadors*. Translated by Malcolm Barnes. New York, 1957.
Deuel, Leo. *Testaments of Time*. New York, 1965.
———, ed. *The Treasures of Time*. New York, 1962.
Dickson, F. P. *The Bowl of Night*. Cambridge, Mass., 1968.
Diringer, David. *Writing*. New York, 1962.
Ditfurth, Hoimar von. *Children of the Universe*. Translated by Jan van Heurck. New York, 1974.
Divine, David. *The Opening of the World*. New York, 1973.
Dobie, J. Frank. *Apache Gold and Yaqui Silver*. New York, 1939.
Doblehofer, Ernst. *Voices in Stone*. Translated by Mervyn Savill. New York, 1961.
Dunaway, Philip, and Mel Evans, eds. *Great Diaries*. Garden City, N.Y., 1957.

Edey, Maitland. *The Missing Link*. New York, 1972.
Edson, Lee. *Worlds Around the Sun*. New York, 1969.
Eiseley, Loren. *Darwin's Century*. Garden City, N.Y., 1958.

Emmerich, André. *Art Before Columbus*. New York, 1963.

Engl, Lieselotte, and Theo Engl. *Twilight of Ancient Peru*. Translated by Alisa Jaffe. New York, 1969.

Eydoux, Henri-Paul. *History of Archaeological Discoveries*. Translated by Joan White. London, no date.

Federmann, Reinhard. *The Royal Art of Alchemy*. Translated by Richard Weber. Philadelphia, 1969.

Ferguson, William M. and Arthur H. Rohn. *Anasazi Ruins of the Southwest*. Albuquerque, 1986.

Fernández-Armesto, Felipe. *Columbus*. New York, 1974.

Finley, M. I. *Aspects of Antiquity*. New York, 1969.

Franzén, Anders. "Ghost from the Depths: The Warship *Vasa*," *National Geographic*, vol. 121, no. 1. Washington, D.C., 1962.

Franzén, Greta. *The Great Ship* Vasa. New York, 1971.

Gaddis, Vincent. *Invisible Horizons*. Philadelphia, 1965.

Gardner, Martin. *Fads and Fallacies*. New York, 1957.

Gay, Carlo. *Xochipala*. Princeton, N.J., 1972.

Ghiselin, Brewster, ed. *The Creative Process*. Berkeley, Calif., 1952.

Gladwin, Harold Sterling. *History of the Ancient Southwest*. Portland, 1957.

Golden, Frederic. *Quasars, Pulsars & Black Holes*. New York, 1976.

Goodman, Edward J. *The Explorers of South America*. New York, 1972.

Gould, Rupert. *Oddities*. New York, 1965.

Gray, George Zabriskie. *The Children's Crusade*. New York, 1972.

von Hagen, Victor. *The Golden Man*. London, 1974.

———. *Realm of the Incas*. New York, 1957.

Hakluyt, Richard. *Voyages*. New York, 1965.

Halliburton, Richard. *His Story of His Life's Adventure*. New York, 1940.

Hamblin, Dora Jane, ed. *The Etruscans*. New York, 1975.

Hart, Henry. *Sea Road to the Indies*. New York, 1950.

———. *Venetian Adventurer*. London, 1942.

Hawkins, Gerald. *Splendor in the Sky*. New York, 1969.

Heer, Friedrich. *The Medieval World*. Translated by Janet Sondheimer. New York, 1969.

Heizer, Robert F. *Man's Discovery of His Past*. Palo Alto, Calif., 1969.

Hencken, Hugh. *Tarquinia and Etruscan Origins*. New York, 1968.

Hermann, Paul. *The Great Age of Discovery*. Translated by Arnold Pomerans. New York, 1958.

———. *Conquest by Man*. Translated by Michael Bullock. New York, 1954.

Herold, J. Christopher. *Bonaparte in Egypt*. New York, 1962.

Herring, Hubert. *History of Latin America*. New York, 1968.
Hibben, Frank C. *Digging Up America*. New York, 1960.
Holand, Hjalmar. *A Pre-Columbian Crusade to America*. New York, 1962.
Holmyard, E. J. *Alchemy*. Baltimore, Md., 1957.
Holzer, Hans. *The Alchemist*. New York, 1974.
Hordern, Nicholas, et al. *The Conquest of North America*. Garden City, N.Y., 1973.
Howell, F. Clark. *Early Man*. New York, 1973.
Howells, William. *Mankind in the Making*. Garden City, N.Y., 1967.
Hoyle, Fred. *Nicolaus Copernicus*. New York, 1973.
Humble, Richard. *Marco Polo*. New York, 1974.
Hus, Alain. *The Etruscans*. Translated by Jeanne Unger Duell. New York, 1961.

Ingstad, Helge. *Westward to Vinland*. Translated by Erik J. Friis. New York, 1969.
———. *Land Under the Pole Star*. Translated by Naomi Walford. New York, 1966.

Janvier, Thomas. *The Aztec Treasure House*. New York, 1918.
Jensen, Hans. *Sign, Symbol and Script*. Translated by George Unwin. New York, 1969.
Jones, Gwyn. *A History of the Vikings*. London, 1973.
———. *The Norse Atlantic Saga*. London, 1964.

Kayser, Joyce. *Phantoms in the Pinyon: An Investigation of Ute-Pueblo Contacts*, 1965.
Kearns, William. *The Silent Continent*. New York, 1955.
Keller, Werner. *The Etruscans*. Translated by Alexander and Elizabeth Henderson. New York, 1974.
Kendrick, T. D. *A History of the Vikings*. London, 1968.
Kesten, Hermann. *Copernicus and His World*. Translated by E. B. Ashton and Norbert Guterman. New York, 1945.
Kidder, Alfred. *Kiva*. Southwestern Archaeology, Vol. 25, No. 4, 1960.
Kirwan, L. P. *A History of Polar Exploration*. New York, 1960.
Koestler, Arthur. *The Sleepwalkers*. New York, 1968.
Kühn, Herbert. *On the Track of Prehistoric Man*. Translated by Alan Houghton Brodrick. New York, 1955.

Lacey, Robert. *Sir Walter Raleigh*. New York, 1973.
La Fay, Howard. "The Maya, Children of Time," *National Geographic*, vol. 148, no. 6. Washington, D.C., 1975.
———. *The Vikings*. Washington, D.C., 1972.

Landström, Björn. *Bold Voyages and Great Explorers*. Garden City, N.Y., 1964.
Lawrence, D. H. *Etruscan Places*. New York, 1932.
Leakey, Louis. *By the Evidence*. New York, 1974.
———. *The Progress and Evolution of Man in Africa*. London, 1961.
Leakey, Louis, and Vanne Morris Goodall. *Unveiling Man's Origins*. Cambridge, Mass., 1969.
Lear, John. *Kepler's Dream*. Translated by Patricia Frueh Kirkwood. Berkeley, Calif., 1965.
Leithäuser, Joachim. *Worlds Beyond the Horizon*. Translated by Hugh Merrick. New York, 1955.
Leonard, Jonathan. *Ancient America*. New York, 1967.
Levitt, Israel. *Beyond the Known Universe*. New York, 1974.
Lewinsohn, Richard. *Animals, Men, and Myths*. New York, 1954.
Lewis, Richard S. *A Continent for Science*. New York, 1965.
Ley, Willy. *Another Look at Atlantis*. New York, 1969.
———. *Watchers of the Skies*. New York, 1963.
———. *Earth and in the Sky*. New York, 1958.
Lothrop, S. K. *Inca Treasure*. Los Angeles, 1938.
Luce, J. V. *Lost Atlantis*. New York, 1969.

Macnamara, Ellen. *The Etruscans*. New York, 1973.
Macvey, John. *Whispers from Space*. New York, 1973.
Magnusson, Magnus, and Hermann Pálsson. *The Vinland Sagas*. New York, 1965.
Mahn-Lot, Marianne. *Columbus*. Translated by Helen R. Lane. New York, 1961.
Manley, Sean, and Gago Lewis, eds. *Polar Secrets*. Garden City, N.Y., 1968.
Maple, Eric. *Domain of Devils*. London, 1969.
Marx, Robert. *The Lure of Sunken Treasure*. New York, 1973.
McNitt, Frank. *Richard Wetherill: Anasazi*. Albuquerque, 1957.
Meyer, Karl E. *The Pleasures of Archaeology*. New York, 1971.
Middleton, Dorothy. *Victorian Lady Travelers*. New York, 1965.
Millar, Ronald. *The Piltdown Man*. New York, 1972.
Mirsky, Jeannette. *The Great Chinese Travelers*. New York, 1964.
———. *To the Arctic*. New York, 1948.
Montague, Ashley. *Man: His First 2 Million Years*. New York, 1969.
Moore, Patrick. *Watchers of the Stars*. London, 1974.
———. *Suns, Myths & Men*. New York, 1968.
Morison, Samuel Eliot. *The European Discovery of America*. New York, 1971.
———. *The Caribbean as Columbus Saw It*. Boston, 1964.
———. *Christopher Columbus, Mariner*. Boston, 1955.
———. *Admiral of the Ocean Sea*. Boston, 1942.

Mountfield, David. *A History of Polar Exploration*. New York, 1974.
Mowatt, Farley. *Westviking*. Boston, 1965.
———. *Ordeal by Ice*. Boston, 1961.
Munro, Dana C. "The Children's Crusade," *American Historical Review*, vol. 19. New York, 1913.
Murphy, Dan. *El Morro National Monument*. Tucson, 1989.

Neatby, L. H. *In Quest of the Northwest Passage*. New York, 1962.
Neider, Charles. *Man Against Nature*. New York, 1954.
———, ed. *Antarctica*. New York, 1972.
Nesmith, Robert. *Dig for Pirate Treasure*. New York, 1958.
Newby, Eric. *World Atlas of Exploration*. New York, 1975.
Noble, David Grant. *Ancient Ruins of the Southwest*. Flagstaff, 1991.
———, ed. *Mesa Verde and Hovenweep*. Santa Fe, 1985.
Nordenskiöld, Gustaf. *The Cliff Dwellers of the Mesa Verde*. Cambridge, 1973.
Norman, Charles. *Discoverers of America*. New York, 1968.
Norman, James. *Ancestral Voices*. New York, 1975.
Nusbaum, Rosemary. *Tierra Dulce*. Santa Fe, 1980.
Nylander, Carl. *The Deep Well*. Translated by Joan Tate. London, 1969.

Ohrelius, Bengt. *The Vasa*. Philadelphia, 1963.
Olson, Daniel M. *Letters of Gustaf Nordenskiöld*. Mesa Verde National Park, 1991.
Outhwaite, Leonard. *Unrolling the Map*. New York, 1972.
Oxenstierna, Eric. *The Norsemen*. Translated by Catherine Hutter. Greenwich, Conn., 1965.
———. *The World of the Norsemen*. Translated by Janet Sondheimer. Cleveland, 1957.

Pachter, Henry. *Magic into Science*. New York, 1951.
Page, Thornton, and Lou Williams, eds. *Wanderers in the Sky*. New York, 1967.
Pallottino, Massimo. *Etruscans*. Translated by J. Cremona. Bloomington, Ind., 1975.
Penrose, Boies. *Travel and Discovery in the Renaissance*. Cambridge, Mass., 1952.
Pericot-Garcia, Luis. *Prehistoric and Primitive Art*. Translated by Henry Mins. New York, 1967.
Pfeiffer, John. *The Emergence of Man*. New York, 1969.
Piggott, Stuart. *Prehistoric India*. London, 1961.
Pohl, Frederick J. *Atlantic Crossings Before Columbus*. New York, 1961.
Pope, Maurice. *Decipherment*. New York, 1975.
Prescott, W. H. *The Conquest of Peru*. New York, 1963.

Quinn, David B. *North America from Earliest Discovery to First Settlements*. New York, 1977.

Rackl, Hanns-Wolf. *Diving into the Past*. Translated by Ronald J. Floyd. New York, 1968.

Ramsay, Raymond. *No Longer on the Map*. New York, 1972.

Rapport, Samuel, and Helen Wright, eds. *Archaeology*. New York, 1964.

———. *Astronomy*. New York, 1964.

Rasky, Frank. *The Polar Voyagers*. New York, 1976.

Read, John. *Through Alchemy to Chemistry*. London, 1957.

Reith, Adolf. *Archaeological Fakes*. Translated by Diana Imber. London, 1970.

Renault, Gilbert. *The Caravels of Christ*. Translated by Richmond Hill. New York, 1959.

Richardson, Emeline. *The Etruscans*. Chicago, 1964.

Richardson, Robert. *The Stars and Serendipity*. New York, 1971.

———. *The Star Lovers*. New York, 1967.

Ronan, Colin. *Astronomers Royal*. New York, 1969.

———. *Astronomers*. London, 1964.

Ross, James Bruce, and Mary Martin McLaughin, eds. *The Renaissance Reader*. New York, 1953.

Runciman, Steven. *History of the Crusades*. Cambridge, England, 1954.

Ruz, Alberto. *Palenque*. Mexico City, 1947.

Sadoul, Jacques. *Alchemists & Gold*. Translated by Olga Sieveking. New York, 1972.

Sagan, Carl. *The Cosmic Connection*. New York, 1973.

Sanderlin, George. *Across the Ocean Sea*. New York, 1966.

de Santillana, Giorgio. *The Age of Adventure*. New York, 1956.

Savours, Ann, ed. *Scott's Last Voyage*. New York, 1975.

Schanche, Don. "The Vasa Affair," *Saturday Evening Post*, Philadelphia, October 21, 1961.

Schreiber, Herman. *Vanished Cities*. Translated by Richard and Clara Winston. New York, 1957.

Scott, Robert. *Scott's Last Expedition*. New York, 1923.

Scullard, H. H. *The Etruscan Cities and Rome*. Ithaca, N.Y., 1967.

Severin, Timothy. *The Golden Antilles*. London, 1970.

Shapiro, Harry L. *Peking Man*. New York, 1974.

Silverberg, Robert. *The Realm of Prester John*. Garden City, N.Y., 1972.

———. *Empires in the Dust*. New York, 1966.

———. *Man Before Adam*. Philadelphia, 1964.

———. *Sunken History*. New York, 1964.

Slater, John M. *El Morro*. Los Angeles, 1961.
Smith, Duane A. *Mesa Verde National Park*. Lawrence, Kansas, 1988.
Smith, Vincent. *The Oxford History of India*. Oxford, England, 1967.
Smith, William. *Northwest Passage*. New York, 1970.
Snow, Edward. *Ghosts, Gales & Gold*. New York, 1972.
Southwestern Monuments Association. *El Morro Trails*. Globe, Arizona, No date.
Sprague, L., and Catherine de Camp. *Citadels of Mystery*. New York, 1963.
Stefansson, Vilhjalmur. *Northwest to Fortune*. New York, 1958.
———. *Great Adventures and Explorations*. New York, 1952.
———. *Unsolved Mysteries of the Arctic*. New York, 1937.
Strayer, Joseph Reese. *The Middle Ages*. New York, 1959.
Strong, Donald. *The Early Etruscans*. New York, 1968.
Sullivan, Walter. *We Are Not Alone*. New York, 1964.
———. *Quest for a Continent*. New York, 1957.
Sykes, Percy. *A History of Exploration*. New York, 1961.

Taylor, F. Sherwood. *The Alchemists*. New York, 1962.
Taylor, John. *Black Holes*. Glasgow, 1974.
Terrell, John. *Pueblos, Gods & Spaniards*. New York, 1973.
———. *Journey into Darkness*. New York, 1962.
Thiel, Rudolph. *And There Was Light*. Translated by Richard and Clara Winston. New York, 1957.
Thorndike, Joseph, ed. *Mysteries of the Past*. New York, 1977.
Time-Life. *The First Men*. New York, 1973.
———. *Cro-Magnon*. Edited by Tom Prideaux. New York, 1973.
Toulmin, Stephen, and June Goodfield. *The Fabric of the Heavens*. New York, 1961.
Treece, Henry. *The Crusades*. New York, 1962.

de Vaca, Cabeza. *Adventures in the Unknown Interior of America*. Translated by Cyclone Covey. New York, 1961.
Vaughan, Agnes. *Those Mysterious Etruscans*. New York, 1964.
de la Vega, Garcilaso. *Royal Commentaries of the Incas*. Translated by Harold Livermore. Austin, Texas, 1966.
Villagrá, Gaspar Pérez. *Historia de la Nueva Mexico*. Albuquerque, 1992.

Waechter, John. *Man Before History*. London, 1976.
Wagner, Kip. *Pieces of Eight*. New York, 1966.
Ward, Anne. *Adventures in Archaeology*. New York, 1977.
Wauchope, Robert. *Lost Tribes & Sunken Continents*. Chicago, 1962.

Wellard, James. *The Search for the Etruscans*. New York, 1973.
Wendt, Herbert. *The First Men*. Translated by Edmund White and Dale Brown. New York, 1973.
———. *From Ape to Adam*. No translator listed. New York, 1972.
———. *Before the Deluge*. Translated by Richard and Clara Winston. Garden City, N.Y., 1968.
———. *In Search of Adam*. Translated by James Cleugh. Boston, 1956.
Wenger, Gilbert R. *Mesa Verde National Park*. Mesa Verde National Park, 1991.
Wetherhill, Al. *As I remember*. . . . The Desert Magazine, May 1945.
Wetherhill, Benjamin Alfred. *The Wetherills of the Mesa Verde*. Lincoln, 1977.
Wheeler, Sir Mortimer. *Civilizations of the Indus Valley and Beyond*. London, 1966.
White, Peter. *The Past Is Human*. New York, 1976.
Whitney, Charles. *The Discovery of Our Galaxy*. New York, 1971.
Wichler, Gerhard. *Charles Darwin*. London, 1961.
Winton, John. *Sir Walter Raleigh*. New York, 1975.
Wood, H. J. *Exploration and Discovery*. London, 1958.
Wright, Louis. *Gold, Glory, and Gospel*. New York, 1970.
von Wuthenau, Alexander. *Unexpected Faces in Ancient America*. New York, 1975.